RACISM
AND
ANTIRACISM

'RACE', EDUCATION AND SOCIETY

RACISM AND EDUCATION
STRUCTURES AND STRATEGIES
EDITED BY DAWN GILL, BARBARA MAYOR AND MAUD BLAIR

'RACE', CULTURE AND DIFFERENCE
EDITED BY JAMES DONALD AND ALI RATTANSI

RACISM AND ANTIRACISM
INEQUALITIES, OPPORTUNITIES AND POLICIES
EDITED BY PETER BRAHAM, ALI RATTANSI AND RICHARD SKELLINGTON

These three volumes, all published by SAGE Publications are Readers for the Open University course ED356 *'Race', Education and Society*

(Details of the course are available from the Student Enquiries Office, The Open University, Milton Keynes, MK7 6AG.)

RACISM AND ANTIRACISM

INEQUALITIES, OPPORTUNITIES AND POLICIES

EDITED BY PETER BRAHAM,
ALI RATTANSI AND
RICHARD SKELLINGTON

SAGE PUBLICATIONS

in association with

The Open
University

SAGE Publications Ltd
6 Bonhill Street
London EC2A 4PU

SAGE Publications Inc
2455 Teller Road
Newbury Park, California 91320

SAGE Publications India Pvt Ltd
32, M-Block Market
Greater Kailash – I
New Delhi 110 048

British Library Cataloguing in Publication data

Racism and antiracism: Inequalities,
opportunities and policies.
 I. Braham, Peter II. Rattansi, Ali
 III. Skellington, Richard
 305.800941085

 ISBN 0–8039–8581–9
 ISBN 0–8039–8582–7 pbk

Library of Congress catalog card number 91–50652

Typeset by Photoprint, Torquay, Devon
Printed in Great Britain by J. W. Arrowsmith Ltd, Bristol

CONTENTS

PREFACE   vii

ACKNOWLEDGEMENTS   viii

PART 1 RACISM: THE POLITICS OF EXCLUSION

Introduction   3

1   The politics of immigration since 1945   *John Solomos*   7

2   The British trade union movement and racism
   A. Phizacklea and R. Miles   30

3   'Same difference': the persistence of racial disadvantage
   in the British employment market   *Colin Brown*   46

4   Women of South Asian origin in Britain: issues and concerns
   Avtar Brah   64

5   Black women and the British state: race, class and gender
   analysis for the 1990s   *Amina Mama*   79

PART 2 INSTITUTIONAL RACISM

Introduction   105

6   Racism and housing: concepts and reality   *Norman Ginsburg*   109

7   New vocationalism, old racism and the careers service
   John Wrench   133

8   Black workers in the labour market: the price of recession
   Richard Jenkins   148

9   An uncaring profession? An examination of racism in
   social work   *Lena Dominelli*   164

10   Black people and the criminal law: rhetoric and reality
   Paul Gordon   179

PART 3 RACISM AND EQUAL OPPORTUNITY POLICY

Introduction   197

11   A political analysis of local struggles for racial equality
   Gideon Ben-Tovim, John Gabriel, Ian Law, Kathleen Stredder   201

12   The theory and practice of equal opportunities policies:
   liberal and radical approaches   *Nick Jewson and David Mason*   218

13   Equal opportunities policy and race equality   *Peter Gibbon*   235

14 Approaches to policy development in the field of equal
opportunities   *Ken Young*   252

15 Racial inequality and the limits of law   *L. Lustgarten
and J. Edwards*   270

LIST OF CONTRIBUTORS   294

INDEX   297

PREFACE

This collection of articles, many of them specially commissioned, is one of three volumes that constitute a major component of the Open University course, 'Race', Education and Society. It is concerned with patterns of differentiation and discrimination across a range of social institutions and practices: the labour market, nationality and migration laws, welfare provision, and so forth. The other two volumes in the series are *Racism and Education: structures and strategies*, edited by Dawn Gill, Barbara Mayor and Maud Blair, and *'Race', Culture and Difference*, edited by James Donald and Ali Rattansi. The former focuses on policies, practices and experiences of schooling, and their implications in sustaining or challenging racism. The latter explores the cultural aspects of 'race', although very much in the light of the critical rethinking of the concept of 'culture' to be found in the emerging traditions of post-structuralism and postmodernism. Although the three books have been designed with the needs of Open University students in mind, each can be read independently and will be of interest to a much wider range of readers who wish to study the social and cultural dynamics of 'race' in Britain today.

In order to include as broad a range of materials as possible, some of the previously published articles have been shortened. Editorial cuts are marked by three dots in square brackets: [. . .]. Editorial interpolations are placed in square brackets. In view of the political significance attached to terminology in this field, no attempt has been made to standardize authors' usage of terms such as 'black', 'Black', 'ethnic minority', 'minority ethnic', etc.

The editors would like to thank the following colleagues for their advice during the preparation of this book: Maud Blair, James Donald, Paul Gordon, Jagdish Gundara, Margaret Kiloh, Barbara Mayor, Paulette Morris and Gaby Weiner. They would also like to thank the following for their assistance in the production of the book: June Evison, Aileen Lodge, Michele Marsh, Gill Marshall, Lesley Passey, John Taylor, Laurily Wilson and Rodney Wilson.

ACKNOWLEDGEMENTS

The authors and publishers wish to thank the following for permission to use copyright material.

Cambridge University Press for extracts from L. Lustgarten, 'Racial inequality and the limits of law' from R. Jenkins and J. Solomos (eds) *Racism and Equal Opportunities in the 1980's*, 1987; and with the Centre for Research in Ethnic Relations and G. Ben-Tovim for G. Ben-Tovim, J. Gabriel, I. Law and K. Stredder, 'A political analysis of local struggles for racial equality' from D. Mason and J. Rex (eds) *Theories of Race and Ethnic Relations*, 1986;

Critical Social Policy for P. Gibbon, 'Equal opportunities policy and race equality', *Critical Social Policy*, 28, **10**(1), 1990;

Harcourt Brace Jovanovich Ltd for P. Gordon, 'Black people and the criminal law: rhetoric and reality', *International Journal of the Sociology of Law*, **16**(3), 1988;

Macmillan Publishers Ltd for J. Solomos, 'The politics of immigration since 1945' from *Race and Racism in Contemporary Britain*, 1989; and K. Young, 'Approaches to policy development in the field of equal opportunities' from W. Ball and J. Solomos (eds) *Race and Local Politics*, 1990;

Manchester University Press for R. Jenkins, 'Black workers in the labour market: the price of recession' from B. Roberts, R. Finnegan, D. Gallie (eds) *New Approaches to Economic Life*, 1985;

New Community for J. Wrench, 'New vocationalism, old racism and the careers service', *New Community*, **16**(3), 1990; and Lena Dominelli, 'An uncaring profession? An examination of racism in social work', *New Community*, **15**(3), 1989;

Open University Press for A. Phizacklea and R. Miles, 'The British trade union movement and racism' from G. Lee and R. Loveridge (eds) *The Manufacture of Disadvantage*, 1987;

Routledge for N. Jewson and D. Mason, 'The theory and practice of equal opportunities policies: liberal and radical approaches', *Sociological Review*, **34**(2), 1986;

South Asia Research Editorial Association for Avtar Brah, 'Women of South Asian origin in Britain', *South Asia Research*, **7**(1), 1987;

Every effort has been made to trace all the copyright holders, but if any have been inadvertently overlooked the publishers will be pleased to make the necessary arrangement at the first opportunity.

PART 1

RACISM

THE POLITICS OF EXCLUSION

INTRODUCTION

Towards the end of his article, 'The politics of immigration since 1945', John Solomos argues that his discussion has shown that, regarding the control of immigration and of migrant labour, it is much too simplistic to see the state as either a cipher for economic forces or as a mirror of popular discontent. Instead he prefers to emphasize the various contexts – social, economic, political and ideological – which have influenced both exclusionary and anti-discriminatory legislation.

Solomos' object is to reveal the role of the state in defining the terms of public debate about immigration policy, a policy which he describes as one of 'ideological racialization'. What this amounts to is to underline what tends to be taken for granted about the subject almost before a word is spoken or a sentence written. For example, is it not axiomatic that 'race' and 'immigration' are synonymous (even though the majority of post Second World War immigrants to Britain may have been white) and is it not equally obvious that harmonious community relations (i.e. race relations) are possible only if strict immigration control is in place?

As Annie Phizacklea and Robert Miles remind us in 'The British trade union movement and racism' this taken-for-granted world is also a product of the habitual hostility of trade unions towards immigrant workers. This was so in the support of the TUC for the Aliens Act of 1904 and it is equally evident in the initial TUC reaction to immigration from the New Commonwealth. We should not assume, of course, that a posture of economic nationalism, however consistently it is expressed, means that the trade unions were able to exert a crucial influence over the passage of immigration control legislation. But the response of trade union leaders to subsequent questions of discrimination in employment – to the particularly sensitive issue of the complicity of the unions themselves in such discrimination, for example – though perhaps more complicated, nevertheless did have a considerable impact. At the time, a policy of inaction was often defended explicitly, if unconvincingly, as a need to maintain a 'colour-blind' approach. The difficulty in this position is that it seems to equate the practice of discrimination with opposing such practice. But this convoluted logic is best understood in the light of the view that many, if not most, union leaders took of their members, that in the matter of 'race' it was better to let sleeping dogs lie.

At one level this raises the question of whether it is sufficient for leaders to reflect the presumed views of their members or whether there is a duty to lead. But at a more fundamental level this relates to the complicity of the trade unions in helping to confine black workers to the poorly paid and less desirable jobs to which, as immigrants from the New Commonwealth, they had been recruited in the first place. The close association that Solomos discerns between 'race' and immigration was certainly not challenged by the trade unions, or more to the point was not challenged until after it was well-established, a state of affairs in which the trade unions played a significant part, as Phizacklea and Miles show. But for this close association to come about, it was first necessary that black immigration should be seen primarily in terms of the problems and hostilities that it was said to arouse – in housing, in employment and elsewhere – and that it be divorced from its economic genesis.

In this sense Solomos gives an accurate assessment of how black migrant labour is generally perceived and of how this perception came about, not only in terms of policy making but also at a more popular level in political and media discourse. Thus when he refers to Enoch Powell's warning of the prospect of racial tensions in Britain following the American experience, this warning, though extreme in its tone is otherwise in accordance with the flavour of political debate. But the various contexts that Solomos mentions should be extended beyond the way black migrant labour is commonly perceived, to encompass other contexts within which migrant labour should be analysed.

It is by no means a rejection of Solomos' political argument to pursue the economics of migration as suggested by Colin Brown in '"Same difference": the persistence of racial disadvantage in the British employment market', an article written specially for this volume. On the contrary, these two aspects of the larger subject are complementary and not mutually exclusive. Thus when we consider the whole, we should recognize that this consists of different aspects or questions and not of a single explanation or truth which must be embraced completely, or jettisoned in favour of another mono-causal or one-dimensional explanation.

If the discussion of the politics of immigration follows the American model and so relates to social tensions, the discussion of the economics of migration draws most obviously on the post Second World War movements of workers from less developed countries into the advanced industrialized countries of North-West Europe.

One seminal explanation of this phenomenon is Böhning's hypothesis that in a post-industrial society, migration becomes what he terms 'self-feeding'. According to Böhning, such a society will run into endemic labour shortages in socially undesirable and low-wage jobs; that because of an inability to change its traditional job-structure, these labour shortages will be met by engaging foreign workers from low-wage countries; and in this way, the social-job structure is further rigidified and an unending and self-feeding flow of migrants is precipitated (Böhning, 1972, p. 55).

There is no mention of 'race' in this scenario, not because Böhning's hypothesis excludes 'race': on the contrary, the rigidification of the social-job structure develops more easily when those in less desirable jobs can be identified most readily. The point is not to deny the importance of racial discrimination as outlined by Brown in article 3, but to indicate what black workers have in common with migrant workers in Europe. Thus, as Brown argues, 'we can only understand the present position of minority workers (in Britain) if we remember that only a generation ago most blacks and Asians . . . were immigrants, and if we know *the causes and conditions of their migration*' (article 3, p. 46, emphasis added). If we then apply Böhning's hypothesis to Brown's evidence that all too often black workers were reluctantly recruited as 'suitable' people to perform 'unsuitable' jobs, we do not deny the salience of 'race' and racism, but simply place it in a wider context.

However, whether we choose to emphasize the political or the economic aspects of migration, we should not – as much of the literature has done – neglect the experience of women either in the process of migration or in the structure of racial disadvantage. We have chosen two articles to illuminate this experience: in 'Women of South Asian origin in Britain: issues and concerns', Avtar Brah investigates the way in which gender divisions have been influenced by colonialism and the international division of labour, and she examines the position of women of south Asian origin in the labour market, in education and within the family. In a more specific discussion Amina Mama, in 'Black women and the British state', analyses the position of black women working in the National Health Service, demonstrating the ways in which they are concentrated in lower-status ancillary jobs.

Reference

Böhning, W. R. (1972) The *Migration Workers in the United Kingdom and the European Community*, Oxford, Oxford University Press.

1 THE POLITICS OF IMMIGRATION SINCE 1945

JOHN SOLOMOS

Introduction

This period has attracted the attention of most researchers on racial issues in Britain, and there is by now a voluminous literature on most aspects of this phenomenon. Looking specifically at the politics literature, two main themes have been highlighted above all else. First, a number of studies have sought to analyse how the question of immigration *per se* has become inextricably linked to black immigration, that is the arrival of migrants from the new Commonwealth and Pakistan (Katznelson, 1976; Freeman, 1979; Layton-Henry, 1984).

This body of work has looked particularly at the political debates about black migration and the role of changing political ideologies in the construction of racial issues.

Second, other research has shown how the successive governments have attempted to regulate and eventually to halt the arrival of black migrants through immigration legislation and other means (Sivanandan, 1982; Macdonald, 1983; Miles and Phizacklea, 1984). According to this body of work arguments about the supposed problems created by the arrival of too many black migrants have been used to legitimize legislative measures which have had the effect of institutionalizing controls on black migrants, thereby excluding potential migrants on the basis of the colour of their skin.

Both these interpretations have been the subject of much controversy and debate, to which we shall refer in the course of this article. The main focus of this article, however, will be to analyse and explain the political and ideological responses to the arrival of migrants from the West Indies, India, Pakistan and other new Commonwealth countries. The first section provides a critical review of the development of political opinions and policy response in the immediate post-war conjuncture. We then move on to assess the impact of state intervention on the patterns of black migration, and to look at how immigration became a focus of political discourses and conflict from the 1940s to the 1980s.
[...]

The post-1945 conjuncture and European migration

During the Second World War the issue of black settlement in Britain became an issue in a number of related, but distinct ways. As a result of the war black workers and soldiers arrived from the colonies to fight in the British army or to help with the war effort (Richmond, 1954; Sherwood, 1984). Additionally, black American soldiers also arrived and attracted a variety of responses (Smith, 1987). At the same time there was concern about two issues. First, the social consequences of the arrival of new groups of black workers and soldiers on the older black seaport settlements. Second, there was increased concern that the arrival of new black migrants could lead to conflict and the institutionalization of a colour bar in a number of towns.

Despite evidence of increased concern about black immigration both during and immediately after the war, debate about immigration in the immediate post-1945 period was not primarily focused on the arrival of black colonial migrants. Despite the arrival of the SS Empire Windrush in 1948 with some 400 British subjects from the Caribbean, there was no large-scale migration from the colonies and dominions at this stage. Most of the migrants arriving in Britain during the immediate post-1945 conjuncture were from other European countries.

The most important source of migrants to Britain from 1945 to 1954 was Europe. Between 1945 and 1951, between 70,000 and 100,000 Irish people entered Britain. Although some concern was expressed later about the entry of Irish migrants, there was surprisingly little debate about this issue at this stage (PREM 11/1409, 1956; Jackson, 1963; Holmes, 1988). [...]

The other significant group of migrants which the Government encouraged was recruited by the British state specifically to resolve labour shortages in certain sectors of the economy. On the European mainland, there were several camps for displaced persons or political refugees who were unable or did not wish to return to their country of birth following the redrawing of political boundaries after the defeat of Germany, and the Labour Government decided to send Ministry of Labour officials to them to recruit workers. The occupants of these camps were or had been, in law, nationals of other countries and were therefore aliens as far as the British state was concerned. But the procedures for admission under the Aliens Order 1920, concerned as they were with the admission of single persons, were not appropriate for what was to become a considerable migration. The result was, in the British context, a unique scheme, the British state undertaking to meet all the costs of recruitment, transport and repatriation on behalf of those capitalists short of labour power and, in a number of respects, it anticipated the contract migrant labour system set up by a number of Western European states in the 1950s and 1960s (Castles and Kosack, 1985; Castles *et al.*, 1984; Miles, 1986). The total cost of the scheme up to October 1948 was £2.75 million (Tannahill, 1958, p. 56).

Those displaced persons who came to Britain were required to sign a contract, the terms of which stated that they would accept work selected by the Minister of Labour and that they could only change that employment with the permission of the Ministry of Labour. Therefore, they became European Volunteer Workers (EVWs). Following health checks, they were admitted initially for one year, an extension being dependent upon the individual complying with the conditions of the contract and behaving 'as a worthy member of the British community' (Tannahill, 1958, pp. 123–8). Many of those recruited were not initially eligible to bring their dependants with them, although most of those who eventually settled in Britain were subsequently joined by their families. The conditions of placement of EVW's in employment varied but usually included the requirements that no British labour was available, that in the event of redundancy EVW's would be the first to be made unemployed, that EVWs should join the appropriate trade union and that they should receive the same wages and conditions as British workers (Tannahill, 1958, p. 57).

[...]

The encouragement given to these two groups of migrants to settle in Britain contrasted with the concern of the Government with the social and political consequences of the relatively small-scale migration from the colonies during this period. What recent research has made clear is that even at this early stage black migration and settlement was politically perceived in a different way from European migration. Privately the Government was considering the most desirable method of discouraging or preventing the arrival of coloured British citizens from the colonies.

Migration, colonial labour and the state: 1945–62

At the end of the Second World War the British state had legislative powers in the form of the Aliens legislation to control the entry into Britain of non-British subjects and their access to the labour market. However, the vast majority of British subjects in the colonies and dominions retained a legal right to enter and settle in Britain. This legal right was confirmed by the British Nationality Act of 1948 which, in response to the granting of independence to India, made a formal distinction between British subjects who were citizens of the United Kingdom and Colonies and those who were Commonwealth citizens, both categories of people having the right to enter, settle and work in Britain (Evans, 1983, pp. 59–62; Bevan, 1986, pp. 112–13). Additionally, citizens of the Republic of Ireland retained the right of unrestricted entry and settlement.

As we have seen already, despite the fact that the vast majority of British subjects from the colonies and independent Commonwealth countries retained the right to enter and settle in the UK, the concern of the state was to encourage the use of migrant labour from Europe to meet the demand for labour. Some British subjects from the colonies did arrive during this period, particularly from the West Indies, but almost as soon as they began to arrive they were perceived as a problem.

The relatively liberal attitude towards the arrival of European workers contrasted sharply with the fears expressed about the social and racial problems which were seen as related to the arrival of coloured colonial workers who were British subjects. Both the Labour Governments of 1945–51 and Conservative Governments throughout the 1950s considered various ways to stop or reduce the number of black migrants arriving and settling in Britain (Joshi and Carter, 1984; Carter, Harris and Joshi, 1987; Dean, 1987).

It was during the period from 1945–62 that the terms of political debate about coloured immigration were established, leading to a close association between race and immigration in both policy debates and in popular political and media discourses.

Contrary to the arguments of some scholars it seems quite inadequate to see this period as an age of innocence and lack of concern about black immigration into the UK (Rose *et al.*, 1969; Patterson, 1969; Deakin, 1970). Throughout this period an increasingly racialized debate about immigration took place, focusing on the supposed social problems of having too many black migrants and the question of how they could be stopped from entering given their legal rights in the 1948 British Nationality Act.

Although much publicity was given to the arrival of 417 Jamaicans on the Empire Windrush in May 1948, and subsequent arrivals by large groups of West Indian workers, the focus on coloured immigration helped to obscure the fact that the majority of immigrants continued to come from the Irish Republic, from white Commonwealth countries and other European countries (Patterson, 1969, ch. 1; Miles and Phizacklea, 1984, pp. 45–8). The concentration on the number of West Indian immigrants, and later on the number of immigrants from India and Pakistan, has been shown to have been an issue of debate within the Cabinet during the period 1950–5, when various measures to control black immigration and to dissuade black workers from coming to the UK were considered. On the basis of a careful analysis of cabinet and ministerial debates about immigration from the colonies a recent study has concluded that the period from 1948 to 1962 involved the state in complex political and ideological racialization of immigration policy (Carter, Harris and Joshi, 1987).

The period between the 1948 Nationality Act and the 1962 Commonwealth Immigrants Act is frequently characterized as one in which the principle of free entry of British subjects to the UK was only relinquished with great reluctance and after considerable official debate. This was not the case. On the contrary, the debate was never about principle. Labour and Conservative Governments had by 1952 instituted a number of covert, and sometimes illegal, administrative measures to discourage black immigration (Carter, Harris and Joshi, 1987).

Additionally, throughout the 1950s the debate about immigration in parliament and the media began to focus on the need to control black immigration. Although both in public debate and in private policy discussions attention was sometimes focused on the behaviour of undesirable black migrants, such as those involved in crime or prostitution, the terms of political debate through the 1950s were also about the desirability of letting into Britain a sizeable number of West Indian or Asian migrants.

The 1958 riots in Notting Hill and Nottingham may have helped to politicize this process further (Miles, 1984; Pilkington, 1988). But it is clear that both before and after the riots themselves the question of control was being integrated into the policy agenda.

With the growing emphasis on the control of coloured immigration the terms of ideological and policy debates about the future of black migration turned on two themes which were to prove influential later on. First, a vigorous debate took place in and out of parliament about the possibility of revising the 1948 Nationality Act so as to limit the number of black workers who could come and settle in the UK. The terms of this debate were by no means fixed purely by political party ideologies, and there was opposition from both Conservative and Labour politicians to the call for controls and the abandonment of the free entry principle. Second, a parallel debate developed about the problems caused by too many coloured immigrants in relation to housing, employment and crime. This second theme became particularly important in the period 1956–8, and in the aftermath of the 1958 riots (*Hansard*, Vol. 596, 1958, Cols 1552–97).

By linking immigration to the social aspects of the colour problem a theme was established which was later to prove influential in shaping both the immigration control legislation and the Race Relations Acts. This was the argument that it was necessary to use direct state intervention to halt the gathering momentum of black migration and to resolve the social problems which were perceived as linked to it.

Controls on coloured immigration had been discussed as early as the late 1940s, and were seriously discussed again in 1954 and 1955. A number of arguments were used in opposition to such controls, and it was not until 1961 that a Bill to control Commonwealth immigration was introduced by the Government. The reasons for the reluctance to introduce controls remains to some extent a matter of speculation, although the release of government documents for the period of the early 1950s has shed some light on this non-decision making process (Joshi and Carter, 1984, pp. 55–63; Rich, 1986, ch. 7). But at least part of the reluctance to introduce controls seemed to result from a concern about whether legislation which excluded black people could be implemented without causing embarrassment to Britain's position as head of the Commonwealth and Colonies, the fear that it would divide public opinion, and a doubt about the legality of controls based on colour in both British and international law (Deakin, 1968, pp. 26–30; Miles and Phizacklea, 1984, ch. 2).

What is clear, however, is that the period from the late 1940s to the late 1950s was not a period of *laissez faire* in relation to black migration. Rather, it was one of intense debate within government departments and in public circles about the impact of black immigration on housing, the welfare state, crime and other social problems.

It is important to note, however, that these debates were not purely about the supposed characteristics of black migrants. They were also about the effect of black immigration on the racial character of the British people and on the national identity. Harris (1988) makes this point clear when he argues that the debates about black immigration during the 1950s reinforced a racialized construction of 'Britishness' which excluded or included people on the grounds of race defined by colour:

> When individuals like the Marquis of Salisbury spoke of maintaining the English way of life, they were not simply referring to economic or regional folk patterns, but explicitly to the preservation of 'the racial character of the English people'. We have developing here a process of subjectification grounded in a racialised construction of the 'British' Subject which excludes and includes people on the basis of 'race'/skin colour.
>
> (Harris, 1988, p. 53)

This process was still in its early stages in this period, but it is impossible to understand the legislation passed to control black immigration during the 1960s and 1970s without referring to the genesis and articulation of political discourse about black immigration during the period from 1945 to 1962.

Immigration and racialized politics

The 1958 race riots, in Nottingham and Notting Hill, are commonly seen as an important watershed in the development of racialized politics in Britain. It is certainly true that the events in these two localities helped to bring to national prominence issues which had previously been discussed either locally or within government departments.

The riots themselves consisted of attacks by whites on blacks but this did not prevent them being used as examples of the dangers of unrestricted immigration. By the time of the 1958 riots, however, the mobilization of opinion in and out of parliament in favour of controls was well advanced, and the disturbances in Nottingham and Notting Hill were used by the pro-immigration controls lobby to support calls for the exclusion or even the repatriation of 'undesirable immigrants'. They were also used in support of the argument that black immigration was a threat to the rule of law in the inner cities and endangered the 'English way of life'. Lord Salisbury used the riots to justify his claim that controls should be imposed on black immigration, and he argued that 'he was extremely apprehensive of the economic and social results, for Europeans and African alike, that were likely to flow from an unrestricted immigration of men and women of the African race into Britain' (*The Guardian*, 3 September, 1958).

It is noticeable that between these events and the introduction of the Commonwealth Immigrants Bill in 1961 a number of important debates on immigration control took place in parliament and at party conferences. (Patterson, 1969; Freeman, 1979, pp. 49–52; Miles, 1984). In parliament a number of Conservative MPs, including Cyril Osborne, organized a campaign in favour of immigration controls, though they made their case against coloured migrants largely through coded language. The Labour Party, along with the Liberals, generally argued against controls, though this was by no means the case for all Labour MPs and local councillors (Reeves, 1983, ch. 7; Layton-Henry, 1984, pp. 31–43).

Outside parliament there was widespread coverage in both the popular and serious newspapers of stories relating to race and immigration issues. There was a flowering of popular debate about housing and social conditions in areas of black settlement, about aspects of employment and competition for jobs, and a resurgence of extreme right groups which sought to use immigration as a basis for political mobilization. The interplay between these processes produced a wide variety of stereotypes and popular images about black people. In September 1958 *The Times* reported that in the areas affected by the riots:

> There are three main charges of resentment against coloured inhabitants of the district. They are alleged to do no work and to collect a rich sum from the Assistance Board. They are said to find housing when white residents cannot. And they are charged with all kinds of misbehaviour, especially sexual.
> (*The Times*, 3 September, 1958)

It was precisely around such concerns that the extreme right groups focused much of their propaganda during and after the riots. There was no need in this context for such beliefs to be substantiated by evidence, but it proved equally difficult to counteract such stereotypes. This weakened the attempts to resist the pressures for immigration controls.

The ambiguities in the presence for controls became even more pronounced during the early 1960s, the period of the passage of the first legislative measures controlling the immigration of citizens of the United Kingdom and colonies, the 1962 Commonwealth Immigrants Act. It is to this period that we now turn.

Immigration controls and state racism

In the previous section we argued that the racialization of the immigration issue during the 1950s laid the basis for the move towards the control of black immigration, an objective which was first implemented through the 1962 Commonwealth Immigrants Act. Part of the dilemma faced by the Conservative Government of the time was how to legitimize a policy which aimed to control black immigration as a more universal measure. William Deedes, who was a Minister without Portfolio at the time, recalls that

> The Bill's real purpose was to restrict the influx of coloured immigrants. We were reluctant to say as much openly. So the restrictions were applied to coloured and white citizens in all Commonwealth countries – though everybody recognised that immigration from Canada, Australia and New Zealand formed no part of the problem.
> (Deedes, 1968, p. 10)

The racialization of the immigration issue was in other words done through coded language: 'commonwealth immigrants' were seen as a 'problem', but 'race' itself was not always mentioned as the central issue. The politicization of such terms was later to lead to a situation where, despite the continuing scale of white immigration, popular common sense perceived all immigrants as black, and 'immigration' became a coded term for talking about racial questions.

Two competing explanatory models have been used to explain the move towards immigration controls. Some scholars have seen this shift as a response by the state to the pressure of popular opinion against black immigration (Foot, 1965; Rose *et al.*, 1969). This is also the main line of argument used by some of the main political figures involved in the crucial debates about control of black immigration (Butler, 1971; Macmillan, 1973). Yet others have argued that the state was responding to the economic interests of the capitalist class, which required the adoption of a migrant labour system which undermined the right of black workers to migrate and settle freely in the UK (Sivanandan, 1982, pp. 101–26).

Both explanations have been widely used in the extensive literature on the politics of immigration, but as we have indicated already it seems inadequate to view the role of the state as purely responsive, whether to popular opinion or to economic interests. Throughout the period 1948–62 the state was actively involved in monitoring and regulating the arrival of black workers, and helped to articulate a definition of the immigration question which was suffused with racialized categories. Additionally, as recent research seems to indicate the Conservative Government came close to agreeing on a policy of controls on black immigration in 1955–6 (Carter, Harris and Joshi, 1987).

The genesis of the demand for the control of black immigration during the early 1950s matured during the period 1955–62 into a concerted campaign within the Cabinet, Parliament, the media and political parties, in favour of action to 'curb the dangers of unrestricted immigration'. This in turn led to the policy debate which developed in the period leading up to the introduction of the Commonwealth Immigrants Bill in 1961 about the formulation of legislation which could exclude black labour from entry and settlement. This process can hardly be interpreted as a move from *laissez faire* to state intervention, since the state and its institutions were already heavily involved in defining the terms of the debate about the problems caused by black immigration.

The 1962 Commonwealth Immigrants Act

[...] The controls announced under the Bill were legitimized by arguments about the need for a halt to black immigration because of the limited ability of the host society to assimilate coloured immigrants. Even though some MPs and commentators were reluctant to accept that the Bill was simply a way of dealing with the immigration of coloured workers, the Labour Party and sections of the media identified the Bill as a response to crude racist pressures. Hugh Gaitskell, as Leader of the Labour Party, led a particularly strong attack on the Bill in parliament and its crude amalgamation of immigration with race (Patterson, 1969, pp. 17–20; IRR Newsletter, May 1962). But despite strong criticism from the Labour Party and sections of the press, the collective pressures against the entry of black British succeeded when the Commonwealth Immigrants Act became law in 1962.

Since it was the outcome of the sustained political campaign against black immigration, it is not surprising that despite claims to the contrary, the main clauses of the Act sought to control the entry of black Commonwealth citizens into the UK. The Act introduced a distinction between citizens of the UK and Colonies and citizens of independent Commonwealth counties. All holders of Commonwealth passports were subject to immigration control except those who were (a) born in the UK; (b) held UK passports issued by the UK Government; or (c) persons included in the passport of one of the persons excluded from immigration control under (a) or (b) (Macdonald, 1983, pp. 10–12). Other Commonwealth citizens had to obtain a Ministry of Labour employment voucher in order to be able to enter the UK.

The changing terms of political debate

Almost as soon as the Act became law there was a widespread political debate about its effectiveness. During the period from 1963 to 1972, when the voucher system was abolished, there was pressure to cut back the number of vouchers allocated, and this was reflected in a fall from a level of 30,130 vouchers in 1963 to 2,290 in 1972. Significantly, no controls were imposed on the entry of citizens of the Irish Republic into Britain. Nevertheless opponents of immigration were quick to call for even tighter controls, and in the political climate of the mid-1960s their voices were a major influence on the terms of political debate about race and immigration.

The opposition of the Labour Party to the 1962 Act was not sustained. When Harold Wilson took office as Labour Prime Minister in 1964 he announced that the Commonwealth Immigrants Act would be maintained. In 1965 the Government issued a White Paper on *Immigration from the Commonwealth* which called for controls to be maintained in an even stricter form, along with measures to promote the integration of immigrants. The White Paper represented a shift in the direction of what some have called a 'Little England' policy (Rose *et al.*, 1969, p. 229), and signalled a convergence of the policies of the Conservative and Labour Parties in favour of immigration controls (Wilson, 1971). This was to be exemplified by the nature of the political debate about race and immigration during the period from 1964 to 1970, when the Labour Party was in power. Three events that represent good examples of this debate are the controversies over the electoral contest in Smethwick in 1964 and the East African Asians during 1968–9, and the political turmoil caused by Enoch Powell's intervention in this debate from 1968 onwards.

Smethwick and immigration

The impact of events in Smethwick during 1964 on the terms of national political debates about race and immigration is sometimes forgotten in hindsight. Yet it is no exaggeration to say that the political turmoil around the issue of immigration in Smethwick and the surrounding area had a deep impact on both the local and national political scene. Popular debate and media coverage was aroused by the contest between the Labour candidate, Patrick Gordon Walker, who was widely seen as a liberal on immigration, and the Conservative Peter Griffiths who fought the election largely on the basis of defending the interests of the local white majority against the 'influx of immigrants' (Foot, 1965; Deakin, 1972). In the volatile political climate of the time one of the slogans commonly heard during the election campaign was 'If you want a nigger for a neighbour vote Labour', and Griffiths was later to defend the use of this slogan as 'a manifestation of popular feeling' about immigration in the area, and refused to condemn those who used it (*The Times*, 1968, p. 139; Griffiths, 1966).

The debate about the implications of Griffiths' victory in Smethwick carried on for some time and was influential on both the Labour Party (*The Economist*, 7 August, 1965; Deakin, 1965; Wilson, 1971; Crossman, 1975) and the Conservative Party (Berkeley, 1977; Layton-Henry, 1980). Within the West Midlands region in particular the events in Smethwick helped to shift political debate and attitudes in both major parties towards a stance which emphasized their support for strict controls on black immigration (Lenton *et al.*, 1966; Deakin, 1972).

East African Asians

One of the features of the 1962 Act was that citizens of the United Kingdom living in independent Commonwealth countries were exempt from control provided they had a UK passport. This included a large number of European settlers as well as a sizeable number of East African Asians in Kenya and Uganda. During the period from 1965 to 1967 a steady flow of this group began to arrive in Britain and when sections of the media and MPs started to call for action to be taken to stop their arrival a heated political debate ensued in late 1967 and early 1968.

The political debate about the right of East African Asians to enter Britain reached its high point in February 1968. As noted above the Labour Party had moved towards acceptance of the need for firm immigration controls during the period from 1963–5, and so it came as no surprise when it responded to this political campaign by introducing the second Commonwealth Immigrants Act in early 1968. This Act sought to control the flow of East African Asians by bringing them under immigration control. Under the new law any citizen of the United Kingdom or colonies, who was the holder of a passport issued by the UK Government, was subject to immigration control unless they or at least one parent or grandparent was born, adopted, naturalized or registered as a citizen of the United Kingdom and colonies in the UK.

The political context in which the Act was passed made it difficult to argue that it was non-racial, as to some extent had been claimed by the Conservative Government which had passed the 1962 Act. *The Times* contrasted the behaviour of the Labour Government to the attitude of the Labour opposition in 1962 and went so far as to call the Act a 'colour bar' and 'probably the most shameful measure that the Labour members have even been asked by their whip to support' (27 February, 1968).

The transformation of the political climate between 1962 and 1968 was, however, clear enough for all to see in the parliamentary debates about the 1968 Act. Given the highly politicized nature of the debate around the Act and the defensive stance taken by the Government, only a few MPs and newspaper commentators saw fit to question the racism which underlay the legalization (Freeman, 1979, p. 56; Miles and Phizacklea, 1984, pp. 59–67). Indeed the period between the 1968 Act and the 1970 election, which saw the return of a Conservative Government, saw a further racialization of the immigration issue. Even though it was difficult to see how immigration could be cut even further than the controls imposed by the 1962 and 1968 Acts, it was precisely during the period 1968–70 that immigration and race relations became issues of partisan political debate on a larger scale than before.

Powellism and political debate

During this period the Labour Government was forced on the defensive by Enoch Powell's famous 'rivers of blood' speech in Birmingham in April 1968, which helped to popularize the common sense racial message that even tighter controls on immigration were not enough to deal with the race problem. In this speech, and in a succession of others over the next few years, Powell sought to warn of what he saw as (a) the dangers of immigration leading to a 'total transformation to which there is no parallel in a thousand years of British history', and (b) the longer term of danger of increasing racial tensions manifesting themselves in Britain on the American model. In the most infamous section of his Birmingham speech Powell said that as he looked into the future he felt deep foreboding about the fate of the nation if present trends were continued, and went on:

> As I look ahead, I am filled with foreboding. Like the Roman, I seem to see 'the River Tiber foaming with much blood'. The tragic and intractable phenomenon which we watch with horror on the other side of the Atlantic, but which there is interwoven with the history and existence of the States itself, is coming upon us here by our own volition and our own neglect.
>
> (*The Observer*, 21 April 1968)

According to Powell's argument the long-term solution to the immigration issue went beyond the issue of immigration controls and was likely to involve the repatriation of immigrants already settled in the UK. Such a line of argument helped to push political debate beyond controls as such and established repatriation as part of the political agenda. Indeed in the same speech Powell used all his rhetorical powers to construct an image of white Britons increasingly becoming isolated and strangers in their own country:

> They found their wives unable to obtain hospital beds in childbirth, their children unable to obtain school places, their homes and neighbourhoods changed beyond recognition, their plans and prospects for the future defeated.
> (Ibid.)

Against this background Powell was able to argue that it was the failure of successive governments to act decisively to halt immigration in the 1950s that had led to a situation where more drastic measures were required to solve the problem.

The furore caused by the speech was such that Powell was forced out of the Shadow Cabinet, and there was extensive media coverage of the issues he raised throughout 1968 and 1969, and in the period leading up to the 1970 General Election (IRR Newsletter, April/May, 1968 and April, 1969). It acted as a focus for those calling not only for tighter controls on black immigration but for action to facilitate the repatriation of those black migrants already settled.

Institutionalizing immigration controls

Within the political climate created by Powell's interventions and the ensuing political debates the continued arrival of the dependants of Commonwealth migrants already settled in the UK helped to keep the numbers game alive, leading to increasing calls in and out of parliament, and the media for more action to halt immigration and to deal with the problems that were popularly seen as associated with it. The combined effect of those two pressures, and the use of immigration as an electoral issue, opened up the possibility of further legislative measures. In 1969 the Labour Government introduced the Immigration Appeals Act, which was officially based on the report of the Committee on Immigration Appeals headed by Sir Roy Wilson (Macdonald, 1983, p. 269). This report accepted the need for restrictions on immigration, but argued that a system of appeal ensured that the restrictions were applied fairly. Although this Act is sometimes interpreted as a positive measure, it institutionalized a process of deportation for those breaking conditions attached to entry. It also legitimized restrictions on the right of entry of those who were legally entitled to settle in the UK through the obligation that dependants seeking settlement in Britain had to be in possession of an entry certificate. Such certificates had to be applied for by an interview at the nearest British High Commission. Applicants had to prove their claimed relationship to the person legally resident in Britain, and if they were unable to do so they could be denied entry. It is under this system that many recent controversial cases have arisen (Moore and Wallace, 1975; CRE, 1985).

The marked shift of the Labour Party towards the idea of firm immigration controls was part of a wider political process, which led to the introduction of the 1971 Immigration Act by the Conservative Government. During the 1970 election campaign the Conservative Party had promised them there would 'be no further large-scale permanent immigration'. When the Immigration Bill was introduced in February 1971 it was legitimized on this basis, but as a number of speakers pointed out during the debates on the Bill it was difficult to see how it would actually reduce the number of primary immigrants further. In essence the 1971 Act qualified the notion of citizenship by differentiating between citizens of the United Kingdom and colonies who were 'patrial' and therefore had the right of abode in Britain, and non-patrials who did not. The most important categories of patrials were:

(a) citizens of the United Kingdom and colonies who had the citizenship by birth, adoption, naturalization or registration in the United Kingdom or who were born of parents, one of whom had United Kingdom citizenship by birth, or one of whose grandparents had such citizenship.

(b) citizens of the United Kingdom and colonies who had at any time settled in the United Kingdom and who had been ordinarily resident in the United Kingdom for five years or more.

Under the Act all aliens and Commonwealth citizens who were not patrials needed permission to enter Britain. Whilst before, Commonwealth citizens entering under the voucher system could settle in Britain, after the 1971 Act came into force they entered on the basis of work-permits. They thus became subject to control by annual work-permit, and thus to the non-renewal of the permit. This change of status has been defined by some scholars as a move towards the migrant worker system of other European countries, with Commonwealth workers who were not patrials (and by definition almost certainly black) reduced to the effective status of short-term contract workers rather than settlers (Castles and Kosack, 1985; Sivanandan, 1982, pp. 108–12).

During the parliamentary debates on the 1971 Immigration Act the amalgamation of immigration with race became an issue of dispute between the Conservative and Labour parties. Although during the late 1960s the Labour Party effectively accommodated itself to a 'White Britain Policy', in 1971 it felt moved to question the treatment of Commonwealth immigrants along the same lines as aliens and the overtly racial criteria which underlay the notion of patriality. Despite the fact that the new Act was rightly seen as racialist because it allowed potentially millions of white Commonwealth citizens to enter under the patriality clause and settle in Britain, a right denied to almost all non-white Commonwealth citizens, successive Immigration Rules issued by the Home Secretary to supplement the 1971 Act have emphasized the intention of the Act to keep out black Commonwealth citizens as opposed to whites (Macdonald, 1983, pp. 25–30). With the exception of the Ugandan Asians who were expelled by Idi Amin in 1972, and some of whom were allowed to settle in Britain during 1972–3, this policy has been consistently pursued ever since. Additionally such measures have emphasized the essentially sexist nature of immigration controls (WING, 1985).

The decade between 1961 and 1971 had seen the introduction of three major pieces of legislation aimed largely at excluding black immigrants. The 1971 Act eventually took away the right of black Commonwealth immigrants to settle, and thus represented an important step in the institutionalization of racist immigration controls.

Immigration and race in the Thatcher years

The policies pursued by the Conservative Government since 1979 represent a further stage in the development of immigration policy. This has involved two main policy changes. First, a number of changes to the Immigration Rules issued under the 1971 Immigration Act have been introduced, with the explicit intention of tightening controls even further. Second the 1981 British Nationality Act was passed under the first Thatcher administration, and came into force in 1983. Debates in parliament on both these issues give a clue to the attempt by the Government to further circumvent the rights of those black Commonwealth citizens with a legal right to enter Britain and to construct the question of nationality along racial lines (*Hansard*, Vol. 5, 1981, Cols 765–1193; *Hansard*, Vol. 31, 1982, Cols 692–761; *Hansard*, Vol. 34, 1982, Cols 355–429; *Hansard*, Vol. 37, 1983, Cols 178–280; *Hansard*, Vol. 83, 1985, Cols 893–989).

The main legislative action of the post 1979 Conservative administrations, the 1981 British Nationality Act, is a case in point. The Government argued that in introducing the Bill it was rationalizing both existing nationality and immigration legislation, in order to create a British citizenship which automatically gives the right of abode in the UK. It did this by dividing the existing category of Citizen of the United Kingdom and Commonwealth into three categories; British citizens; British Dependent Territories citizens; British Overseas citizens. Although the Government argued that the Act would make immigration control less arbitrary, public and parliamentary responses criticized it for reinforcing racial discrimination (Layton-Henry, 1984, pp. 157–9). Indeed the category of 'British Overseas citizens' effectively excludes British citizens of (mostly) Asian origin from the right of abode in the UK. In this sense it seems correct to argue that the 1981 Act 'enshrines the existing racially discriminatory provisions of immigration law under the new clothing of British citizenship and the right of abode' (Macdonald, 1983, p. 69).

A government document prepared for the OECD conference on immigration policy states the broad policy objectives in traditional terms, but links them closely to other areas of concern:

> In recent decades, the basis of policy in the United Kingdom has been the need to control primary immigration – that is, new heads of households who are most likely to enter the job market. The United Kingdom is one of the most densely populated countries in Europe. In terms of housing, education, social services and, of course, jobs, the country could not support all those who would like to come here. Firm immigration control is therefore essential, in order to provide the conditions necessary for developing and maintaining good community relations.
>
> (OECD, 1986, p. 1)

In practice, therefore, the strategy pursued since 1979 has continued to legitimate the supposed link between 'firm controls' and 'good community relations'. The signs are that this amalgam will continue to guide the thinking of the mainstream of the Conservative Party.

At the same time the Government has steadfastly refused to strengthen the 1976 Race Relations Act or to adopt a more positive approach against discrimination and racism. Even after the Scarman Report of 1981 called for a coordinated and government-led policy against racial disadvantage, a call repeated a number of times since by Lord Scarman and others, the response of the various agencies of the state has been at best limited. Rather it has continued to emphasize the need for tight immigration controls because 'of the strain that the admission of a substantial number of immigrants can place on existing resources and services' (Leon Brittan, *Hansard*, Vol. 83, 1985, Col. 893).

The logic of this approach is to displace conflicts and strains in race relations on to the black communities as a whole or specific sections of them. This in turn has allowed the commonsense ideas which see blacks as an 'enemy within' and a threat to social stability to take further root.

If the main rationalization of the immigration laws and the race relations acts was the objective of producing an atmosphere for the development of good race relations and integration, it needs to be said that they failed to depoliticize the question of black immigration. The racialization of British politics proceeded apace during the 1970s, and took on new forms in relation to specific issues or groups, e.g. education, the police, young blacks and urban policy (CCCS, 1982; Miles and Phizacklea, 1984; Jacobs, 1986). The restrictions imposed by the 1971 Immigration Act, and the successive Immigration Rules issued under this Act throughout the last fifteen years, have seemingly fulfilled the ostensible objective of post-1962 policies, which has been to control primary immigration and restrict secondary immigration, but the politicization of race has continued during this time.

What explains this racialization of political discourses in a context of firm immigration controls? A number of issues are involved, and not all of these can be analysed here, but at least two are worth noting. First, debates about immigration and race have taken place within a broader context of social, political and economic change which has influenced the ways in which such debates have developed. The rapid transformation of many inner city localities over the last two decades, particularly in relation to the economic and social infrastructure, has provided a fertile ground for the racialization of issues such as employment, housing, education and law and order (Hall *et al.*, 1978; Phizacklea and Miles, 1980, pp. 42–68; Solomos, 1986). This racialization process has moved public and political debate beyond the question of immigration *per se*, with the focus moving towards the identification and resolution of specific social problems linked to race. But the link with the immigration question is maintained at another level, because it is the size of the black population, whether in the schools or the unemployed queue which is identified as the source of the problem (Macdonald, 1983; Castles *et al.*, 1984).

Second, the continuing racialization of British politics in the context of firm immigration highlights the way in which political language is often a way of emphasizing what one wants to believe and avoiding what one does not wish to face (Edelman, 1977; Katznelson, 1986). Thus, although calls for more controls on immigration are often laced with references to the number of immigrants or to the large numbers who could potentially arrive and swamp British culture, such statements are not necessarily based on the facts in any recognized sense. Rather references to statistics and reports are often highly selective and emphasize symbolic fears about the present or future. Good examples of this process are the debates which occurred during the mid-1970s about the Hawley Report on immigration from the Indian subcontinent (1976) and the Select Committee on Race Relations and Immigration report on *Immigration* (1978). In both cases the debates about these reports in parliament, the media and in other contexts focused on the dangers of massive numbers of immigrants arriving and the possible social and political consequences; and this despite the fact that firm controls on immigration had been implemented during the 1960s. Perhaps a more recent phenomenon is the case of the visa controls introduced in 1986 for visitors from India, Pakistan, Bangladesh, Nigeria and Ghana on the basis of controlling the number of illegal immigrants from these countries. The fact that only 222 out of

452,000 visitors from the five countries absconded as illegal immigrants in 1985, did not prevent the symbolic use of visa controls as another means of 'holding the tide' of immigration (*The Guardian*, 2 September, 1986).

[. . .] The symbolism of the language used by Enoch Powell in 1968–9 to warn of the dangers of immigration, was reworked by the late-1970s around the issue of the 'enemy within'; who was in many cases no longer an immigrant but born and bred in Brixton, Handsworth, Liverpool and other urban localities. The generation and amplification of the mugging issue in the early 1970s, confrontations between the police and young blacks, and the identification of young blacks as an alienated group within the black communities and British society generally, helped to construct a new racialized discourse about black youth (Solomos, 1988). Increasingly this group was identified as drifting into either criminal activities or radical political activities which brought them into direct contact, and hence conflict, with the police. Just as in the 1950s and 1960s the numbers game mobilized a conception of the problem which focused on the need to keep black immigrants out, now the language of political debate seemed to shift towards the view that black youth were a kind of social time-bomb which could help undermine the social fabric of the immigration/race relations amalgam and possibly society as a whole.

Unrest and disorder in the inner cities

The experience of the 1981 and 1985 riots is an example of the power of immigration as a political symbol, even though there was no evidence of a causal relationship between the two processes. During both periods one of the central themes in public and parliamentary debates about the riots was the question of race. A number of the popular papers and MPs focused on the role that young blacks played in the riots, and the linkage between the emergence of forms of violent protest and the growth of immigrant communities and alien values (Solomos, 1986). Indeed in the context of both the parliamentary debates and the popular press Enoch Powell and other MPs and commentators constructed an interpretation of the riots which saw them as intimately linked to the size and concentration of the black population in certain localities. Powell proclaimed the 1981 riots as a vindication of his warnings about immigration since 1968 (*Hansard*, Vol. 8, 1981, Cols 1313–14). In 1985 he repeated this assertion and linked it to a renewed call for repatriation as the only effective solution to the problem (*Hansard*, Vol. 84, 1985, Cols 375–6). Similar arguments were made by other MPs and press commentators during both 1981 and 1985. The extreme implications of this analysis were rejected by both the Government and Opposition, along with other sections of political opinion. But there seems little doubt that the riots since 1981 represent an important watershed in the racialization of British politics. They have helped to strengthen the commonsense notion that black youth are a danger to the stability of domestic race relations.

Prospects for reform

The shift we have noted in the previous section from a preoccupation with immigration and the numbers game as such to the question of the enemy within and related images of social disorder is an important development. At least in relation to the disorders experienced in 1981 and 1985 it highlights the complex processes through which racialized political discourses are working in contemporary Britain. But we should emphasize that we are far from suggesting that immigration will become less important as a political issue. Rather we see the growing usage of political symbols which depict blacks as an enemy within as inextricably linked with the history of state responses which we have analysed here. Indeed the post-1979 Conservative administrations have continued to mobilize the immigration question as a political symbol, and to legitimate the maintenance of racially specific controls as a necessary response to the fears of ordinary people about too much immigration.

Since 1979, however, the Labour Party and the minority parties have shown some signs of questioning the basis of this approach (Fitzgerald and Layton-Henry, 1986). The Labour Party, which was responsible for the introduction of the 1968 Commonwealth Immigrants Act, has seemingly come round to the view that current immigration laws are racist, and it aims to introduce its own legislation when in power to ensure that controls are both non-racist and non-sexist. In a parliamentary debate on immigration in July 1985 Gerald Kaufman affirmed that the intention of a future Labour administration would be to (a) maintain firm controls on immigration and (b) ensure that such controls were applied equally to all immigrants regardless of 'race' (*Hansard*, Vol. 83, 1985, Cols 909–10). He accused the Conservatives of trying to identify immigration with race, when recent history questioned this assumption:

> Viewed objectively, immigration should be neither a problem nor an issue in Britain. Substantial primary immigration ended at least a decade and a half ago, and there is no prospect of it starting again. In most years there is a net emigration from the United Kingdom. In 1983–4, 45 per cent of so-called immigrants are Britons returning to the United Kingdom. In that year only 15.5 per cent of immigrants came from the West Indies, Africa and the Indian subcontinent – the areas from which, according to the Government, there is the greatest pressure to migrate to the United Kingdom.
> (Ibid., Col. 910)

This approach represents a marked shift from the actions of Labour Governments during 1964–70 and 1974–9, but it is difficult to say what is meant by non-racist immigration controls and how a future Labour administration could effectively break away from the logic of politics since 1962 – which has been to construct black immigration into a problem. Certainly over the post-1981 period, in the aftermath of the riots, a strong black and anti-racist lobby has emerged within the Labour Party. This lobby is pressing the party into a firm commitment to implement the reforms (Fitzgerald and Layton-Henry, 1986, pp. 110–14).

In the context of the current political climate, however, it is hard to see how a de-politicization of the immigration/race question can come about. Growing urban unrest and violence create a space for the Powellite imagery of a racial civil war to take root in popular common sense, for the real fears of the white population to be defected on to the enemy within. Promises of a fundamental break from its past practice by the Labour Party have to be set against the wider political background.
[...]

The significance of politics

The above discussion has demonstrated that it is far too simplistic to see the state as a reactive instrument of either economic forces or popular pressures in relation to the control of immigration and the management of migrant labour. Rather, we have highlighted the social, economic, political and ideological contexts which have helped to shape state legislation in this field and to bring about the present articulation between racially exclusionary practices and social policies against discrimination.

In a broad sense the state interventions described above can be seen as making a contribution to the reproduction of the dominant social relations of contemporary Britain, particularly through the regulation of migrant workers and the reinforcement of racialized and ethnically-based social divisions. But such a generalization does not capture the complexity of the role of the state in relation to immigration and other important issues on the political agenda of the period we have covered. Far from the state simply responding to pressures from the outside, we have shown throughout this article that it has played a central role in defining both the form and the content of policies and wider political agendas. Indeed the state and its agencies have become the locus of struggles over the form of the political regulation of immigration and the management of domestic race relations.

Summary and conclusion

[. . .] The story of post-1945 responses to immigration that we have covered here shows how popular responses and state policy-making have been shaped by specific contexts and political situations. The circumstances which bring about specific types of policy response are not given but are the product of struggles and contradictions, both within and outside state institutions. During the period covered here state responses to migration have by no means been uniform, although there are trends that can be delineated.

We still need to know more about the dynamics and the limits of state intervention in this field, the interplay between state policies and political mobilization around racial issues. A more adequate understanding of these processes is required if we are to understand how the interplay between immigration and the state has produced a situation whereby racist immigration controls have become institutionalized.
[. . .]

References

Berkeley, H. (1977) *The Odyssey of Enoch*, London, Hamish Hamilton.

Bevan, V. (1986) *The Development of British Immigration Law*, London, Croom Helm.

Butler, Lord (1971) *The Art of the Possible*, Harmondsworth, Penguin.

Carter, B., Harris, C., Joshi, S. (1987) 'The 1951–55 Conservative government and the racialisation of black immigration', *Policy Papers in Ethnic Relations*, No. 11, University of Warwick, Centre for Research in Ethnic Relations.

Castles, S., with Booth, H. and Wallace, T. (1984) *Here for Good: Western Europe's new ethnic minorities*, London, Pluto Press.

Castles, S. and Kosack, G. (1985) *Immigrant Workers and Class Structure in Western Europe*, London, Oxford University Press.

CCCS Race and Politics Group (1982) *The Empire Strikes Back: race and racism in 70s Britain*, London, Hutchinson.

Commission for Racial Equality (CRE) (1985) *Immigration Control Procedures: report of a formal investigation*, London, Commission for Racial Equality.

Crossman, R. (1975) *Diaries of a Cabinet Minister*, Volume 1, London, Hamish Hamilton/ Jonathan Cape.

Deakin, N. (1965) *Colour and the British Electorate*, London, Pall Mall Press.

Deakin N. (1968) 'The politics of the Commonwealth Immigrants Bill', *Political Quarterly*, **391**, pp. 24–45.

Deakin, N. (1970) *Colour, Citizenship and British Society*, London, Panther.

Deakin, N. (1972) *The Immigration Issue in British Politics*, Unpublished PhD Thesis, University of Sussex.

Dean, D. (1987) 'Coping with colonial immigration, the Cold War and colonial policy', *Immigrants and Minorities*, **6**(3), pp. 305–4.

Deedes, W. (1968) *Race Without Rancour*, London, Conservative Political Centre.

Edelman, M. (1977) *Political Language: words that succeed and policies that fail*, New York, Academic Press.

Evans, J. M. (1983) *Immigration Law*, London, Sweet and Maxwell.

Fitzgerald, M. and Layton-Henry, Z. (1986) 'Opposition parties and race policies: 1979–83' in Layton-Henry, Z. and Rich, P. (eds) *Race, Government and Politics in Britain*, London, Macmillan.

Foot, P. (1965) *Immigration and Race in British Politics*, Harmondsworth, Penguin.

Freeman, G. (1979) *Immigrant Labor and Racial Conflict in Industrial Societies*, Princeton University Press.

Griffiths, P. (1966) *A Question of Colour*, London, Leslie Frewin.

Hall, S., Critcher, C., Jefferson, T., Clarke, J. and Roberts, B. (1978) *Policing the Crisis: mugging, the State, and law and order*, London, Macmillan.

Harris, C. (1988) 'Images of blacks in Britain: 1930–60' in Allen, S. and Macey, M. (eds) *Race and Social Policy*, London, Economic and Social Research Council.

Holmes, C. (1988) *John Bull's Island*, London, Macmillan.

Jackson, J. A. (1963) *The Irish in Britain*, London, Routledge.

Jacobs, B. (1986) *Black Politics and Urban Crisis in Britain*, Cambridge, Cambridge University Press.

Joshi, S. and Carter, B. (1984) 'The role of Labour in the creation of a racist Britain', *Race and Class*, **25**(3), pp. 53–70.

Katznelson, I. (1976) *Black Men, White Cities*, University of Chicago Press.

Katznelson, (1986) 'Rethinking the silences of social and economic policy', *Political Science Quarterly*, **101**(2), pp. 307–25.

Layton-Henry, Z. (1980) 'Immigration', in Layton-Henry, Z. (ed.) *Conservative Party Politics*, London, Macmillan.

Layton-Henry, Z. (1984) *The Politics of Race in Britain*, London, Allen & Unwin.

Lenton, J. *et al.* (1966) *Immigration, Race and Politics: a Birmingham view*, London, Bow Publications.

Macdonald, I. (1983) *Immigration Law and Practice in the United Kingdom*, London, Butterworth.

Macmillan, H. (1973) *At the End of the Day*, London, Macmillan.

Miles, R. (1984) 'The riots of 1958: notes on the ideological construction of "race relations" as a political issue in Britain', *Immigrants and Minorities*, **3**(3), pp. 252–75.

Miles, R. (1986) 'Labour migration, racism and capital accumulation in Western Europe since 1945', *Capital and Class*, **28**, pp. 49–86.

Miles, R. and Phizacklea, A. (1984) *Racism and Political Action in Britain*, London, Routledge.

Moore, R. and Wallace, T. (1975) *Slamming the Door: the administration of immigration control*, Oxford, Martin Robertson.

OECD (1986) 'United Kingdom', National Report for OECD Conference on the Future of Migration, Paris, February.

Patterson, S. (1969) *Immigration and Race Relations in Britain 1960–1967*, London, Oxford University Press.

Phizacklea, A. and Miles, R. (1980) *Labour and Racism*, London, Routledge.

Pilkington, E. (1988) *Beyond the Mother Country: West Indians and the Notting Hill white riots*, London, I. B. Tauris.

PREM 11/1409 (1956) 'Immigration from the Irish Republic', London, Public Records Office.

Reeves, F. (1983) *British Racial Discourse*, Cambridge, Cambridge University Press.

Rich, P. (1986) *Race and Empire in British Politics*, Cambridge, Cambridge University Press.

Richmond, A. (1954) *Colour Prejudice in Britain: a study of West Indian workers in Liverpool, 1942–51*, London, Routledge and Kegan Paul.

Rose, E. J. B. and Associates (1969) *Colour and Citizenship: a report on British race relations*, London, Oxford University Press.

Select Committee on Race Relations and Immigration (1978) *Immigration*, London, HMSO.

Sherwood, M. (1984) *Many Struggles: West Indian workers and service personnel in Britain 1939–45*, London, Karia Press.

Sivanandan, A. (1982) *A Different Hunger*, London, Pluto Press.

Smith, D. (1987) 'Knowing your place: class, politics and ethnicity in Chicago and Birmingham 1890–1983' in Thrift, N. and Williams, P. *Class and Space*, London, Macmillan.

Solomos, J. (1986) 'Trends in the political analysis of racism', *Political Studies*, **34**(2), pp. 313–24.

Solomos, J. (1988) *Black Youth, Racism and the State*, Cambridge, Cambridge University Press.

Tannahill, J. A. (1958) *European Volunteer Workers in Britain*, Manchester, Manchester University Press.

Wilson, H. (1971) *The Labour Government 1964–70*, London, Weidenfeld and Nicolson.

WING (1985) *Worlds Apart: women under immigration and nationality law*, London, Pluto.

Source: Solomos, J. (1989) *Race and Racism in Contemporary Britain*, London, Macmillan.

2 THE BRITISH TRADE UNION MOVEMENT AND RACISM

A. PHIZACKLEA AND R. MILES

In theory, indigenous workers and their various organizations (trade unions and political parties) can react to the recruitment of labour from outside national boundaries in a number of ways. First, indigenous labour might attempt to prevent the entry of migrant labour by demanding immigration controls. This would bring the organizations of the labour movement into direct conflict with the state and capital, a conflict in which the labour movement is unlikely to be successful if capital believes migrant labour to be essential to its reproduction. Assuming, then, that this response is unsuccessful, the second and equally defensive response is to ensure that the migrants are excluded from the better-paid and more secure areas of wage labour. If successful, this creates a *labour aristrocracy* out of indigenous labour, leaving migrant labour in a *buffer* position, cushioning indigenous labour against the worst effects of subsequent cyclical recession and unemployment. We shall see later that British trade unions ensured that the Labour government in the immediate post-war period imposed certain restrictions on the recruitment of foreign (as distinct from New Commonwealth) migrant labour. Such a strategy is not, however, inconsistent with the demand that migrant labour is paid the rate for the job in order to prevent undercutting, although such a safeguard can only be effective if migrants are directed to sectors of work where the labour movement can ensure that it can be enforced.

Both these responses can be described as expressions of economic nationalism. In both cases the labour movement adopts the national boundary as the marker of the limit of its responsibility and jurisdiction. Such responses also spring from the knowledge and the fear that migrant labour has in the past, and could in the future, be used to undercut and force down wages by swelling the ranks of those seeking wage labour. This in turn, undermines hard-won safeguards that labour has extracted from capital, and worse, it can lead to the displacement of indigenous labour altogether. Such outcomes have their origin in the fact that capital operates on an international scale and is always seeking to reduce its variable cost of production, the cost of wage labour.

This leads to the third, international, response which, unlike the previous two, puts into practice the principle of the international solidarity of the working class. Rather than oppose migration or attempt to turn migrant labour into a *buffer*, the labour movement could oppose imperialist expansion which entails the uneven development of capitalism at an international level and the enforced (in terms of economic compulsion) migration of workers to the industrializing and advanced industrial zones of the world economy. Additionally, it could oppose all restrictions that the state may attempt to impose on migrant labour, not only as a matter of principle, but also because such restrictions create, for example, conditions for illegal migration and, hence, the creation of an even more vulnerable fraction of the working class (Portes, 1978). But in the absence of an internationalist response, the labour movement actually conspires with capital to create the conditions for the emergence of a concentration of migrant workers in low-wage, low-skill jobs and who may become the object of racism.

These three responses are not mutually exclusive; we set them out in this formal way in order to provide a yardstick with which to assess the historical evidence of the response of the trade union movement in Britain to labour migration. First, we will briefly review events in the nineteenth century. Second, we will consider the response of the trade union movement to Asian and Caribbean migration since the 1950s by considering the record of the Trades Union Congress (TUC), paying particular attention to the conflicts between the leadership of the TUC and rank-and-file delegates in acknowledgement of the fact that the response of the trade union movement cannot be reduced to that of the policy and practice of the official leadership. Third, we will consider resistance to trade union racism including certain initiatives taken by individual trade unions.

Labour and migration in the nineteenth century

In the nineteenth century, Irish labour constituted a latent reserve army of labour for the development of British capitalism (Miles, 1982). Irish agriculture was experiencing important changes in production relations, while the nascent Irish textile industry of the eighteenth century was, with the partial exception of linen, destroyed by the import of cheap textiles. The result of both processes was an increase in the proportion of the Irish population unable to make a living in Ireland, making it willing to consider the possibility of migration to where a living wage was more likely to be found. The failure of the potato crop between 1845 and 1849 only extended this to a larger proportion of the Irish population. Irish labour in Britain increased the pool of cheap labour available to capital to hold down wages and break strikes. One result was physical conflict between indigenous and Irish labour. The Irish were labelled as a 'race', distinguishable by reference to supposedly physical and emotional characteristics (Curtis, 1968, p. 53). They were blamed for the appalling social conditions found in the areas of new, industrial settlement, a view that became sufficiently common for it to be reflected in the early writing of Frederick Engels (1969, p. 123): 'Whenever a district is distinguishable for especial filth and ruinousness, the explorer may safely count upon meeting those Celtic faces which one recognises at the first glance as different from the Saxon physiognomy of the native.' There is no doubt that sections of the British working class were extremely hostile to the presence of Irish workers. The historical record, (for example, Handley, n.d.) contains references to mob violence involving hundreds of people, the systematic destruction of property, and deaths, most of the incidents occurring in the West of Scotland and North-West England. This hostility was neither formally nor systematically organized by the labour movement. This was because a large proportion of the labour force had no vote at the time, because those workers engaged in the opposition were themselves rarely organized and because the organized labour movement, such as it was in the middle of the nineteenth century, had little influence on national politics (Nugent and King, 1979, p. 31). The significance of these points is demonstrated by the evidence of the organized trade union opposition to the arrival in Britain of Jewish political refugees after 1880. The organized trade union movement agitated for and supported the passage of the Aliens Act 1904 in an attempt to prevent the arrival of further 'alien' refugees. In doing so, it allied itself with those political forces whose concern to keep 'British workers in British jobs' took the form of a barely disguised racism.

The TUC and new Commonwealth migration

Since 1900, the trade union movement has grown in size and strength, along with its political creation, the Labour Party. Since the Second World War, trade union leaders, in particular General Council members of the Trades Union Congress, have been increasingly drawn into participation in the state machinery (a trend that was reversed only after the 1979 general election). Given the primarily defensive and reformist role of trade unions, operating within the parameters of the British nation-state, there is nothing particularly contradictory about this collaboration. This is the context in which one might expect the principle of the international brother- and sisterhood of the working class to be sacrificed in defence of the British working class and so, ultimately, British *capitalism* (see Miles and Phizacklea, 1977, p. 34 for a fuller discussion of this point). But having accepted the defensive role of trade unionism, the post-war attitude and practice of leading sections of organized labour cannot be explained as a reaction to the presence of a group of workers whose presence might be used to undercut and undermine hard-won gains because racism ensured that, for the period up to the mid-1970s, Asian and Caribbean labour has rarely been in a position to act as competition to indigenous labour. Asian and Caribbean labour came largely to fill jobs vacated by indigenous workers or new deskilled jobs created by the introduction of new technology (Fevre, 1984; Brooks, 1975; Phizacklea, 1983). Nevertheless the complete lack of concern shown by leading sections of organized labour for the material disadvantage experienced by Asian and Caribbean labour implicitly condones the conditions which create a pool of subordinated labour power.

Immediate post-war labour shortages in Britain were met by the recruitment of European Volunteer Workers (EVWs) and other European labour. As far as the state and capital were concerned, the great advantage of this labour was that, by being 'alien', it could be allowed entry into Britain on terms and conditions which ensured that it could be directed to specific areas of work. British unions were anxious to ensure that foreign workers did not threaten the pay and conditions of indigenous workers by being employed as a cheap labour force. Part of these agreements worked to the advantage of the EVWs (such as the stipulation that foreign workers should be paid at the same rate as British workers); other parts, however, clearly disadvantaged the foreign worker – those which imposed quotas on the number of foreign workers to be employed in any particular section of the industry, those which stipulated that foreign workers should be the first to be dismissed in cases of redundancy and those which restricted the foreign workers' prospects of promotion (Tannahill, 1958).

A White Paper of 1947 explicitly states that the colonies were not seen at that time as a source of labour precisely because colonial labour, by virtue of the law which allowed such labour free entry and the right of settlement, could not be directed to specific jobs (Cmnd. 7046). Privately, the Labour government went further. A Cabinet Committee recommended controlling the entry of 'coloured' British subjects into Britain (Joshi and Carter, 1984). Nevertheless, throughout the early 1950s, there was a small flow of migrant labour from the Caribbean attracted by the shortage of labour in certain sectors and, in one instance, by the direct advertising in the Caribbean by London Transport (Brooks, 1975).

Despite the reality of full employment, as early as 1954 the General Council of the TUC was implicitly defining immigration from the Indian subcontinent and the Caribbean as a problem and suggesting that it should be controlled. At the 1955 Congress, we therefore witness a split emerging between the position being adopted by the General Council and that of a proportion of the rank-and-file delegates. For the General Council, the problem was uncontrolled 'immigration', not because British workers were experiencing unemployment (which they were not), nor because they were racist (which a large proportion of them were), but because the migrant labour was somehow or other a problem in itself. For those opposed to this position, their argument concentrated upon the emerging evidence of racial discrimination experienced by the migrants, although their concern was that this discrimination had the potential to create a pool of cheap and flexible labour power (see TUC, 1955).

So, from the earliest stages of labour migration from the Indian sub-continent and the Caribbean, General Council opposition was not principally based on *economic nationalism*. Its response ignored the growing evidence of the expression of racism by indigenous workers under cover of regularly repeating the myth of the tradition of British working-class 'tolerance'. That this was a myth was partly reflected in the fact that the object of the General Council's concern about labour migration was posed as the 'immigrants' refusal to 'integrate'. In turn and in spite of the supposedly principled opposition to racial discrimination, the TUC came to accept implicitly between 1968 and 1973 the racism implemented by the state in the form of the law on immigration control (see Miles and Phizacklea, 1977 pp. 21–39).

These tendencies, and the contradictions which they represented, were clearly expressed at the 1958 Congress, held in the midst of the attacks on West Indians by local British residents in Nottingham and London (Miles, 1984). In responding to these attacks, there was, first, evidence of the rank-and-file tendency which acknowledged the reality of racism and racial discrimination within British society, although it was never admitted that trade unionists themselves might be guilty of such attitudes and practices. Those who argued this also claimed that the trade union movement was well placed and, indeed, had a duty to combat such expressions. Second, the alternative perception, which one can identify as characteristic of the General Council's position, was perfectly illustrated by the speech of the General Secretary, Sir Vincent Tewson. He claimed that the responsibility for the 'riots' had to be laid at the door of the fascists who had been active in these areas. This was a convenient way of externalizing the cause by directing attention away from the evidence of the pervasive climate of racism and of the existence of racist beliefs and practices within the ranks of the trade union movement. And, in order to square the circle, Tewson claimed that some of the responsibility must be borne by the immigrants themselves because of their unwillingness to 'integrate'. He rounded off his speech by expressing his 'personal view' that immigration should be controlled (TUC, 1958, p. 460).

However, Tewson was not expressing a personal view. The General Council as a whole had discussed 'immigration' at the National Joint Advisory Council which advised the Minister of Labour. The Council's subsequent report of this meeting recorded that they had suggested that Britain adopt 'some measures of control over would-be immigrants for whom no job is waiting or is likely to be available' (TUC, 1958, p. 125). It was left to the Conservative Minister of Labour to reply subsequently that the government 'were unwilling to contemplate a departure from the traditional readiness of this country to receive citizens of British status'

(TUC, 1958, p. 125). Thus, those trade unionists placed at the heart of the collaborative machinery of government and in a position of leadership within the trade union movement were amongst the earliest advocates (along with a small group of racist Conservative MPs) of racist immigration controls. However, in order to ensure that this motivation was obscured, Tewson argued that the Government could maintain the appearance of 'traditional readiness' by ensuring that 'there should be gates in their land of origin' (TUC, 1958, p. 460).

One can see, therefore, the emergence of certain tendencies within the response of the Trades Union Congress to the presence of migrant labour from the Indian subcontinent and the Caribbean in the early years of the migration. The attitudes and practice of the TUC in succeeding years reflected these early tendencies. The position taken by the leadership remained dominant and the limited rank-and-file opposition was quiescent throughout the early years of the 1960s as the framework of state racism began to be erected (Miles and Phizacklea, 1984, pp. 45–78). The first real challenge emerged in the course of the attempt of the Labour Government to ameliorate its support for racist immigration control with a strengthening of the law prohibing racial discrimination: its first legislative intervention had not considered it relevant to allow the law to apply to discrimination in employment. The General Council of the TUC was opposed to the Government's plans. Hence, the submission of a motion to the 1969 Congress supporting the government's plans and calling for positive action by the trade unions to combat discrimination was a direct challenge to the General Council's belief that 'integration' was the problem which required attention and not discrimination. The strength of the rank-and-file opposition to the General Council's position was such that it had to employ procedural means to prevent the motion receiving majority support (TUC, 1967).

Although the General Council finally conceded on the question of its opposition to the Labour Government's plans to strengthen the law which made discrimination illegal, it continued to act resolutely in line with its identification of the immigrants' refusal to 'integrate' as the main problem requiring attention. It was therefore more than willing to collaborate with government-initiated organizations which were set the task of improving 'race relations' while at the same time refusing to oppose the Commonwealth Immigrants Act 1968 and the Immigration Act 1971 on the grounds that they implemented racism in the sense that they were racist in intent and effect (TUC, 1969; 1970; 1971; 1972). It was not until 1973 that a motion from the floor of Congress was carried which requested that the next Labour Government repeal the racist legislation of 1971 (a request that the 1974–9 Labour Government chose to ignore). This was the first time that a motion from the floor of Congress had been successful in changing the emphasis of TUC policy towards Asian and Caribbean workers in Britain (TUC, 1973, p. 585).

That this happened was due in part to the activity of some trade unionists throughout Britain aimed at combating racism and racial discrimination. For many, the matter was, and is, a matter of principle and they have strenously campaigned to change the policies of their own unions and that of the TUC. But such workers remain a minority within the ranks of organized labour. Nevertheless, the criticisms voiced by them, and the anti-racist campaigns that they have initiated at the local level, represented one important force in ensuring further changes in TUC policy and practice in the mid-1970s (Miles and Phizacklea, 1978). These changes, which were reflected in both policy and organization, involved recognizing the existence of racism in the labour movement as a significant force which required attention, and the effects of racism and discrimination on the material circumstances of the now settled migrants and their British-born children. However, there remains very little real evidence that organized labour in Britain has seriously confronted the issue of racism within its own ranks and the reality of material disadvantage amongst those who have been the object of racism and discrimination.

Rank-and-file pressure within the trade union movement was not the only factor which forced a limited reappraisal of TUC policy and practice. A second was the growth of support for organized fascism in the form of the National Front in the early 1970s. The trade union leadership became increasingly concerned about this growing support, being mindful of what fascism in power in Germany and Italy had meant for the trade union movement. The fact that fascism had gone hand in hand with the destruction of independent trade union organization between the two world wars was one important motivation to begin to be seen to take a principled stand of opposition towards racism, not only in Britain, but also within the labour movement. The third factor was the occurrence of a number of industrial disputes in the early 1970s which sprang from the resistance of Asian and Caribbean workers to exploitation and trade union racism. These disputes clearly demonstrated even to the most short-sighted and reactionary trade union leader that racism was rife within its own ranks.

Resistance to trade union racism

These industrial disputes clearly demonstrated what some rank-and-file activists and large numbers of Asian and Caribbean workers had been claiming for more than fifteen years – that fellow workers, trade union officials and employers often colluded or were actively engaged in discriminatory and exclusionary practices which confined Asian and Caribbean workers to low-paid, low-skill jobs or excluded them altogether from the labour market.

In October 1972, Indian workers at Mansfield Hosiery Mills, Lough-borough, went on strike to press a claim for higher wages and for the right of promotion to jobs reserved for white workers. The National Union of Hosiery and Knitwear Workers at first refused to back the strike and when it was eventually forced to do so following an occupation of its offices by the Indian strikers, it refused to call out fellow workers who, of course, were not supporting a strike which had as one of its aims the elimination of a privilege gained by a racist practice. The dispute was protracted and bitter, and notable for the fact that it demonstrated the importance of the material and political support given to the strikers by the Indian community and for the fact that it prompted one of the union officials to later declare his disgust at being unable to support 'his own people'. The Commission for Industrial Relations was ordered to report on the dispute and, as a result of its efforts, the complicity of the trade union in implementing racist practices was set down in official print for all to see (Commission for Industrial Relations, 1974). But, even more significantly, the report warned that if action was not taken to eliminate such practices, there was a real danger that those excluded from promotion to the ranks of the skilled and the higher paid by their own union might take the logical step of forming their own.

The implication was clearly stated, and then underlined by further, similar disputes at Harwood Cash Lawn Mills in Mansfield, E. E. Jaffe and Malmic Lace in Nottingham, Standard Telephone and Cables in Southgate and Perivale Gutterman in Southall, all in 1973. Then, in 1974, the resistance to racism practiced by trade unions was carried into the ranks of the largest union in Britain, the Transport and General Workers Union. The Imperial Typewriter factory in Leicester employed over 1500 workers of whom about two-thirds were Asian (many of whom were women). The strike again originated in racial discrimination and again the striking Asian workers were refused the support of their union, forcing them back onto the assistance willingly provided by the Asian community (see Moore, 175). The dispute was also notable for the active role played by the neo-fascist National Front, and the support that it gained by arguing that 'white' workers should remain true to their 'race'. On this occasion, the issue of trade union collaboration in racism and discrimination was placed on the desk of one of the leading trade union officials, Jack Jones. The evidence illuminated by the resistance of Asian and Caribbean workers was so clear and so substantial that it could no longer be completely swept under the carpet, not even that of the General Council of the TUC. This was the third factor which pushed the TUC into mounting an anti-racist campaign in collaboration with the Labour Party in 1976 and into stating that it would press all affiliated unions to negotiate equal opportunity policies with employers, as well as encourage both government and CBI to pursue such policies (Miles and Phizacklea, 1978).

Racism at work

In theory these initiatives of the mid-1970s represent a commitment to recognize and combat racism within trade union ranks and pursue measures aimed at ameliorating, even eradicating, the material disadvantage of West Indian and Asian workers. In practice, what has been their effect? There is no easy answer to that question. In the short term, the propaganda initiative and the large demonstration that was organized in London in Autumn 1976 indicated the potential scale of opposition that could be mobilized against racism and fascism, and that was not without political effects. In the longer term, what is of equal importance is that such an initiative changes racist attitudes and practices, first of all in trade union ranks and on the shop-floor. The fact that the TUC and Labour Party anti-racist campaign did not survive for long after the demonstration, and that anti-racist activity seemed to die away with the collapse of the National Front vote in the general election of 1979 suggest that the impact on racist attitudes and practices was slight. This is confirmed if the Commission for Racial Equality's formal investigation in 1981 into certain activities of BL Cars Ltd is taken as a measure of the success or failure of those initiatives. We choose to draw attention to this investigation for reasons suggested by the Commission itself:

> We are dealing with a major employer in a multi-racial labour market, not only in the West Midlands but in other parts of the country too; and we are dealing with shop stewards of a major union with many ethnic minority members.
>
> (Commission for Racial Equality, 1981, p. 1)

BL Cars has had a corporate equal opportunity policy since June 1976 and at the plant in question an Equal Opportunities Handbook was circulated to all staff at supervisory level and above. The policy of the AUEW is contained in conference resolutions condemning racial discrimination. However, while such resolutions are binding on members by virtue of being union policy, no specific instructions about how such a policy should be implemented had been provided for either officials or members. The CRE's decision to conduct an investigation followed allegations by an employee of BL Cars that in July 1977 the fitters in the

> Machine Tool Section held a meeting at which they passed a resolution refusing to accept the employment of black fitters, that the two shop stewards for the Section informed their Superintendent of this resolution, and the Superintendent then decided not to recruit a black applicant, Mr. Jones.
>
> (CRE, 1981, p. 4)

The company and the shop stewards were given the opportunity of making representations prior to any investigation by the CRE taking place. The company simply denied that any discrimination had taken place, while the shop stewards stated that they had simply 'passed on' to the superintendent responsible for recruitment the section's views which opposed 'coloured people' joining that section. In other words, the company was denying that it practised discrimination while the shop stewards admitted to their racism. But after the investigation began, the company offered a different interpretation of events. It claimed that the applicant, Mr Jones, had been rejected not because of his 'race' but because he lacked the required experience. This claim is contradicted by the fact that 'whites' with similar experience had been taken on before and after his rejection, and by the fact that Mr Jones was a time-served and experienced fitter and held a Section 1 AUEW membership card (denoting skilled membership) necessary for recruitment into the section in question.

Towards the end of the investigation, the company produced a new line of argument. It continued to insist that it was not guilty of discrimination, and then argued that Mr Jones had not been appointed because workers in the section refused to work with him. This argument, while being internally contradictory, also contradicts the commitment of the company in 1976 to abide by the provisions of the Race Relations Act of the same year and their self-presentation as an equal opportunity employer. These commitments are shown to be worthless, not only by the specific decision taken in the case of Mr Jones, but also by the fact that the superintendent responsible for recruitment was shown to have received no training concerning the implementation of the equal opportunity policy.

As far as the AUEW was concerned, the behaviour of its shop stewards and officials was consistent with the position adopted by leading sections of organized labour. Moreover, the behaviour and openly expressed opinions of the membership in the machine tool section indicate that, at least on this issue, the position of the leadership reflects what is probably the view of the majority. Hence, we find a formal commitment to internationalism in the form of 'principled' opposition to racial discrimination at the level of official policy which is subsequently contradicted by both the open expression of racism (and the use of the shop-floor machinery to put it into practice) and the refusal of the officials to take any action to combat that racism. The overall result is a blatant breach of the 1976 Race Relations Act.

As a result of the investigation, both the company and the AUEW shop stewards were served with non-discrimination notices requiring them not to commit any discriminatory acts in the future. This is the limit of the CRE's action in such cases and demonstrates that the real weakness of the 1976 Race Relations Act lies in the area of enforcement. The investigation as a whole serves to underline the rigidity of racism in contemporary Britain and the type of attitude and practice prevalent amongst organized labour in support of the structure of racism. The 'skilled' workers in question had a very clear idea of who could and who could not fill the vacant places in their 'reservation'. 'Skill' was long ago defined so as to exclude female workers (Phillips and Taylor, 1980), and now it is clearly defined so as to exclude West Indian and Asian workers. The investigation also demonstrated the extent of collaboration between management and workers in putting racism into practice.

Racism and trade union practices in the 1980s

We are suggesting, therefore, that the principled statements and limited policy initiatives of the 1970s were largely declaratory in nature. Although this represented a positive advance when compared with the 1950s and 1960s, on the shop-floor it was business as usual. Racist practices in the work-place had not been curtailed and consequently the material disadvantage of Asian and Caribbean workers had not been tackled by the trade union movement. In the 1980s this remained largely the case but we have witnessed some concern amongst some unions to increase the participation and representation of Asian and Caribbean workers and the restatement of a commitment amongst the same unions to tackle racism within their own ranks and the wider society.

These developments have occurred within a context of mass unemployment, falling union membership rolls and a situation where less than half of Britain's work-force is now organized through TUC-affiliated unions. Asian and Caribbean workers have been the frontline victims of deepening recession, redundancy and unemployment because the type of jobs they do and the industries in which they are most commonly found have suffered most as a result of these processes (Smith, 1981). Nevertheless they continue to exhibit a higher level of unionization than their fellow workers (Brown, 1984, p. 169) and to resist exploitation, often in the face of union indifference (see Bishton, 1982).

The cynical response within this context must therefore be, can unions any longer *afford* to ignore the needs of Asian and Caribbean workers and the racism within union ranks? Certainly this cannot have been far from Ken Gill's mind when he argued in 1981 that TUC Congress policy

> demands the removal of direct and indirect discrimination at the workplace; more, it demands that trade unions themselves look at their own structures and organisations, and break down the barriers within the unions to advance to decision making bodies, to Executives and to officialdom. If in your industry or your occupation

there are no blacks, why? If there are no black lay or full-time officers in your organisation, why? If there are no black activists, why? All those questions have to be asked within our movement.

(quoted in Lancashire Association of Trades Councils/CRE, 1985, p. 31)

In the same year the TUC launched the *Black Workers' Charter*, urging unions to find answers to those questions and actively to combat the obstacles which prevent Asian and Caribbean workers from achieving elected office within unions. The Charter also urges unions to set up advisory committees on implementing equal opportunities, to negotiate for the adoption of the TUC model equal opportunity clause and to monitor the impact of such clauses. In addition, the TUC held a major conference of national representatives in July 1985 to review the progress made by trade unions in implementing effective equal opportunities policies. The TUC has urged unions to adopt ethnic monitoring (Labour Research Department, 1985) to make full use of the CRE's *Code of Practice* in negotiating comprehensive equal opportunities policies, to take up the grievances of ethnic minority members and to tackle racial discrimination. In addition, since 1983 the TUC has run courses at national and regional level for full-time and lay officials on the impact of racism for their members.

But in its 1985 report, NUPE's Race Equality Working Party argues that the trade union movement has voiced its opposition to racial discrimination and all forms of division amongst working people but it is a fact that there has been very little concerted action to put policies into action (National Union of Public Employees, 1985, p. 10). A year previously, the GLC Anti-Racist Trade Union Working Group went further, acknowledging the flurry of anti-racist activity but concluding:

They [black people] are sick and tired of being fobbed off with all the other reasons, complications and excuses for inaction. We consider that few substantial advances have been made by unions in combating racism in Britain to-day ... It is our view that because of their past practices and attitudes trade unions have abrogated their responsibilities and obligations to their black and minority group members. They have done this knowing full well that black people have for many years joined and would continue to do so.

(GLC, 1984, p. 32)

The Report goes on to argue that 'colour-blindness' is a result of union racism. Harsh words, but the results of the GLC survey and others, namely the joint Lancashire Association of Trades Councils and CRE study (1985), the report to the West Midlands Regional TUC (Lee, 1984), Labour Research Department (1985) and NUPE (1985), bear this out. There is considerable evidence to show underrepresentation of Asian and

Caribbean workers in lay and full-time positions within trade union structures.

The 1982 PSI Survey had revealed that, while Asian and Caribbean workers were generally more likely to join unions than other workers and attend meetings with about the same frequency, Asian and Caribbean members are much less likely than white members to hold an elected post: 11 per cent of white men against 4 per cent of Asian and West Indian men and, for women, 6 per cent for whites against 3 per cent for Asian and West Indian women (Brown, 1984, p. 170). No union has an officer whose responsibility it is to work entirely with the position and circumstances of minority members or combat racist practices and procedures in the union and elsewhere. Of the thirty-three major national unions in the Labour Research Survey only thirteen had any full-time Asian or Caribbean officers at all and most of these had no special responsibility for Asian and Caribbean members (Labour Research Department, 1985 p. 23). Whether or not Asian or Caribbean officials should be solely responsible for such issues is another matter. In January 1985, NUPE had no ethnic minority full-time officers even though, like most of the other public service unions, a significant proportion of its membership is Asian or Caribbean (NUPE, 1985). Just how many are 'black' NUPE does not know, because in turn, like most other unions, it does not keep ethnic records of its membership (in fact at the time of writing only the National Association of Probation Officers appears to do so). In addition, out of those unions who responded in the GLC survey (twenty out of fifty contacted) only two said that such an exercise was currently taking place (GLC, 1984, p. 31).

The issue of representation cannot be divorced from the question of ethnic record-keeping. In the absence of ethnic records, unions do not know how far their membership reflects the presence of minority workers in the labour market, nor whether the number of minority officers reflects the proportion of minority members. The GLC report argues that unions may not acknowledge the existence of Asian and Caribbean members in the absence of records, nor take measures to counter the effects of racist practices or procedures which discriminate against them. The colour-blind attitude of unions is highlighted in the GLC report by answers to the question: 'In what ways is encouragement given to members of black and ethnic minority groups a) to participate actively in your union's activities, b) play a leading role in your union?' The Transport and General Workers Union gave the following response: 'All members are equal, therefore no problems. To have it separate means we are fighting the race issue rather than the class issues' (GLC, 1984, p. 24). As the report goes on to point out, the TGWU's record in disputes such as Imperial Typewriters does not bear this out. Racism can masquerade in the guise of colour-blindness, when there is clear evidence of cases of continuing discrimination and allegations of lack of support for Asian and Caribbean members from their unions (see GLC, 1984, p. 15).

The response of Asian and Caribbean trade unionists has not been withdrawal or separate organization. There is a long tradition in Britain of Asian and Caribbean workers associations, the most notable, of course, being the Indian Workers Association whose first branch was set up in Coventry in 1938 (John, 1969, p. 45). Such groups have always encouraged their members to join and be active in mainstream unions and have discouraged separatism. More recently, a number of groups such as the Black Trade Union Solidarity Movement and the Black Workers Association have been established to pressurize unions into setting up or stepping up their anti-racist activities inside and outside the unions. But there are also 'black' members' groups within trade unions which have TUC approval, NALGO having established 'black' workers' groups in some branches.

Conclusion

In drawing a conclusion from this evidence, it is relevant to emphasize the degree of commitment of Asian and Caribbean workers to the trade union movement. All the evidence shows that Asian and Caribbean workers are just as likely to join a trade union as those they work alongside and, in some sectors, to have a higher level of membership. There is no evidence to show that Asian and Caribbean workers have acted as strike-breakers (unlike 'white' workers in the case of the Imperial Typewriters strike in 1974) nor that they have been willing recruits in attempts by management to reduce wages. And, in the various disputes in the public sector arising out of low pay and state wage controls, Asian and Caribbean workers have been prominent in the strike action and picketing (Phizacklea and Miles, 1980).

This record demonstrates a positive commitment to the trade union movement by Asian and Caribbean workers, both male and female, a commitment that arises from two important facts. First, these workers came, as migrants, to Britain to serve as wage labourers in particular sectors of the British economy. In addition, they also had to deal with the difficulties resulting from racism. It is for both reasons that Asian and Caribbean workers have willingly joined and (as the disputes at Grunwick Film Processing in 1976–77 and Kewal Bros in 1984, to name but two, have shown) willingly fought to join trade unions. Second, many migrants brought with them from the Caribbean and Indian subcontinent a tradition of labour organization, and, for some, a tradition of resistance to colonialism.

This record highlights the regressive role that the British trade union movement has played in dealing with racism and, particularly, its expression within the working class. We find an abstract commitment to internationalism in the limited form of a declaration of opposition to racial discrimination, but this commitment is contradicted by the history of the actions of leadership and rank-and-file membership. The trade union movement is therefore responsible for having assisted in the process of confining a large proportion of Asian and Caribbean labour to the low-paid, low-skill section of the economy in much the same way that women have been so confined.

Trade unions' defensive role conducted within the boundaries of a nation-state can explain their predisposition to policies of economic nationalism. But we are left to conclude that racism itself was, and remains, an important determinant of the policy and practice of the labour movement. At the same time, this policy and practice has not gone unchallenged from within the ranks of the labour movement: different groups of rank-and-file workers have, in various ways, been engaged in resistance against the support given to working-class racism within the trade union movement.

References

Bishton, D. (1982) *The Sweat Shop Report*, Birmingham, All Faiths For One Race.

Brooks, D. (1975) *Race and London Transport*, London, Oxford University.

Brown, C. (1984) *Black and White Britain: the third PSI survey*, London, Heinemann.

Commission for Industrial Relations (1974) *Mansfield Hosiery Mills Ltd*. Report no. 76, London, HMSO.

Commission for Racial Equality (1981) *BL Cars Ltd: report of a formal investigation*, London, CRE.

Curtis, L. P. (1968) 'Anglo-Saxons and Celts: a study of anti-Irish prejudice in Victorian England', University of Bridgeport, CT.

Engels, F. (1969) *The Conditions of the Working-Class in England*, London, Panther.

Fevre, R. (1984) *Cheap Labour and Racial Discrimination*, Aldershot, Gower.

Greater London Council Anti-Racist Trade Union Working Group (1984) *Racism within Trade Unions*, London, GLC.

Handley, J. (n.d.) *The Irish in Scotland*, Glasgow, John Burns.

John, D. (1969) *Indian Workers' Association in Britain*, Harmondsworth, Penguin.

Joshi, S. and Carter, B. (1984) 'The role of Labour in the creation of a racist Britain', *Race and Class*, **25**(3), pp. 53–70.

Labour Research Department (1985) *Black Workers, Trade Unions and the Law: a negotiator's guide*, London, LRD Publications.

Lancashire Association of Trades Councils/CRE (1985) *Trade Union Structures and Black Workers' Participation*, London, CRE.

Lee, G. (1984) *Trade Unionism and Race*, Birmingham West Midlands Regional TUC.

Miles, R. (1982) *Racism and Migrant Labour*, London, Routledge and Kegan Paul.

Miles, R. (1984) 'The riots of 1958: the ideological construction of "race relations" as a political issue in Britain', *Immigrants and Minorities*, **3**(3), November, pp. 252–73.

Miles, R. and Phizacklea, A. (1977) 'The TUC, black workers and new Commonwealth immigration, 1954–1973', CRER Working Papers, University of Warwick.

Miles, R. and Phizacklea, A. (1978) 'The TUC and black workers, 1974–76', *British Journal of Industrial Relations*, **16**(2), pp. 195–207.

Miles, R. and Phizacklea, A. (1984) *White Man's Country*, London, Pluto.

Moore, R. (1975) *Racism and Black Resistance in Britain*, London, Pluto.

National Union of Public Employees (1985) *The Report of the Race Equality Working Party*, London, NUPE.

Nugent, N. and King, R. (1979) 'Ethnic minorities, scape-goating and the extreme right' in Miles, R. and Phizacklea, A. (eds), *Racism and Political Action in Britain*, London, Routledge and Kegan Paul.

Phillips, A. and Taylor, B. (1980) 'Sex and skill. Notes towards a feminist economics', *Feminist Review*, No. 6.

Phizacklea, A. (ed.), (1983) *One Way Ticket*, London, Routledge and Kegan Paul.

Phizacklea, A. and Miles, R. (1980) *Labour and Racism*, London, Routledge and Kegan Paul.

Portes, A. (1978) 'Towards a structural analysis of illegal (undocumented) immigration', *International Migration Review*, **12**, pp. 469–84.

Smith, D. (1981) *Unemployment and Racial Minorities*, London, Policy Studies Institute.

Tannahill, J. (1958) *The European Volunteer Workers*, Manchester University Press.

Trades Union Congress (1955) *Report of Proceedings of the 87th Annual Trades Union Congress*, London.

Trades Union Congress (1958) *Report of Proceedings of the 90th Annual Trades Union Congress*, London.

Trades Union Congress (1967) *Report of Proceedings of the 99th Annual Trades Union Congress*, London.

Trades Union Congress (1969) *Report of Proceedings of the 101st Annual Trades Union Congress*, London.

Trades Union Congress (1970) *Report of Proceedings of the 102nd Annual Trades Union Congress*, London.

Trades Union Congress (1971) *Report of Proceedings of the 103rd Annual Trades Union Congress*, London.

Trades Union Congress (1972) *Report of Proceedings of the 104th Annual Trades Union Congress*, London.

Trades Union Congress (1973) *Report of Proceedings of the 105th Annual Trades Union Congress*, London.

Source: Lee, G. and Loveridge, R. (eds) (1987) *The Manufacture of Disadvantage*, Buckingham, Open University Press.

3 'SAME DIFFERENCE'
THE PERSISTENCE OF RACIAL DISADVANTAGE IN THE BRITISH EMPLOYMENT MARKET

COLIN BROWN

Understanding the history of racial minorities at work in Britain – at least since the Second World War – is both simple and complex. It is simple because just three factors have an overwhelming importance: the requirements of the economy, white racism, and the enterprise of the racial minorities. It is also complex because of the changing ways in which those factors have been mediated through the actions of different individuals, groups and institutions. The underlying processes are racial exploitation and exclusion, economic migration, and community consolidation, but the picture we see is made up of many histories: of individuals from racial minorities, their families, their communities, employers, the white public, the government and other public agencies, politicians of all parties, openly racist organizations, and people campaigning against racism. The story is most easily digested in three pieces – three phases of British race relations. As far as the minority communities are concerned, I am simply talking about the period of migration to Britain, then the period of putting down roots, then the period of trying to take up rights to live and work as equal citizens.

Migration and the original patterns of employment

There has been a substantial black presence in the British labour market for over thirty-five years, so it is inappropriate to discuss today's scene in terms of 'immigrants' and 'newcomers'. But we can only understand the present position and experience of minority workers if we remember that only one generation ago most blacks and Asians in Britain were immigrants, and if we know the causes and conditions of their migration.

In the 1950s and 1960s migrants came to Britain to find jobs. Until 1962 there were no restrictions on the entry of people from the Commonwealth, and even after the introduction of controls people were still drawn here to meet the needs of the expanding economy. The vacancies resulted from the overall rebuilding and growth of industry and the public services after the Second World War, and labour shortages were acute. There was also substantial emigration of white Britons at the time, and even after taking account of the Commonwealth immigration the total result was a net outflow of people from Britain throughout the 1950s. A well-known quote from a Midlands industrial employer sums up the demand: 'The big influx of labour began in 1954. At this time you couldn't get an armless, legless man never mind an able-bodied one' (Rose *et al.*, 1969).

But for the immigrant workers the openings were mainly where jobs had been left behind by white workers moving to better employment. Migrants moved into public service employment, which was falling behind private industry in wage levels, and into industrial jobs with long hours, shiftwork or unpleasant conditions. For employers and for the white workforce, the invitation to immigrant workers was not an open one, but a last resort. Employers made this clear in interviews during the first of the Political and Economic Planning (PEP) studies:

> ... the initial decision to employ them was almost invariably taken reluctantly, apprehensively and after a perhaps prolonged struggle with shortages of staff and unsuccessful attempts to recruit enough white employees. Inevitably the sectors in which circumstances had forced employers to accept coloured employees, through the shortage of white personnel, had been those of acute manpower shortage or those in which the type or location of the jobs were especially unattractive to white people.

> (Daniel, 1968)

Underlying this pattern of recruitment was the assumption that non-whites were naturally less desirable people. Until 1968, racial discrimination in employment was lawful, and openly discriminatory advertisements were common, as were 'no coloureds' instructions to state and private employment agencies. The same was true for public and private housing: landlords and agents were at liberty to turn people away on grounds of their colour, and often did so. What cannot be over-emphasized is how *natural* and *legitimate* this preference was perceived to be at the time, even among those who felt they were 'progressive' about the matter. The following employers' comments from the first PEP report should be seen in this context:

> We haven't got to the point where we have to take them on.
> I suppose if things got bad enough we would.

> We're very lucky here, we've managed to keep the buses white.

I have said we do not discriminate and I stand by that statement. However, there are circumstances when it is impossible to employ a coloured person, despite his qualifications . . . the higher the level the greater the pressure and practical considerations that inhibit the employment of coloured people.

As far as promotion goes, once through the gates everyone has equal opportunity and, providing it was all right with the other workers, an immigrant would be promoted if suitable. I should say though that here [in this firm] the immigrant has a limit – it's going to be concerned with labouring and repetitive work.

Thus many white British people's ideas about immigrant workers were classically racist (because they rested on the assumption that whites were naturally preferable) but were also economically instrumental. Dark-skinned immigrants were seen as undesirable but necessary, in their allotted place, and it was not just employers who took this view. Governments, both Labour and Conservative, in the 1940s and 1950s wrestled, secretly at first but openly later, with the impossible equation of ensuring labour supply, supporting free movement within the Common-wealth, and discouraging black settlement.

The overall job patterns of immigrant workers evidenced their treatment as an inferior but necessary labour supply. At the end of 1966, a PEP survey of nearly a thousand immigrants showed that over 90 per cent were doing manual work; this was the case even among those who had held non-manual jobs before migration to Britain. The 1966 Sample Census revealed other details of this pattern: comparisons in London and the West Midlands showed that there were far more semi-skilled and unskilled manual workers, and far fewer managers and supervisors, among the immigrants than among the white population (Table 1). However, the Census also showed a notable proportion of Indian and Pakistani self-employed and professional workers, while there were few Caribbeans in those occupations. In part the figures here give a false impression: the Census slightly inflated the numbers of Indians and Pakistanis in higher jobs because they also included some whites born in those countries during the days of Britain's imperial administration. But this is only part of the explanation. The table is also early evidence of a difference between the migration from the east and the migration from the west: people from the Indian subcontinent came from a much wider variety of backgrounds than those from the Caribbean. Some Indians and Pakistanis were from rural villages while others were from large cities; some were farmers with poor levels of literacy while others were educated professionals, some of whom did get white-collar, medical or technical jobs, or started their own businesses. It should be stressed, however, that the general pattern was downgrading: many well-educated Asian immigrants had to take jobs far beneath those they were qualified for.

In 1966 statistics also showed that immigrants were absorbed into

Table 1   1966 Sample Census: job levels of men, by birthplace (column percentages)

	India	Pakistan	Caribbean	England and Wales/total population
London				
% Self-employed and professional	12	10	2	11
% Managers and supervisors	8	4	2	15
London, selected boroughs				
% Semi-skilled and unskilled manual			52	26
West Midlands				
% Self-employed and professional	6	2	1	8
% Managers and supervisors	2	1	0.4	12
West Midlands, selected wards				
% Semi-skilled and unskilled manual	51	80	48	28

Note: India and Pakistan figures for London selected boroughs not available.
Source: Rose *et al.*, 1969.

distinctive sectors of the economy. Overall, they were disproportionately concentrated in manufacturing, transport and communications industries, but there were differences between groups from the various countries. Men from the Caribbean, for example, were more concentrated in transport than men from India and Pakistan, who were more clustered in manufacturing industry.

Commonwealth immigrants in later years came to Britain for other reasons. Many women, children and elderly relatives joined men who had settled in Britain first; the migration in its early years was dominated by men, although this was much more the case for people from the Indian subcontinent than for people from the Caribbean, among whom a substantial proportion of the 'primary migrants' were women. In Britain in 1962, over 90 per cent of Pakistanis, 70 per cent of other Asians and 54 per cent of Afro-Caribbeans were men. By 1974, these figures were 65 per cent, 56 per cent and 50 per cent respectively. Another important phase of immigration began when Asians were driven from East Africa in the late 1960s and early 1970s. Many had British citizenship and Britain was therefore a natural destination (although special immigration legislation was rushed through to limit their numbers). Although a substantial proportion of 'African Asians' had previously worked in professional and business occupations, many were first absorbed into the British economy as manual workers, like their predecessors.

Immigrant workers came to areas where both jobs and housing were available to them. Kept out of council housing by local residence rules and by racial discrimination, and unable to afford expensive owner-occupied property, many immigrants had to lodge in privately rented properties in central areas, or to buy cheap, run-down property for multi-occupation in the same areas. In the 1950s and 1960s, houses and flats in the inner cities occupied a much lower position in the housing market than they do now. The conurbations of London, the West Midlands, South East Lancashire and West Yorkshire provided work and accommodation, but within those areas immigrants were concentrated in particular districts, mostly in the inner cities. Like immigrant jobs, immigrant housing was often what luckier white Britons had left behind. Immigrants naturally tended to come to areas where there were already others from their own families and their own communities, so the initial geographical pattern was self-reinforcing. The combination of these processes of finding niches of available employment and accommodation and building upon opportunities opened up by pioneer migrants resulted in a distinctive residential distribution, which was quite different from that of the general population and which had complicated repercussions for employment in later years.

Consolidation and segregation

As time passed the minority ethnic groups lost the appearance of migrant workers and started to become settled communities. The ratio of men to women gradually balanced out, and families began to be built anew. 'Secondary migration' of wives, children and other dependants complemented the birth of other children as new households formed through marriage, and the British black and Asian population grew rapidly. Shops, places of religious worship and other services for the communities developed. Although the sizes of the different ethnic communities were small, their geographical concentration made it possible for these facilities to be established and to work successfully. Had immigrant settlement been spread evenly around the country, the numbers in any one town or district would have been so tiny that it would have been impracticable to set up churches, mosques or temples, and the demand for Asian and Caribbean foods and other products would have been insufficient to support any local commercial development. Housing tenure patterns also reflected the settling-down of families and communities: more houses were being bought and, among the earliest immigrants, families were moving into council accommodation. The overall trend was a gradual move away from privately rented property, a housing sector which in Britain was becoming more and more associated with short-term tenancy.

By the beginning of the 1970s immigration legislation had effectively bolted the door on further non-white migration for work. In response to the racist disquiet of the white public and many politicians, a succession of Acts and changes of administrative rules had ended the period when employers filled vacancies with workers from the Commonwealth. Thus it was clear that the minority communities were here to stay (unlike their counterparts elsewhere in Europe, where migrant workers were granted only temporary status, and had few rights) but it was also clear that the Government was calling an end to immigrant recruitment. During the 1960s non-white migration was controlled by a system of vouchers issued by the Ministry of Labour. One way to look at this period of control is as a botched attempt to solve the equation mentioned above: it cut back on black settlement, and made some concessions to labour supply needs, but at the expense of free movement. It can also be seen as an intermediary phase of immigration control within a framework of changing demands for labour in Britain: in the 1950s there was a desperate demand for workers, and unrestricted immigration suited the economy; in the 1960s economic expansion was punctuated by economic crises which demanded that immigration should be permitted but controllable; later, more stringent controls halted the flow to suit the troubled economy which had little need for further supplies of labour.

The extent of entry controls followed the needs of the labour market, with the 1960s being the period when the state could pitch the level of immigration at the level it wanted. It remains an open question what would have happened to the number of vouchers issued annually if Britain's faltering economic performance had been rekindled and had returned to uninterupted growth. The voucher system itself was an open acknowledgement that labour demand was driving the conditions of entry: priority was given first to people who already had jobs to come to (Category A) and next to people with special skills short in Britain (Category B). Last priority was the largest group of applicants – those without special skills (Category C) who were dealt with as a simple queue. By the mid-1960s no vouchers at all were being issued to the third group – in other words, *all* primary migration comprised people hand-picked for work by employers or by civil servants.

The change from open immigration to the voucher system was accompanied by a swing from a predominance of Caribbean migrants to a predominance of Asian migrants. This is a peculiar historical conjunction which has never been satisfactorily explained. Between 1962 and 1967 Category A vouchers were issued to Asians and Caribbeans almost equally (about 10,000 each), but the number of other vouchers differed hugely between the two groups: Asians were issued 74 times more B vouchers than were issued to Caribbeans, and seven times as many C vouchers. Smith (1977) argued that the disparity was much too large to be explained purely by differences between the qualification levels of potential migrants from the two sending areas, and that official policy to

Table 2   Job levels of white men and minority men in 1974 (column percentages)

	White	Afro-Caribbean	Indian	Pakistani Bangladeshi	African Asian
Professional/ employer/manager	23	2	8	4	10
Other non-manual	17	6	12	4	20
Skilled manual	42	59	44	33	44
Semi-skilled and unskilled manual	18	32	36	58	26
Total	100	100	100	100	100

Source: Smith, 1977.

change the racial balance of the migration could not therefore have been based on qualifications alone.

In general this second period of post-war immigrant history was characterized on the part of the British state by smoothly-phased closure, and on the part of the immigrant communities by social consolidation. What characterized the behaviour of the white population was racial discrimination, and in the employment sphere this supported the persistence of a high degree of racial segregation in the labour market. In the 1960s and 1970s an employment pattern developed which, while taking black and Asian people into a broader range of occupations than they were originally recruited to do, was clearly centred on jobs that were deemed fit for ethnic minority workers rather than for white workers. Tables 2, 3 and 4 give an indication of this segregation in the mid-1970s. Low penetration of white-collar occupations was the most striking characteristic of the black and Asian labour force, with four-fifths of men still doing manual work. The comparison restricted to men with degree-standard qualifications shows that even among the highly educated the racial inequalities were huge. Even crude classification by industrial sector gives some idea of the particular patterns that had become established for the different minority groups: obvious examples are the

Table 3   Job levels of white men and minority men with degree-standard qualifications in 1974 (column percentages)

	White	Minority
Professional/employer/manager	79	31
Other non-manual	22	48
Skilled manual	0	14
Semi-skilled and unskilled manual	0	8
Total	100	100

Source: Smith, 1977.

Table 4   Type of industry of white and minority workers (men and women) 1974 (selected industries) (column percentages)

	General Popn	Afro-Caribbean	Indian	Pakistani Bangladeshi	African Asian
Vehicles/ shipbuilding	4	6	12	12	6
Textiles	2	1	10	26	6
Transport/ communications	7	10	12	5	11
Professional/ scientific (includes NHS)	12	19	6	2	3

Source: Smith, 1977.

extent of engineering factory labour among Indians and Pakistanis, textile manufacture among Pakistanis, hospital work among Afro-Caribbeans, and public transport among most minority groups. Industrial differences between the regions meant that the jobs available to former immigrants and their families were determined in part by their pattern of geographical settlement, but even within each region the ethnic minority workforce occupied a distinct and inferior position. For example, 24 per cent of minority men in the South East had non-manual jobs, a much higher proportion than the 5 per cent of minority men elsewhere in the country; however, the corresponding figure for white men in the South East was 47 per cent, and 36 per cent elsewhere.

The extent of discrimination faced by blacks and Asians when trying to get jobs was demonstrated by a series of tests in the 1960s and 1970s (Daniel, 1968; McIntosh and Smith, 1974). These studies, which involved people of different ethnic origins making trial applications for advertised vacancies, showed that a substantial proportion of employers rejected black and Asian applicants (before interview) in favour of equally qualified whites. There was little difference between the levels of discrimination faced by the Asian and Afro-Caribbean applicants. Furthermore, the inclusion of Greek immigrants in one of the studies revealed that foreigners who were not classed as 'coloured' did not suffer discrimination to the same extent: most of the discrimination was based on a crude response to skin colour. Trapped within restricted channels of the labour market and having job opportunities limited by racial discrimination, black and Asian workers had to settle into an established, inferior location within the economy in the same way that they settled into familiar but poor residential districts. The process of consolidation was therefore at one and the same time positive and negative – enabling but limiting, guiding but segregating, insulating but estranging.

During this period of settlement another feature of the distinctive place of

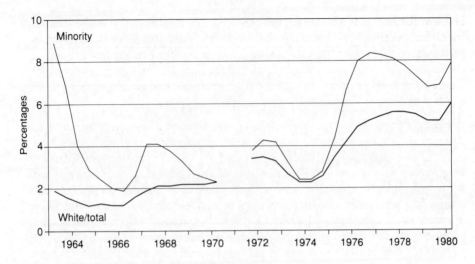

Figure 1   Minority unemployment and general unemployment in the 1960s and 1970s (unemployment rate for men and women; registered unemployed)

Source: S. Field *et al.* (1981) *Ethnic Minorities in Britain*, London, Home Office Research Study No. 68.

racial minorities in the British labour market became clear: vulnerability to unemployment. Although unemployment generally tends to be higher among the minorities than among whites, it is the relative movement of unemployment rates over time that is most revealing. When unemployment rises among the general population, it rises much faster among the minorities, to a higher peak; and as the national trend goes into reverse and jobs become more plentiful, minority unemployment falls faster than among whites. Figure 1 illustrates this for the period 1963–1980. This sensitivity to the economic cycle has been partly a consequence of the concentration of black and Asian manual workers in industries that have suffered badly over the last twenty-five years, such as textiles and traditional engineering, partly a consequence of the marginal nature of many of the jobs held by ethnic minorities, and partly a consequence of racial discrimination. Over the long term, the industrial structure of Britain has been shifting away from heavy manufacturing and towards services, and some of the sectors into which immigrants were recruited have been shrinking, most quickly during the economic slumps. The decline of fabric and clothing manufacture and the heavier 'metal-bashing' industries has affected some groups of minority workers, particularly outside the London area, and this has contributed to their high recessional unemployment rates. Most of the minority groups in Britain, however, have been relatively well-placed in terms of the actual industries in which they work, and their job losses have more to do with their own insecure position than with the problems of the industry itself. In recession, employers shed semi-skilled and unskilled jobs more readily than others, but when undergoing regeneration they can fill posts at this level quickest; thus the social groups who are disproportionately located in these occupations become the first out and the first back during contraction and expansion. Black and Asian workers suffer from this in a compounded way, because of racial discrimination. They are often more likely to be made redundant than white workers, and once they are out of a job it is harder for them to find another.

Although there is no evidence to suggest that employers' *propensity* to discriminate rises when jobs are in short supply, it is a simple matter of logic to see that there is more *opportunity* to discriminate at such times. Employers who are so keen to recruit that they advertise overseas are not in a position to exercise any choice based on racial prejudice, but employers who daily sift through piles of applications for a small number of vacancies can take their pick. Between these two extremes the economic viability of racial exclusion varies, irrespective of the underlying racial hostility of the employer. It is therefore an important lesson that an increase or a decrease in ethnic unemployment does not on its own indicate anything about the underlying degree of discrimination or the level of racism in Britain. The arithmetic of labour supply and demand applies in a particularly cruel way to minority workers, since the full force of racial discrimination is triggered only when jobs are already in short supply.

From the mid-1960s to the mid-1970s legal moves were taken to control racial discrimination. Three Race Relations Acts progressively marked out the domains of life in which discrimination is now unlawful, and established the mechanisms and institutions of enforcement. The first Act, passed in 1965, did not cover employment or housing, but both were brought into the scope of the law by the second Act in 1968. The third Act, passed in 1976, changed the basis of enforcement. Until then the procedure for handling complaints about discrimination was a system of conciliation, and all cases were handled by a central agency, the Race Relations Board. The new Act enabled individuals to take cases of alleged employment discrimination to industrial tribunals to seek damages, and replaced the Race Relations Board (and another body, the Community Relations Commission, which had worked in other ways to foster good race relations) with the Commission for Racial Equality (CRE), a new agency which was able to assist individual complainants to take their cases to tribunals. The CRE was also given powers to act as an enforcement agency itself by mounting *formal investigations* into the activities of employers suspected of discrimination and issuing *non-discrimination notices* to those found to be in breach of the Act. The 1976 Act also outlawed policies and practices that were discriminatory in outcome, regardless of their formulation and original intent; action could therefore be taken against employers both for direct and indirect discrimination.

All three Acts were products of Labour administrations, responding in part to liberal and left-wing pressure to balance the entry restrictions with some moves to reduce the now obvious injustices of discrimination and segregation. The development of anti-discrimination legislation has to be considered alongside the increasing controls on non-white immigration to Britain. Politicians felt that the base on which the Race Relations Acts rested was the end of immigration; they believed public support for (or, more accurately, public acquiescence to) legal measures to promote racial justice could only be maintained by assuring white people that 'coloured' immigration would be firmly controlled. Indeed, the Home Secretary's opening speech for the second reading of the 1965 Bill began with the reassurance that he was considering further restrictions on immigration. From another Labour MP came the most articulate expression of the twin-plank policy of keeping out further migrants but giving fair treatment to those already in Britain: 'without integration, limitation is inexcusable; without limitation, integration is impossible' (Hattersley, 1965). The effect of the 'keep them out – treat them equal' argument on British race relations is a practical matter of some importance. The formula had such appeal that it became the broad consensus in Westminster and in the country, but at its heart was the familiar notion that immigrants were undesirable if they were not white – and it is hard to see this assertion in any terms other than an official endorsement of racism. The government's challenge to racism within Britain's borders was therefore built on an open expression of racism at those borders, and the significance of this contradiction has been more than formal: for most of the white population the primary (and popular) element of the policy has been the ending of non-white immigration, a strategy which conforms with the opinion that black and Asian people cause problems by their mere presence in the country.

The impact of the Race Relations Acts on discrimination in the job market was at first encouraging but in the long term disappointing. Openly discriminatory advertisements disappeared after the 1965 and 1968 Acts, and a public feeling that discrimination was no longer acceptable did bring about a reduction in its extent (possibly helped by an unrealistic alarm about the powers of the Race Relations Board); the second PEP study (Smith, 1977) showed evidence of a general reduction. But it was not the beginning of a steady erosion: direct discrimination seemed to become set at a new level that was lower but still substantial, and progress towards equality in actual outcomes in the labour market was painfully slow. By the early 1980s, the distinctive black and Asian employment patterns were still firmly set, and the gap between majority and minority unemployment levels was becoming wider as the national jobless total grew. The Policy Studies Institute (PSI), the successor to PEP, conducted a third survey in 1982 which showed how much racial inequality persisted (Brown, 1984).

Table 5 shows that in 1982 there were still disproportionately large numbers of black and Asian workers, both male and female, in lower manual occupations, and Table 6 shows that within industry the contrast

Table 5   Job levels of employees, 1982 (column percentages)

	Men			Women		
	White	Afro-Caribbean	Asian	White	Afro-Caribbean	Asian
Professional employer/manager	19	5	13	7	1	5
Other non-manual	23	10	13	55	52	35
Skilled manual/ manual supervisor	42	48	33	5	4	8
Semi-skilled and unskilled manual	16	35	40	32	43	51
Total	100	100	100	100	100	100

Source: Brown, 1984.

between white and minority workers was particularly acute: in this sector about 55 per cent of white men and women were in non-supervisory manual jobs, but the figure for minority men and women ranged between 78 and 91 per cent. Because it was these types of job that suffered most during the redundancies of the late 1970s, unemployment soared among blacks and Asians: by 1982 the overall unemployment rate for minority groups together was approaching 20 per cent, nearly double the white rate.

Table 6   Job levels of employees in industry and manufacturing, 1982 (column percentages)

	Men			Women		
	White	Afro-Caribbean	Asian	White	Afro-Caribbean	Asian
Professional employer/manager	13	3	5	6	–	1
Other non-manual	15	2	4	35	19	6
Manual supervisor	13	9	5	2	3	2
Skilled manual	40	43	32	17	13	9
Semi-skilled and unskilled manual	17	43	53	38	65	82
Total (all employees in engineering, vehicles, shipbuilding, manufacturing and mining)	100	100	100	100	100	100

Source: Brown, 1984.

Becoming equal citizens?

During the 1980s the black and Asian population of Britain reached over two million people, of whom about half were born in this country: a largely settled population of families for whom migration was mostly a memory of some fifteen, twenty or more years earlier. The consolidation of communities continued, with a concentration of ethnic residence in familiar areas absorbing most of the population growth, rather than a substantial movement out to other areas. Hardly any black and Asian people looking for jobs were new to the country; jobseekers no longer had to contend with problems stemming from their recent arrival. Laws against discrimination in employment had been in place for over a decade. Against this background of stability and formal rights, Britons from the minority ethnic groups were expectant that they could take up the same opportunities in employment as enjoyed by white people. All the evidence suggests that there have been changes in the employment patterns of black and Asian people over the last decade, but that they are not converging with the employment patterns of whites, and that earlier injustices and imbalances continue to set the boundaries within which change can occur. Different processes are occuring among different groups and the trends are complicated, but they are easier to understand if they are split into four areas: unemployment, self-employment, job levels and racial discrimination.

Unemployment

The major feature of ethnic minority experience in the labour market in the past decade has been mass unemployment: their overall jobless rate continued to climb during the early 1980s, passing the 20 per cent mark in 1983 and not falling below it again until 1987. As explained above, the rise in unemployment among minority workers is always greater than among the rest of the workforce, and Figure 2 shows that it happened during this period. Separate comparisons of unemployment rates among people with particular levels of qualifications have shown that the ethnic differences cannot be explained by educational differences – in fact the unemployment gap between whites and minorities is greater among people with higher qualifications. In some ways the areas in which black and Asian people live appear to have had an impact on the extent they are unemployed: many live in areas that have high local unemployment rates. But comparing the regional distribution of whites and minorities leaves one with the conclusion that, overall, the geographical differences are as likely to favour the minorities as to disadvantage them. Even at a local level, the high-unemployment districts are often within the same 'travel-to-work areas' as districts with much lower unemployment – suggesting

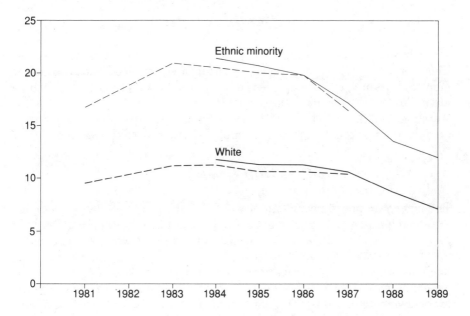

Figure 2   Unemployment rates for whites and minority ethnic groups, 1981–1989

Source: Labour Force Surveys 1981–1989. GB Labour Force definition of unemployment shown 1981–1987; ILO definition shown 1984–1989.

an explanation that ethnic minorities live among other disadvantaged people, rather than a causal relationship between their residential location and their high unemployment.

Behind the overall unemployment rate for minorities have been some important differences between the ethnic groups and age groups: among Afro-Caribbeans and among Pakistanis and Bangladeshis the rate has been much higher than among Indians; and for young people the rate has been much higher than for older people. Among Afro-Caribbeans aged 16–24 unemployment exceeded 30 per cent for a time, and exceeded 40 per cent among Pakistanis and Bangladeshis in that age group.

After 1986 unemployment began to fall as the job supply improved, and the gap between whites and the minorities began to close. This was the result partly of a general economic improvement and partly of the changing population structure of Britain. The 'demographic downturn' means that the number of 16–19 year-olds available for employment will fall by nearly 600,000 between 1987 and 1995. The kinds of jobs that young, inexperienced people would usually fill are the same as those to which ethnic minorities have been recruited, and the shortage of workers in this part of the market benefits the ethnic minorities – in numbers if jobs, but not necessarily in the quality of jobs.

Self-employment

There has been a considerable increase in self-employment among Asians since the mid-1970s. Now about a quarter of economically active Indian men in Britain are self-employed, almost double the proportion of white men. The figure for Pakistanis and Bangladeshis (17 per cent) is less startling, but is still higher than average. By contrast, among Afro-Caribbeans the proportion of self-employed is lower than average.

Job levels

The large number of people out of work and the relatively large group of self-employed among Asians makes it very difficult to see trends in the gap between the job levels of white and minority workers. The high unemployment rate interferes with the comparisons over time because it has affected some types of job more than others: if it were not for the job losses, many of those without employment would appear in the tables in lower-level occupations, so their 'removal' has *artificially* inflated the percentage in better jobs. The self-employed also cause problems because in the available statistics they are included with employees, and are classed in the top occupational categories; therefore the move into self-employment will raise the proportions of Asians in top jobs by definition, and this might be misinterpreted as evidence of better treatment of employees at the hands of white employers. Thus, perversely, two processes which involve minority workers moving outside the mainstream of employment (voluntarily or involuntarily) can give the impression that minorities are becoming more closely integrated into the mainstream. But even among those who are employed, there has been a drift upwards in the average job levels of blacks and Asians over the 1980s. The general shift away from manufacturing and towards services is also particularly apparent in the changing industrial profile of minority workers. The improvement in job levels among employees is largely due to changes in the job patterns of young people. Overall, however, the gap between white and minority job levels is still large: among black and Asian workers there is still a disproportionately large number of semi-skilled and unskilled manual workers.

Racial discrimination

There was no evidence during the 1980s to suggest that the extent of discrimination fell at all. Repeats of the application trials by PSI in 1984 and 1985 produced figures for the minimum level of employer discrimination that were no lower than in 1973 and 1974 (Brown and Gay, 1985): the research, carried out in London, Birmingham and Manchester, showed that at least one third of private employers discriminated against Asian applicants, Afro-Caribbean applicants or both. A less systematic but altogether more dramatic illustration of racial discrimination was given in a series of BBC TV programmes in 1988 relating the experiences of two men, one black and one white, searching for work and accommodation in Bristol. With hidden cameras and microphones they revealed discrimination on a wide scale.

In addition to these reports on direct, deliberate discrimination there has been research in the late 1980s and in 1990 detailing the disadvantage still suffered by ethnic minorities in employment because of both direct and indirect discrimination. These are of particular concern because they have concentrated on entry into and progress within the more professional occupations. The areas covered were accountancy (CRE, 1987a), graduate employment (CRE, 1987b), and journalism (Alibhai, 1990). Equally worrying is the evidence that young blacks and Asians have found themselves excluded from the parts of government training schemes that are most likely to lead to permanent employment, and diverted by the Careers Service away from employers that choose to exclude minorities (Cross and Smith, 1987; Wrench, 1990). At all levels of employment, therefore, there is evidence of continuing widespread discrimination.

The lack of substantial improvement in the general position of blacks and Asians within the labour market is all the more disappointing because the past decade has been a period of apparent political breakthroughs for Britain's minorities. The number of elected local councillors from the minority communities has risen steeply; race equality became a real issue in local politics in urban areas, and, occasionally, a national issue, particularly after the inner-city disturbances at the beginning of the decade; by 1991 there were three black MPs and one Asian MP, all of whom have worked to raise the public profile of race equality issues; the provisions of the Race Relations Act 1976 have facilitated 'positive action' by employers on race equality; and some large employers – particularly in the public sector – have openly paid a good deal of attention to reviewing policy and practice to eliminate direct and indirect discrimination. The small progress that has taken place has therefore involved an enormous expenditure of effort by ethnic minority organizations and by others campaigning and working alongside them; and, at an individual level, it has involved painful battles against discrimination and indifference to gain qualifications and employment, or the enterprise and hard work of building a business.

The patterns of employment among blacks and Asians are shifting, and there is now greater diversity among them than before. Examples of success in business, in the professions and in politics are now easier to point to; in particular, business and commerce seems to have reached a 'critical mass' within some sections of the Asian communities, sufficient to sustain its own growth and to insulate itself partially against discrimination. But these achievements have been in spite of the general experience of hostility, stereotyping and exclusion, and they should not blind us to the other realities of minority employment. Considering the years that have passed and the work that has been put in, the surprising fact is not that some people have hewn a niche in the business world or become professionally qualified, but that so few have been allowed to succeed. At the risk of labouring the point, we should note that progress has been most evident where the acceptance, endorsement and help of white employers has been least required: in self-employment and in the professions. Even the contrast between business and the professions is illuminating in this respect. Although entry to the professions has been achieved by many (because it is possible to do this by individual work and study), progress within them has been restricted because it relies on the decision-making of white superiors, as shown in the reports mentioned above.

Prospects for the future cannot be expected to rest on this circumvention of racial discrimination. It is unrealistic to expect the whole black and Asian population to develop strategies of dealing with racism by avoiding it. We therefore have to turn to the reduction of discrimination as a priority for public policy. As a nation we have to confront the fact that racial hostility underlies the persistence of racial discrimination, and that it is unlikely to wither with time. In Britain, race has been in the headlines in the late 1980s and in 1990, but they have not brought encouraging news about the mood of the white public or politicians. Racist assaults and harassment have been on the increase; white parents demanding to transfer children to all-white schools have been appeased by the Government and encouraged in the press; local authorities attempting to introduce equal opportunities programmes in their delivery of services have been targets of campaigns of vilification and lurid misreporting in the media; the possibility of Chinese immigration from Hong King has been greeted by openly racist opposition; and the *Satanic Verses* affair has been used by many writers as an opportunity to express their pent-up hostility towards Asian Muslims in Britain. In all, it would be difficult to argue that racial hostility among British white people is in decline. In the absence of any vigorous action from central government, the chances of any real reduction in the extent of racism and discrimination are slim.

Meanwhile, the downward trend in minority unemployment depends on the improvement in the job supply. Although the demographic component of that improvement is assured for several years, the economic component is already wearing thin. In 1990 general unemployment began to rise again, and it is not yet known what effect this will have on blacks and Asians; the overall convergence of white and minority unemployment rates had already stopped by 1989, so there are grounds to expect that the old pattern of disproportionate impact will reappear. And nobody knows what effect European labour mobility will have on the domestic job market after 1992. Even if the economic future does swing the labour market in favour of the ethnic minorities, the principal improvements are likely to be in numbers of jobs, and not in the quality of jobs when compared with the rest of the population. It should be remembered that the original migration to Britain was the consequence of a labour shortage, and that process did not put the minorities on an equal footing with whites – rather, as we have seen, it established the inequalities that have persisted since. If there is to be a fourth phase in the history of British blacks and British Asians, a phase of moving to real equality of opportunity, it will take more than a reliance on the vicissitudes of national and international economic performance to bring it about.

References

Alibhai, Y. (1990) 'Still papering over the cracks', *The Guardian*, September 10.

Brown, C. (1984) *Black and White Britain: the third PSI survey*, London, Heinemann/Gower.

Brown, C. and Gay, P. (1985) *Racial Discrimination: 17 years after the Act*, London, Policy Studies Institute.

Commission for Racial Equality (1987a) *Formal Investigation: Chartered Accountancy Training Contracts*, London, CRE.

Commission for racial equality (1987b) *Employment of Graduates from Ethnic Minorities: a research report*, London, CRE.

Cross, M. and Smith, D. (eds) (1987) *Black Youth Futures: ethnic minorities and the youth training scheme*, London, National Youth Bureau.

Daniel, W. W. (1968) *Racial Discrimination in England*, Harmondsworth, Penguin.

Hattersley, R. (1965) 'Defending the White Paper', *The Spectator*, 20 August.

McIntosh, N. and Smith, D. J. (1974) *The Extent of Racial Discrimination*, London, Political and Economic Planning.

Rose, E. J. B. *et al.* (1969) *Colour and Citizenship: a report on British race relations*, London, Oxford University Press.

Smith, D. J. (1977) *Racial Disadvantage in Britain: the PEP report*, Harmondsworth, Penguin.

Wrench, J. (1990) 'New vocationalism, old racism and the careers service', *New Community*, 16(3), pp. 425–40.

4 WOMEN OF SOUTH ASIAN ORIGIN IN BRITAIN
ISSUES AND CONCERNS

AVTAR BRAH

The social reality of Asian women's lives in Britain is constituted around a complex articulation of the economic, political and ideological structures that underpin the interrelationship between race, class and gender. To understand fully the life experiences of Asian women in Britain, it is necessary to analyse the social processes through which gender divisions have been constructed and reproduced against the background of colonialism and imperialism. It is important to take into account the historical basis of the international division of labour and the role of women in the global economy. These are linked processes – some complementary, others contradictory. The question is not whether patriarchal relations pre-date capitalism, for they do, but rather how these social relations have been reshaped within the context of capitalism and imperialism. Capitalism, patriarchy and imperialism are *not* independent albeit interlocking systems – they are part of the same structure. Capitalist social relations are themselves patriarchal and imperialist in form.

When we speak of South Asian women in Britain we are referring to a very heterogeneous category of people. Asian women have come to Britain from different parts of the world, most notably from India, Pakistan, Bangladesh, Uganda, Kenya and Tanzania. While those who have migrated from the Asian subcontinent are predominantly from the independent proprietor class of peasants, their counterparts from East Africa are overwhelmingly urban, middle-income families. Asian women are further differentiated according to religion, linguistic group, caste and sect. There are three main religions – Islam, Hinduism and Sikhism – and five major languages – Punjabi, Gujarati, Bengali, Urdu and Hindi – represented among Asians in Britain. Each religious and linguistic group is in turn differentiated along various castes and sects. The cultures of these groups and the sex/gender systems of which they are a part are correspondingly different.

As is now well known, the post-war Asian migration to Britain was part of the wider labour flow from the European periphery and the Third World to advanced Western Europe. Asian workers were recruited to Britain in response to the chronic labour shortages that accompanied the post-war economic expansion. The economic boom made it comparatively easy for white workers to secure better-paid jobs or obtain places on skill apprenticeships and training schemes. This led to the most pronounced labour shortages occurring in those sectors of the economy where working conditions were poor and the work was low-paid. It was mainly for this work that immigrant labour was recruited. Thus Asian workers in Britain came to be disproportionately represented in textiles, clothing and footwear, metal manufacture, transport and communications, and the distributive trades. Within these mainly manual occupations Asian workers tend to be concentrated in unskilled and semi-skilled jobs. The class position of Asians in Britain is a key determinant of their life chances.

Apart from the case of Asians who arrived together as families after being evicted from Uganda by the then President Amin, Asian women generally migrated later than the men. Various factors have influenced the timing of female immigration, e.g., the variation in the timing of the principal period of migration of men from India, Pakistan and Bangladesh, and the series of legal and administrative measures introduced by successive British governments to reduce black immigration. On the whole, migration of women from India has preceded that of women from Pakistan and Bangladesh. Indeed, the relatively high ratio of men to women among these latter groups suggests that a substantial proportion of Bangladeshi and Pakistani families are still waiting to be reunited.

Because of the variation in timing of migration, some of the issues and concerns facing different categories of Asian women are correspondingly different, even though their structural position as black women will expose them to many common experiences. For example, many Sikh women from India have been resident in Britain for over two decades whereas a significant number of Bangladeshi women are newcomers to the country. A high proportion of the Sikh women are engaged in waged work. They have been involved in a number of industrial struggles. In the current recession many have lost their jobs or are faced with the prospect of losing their jobs. A key area of concern for these women is the issue of unemployment. Many of the recently arrived Bangladeshi women, on the other hand, are facing exclusion from the labour market even before they have had the opportunity to seek paid employment. Similarly, the housing problems of the long-established Sikh families living in owner-occupied properties are qualitatively different from those of Bangladeshi families in East London, who have been housed in poor quality council flats on estates where racial violence is a common feature of daily existence. Bangladeshi women on these estates lead a life of acute isolation and fear of racial attacks.

It is not possible to do justice to the complexity of Asian women's experience in a short survey article of this kind. My intention here is to sketch an overview by analysing their position within wage-labour, the family and education. I examine how patriarchal racism underpins Asian women's experience within each of these sites, and how it articulates with racialized discourses, policies and practices of the state such as those centred around immigration controls. I argue against European orientalist ideologies which construct Asian women as 'passive'. Instead, I am concerned to show the many and different ways in which women of Asian origin in Britain are actively challenging and struggling against their specific oppressions.

Asian women and wage-labour

The use of Asian women's labour in the heart of the metropolis is not simply a post Second World War phenomenon. As early as the beginning of the eighteenth century, British employees of the East India Company were wont to import Asian women to Britain as domestic servants. These ayahs were required to minister to every whim and need of the white family and children during the long and arduous journey back to Britain. Some were kept on by these families as domestics, while others were discharged upon arrival without a return passage to India and left to fend for themselves. Many lived in squalid lodging houses, faced racism and were grossly exploited.[1]

Colonial exploitation and unequal development of capitalism were major determinants of the migration of labour from the former colonies to Britain during the post Second World War period. As noted earlier, the initial migration from the subcontinent was almost entirely male. Asian women came as dependants of husbands or fathers. Soon, however, the concentration of Asian men in low-paid occupations had the effect of drawing Asian women into the labour market. Their wages were an essential requirement for the payment of mortgages, rents and for meeting the continually rising cost of living. A recent survey has shown economic activity in the 25–34 age group of Hindu and Sikh women to be higher than amongst white women.[2] In the case of the Muslim sample, however, less than a fifth of those eligible for work were in employment. It is worth stressing that this figure is probably an underestimate since a substantial proportion of Muslim women are involved in home-working – a form of paid work that tends to fall outside the net of statistics. A reason most commonly put forward for the lower economic activity rates for Muslim women is that Muslim families do not permit female members to work outside the home. Such exclusively 'culturalist explanations' are, however, inadequate for they do not take into account factors such as the later migration of Muslim women from Pakistan and Bangladesh compared with Hindu and Sikh women from India; the differences in economic activity levels of Muslim women from Africa as compared with Muslim women from the subcontinent; the regional variation in the levels of Muslim women engaged in wage-labour in the south-east and south-west of England compared with Yorkshire and the West Midlands; the socio-economic position of the women prior to migration and the different time period in which these women entered the modern job market in their countries of origin; and the structure of the local labour markets in the areas of Muslim settlements in Britain. Moreover, research on young Asian women fails to show any marked difference in job aspirations of young Muslim women with non-Muslims, thus bringing into focus the significance of generational issues.[3] When all such factors are taken into account, the influence of religion and family ceases to acquire the overarching determinancy often ascribed to it in Western discourses about Asian women.

However, this is not to underplay the role of the ideology of domesticity and femininity in structuring the labour market situation of both black and white women. The expectation that household duties and child care are primarily the women's responsibility, and ideas about the appropriateness of particular types of work outside the home for women determines the kind of waged work women do, whether they do it full-time or part-time, whether or not their work is recognized as skilled or unskilled (for the definition of skill is itself socially constructed) and the level of remuneration awarded for the paid work that women do. Thus, for instance, a higher proportion of women than men in Britain are engaged in part-time work; women are concentrated in service industries; within particular occupations women tend to be employed at lower grades; women are concentrated in low-paid work and this work is often defined as unskilled even when it involves complex competencies.[4] Asian women's position in the labour market is affected not only by gender ideologies, but also by their structural location as black workers. On average, Asian men earn substantially less than white men. This has meant that a higher proportion of Asian women than white women have had to take up full-time employment from sheer economic necessity and not just from choice. Even in industries where female labour predominates, Asian women are concentrated in the lowest-level jobs. In contrast to the overall pattern of women's concentration in the service industries, Asian women are more commonly found in the low-paid, semi-skilled and unskilled work in the manufacturing sector, particularly in the clothing and textile industries which have recently been in decline.[5]

Over the last decade Asian unemployment has risen dramatically. The rate of unemployment among Asians is substantially higher than whites, with a figure twice as high for Asian women compared with white women. There are several reasons for this, including the concentration of Asian workers in industries and skill levels which have been on the decline. The restructuring of the world economy involving an accelerating trend towards the internationalization of capital and labour has been particularly significant for Asian women and men, for a large segment of the Asian work force is found in occupations which are vulnerable to technological change and relocation.[6] At the same time there has been a growth in the sweatshop economy which enables some of the multinational corporations to have access to cheap and disposable labour from the unemployed and underemployed. Many Asian women work in this economy, especially as home-workers, who have been characterized as one of the most exploited groups of workers.

The employment profile of Asian women and men has changed little over the last three decades. There is now a large body of evidence which points to discrimination against these workers in terms of access to employment, promotion and training.[7] It has also been found that young Asians, born and brought up in Britain, are no less subject to racism than their parents have been. For example, Asian young women's and men's search for jobs is often less successful even when they have equivalent or better qualifications than their white counterparts.[8]

On a number of occasions since the early 1960s Asian workers have had to take industrial action in order to improve their work conditions. Low wages, different rates for the same job paid to Asian and white workers, allocation of worst tasks to Asians in the production process and racial as well as sexual harassment were some of the key issues around which the major industrial struggles of the period were initiated by Asian workers. Asian women have played a central role in all of these struggles. The Imperial Typewriters strike of 1974 in Leicester in the Midlands and the Grunwick strike of 1977 in London were mainly led by women, while all the strikers at Chix Sweet factory in Slough and at Fritters in North London were women, as the majority of the work-force was female. Women have also been the backbone of such strikes through their activities to mobilize support for these struggles among the Asian communities. In the strike at Woolfe's rubber factory in the mid-1960s and at Imperial Typewriters, for instance, community solidarity proved to be as crucially important as the bonds of labour. These struggles highlighted endemic racism both among white fellow-workers and in the trade union movement.[9]

Patriarchal racism, culture and family

This section is divided into two parts; in the first part my aim is to show that the legitimation of state racism in post-war Britain has been secured in an important way around particular ideological constructions of South Asian marriage and family systems. I illustrate this point with specific reference to the introduction and implementation of immigration controls. I also consider, albeit briefly, the effects of immigration policy on Asian communities, particularly women. Furthermore, I suggest that there is considerable continuity between the colonial and contemporary racialized discourses on Asian women's position within the family. In this way, the first part provides an outline of some of the broad issues which structure family life. In the second part, my focus is much more on the family as a lived experience.

(a) *The Asian family and state racism*

The trajectory of Britain's anti-black racism is closely bound up with the history of the development of capitalism and its relationship to colonialism and imperialism. Ideologies of 'race' have featured centrally in the historical constitution and contemporary elaboration and reorganization of the international division of labour, and they have been pivotal in the reproduction of a racially divided British working class.[10] The Raj was legitimated by the ideology of the 'civilizing mission' which constructed Indian cultures as inferior, barbaric, steeped in superstition and emotion rather than based on rationality, and so on. These discourses were elaborated around the notions of 'the family' as carriers of these cultures, and around representations of Indian women as ruthlessly oppressed creatures who must be saved from their degradation. The British claimed they were a liberalizing force in the colonies, especially for women, yet as Liddle and Joshi show, colonial policy on issues concerning the position of women was shot through with contradictions. While they liberalized the law on some issues, on others their policies had the effect of either reinforcing existing gender inequality or creating a new form which was as oppressive to women, if not more. Liddle and Joshi argue that the British were not interested in women's position for its own sake, but in the way that gender divisions mediated the structure of imperialism.[11]

There would seem to be a remarkable continuity between the imperial discourses on Asian women and those which socially construct Asian women's experience in post Second World War Britain. Many of the contemporary academic, political and popular discourses on Asian women also present us as 'docile' and 'passive' victims of archaic 'traditional' customs and practices, and of domineering Asian men. These discourses pathologize Asian family life, presenting the family, rather than racial, sexual and class inequalities as the main cause of the problems faced by Asian women. They operate within a totally reified concept of culture as some kind of baggage to be carried around instead of a dynamic and potentially oppositional force which stands in a complex relationship with the material conditions of society. To posit a continuity between imperial discourses and the contemporary ones is not necessarily to suggest an identity between the two. As Stuart Hall has argued, present-day racism is the racism of a declining social formation and not of the 'high imperial noon'. It is embedded within the economic, political and cultural crisis experienced at the heart of the metropolis.[12] It has its own specificity [. . .] The new discourses draw upon the old but connect with new repertoires within changed social conditions.

Ideological constructions of Asian marriage and family systems as a 'problem for British society' have played a central role in the legitimation of state racism in post-war Britain. One clear illustration of this can be found in the development and implementation of immigration control. Over the last twenty years successive British governments have introduced increasingly restrictive immigration legislation designed to reduce black, in particular Asian, immigration. The Immigration Acts together with the Nationality Act of 1981 divide the world into patrials (mainly white) with rights normally associated with citizenship and non-patrials (mainly blacks) who are subject to immigration control, deportation and restrictions on taking employment. The history of immigration control is a case study in how common-sense racism was appropriated into the mainstream of British parliamentary politics with the result that patriarchal racism is now institutionalized within the state apparatus. Notions of race and culture were central themes in the parliamentary and nationality legislation. Racist images of 'tidal waves' of potential immigrants from the subcontinent were invoked to justify these controls.

Immigration law defined men as prospective workers who posed a threat to the indigenous labour market, but the women and children were regarded as 'dependants'. The so-called 'Asian arranged-marriage system' was singled out as a mechanism potentially to be used by the Asians to circumvent immigration restrictions. Hence, every single Asian woman settled in Britain was regarded as a prospective sponsor of a fiancé from the subcontinent. The Immigration Rules governing the entry of foreign husbands and fiancés were changed five times between 1969–1983 with the primary aim of preventing black and immigrant women from having their partners join them in Britain while allowing white women the right to do so. In 1985, the European Commission of Human Rights decreed that the British Immigration Rules discriminated on the grounds of sex. The Government has responded by amending its rules to give women equality, but by making it equally difficult for a man to bring his wife or fiancée.[13]

The particular nature of British immigration control means that every Asian arriving in British ports of entry can expect to be treated with suspicion. Asian marriages involving a partner from the subcontinent are subject to the 'primary purpose' clause which decrees that the couple have to 'prove' that their marriage is 'genuine'. Such couples are made to submit themselves to acutely embarrassing forms of surveillance. Reports of harassment at the hands of the immigration service are widespread. Although it is claimed that the practice has been discontinued, there have been cases of Asian women being subjected to 'virginity tests', and Asian children to X-ray examinations in order to establish their age. Work places with an Asian workforce have been raided by the police and the immigration service in search of alleged illegal entrants or overstayers. As a result of the immigration and nationality legislation many Asian families are separated. Some wives have been waiting in countries such as Bangladesh for several years to be reunited with their husbands. There have been cases of Asian women with children legally settled in Britain for many years who became liable to deportation when a mar- riage broke down or a husband died because the wife was considered legally the husband's dependant. There have been a number of success- ful anti-deportation campaigns which have been led by Asian women. South Asian and other female victims of immigration control have now become more formally organized into the Immigration Widows' Campaign Group. There is also an invidious link between immigration controls and social security benefits which results in discrimination against black claimants.[14]

(b) The family as lived experience

Feminists have argued that the institution of the family is one of the major contributory factors in the subordination of women. Family life is an area of ambivalence for women. It is where women's labour and emotions are appropriated in the name of 'love'. Patriarchal ideology constructs home as the 'rightful' place for the women to be. Marriage constitutes a pivotal mechanism in the regulation and control of female sexuality. Yet the domestic unit remains important for women. This is due to a variety of reasons, not least the need for intimacy, and the lack of viable options for the majority of women. For Asian women family support becomes essential also in their struggles against the onslaughts of racism.

When women acknowledge the importance of family life they do not, however, necessarily accept as legitimate the hierarchical organization of the household, or the exercise of male power. In a study of Asian and white adolescent girls and boys and their parents, I found the influence of the ideology that housework and child-care were primarily a 'woman's job' to be strong among Asians and whites alike. The general view was that the man should assist the woman with 'her' domestic duties to a degree whether or not the woman was engaged in paid work, and whether or not she worked part-time or full-time. The tasks with which the men were prepared to help were limited to occasional washing-up, vacuum-cleaning, and minding the children for limited periods. The majority of the girls and their mothers colluded with this ideology of domesticity, with one white girl saying, 'I like a man to be a man – wouldn't like him to be running around with a duster.' But at the same time they did not completely acquiesce and deployed a variety of strategies to avoid doing all the work themselves.

In comparison with the white mothers a greater proportion of Asian women were in full-time paid work. Not surprisingly they complained about the 'double-shift'; in the words of one woman, 'It's a dog's life. There are bills after bills to be paid. You wear yourself to the bone with work.' Many Asian women lamented the absence of support in Britain of other women from an extended household. Where extended households did exist, domestic work was indeed shared amongst the women, but it was no less onerous since there were now more members of the household to cater for. The strongest opposition to the sexual division of labour in the home came from Asian girls, with half of the sample rejecting the notion of nominal help from men and insisting that housework should be shared on an equal basis. Clearly both Asian and white women's views embody elements of collusion, resistance and opposition.[15]

Similarly statistics show that marriage remains popular in Britain despite the high rate of divorce. This orientation was reflected among both white and Asian adolescents whom I interviewed. Yet, whilst they did not reject marriage, the girls in particular wanted their own marriage to be established on a more egalitarian basis with both partners having an equal say in the decision-making. The great majority of the Asian adolescents expected their marriages to be arranged – a prospect they accepted because, unlike the media portrayal of bullying Asian parents ramming arranged marriages down the throats of their children, many adolescents felt confident that they would not be forced into a marriage that they did not want. It was evident that this confidence was not misplaced as most parents declared that they would not countenance forcing their children into a marriage against the latter's wishes. A significant majority of the parents saw the whole process as a joint undertaking between the parents and the young person. This is not to suggest that there were no determined parents or anxious adolescents, but rather that in a great many households there was scope for negotiation between the generations. The emotional and psychological support provided to the individual by their families was important in structuring the adolescents' response that they did not wish to 'let the family down'. The Asian girls argued that what little they had seen of the process which led to white girls marrying did not convince them that the latter had 'more freedom' than themselves. In saying this the girls highlight the problematic nature of marriage for all women.[16] And, as Parita Trivedi has argued, Asian women want to make their own choices as to how and why they challenge their own marriage systems rather than accept a racist definition of such marriages.[17]

In a recently published work on adolescent girls in British schools, Sue Lees shows the importance of the concept of reputation in structuring women's sexuality. She demonstrates how the term 'slag' and its equivalents are used by both boys and girls to cast doubts on a girl's reputation. She argues that:

> . . . While everyone apparently knows a slag and stereotypically depicts her as someone who sleeps around, this stereotype bears no relation to the girls to whom the term is applied . . . What is important is the existence of the category rather than the identification of certain girls . . . All unattached girls have to be constantly aware that the category slag may be applied to them.

There is no hard and fast distinction between the categories since the status is always disputable, the gossip often unreliable, the criteria obscure. If a girl does get the reputation of being a slag, all the girls interviewed agreed that the one thing she could do about it to redeem herself would be to get a steady boyfriend.[18]

Of course, Lees' last sentence cannot apply to Asian girls (although she claims to have them in her sample) because having a boyfriend in their case in itself constitutes a transgression from certain norms of 'respectability'. Nevertheless, the importance of Lees' study lies in illustrating how, even in the 1980s when women are supposed to have made considerable gains towards sexual equality, notions of respectability can have the power to control female sexuality through sheer innuendo. It is important to stress that notions of female sexuality in Britain are racialized concepts. Asian women's sexuality is categorized broadly in three ways. First, there is the image of the exotic oriental woman – sensuous, seductive, full of Eastern promise. Her sexuality is projected as suitably controlled but vulnerable. This image is most explicitly available in the portrayal of airline 'hostesses' in advertisements. The second type of representation is almost an antithesis of the first. Here Asian women are characterized as 'ugly', 'smelly', 'oily-haired', etc. This image plays a vital role in the substantial exclusion of black women from 'glamorous jobs' where women's femininity is required to be visible. In the third construction, Asian women's sexuality is portrayed as licentious. All three elements are captured in the following quotation from a *Guardian* article of 5 September 1985, in which a nineteen-year-old Asian girl, Sunjita, describes her experience:

If I'm with a white boy, say just on the way home from college, they shout in the street, 'What's it like to fuck a Paki?', or if I'm on my own with other girls it's, 'Here comes the Paki whore, come and fuck us Paki whores, we've heard you're really horny'. Or maybe they'll put it the other way round, saying that I am dirty, that no one could possibly want to go to bed with a Paki . . . I don't think any white person can possibly identify with what it's like.

Such racialized discourses 'privilege' white women over black women even as they subordinate both sections of women and at the same time render lesbian sexuality largely invisible. Of course, these definitions are repudiated by Asian women in a variety of ways, and, in any case, white people do not always constitute 'significant others' in the formation of Asian women's sexual identity. Nevertheless, such dominant definitions have powerful effects when translated into social policy or when they become the 'professional common sense' of teachers, social workers, health visitors and others working within agencies of social welfare. The actual lived experience of the family often bears little resemblance to the stereotypic notions which structure professional values and perspectives.

Schooling and Asian girls

The consequences of sexism in schooling are now well known. Attention has been drawn to the under-representation of girls in key science subjects, the invisibility of women in key content areas of the curriculum, the tendency on the part of teachers to pay more attention to boys, the role of education in contributing to a gender-divided occupational structure, and the pressure on girls to see their lives primarily in terms of marriage and the family.[19] In the case of Asian girls these effects are further compounded by racism. Racism in schools operates in a variety of complex ways. It may be direct or indirect, conscious or subconscious. It can operate through implicit stereotyped assumptions made by teachers or other educationists about Asian girls and boys, or it may be institutionalized in the routine structures and practices of the school, as, for example, when the school curriculum neglects, negates or misrepresents the history and cultures of Asian and other black groups.

There is a tendency among teachers to see most problems encountered by Asian girls as being the result of 'intergenerational conflict'. Yet there is no evidence to support the implied assertion that conflict levels are higher amongst Asian families than among white families. Asian parents tend to be protrayed as 'authoritarian', 'conservative' and supposedly 'opposed to the liberating influence of schools'. But there is as much variation among Asian parents on issues concerning the education of their children as can be expected in any other group of parents. There are many problems with 'culturalist explanations', not least that they can have the effect of blaming the victim as well as providing legitimacy to the ideology which claims superiority of Western cultural traditions over non-Western values.

As we noted earlier, girls in general tend to receive less attention from teachers than boys. In the case of Asian girls, the prevailing stereotype of them as 'passive' can lead some teachers to pay an even lesser degree of attention to this category of girls. There are other ways in which cultural stereotyping can work against the interests of Asian girls. For instance, teachers who may assume Asian parents to be opposed to their daughters going into further or higher education, may discourage these girls from studying subjects at O and A levels, and from pursuing academic careers. Yet many Asian parents are very keen for their daughters to gain higher-level qualifications. There is evidence that Asian girls who may require additional support in English can find themselves presented with a restricted curriculum as if they were remedial learners. Asian girls in schools can also experience ridicule from white pupils if they wear Asian style of dress.[20]

Of course, educational disadvantage also accrues if, as is common, the formal and hidden curriculum of the school is Euro-centric; the cultures and identities of Asian children are devalued; if there are very few Asian teachers in the schools and even fewer Asian people in the power hierarchy of the education system; if the ideology 'black people are problems for white society' is not challenged, and generally if no connection is made between the educational process and the broader social context to the arrival and settlement of Asian and other black groups in post-war Britain.

Asian women organizing

Despite the Western stereotype of the abjectly submissive Asian woman, we have a long history of resistance and struggle in the subcontinent and in Britain. A significant number of South Asian organizations existed in Britain even during the colonial phase, and many female and male activists made an important contribution to Britain's intellectual and political life. Women such as Renu Chakraverty and N. C. Sen were prominent activists of the time.[21]

Since the Second World War, Asian women have continued this tradition of resistance and struggle, although their responses may not always take the form familiar to a Western observer or be crystallized around issues defined as relevant from a Western frame of reference. As we have already seen, Asian women have been at the forefront of several major industrial struggles and have been the principal protagonists in a number of well-publicized immigration campaigns. Asian women have also played a crucial role in a variety of defence campaigns launched in support of people arrested while defending communties against fascist attacks. Over the years racist attacks have become a common feature of life in several parts of Britain. The 1981 Home Office Survey estimated that in any one year about 7,000 incidents would be reported to the police in England and Wales. According to a study made by the Policy Studies Institute, the above figure could well be a severe underestimate and the actual frequency of racial incidents could be as much as ten times higher.[22] These attacks have included arson and murder, yet few attackers have been convicted. On the other hand, Asians taking measures to protect themselves and their communities have been subjected to the heavy hand of the criminal justice system. It is only after extensive campaigning that many of the defendants in some of the well-known cases, for example, Southall 344, Bradford 12 and Newham 8, were acquitted.

Asian women have also been actively engaged in placing the question of reproductive rights firmly on to the political agenda. There have been campaigns against the use of the contraceptive drug Depo-Provera against black and Third World women, and working-class women in general. This intervention has challenged the narrow focus of the National Abortion Campaign upon abortion rights when certain categories of women may be subjected to forced sterilization. Racist ideologies about the reproductive capacities of Asian women abound within the whole spectrum of the agencies of the Welfare State ranging from the social services and the National Health Service to education welfare. Both as clients and workers Asian women are increasingly uniting to fight back against the oppressive practices of these institutions.

A major priority for women is the need to fight male violence in its variety of manifestations including rape, incest and domestic violence. These issues are a focus of activity for several Asian women's groups across the country. Separate refuges have been set up for Asian women so as to enable these victims of violence to work out their futures in a supportive environment of other Asian women facing similar problems. Protest demonstrations have been held, conferences organized and campaigns mounted to highlight the issues. A range of political opinion is represented among the Asian women whose efforts have led to the growing emergence of an organized revolt.

Within the private sphere of home, Asian women combine with other female kin and friends to create a dynamic and lively social and cultural life. These female cultures are not devoid of contradictions, tension, rivalry or inter-generational difference, but they provide structures of support and space within which to construct gender-specific leisure activities. They are a means of negotiating and/or combating hierarchies of power in the household and in a wider community. These cultures are the affirmation of a positive sense of the female identity.

The organizing activities of Asian women take a variety of forms. Recently a directory listing Asian women's groups in London has been published. They range from religious organizations to collectives of feminists. Whatever their political perspective, these groups seek to develop support networks for one another, organize social and cultural activities, provide information and advice (for example, on immigration, law and social welfare) and offer space to women to organize and campaign on issues they see as relevant. These self-help groups speak to the shared experience of Asian women and address issues of common concern in an atmosphere of trust and self-respect. It is not easy to categorize these groups along some conventional notion of a political continuum from the 'right' to the 'left'. The multi-faceted nature of our oppression demands resistance at so many different levels that such labels become quite problematic. Organizations whose *raison d'être* is religious or caste exclusivity, for example, will actively support and/or join in with members of other religions and castes in a range of antiracist activities. Similarly major work-place struggles involving Asians have relied on support from diverse sections of the Asian communities.

Whilst it is important to acknowledge the broad base of support among Asian women for tackling the concrete manifestation of their specific forms of subordination, there is equally a need to distinguish between those forms of mobilization which are primarily concerned with specific, largely single issues, and others which derive from a wide-ranging feminist analysis of the condition of being Asian and female in Britain. The two, of course, are not mutually exclusive, but nor are they identical. Asian feminism is one of the most creative and vigorous forces within contemporary black politics in Britain. It draws upon the political traditions of women and men in the subcontinent, but its identity is organically rooted within the British social and political dynamic. Asian feminists have had to address issues surrounding the ways in which factors such as caste, class and religion configure in the British situation. We have placed great emphasis on the need for unity between women of different castes, religions and regional backgrounds in the subcontinent, while recognizing the specificity of each experience. A number of Asian feminist groups were jointly formed with black women of African-Caribbean origin as an expression of solidarity against the shared experience of anti-black racism. This combined black feminism has posed a major challenge to the theory and practice of the whole feminist and socialist movement. Black feminists have sought to gain priority for issues which underpin our particular oppression in the context of the international dimension of race, class and imperialism. The aim has been not to assert the primacy of one form of oppression over the other, but to examine how they articulate. On this, black activists in general have had continuing skirmishes with those sections of the white left who continue to assert the primacy of class over race and gender.

Notes

1 Rozina Visram, *Ayahs, Lascars and Princes* (London, 1986).

2 Colin Brown, *Black and White Britain* (London, 1984).

3 Avtar Brah, 'Unemployment and racism: Asian youth on the dole' in Sheila Allen *et al.* (eds), *The Experience of Unemployment* (London, 1986).

4 Veronica Beechey and Elizabeth Whitelegg (eds), *Women in Britain Today* (Milton Keynes, 1986).

5 Ibid.

6 Cf. Colin Brown, op.cit.; Swasti Mitter, *Common Fate, Common Bond: women in the global economy* (London, 1986).

7 Cff. W. W. Daniel, *Racial Discrimination in England* (Harmondsworth, 1968); D. J. Smith, *Racial Disadvantage in Employment* (London, 1974).

8 Cf. D. Brooks and K. Singh, *Aspirations versus Opportunities: Asian and white school leavers in the Midlands* (London, 1978); G. Lee and J. Wrench, *Skill Seekers* (Leicester, 1983); B. Troyna and D. I. Smith (eds), *Racism, School and the Labour Market* (Leicester, 1983).

9 Avtar Brah, 'Culture and identity: the case of South Asians', in the Open University (1982) E354 *Ethnic Minorities and Community Relations*, Units 8–9, *Minority Experience*, Milton Keynes, The Open University. Pratibha Parmar, 'Gender, race and

class: Asian women in resistance', in *The Empire Strikes Back*, Centre for Contemporary Cultural Studies, University of Birmingham (London, 1982).

10 Ibid.; Stuart Hall *et al.*, *Policing the Crisis* (London, 1978).

11 Joanna Liddle and Rama Joshi, 'Gender and Imperialism in British India', *South Asia Research*, **5**(2), November, 1985, pp. 147–63.

12 Stuart Hall, 'Racism and reaction', in *Five Views of Multiracial Britain* (London, 1978).

13 *Right to be Here: a campaigning guide to the imigration laws* (London, 1986).

14 Paul Gordon, 'Racism and social security', *Critical Social Policy*, Issue 17, Autumn, 1986.

15 Avtar Brah, 'Inter-generational and inter-ethnic perceptions amongst Asian and white adolescents and their parents', PhD thesis, University of Bristol, 1979.

16 Cf. Diana Leonard and Mary Ann Speakman, 'Women in the family: companions or caretakers', in Beechey and Whitelegg, op.cit.

17 Parita Trivedi, 'To deny our fullness: Asian women in the making of history', *Feminist Review*, 17, Autumn, 1984.

18 Sue Lees, *Losing Out: sexuality and adolescent girls* (London, 1986), p. 36.

19 Cf. Rosemary Deem, *Schooling for Women's Work* (London, 1980); Dale Spender, *Invisible Women: the schooling scandal* (London, 1982).

20 Avtar Brah and Rahana Minhas, 'Structural racism or cultural difference: schooling for Asian girls', in Gaby Weiner (ed.), *Just a Bunch of Girls* (Milton Keynes, 1985); Pratibha Parmar and Nadira Mirza, 'Stepping forward: work with Asian young women', in *Gen*, Issue 1, Autumn, 1983.

21 Pervaiz Nazir, *The Life and Work of Rajani Palme Dutt* (London, 1986); Liddle and Joshi, op.cit.

22 Colin Brown, op.cit.; Home Office, *Racial Attacks* (London, 1981).

Source: Brah, A. (1987) 'Women of South Asian origin in Britain: issues and concerns', *South Asia Research*, **7**(1), May.

5 BLACK WOMEN AND THE BRITISH STATE
RACE, CLASS AND GENDER
ANALYSIS FOR THE 1990S

AMINA MAMA

Concepts and issues

This article looks at the material situation of black women in Britain and the way in which the changing British State constructs and reconstructs their positions, first as workers who contribute to the nation, its economy and its public services, and then as citizens, and as consumers of public services. The situation of black women is analysed against the backdrop of debates around race, class and gender, with a view to setting out the terrain on which black women must develop strategies for the 1990s.

In Britain since the end of the 1970s we have seen the emergence of a political discourse calling for unity between the Caribbean, African and Asian communities ('Afro-Asian unity'). At this time a number of black and black women's organizations defined their constituencies to comprise members from all three communities (e.g. Brixton Black Women's Group, Southall Black Sisters, Brixton Defence Campaign and others). OWAAD, the national umbrella of black women's organizations changed from being an 'Organisation for Women of Africa and African Descent' to an 'Organisation for Women of African and Asian Descent'. This was in keeping with its shift in focus from anti-imperialist solidarity work with women from African liberation movements to a greater emphasis on British race and gender politics. There also continued to be Asian and Asian women's organizations which did not include African or Caribbean people, and Black organizations which did not include Asians (e.g. East London Black Women's Organisation, Camden Black Sisters, Africa Liberation Committee, Grassroots). Modood (1988) argues that in Britain there have been factors which make the positive concept of blackness 'harmful' to Asians. He asserts that it was only ever accepted by a minority of 'activists', and claims that there was a hierarchy of blackness implied within the term, which favoured those who were 'more black' by virtue of having (at some point) come from Africa. He completely overlooks the fact that there are many black-identified people, from many communities across Europe and the Americas, who do not link their black identity with Africa.

During the 1980s, the emphasis on common experience (of racial oppression in particular) as the rationale for black unity led to a further change in the meaning of the term black, as it came to mean 'people affected by racism'. There were actually debates about whether Irish people and other migrant groups should be defined as 'politically black' on account of their experience of British colonialism.[1]

The concepts 'ethnicity' and 'culture' have also seen changing meanings through both theoretical discourses and state ideologies in the 1980s. While oppressed minorities have to engage in a struggle to establish their cultural identities and collective histories, in Britain the issues of race and culture have been played off against each other in quite negative ways, so that specific expressions of 'African-ness' 'Caribbean-ness' and 'Asian-ness' were initially often misunderstood and treated as if these jeopardized the politics of black unity. Elsewhere (Mama, 1989a) I have discussed the culturalization or ethnicization of race as a state-orchestrated process which, by focusing on the language, food, habits and clothing of black (African, Asian or Caribbean) people, masks and denies the fact of discrimination. Systematic and institutionalized racism is thereby reduced to cultural misunderstanding and is so depoliticized. Even more mystifying was the manner in which class politics have been superseded by the new identity politics of gender, ethnicity, sexuality and disability.

One aspect of the changing policy climate has been the development and then retraction of ethnic funding. The narrow focus on specific cultural and ethnic needs has produced a fragmented and competitive identity politics which failed to advance the antiracist praxis that guided black struggles into the 1980s. This is not to suggest that diverse positive cultural identifications are incompatible with a politics of black unity. However, it is now clear that in the early 1980s 'black unity' was more of an aspiration than an actuality. Furthermore, it is now also clear that the contradictory policy climate of municipal socialism *and* Thatcherism generated a scramble for the suddenly available but limited funding for ethnic needs, which did not help.

The minority communities remain largely separate, although amongst the younger generation there is evidence that new, syncretic black identities are being formed, and that at least some of these are inclusive rather than exclusive. There is a need for further research and analysis of the different historical, cultural and material constitution of black identities.

In Britain, politics has developed to include black people of African (from the African continent), Caribbean (from the Caribbean region) and Asian (mostly from South Asia, i.e. India, Pakistan and Bangladesh, but also from Africa and the Caribbean) descent. What these groups share from the past is a history of oppression by British colonialism and racism. What they share in the present is their situation as minorities that are subjected to different forms and degrees of class, gender and racial oppression (Mama, 1984). For many, but not all, black people this experience facilitates a change in consciousness that diminishes the ancestral and colonial divisions of class, skin tone and caste. This climate manifests 'inside' these communities in positive and negative ways that demand further analysis.

It would seem that the phenomenon of the more inclusive articulation of black identification and political consciousness is linked to historical experience of European and North American imperialism and racism. Race, class and gender divisions do not simply fade away or decrease with the advent of parliamentary democracy and the Welfare State. Rather, they continue to be reproduced in new forms and given new material weight in socio-economic life, manifesting clearly in the increasingly complex mechanisms of social regulation and administration, in the allocation of resources and in the delivery of social welfare services.

The remainder of this article discusses the relationship between black women and the British state with particular reference to the Welfare State. These relations are cast in an historical framework which incorporates the effects of the rapidly evolving character of racism within Britain in the 1990s, and how this manifests through gender to structure and circumscribe the lives of black women.

Working for the state

In Britain, women have very often found paid employment by working in the public sector (Showstack-Sassoon, 1987; Hernes, 1987). This has meant that they have been highly vulnerable to the public service cutbacks that have characterized the 1980s. Women comprise 47 per cent of public service employees, but 78 per cent of NHS and 86 per cent of local authority health and social service employees (Glendinning, 1987). Apart from causing job losses, cuts in public services also increase women's unpaid work, since the burden of community care, looking after the elderly, the sick and the mentally ill, for example, continues to fall on women's shoulders. The lack of childcare provision also increases domestic labour burdens and makes it impossible for many to find suitable waged labour, forcing many to engage in exploitative homeworking, or to take up poorly remunerated part-time work.

Black women have a long history of being employed by the state, notably in the Welfare State and transport services. A decade of monetarist economic policies has had political-ideological and material consequences on social relations. There has been a restructuring of forces that have a history of domestic and international exploitation in the interests of finance and capital. The apparatuses of the state that maintained British supremacy at horrendously destructive costs to black people on the African, Asian and American continents during slavery and colonialism continue to uphold the interests of internationl capitalism today. International imperialist and local racist discourses change form but continue to thrive and, in times of reaction, to proliferate, throughout both the state structures and civil society.

Black women's relations to the state are discussed here primarily with reference to their status as workers in the British National Health Service. The majority of black women working in these institutions are of African and Caribbean descent. Asian women workers are employed in quite different sectors of the labour market – in manufacturing, garment industries and often as homeworkers and in other undocumented forms of work which are more fully discussed elsewhere (see Chapter 4 above, Brah; Bruegel, 1989).

Some characteristics of the relations of various groups of black women to the British labour market emerge in race analyses. However, most of the historical literature is gender blind and does not address the situation of black women (Philips, 1975; Shyllon, 1974; Gutzmore, 1975; Williams, 1944). Gender must be simultaneously considered if we are to develop a complete picture. It is not simply a matter of going into detail about black women as a subgroup of women, or as an addendum to black people. The positions of black and white women and men are inextricably related and often resonate against each other. Black women enter the labour market facing the dual constraints of race and gender. They have played specific roles in the rationalization processes of British capitalism both at wider societal level and within the various black communities.

Studies of the post-war period were often discussions of 'immigrants', and therefore negated the black presence in earlier centuries. A second deficiency is that little of this material is gender-differentiated although there are a few publications on female 'immigrant' labour (e.g. Foner, 1976; Phizacklea, 1983). Peach, for example, presumed female migration to have been a passive following of menfolk. He put the proportion of 'women and children' at over 40 per cent of the total between 1955 and 1964 (1972, p. 45). Since that time it has been recognized that while this may be partially true for some Asian groups, a substantial proportion of Caribbean and African women migrated independently in search of better prospects. Furthermore, women were specifically recruited from both Africa and the Caribbean (also from other former colonies) to take up low-paid jobs that came vacant with the upward mobility of the local working classes. The National Health Service (NHS) and the then Ministry of Labour were in consultation with the Colonial Office as early as 1944 to organize recruitment, and by 1948 local selection committees constituting a centralized recruiting system had been set up in sixteen countries (including Nigeria, Sierra Leone, British Guyana, Trinidad, Mauritius and Jamaica). If nurses and ancillary workers (mostly women) were recruited from Africa and the Caribbean, doctors and dentists (mostly men) were recruited primarily from the Indian subcontinent. Increasingly restrictive immigration legislation did not hinder recruitment, since quota systems allowed the NHS to continue importing unskilled labour for ancillary jobs, and skilled labour was not restricted (Doyal *et al.*, 1981).

The NHS is a major component of Britain's Welfare State. Its birth was fundamentally a fruit of wartime class collaboration and social democratic consensus, and financed by the post-war boom. The late 1940s was also a time when workers, like soldiers before them, were recruited from the colonies to staff the boom and facilitate white upward (and outward) mobility, while keeping wages to a minimum that would have been unacceptable to the increasingly unionized white working class. Black female labour was therefore allocated by the market to specific purposes.

Labour Force Survey figures averaged over the years 1986–88 show that ethnic minority groups make up 4.8 per cent of the working age population in Britain. Each main ethnic group has distinct patterns of involvement in the labour market. Women of West Indian or Guyanese origin have the highest rates of involvement at 73 per cent, as compared to 69 per cent of white women. Women of Indian origin have an activity rate of 57 per cent, while women of Pakistani or Bangladeshi origin have the lowest recorded rate at only 20 per cent. This pattern varies with age, with older women of Guyanese and West Indian origin showing an even higher rate of 77 per cent, whereas for white women economic activity rates decline with age (*Employment Gazette*, March 1990).

The location of various groups of black women in the labour market reflects and compounds the dimensions of inequality intrinsic to British society. In accordance with racial stratification, in general, black women are to be found in the lower echelons of all the institutions where they are employed, where the pay is lowest, and the hours are longest and most anti-social. In accordance with gender divisions, black women tend to be employed in particular sectors of the Welfare State: catering, and cleaning, nursing and hospital ancillary work. Jobs in the 'caring' professions (nursing, community and social work) exploit oppressive notions of 'femininity'. Racial stratification, however, ensures that the areas where black women (particularly of African and African-Caribbean descent) have most commonly been employed actually involve physically heavy labour, as in the case of nurses, ancillary workers and cleaners.

Many professional black women have been employed as nurses in the NHS, usually as State Enrolled Nurses (SENs) rather than as State Registered Nurses (SRNs), despite the fact that the lower status SEN qualification is unrecognized in many of the countries of origin to where it was originally assumed nurses would return when no longer required. National data on overseas nurses in the NHS are not available, and the studies that have been done include the large and fluctuating proportion that have been recruited from Ireland, Malaysia and the Philippines. In the hospitals they studied, Doyal *et al.* (1981) found 81 per cent of the qualified nursing workforce to be from overseas. Within this group, Irish and Malaysians were more often SRNs, ward sisters and nursing officers, while Caribbean and Filipino women were more often SEN or nursing auxiliaries. With regard to ancillary and maintenance workers the same study found that 78 per cent of ancillary workers were from overseas, more than half of whom were women. Within this group, 84 per cent of domestic and catering workers were from overseas. Amongst these overseas workers, 78 per cent of domestic and 55 per cent of catering workers were women.

Immigrants have provided a crucial source of cheap labour, enabling the NHS to meet the demands of Britain's changing demography (Doyal *et al.*, 1981). The ever-increasing numbers of geriatric and chronically mentally and/or physically handicapped people has resulted in a growing demand for long-term care in unpopular areas of health care; migrant labour has been used to meet this demand without dramatically increasing costs. Unsurprisingly then, the evidence indicates that black nurses (like black doctors, most of whom are male) are disproportionately employed in unpopular specialities such as geriatrics and mental health (Radical Statistics Health Group, 1987). Women doctors (most of whom are white) are similarly employed in low-prestige areas of the NHS, in areas which are assumed to suit their 'special qualities' (Allen, 1988).

The recession of the early 1980s and subsequent Conservative legislative and political changes have affected black workers disproportionately across the board. 'Restructuring' involves closing down old, declining areas in favour of new expanding ones. It so happens that it is exactly those sectors of the labour market that have employed black people – namely the Welfare State and other public service sectors that are suffering from residualization and privatization. At the same time persistent discrimination ensures racist recruitment patterns in those areas being expanded and developed, namely the financial and banking sector and newer high technology industries. In view of resurgent recession at the beginning of the 1990s, racist redundancy policies must also be taken into account.

The NHS has been a focus of public expenditure cuts. Between 1979 and 1986 alone, 286 NHS hospitals were closed, and the number of hospital beds cut by 50,470, or by 14 per cent (Fabian Society, 1989). The resultant long waiting lists have led to public outrage, but not to any reversal of the policy. Instead, the 1990s have seen the introduction of experimental 'free market healthcare schemes'. The government strategy appears to involve whittling away as much as possible while privatizing, and it is the areas where many black women work that have been the first to be contracted out. For workers, privatization means an intensified exploitation: longer hours, less bargaining power, lower wages and fewer people employed on these inferior terms. Little wonder that black women workers were amongst the first to protest against the changes (*Caribbean Times*, issue 158, March 1984).

This period also saw an upsurge in 'fishing raids' by immigration authorities into workplaces, and the subsequent deportations of Filipino nurses. This highlights the way in which the British state continues to use immigration legislation to regulate black workers according to demand, much as the Ministry of Labour used the Colonial Office to execute earlier recruitment strategies. The current context of high unemploymnt means that inferior jobs are becoming attractive to white British workers who previously enjoyed the luxury of regarding these as 'below' them.

Irene Breugel's analysis of the data from the Greater London Council's Living Standards Survey (1981–1986) shows that 'black women are not only at the bottom of the pile, but their position has got worse relative both to black men and white women over the last few years' (1989, p. 49).

Her argument takes on even greater weight when she comes to consider pay differentials, taking working hours and regional variations into account. Her evidence shows that white women earn 23 per cent more per hour than black women, and that black women in London earn only 63 per cent of the average black man's weekly wage (the comparable figure for white women is 72 per cent). Importantly, this more detailed analysis of the figures puts to rest the thesis that race and gender somehow 'cancelled out' to privilege black women *vis-à-vis* black men (e.g. Brown, 1984). Having higher qualifications does not reduce the discrimination that black women experience, since earnings differentials persist up the occupational scale. Women of African and Caribbean origin nonetheless continue to work and study, and are proportionately more highly qualified than white, women and men and Indian, Pakistani and Bangladeshi women (*Social Trends*, 1991, **21**, p. 60).[2]

To conclude this section, it needs to be pointed out that the black woman's status as a worker is particularly important because, at least in the African and Caribbean communities, significantly more women are breadwinners and household heads. African and Caribbean women have more dependants than white women and are more likely to have unemployed partners. For those with working partners, black male wage levels are often so low that African and Caribbean women's wages are still crucial to households in these communities, which continue to be disproportionately vulnerable to labour market fluctuations.

In short, black women have particular relations to the British state, firstly as workers to capital's needs, and secondly to the legislative apparatus, particularly through immigration legislation which is used to mediate this relation and keep it on terms that undermine our interests as workers. The sexist and racist devaluation of black female labour in Britain is not only historical but also a contemporary fact, and the situation, far from improving, appears to be deteriorating. The 1990s strategies for coping with economic crisis have been particularly detrimental to black women workers in the NHS, and this pattern is likely to be repeated in other public service sectors undergoing similar changes.

The Welfare State and black women as clients

Apart from being workers, as discussed above, black women have a second relation to the state: that of citizens and consumers. In this section, discussion will focus on the National Health Service and Local Authority public housing provision, with some reference to the social services provided by the Department of Health and Social Security. The Welfare State's primary purpose is to ensure the reproduction and maintenance of the nation's labour force, so supplementing domestic labour that has largely fallen to women with the development of patriarchal capitalism.

British welfare developed after the war, during a period of social democratic consensus (e.g. Jacobs, 1985). The fact that this was never really supported by the political right in Britain helps us to understand why residualization of the Welfare State has been so central to the conservatism of the 1980s. A race and gender analysis of British welfare service delivery further underscores the point that, contrary to much popular opinion, basic material and social support have never actually been presumed to be something that citizens are entitled to in Britain. Rather, healthcare, education, housing, social security and services have been differentially delivered to different groups by hired custodians of public resources. While sections of the political left, along with some professional associations (the British Medical Association, for example) became increasingly alarmed and vociferous about the erosion of healthcare, the history of the development of welfare and the circumscribed nature of access to it demonstrates that provision has always been constituted along social divisions. Class, race and gender discrimination have often operated through notions and judgements about who are 'really deserving' and who are 'undeserving'. In short, the Welfare State has never existed universally for the public, but has operated to exclude minorities and uphold dominant ideologies about the family, motherhood and sexuality, often behaving punitively and coercively towards women, towards black people, towards black women, towards lesbian and gay people and towards other marginalized groups through various ideological mechanisms and administrative practices. This is evidenced most clearly in the differential service delivery to black people (this argument is developed in Mama, 1989a, 1989b). Here we will focus on service delivery to black women in particular.

Health services

Gender analysis shows how the attrition of services affects women disproportionately because, in accordance with their ascribed reproductive, caring and nurturing roles, women come into more frequent contact with health services than men, both directly and in accompanying relatives. Women are the ones who attend family planning clinics for contraceptive and fertility advice, antenatal clinics and hospitals for deliveries and post-natal care. A race analysis highlights the fact that cuts in services have been accompanied by increasingly stringent policing, and health services have become check points for the enforcement of new immigration laws. This linking up between the immigration department and public services particularly affects black people. During the inner city disturbances of the early and mid-1980s, community groups complained that hospitals were turning injured black people over to the police when they sought medical attention.

Black women have not only resisted the job losses in their capacity as workers, but have also been active defending their interests as clients in the 'No Pass Laws to Health' campaigns, which protested against the racist policing of services.

I would argue that the quality of healthcare provided to black women is in many ways a continuation of historically rooted patterns of racism and sexism. Looking at earlier periods, we can see that dominant ideas about black women's sexuality have fundamentally influenced our relationship to British state and society. In earlier centuries, black female sexuality and reproductive powers were regarded as the property of the slave-owning class. Historically, black female reproductive powers have been controlled according to the needs of the capitalist labour market. Slave women, apart from being labourers themselves, also had the task of reproducing the slave labour force, particularly when legislation obstructed their wholesale importation, a pressure fuelled by the low life expectancies of slaves (Davis, 1981). Contrary to the sexist mythology that slave women had an 'easier time' as a result of their sex, rape was an additional form of punishment and coercion. Slave women, 'breeders' were compelled to reproduce as fast as biology would permit, but given none of the status or care associated with white motherhood. Pregnant and mothering slave women had to work the fields and were subjected to the same maltreatment as everyone else.

> A woman who gives offence in the field and is large in family way is compelled to lie down over a hole made to receive her corpulency, and is flogged with the whip or beat with the paddle, which has holes in it; and at every stroke comes a blister. One of my sisters was so severely punished in this way, that labour was brought on, and the child was born in the field. This very overseer, Mr Brooks, killed in this manner a girl named Mary.

(quoted in Davis, 1981)

The racist myths about African sexual prowess were used to fuel large-scale sexual abuses: the castration of men and the rape and violation of women. For example in the nineteenth century, a certain J. J. Virey commented:

> Negresses display no common proficiency in the art of exciting the passions and gaining an unlimited power over individuals of a different sex. Their African blood carries them into the greatest excesses.
>
> (Virey, 1837, cited in Rogers, 1945)

The proximity and intimacy that domestic slaves were forced to live and work in would have facilitated regular and repeated abuse from their masters.

In the present era, concern has been centred around the limiting of black female fertility. The economic fluctuations in Western states and hence the global economy, and the fluctuations in demand for cheap labour must be taken into consideration in analysing the way in which gender structures relations between black women and the British state. While the absolute birth rate in Britain shows a decline similar to other Western European countries, and net emigration remains significantly higher than immigration, the popular consciousness may continue to be haunted by spectres of being overrun by 'nig-nogs' and 'pakis', just as in earlier centuries the bourgeoisie suffered from paranoia over the 'swarming hordes' beneath them on the social scale. Black birthrates are indeed higher, and the age profile of the black communities is generally younger, but this only presents a problem to those clinging to Hitlerian notions of 'racial purity' and old dreams of empire and a new white nation (see also Gilroy, 1987). Similar concerns underlie the convoluted changes in immigration legislation, which have consistently sought to specifically exclude black people, while not hindering the entry of whites to the same extent.

The preoccupation with black women's sexuality can be most blatantly seen in the (1970s–80s) practice of so-called 'virginity testing' of Asian fiancées by medical practitioners at Heathrow airport. 'Non-virgins' could be accused of entering under false pretences on the basis that 'Asian tradition' was claimed to preclude marrying 'non-virgins', and deported. Rather than upholding 'Asian tradition' it is more likely that the Immigration department intended to deter Asian women from travelling to Britain.

At the present time, since the borders have been all but closed to black immigration for years, concern has shifted to the monitoring, regulation and control of those already inside the country, and the struggles over reproductive rights indicate one way in which health services have participated in this. As a result, black women have fought many battles over their reproductive rights, often having to protest against the emphasis on curtailing their fertility. Disturbing evidence about the long-acting contraceptive Depo-Provera provoked campaign action and protests from the black women's movement during the early 1980s, and campaigns against the use of Norplant on African and Asian women in the 1990s.

The quality of maternity care and other support delivered to black mothers also leaves much to be desired, but has yet to be systematically studied.

Thorogood (1989) found black (Caribbean) women frequently changed their GP because of dissatisfaction, which they attributed to the overall deterioration in the NHS. Existing research (such as it is) indicates class, race and gender dynamics in both access to and distribution of resources and quality of care (e.g. Townsend and Davidson, 1982; Whitehead, 1987).

Social Services

Black women most frequently come into contact with social services through their status as mothers and the legislation concerning children. The high proportion of single parents (the vast majority of whom are women) and working mothers in the Caribbean community, for example, can combine with the above mentioned racist sexual fantasies about women of African origin to produce the assumption that they are immoral and irresponsible parents. The high proportion of children of African and Caribbean parentage in state custody can additionally be attributed to the material conditions of many black women's lives: exploitative jobs, inferior housing and poverty combine with racist assessments about whether women are 'fit' to parent. Inadequate childcare facilities affect all women (including all the grandmothers and girls who stand in for working mothers). Britain has one of the lowest rates of childcare provision in Western Europe, so that many single parents simply cannot go out to work unless they are able to obtain childcare support from relatives or friends.

The 1980 and 1986 Social Security Acts make it a civic duty for officers to detect 'illegal' migrants. Failure of sponsors to meet their obligations to relatives became a criminal offence in 1980, when the Department of Health and Social Security was given the power to take sponsors to court. The 1981 Nationality Act excluded further categories of people from the ill-defined 'recourse to public funds' and together with the 1986 Social Security Act has severely reinforced institutionalized racism in a number of ways. For example, Dominelli has pointed out that the manual used by DHSS officers at the local level suggests that checks should be carried out 'if a person comes from abroad' (Dominelli, 1989).

The London Race and Housing Research Unit's domestic violence project (Mama, 1989b) included a section on social services responses to abused black women in London. In a sample of 100, one third of victims had some contact with social services, and this was not evenly distributed among the different ethnic groups: half of the Asian women had contact, as compared to only 20 per cent of Caribbean women and 33 per cent of the African women. The amount of service uptake corroborated the different group perceptions of social services: none of the Caribbean women interviewed described them as supportive or positive, although a number of the Asian women did. Social workers assisted some of the younger Asian women in leaving violent marriages, but for the Caribbean women, contact often centred around concern for a child on the 'at risk' register.

The same study of statutory services also indicated that women seeking homes are often pressured into contact with social services, and this can have its own consequences:

> [The housing officer] stressed that he wanted me to make an appointment for me to see a social worker. He came to my flat and left a note saying that he had made an appointment for me the following Monday. I felt I didn't need a social worker because I didn't have a social problem, I had a housing problem. I didn't feel that a social worker's intervention was necessary. So I didn't keep the appointment. The social worker got the police and together they broke down the door of the place I was staying at. When I came back the door was ajar and I couldn't lock it. They had left a note on the table saying that they had done this because I didn't keep my appointment with the social worker.
>
> (Mama, 1989b, pp. 95–6)

A better-known case is that of Lisa Huen, a woman of Chinese origin who was married to a British citizen who became extremely violent. At one point she had to place her young son in care temporarily because her injuries were so severe that she could not look after him. Subsequently Women's Aid grew so concerned that they alerted the social services, who advised that they would take her son into care if she remained in the violent marital home. Whereas this may well have been good advice, when she did leave her husband, Lisa became the subject of a deportation order which was subsequently withdrawn after a successful campaign.

Housing departments often require social reports from women seeking housing as a result of domestic violence, despite the fact that women may not want or need social work intervention. Once children have been removed, obtaining housing becomes even more difficult, since single people without children are regarded as lower priority cases. Insistence on social reports selectively deprives the many black women who resist the intrusions of social workers. The experience of those who do find themselves involved with social workers suggests that their reluctance is not unfounded. Women are being passed around between various agencies instead of having their problems identified and their expressed needs met. At the same time, there were other cases where women may have benefited from social workers support but this was not available for them.

Unfamiliarity with the legal intricacies involved in retrieving children from the state agencies, and the racism of officials creates particular problems for West African families. The lack of daycare facilities, the unsuitability of access to those that do exist and the high cost, force many to have children privately fostered. Researchers have ignored these factors, and have instead focused on the role of 'West African culture'. According to such culturalist arguments, it is 'tradition' that leads Africans to have their children fostered. It should not be necessary to point out that African mothers are fully aware that sending young children to English foster families or institutions is not the same thing as sending them to live with a close and trusted relative (which, in any case traditionally occurs when they are older). Ellis (1978) unashamedly suggests that it would be better for Africans to leave their children in their countries of origin, despite the fact that this may mean not seeing them for many years. In any case, Goody's study on the delegation of parenting by black families in the Caribbean, West Africa and London (1978) found the reasons given for fostering in the British context to be quite different from those in West Africa, where sophisticated systems of kinship obligations and ties are involved. Furthermore, there is no basis for assuming that sending children to live in other countries is an option for African women living in Britain, many of whom have themselves grown up in Britain.

Misportrayals and misunderstandings like those propagated in the literature compound the racism of social service officials, precipitating and sustaining disputes between the state and black parents or between white foster parents and parents of African and Caribbean origin.

The issue of what sort of social work intervention is appropriate requires a great deal of attention and the development of strategies that do not compound the oppressed situation of black women. Growing evidence highlights the negative consequences of placing black children in the inappropriate and substandard environments that state care frequently offers (e.g. Ahmed, Cheetam and Small, 1987). Yet often children are taken away from their mothers in situations where minimal material support for the mother could have forestalled such drastic action. The freeze on child benefit between 1987 and 1991 further deprived poor families. There is also evidence that black people are additionally deprived of their entitlements by the humiliating treatment meted out by officials in DHSS offices (*The Independent*, 5 February, 1991).

Psychiatry and mental health care

The psychiatric aspects of the Welfare State are of particular concern to black people. Forty per cent of all black people in NHS beds are there as psychiatric patients (Black Patients and Health Workers Group, 1983).

Studies have repeatedly indicated the over-representation of Caribbean people of African descent amongst those in psychiatric hospitals as a result of compulsory detention orders, showing that they are two to three times more likely than whites to be admitted as a result of such orders. One study conducted in Nottingham estimated that 'Afro-Caribbean' people (people with African-Caribbean origins) were ten times more likely to be diagnosed as schizophrenic (Harrison *et al.*, 1989).

The Mental Health Act 1983 retains the compulsory detention powers of earlier Acts (persons involved in criminal proceedings or under custodial sentence are dealt with under Part III, while civil cases are covered under Part II). The admission of black patients is more likely to be through police and social services referrals than the result of referral by general practitioners, and the diagnoses accounting for these racial differentials are schizophrenia and other psychotic disorders. Several researchers have found the pattern to be more pronounced for the British-born Caribbean community than for those who migrated to Britain, and so the differences cannot be attributed to the 'stress of migration' as earlier analyses suggested. Nonetheless, one recent study found young African-Caribbeans to have the highest admission rates under the noncriminal (Part II) sections of the Act (seventeen times higher than whites, as compared to nine times higher for British born African-Caribbean). Under Part III young 'Afro-Caribbean migrants' had a compulsory detention rate twenty-five time higher than young whites (Cope, 1989).

The historical relations of African people to psychiatric medicine are relevant here. During slavery, for example, many were diagnosed as suffering from 'drapetomania' (an incurable urge to run away) (Thomas and Sillen, 1972). During the colonial period the psychiatrist J. C. Carothers was sent in to study the mental health sources of the Kenyan rebellion waged by the Land and Freedom Army (the Man Man) (Carothers, 1953). The 'pathologization' of black resistance has two notable ideological concomitants: first, it discredits revolutionary or rebellious ideas and actions and, secondly, it conflates these with madness.

Today, as in the past, categorization, diagnosis and treatment of black people continue to be problematic. For example, 'West Indian psychosis' and 'cannabis psychosis' are new categories created to include behaviour that does not fit existing diagnostic categories. Paranoia (for example, imagining that white neighbours are hostile and threatening) and 'religious mania' feature strongly in diagnoses while 'marital psychosis' is said to occur in young Asian women facing arranged marriages (Littlewood and Lipsedge, 1982). There is evidence to suggest that behavioural disturbances may be individual responses to unbearable social situations, but it is also clear that psychiatric interventions need to be considered against the background of often coercive and disruptive state interventions into black family and community life, described above.

Not only do diagnostic and admission routes show race differences. The treatment that black people receive in NHS psychiatric facilities also differs substantially from that received by whites. Black (particularly African-Caribbean) people receive more physical treatments (electro-convulsive therapy, oral and injected drugs), and at higher dosages. They receive less nonphysical treatment (therapy, counselling, etc.), and are less likely to see consultants or other highly-qualified stafff (Littlewood and Lipsedge, 1982).

Gender analyses of mental healthcare have challenged the diagnosis and treatment of women, arguing that psychiatry is effectively a sophisticated form of social regulation, controlling and even punishing women for not conforming to contradictory gender norms. More directly, research suggests that both clinical psychologists and psychiatrists tend to see 'adult women' as more pathological than 'adult men' (Broverman *et al.*, 1970). Women have significantly higher rates of diagnosed depression which are linked to their marital status (Brown and Harris, 1981) but the extent to which this is a result of diagnosis, actual levels of depression, or the oppressive life circumstances of women is still a subject of debate. In terms of treatment, objections have been raised about the containment of emotional misery through prescription of tranquillizers and anti-depressants to women across the classes.

The British literature omits consideration of black women. Studies of race and mental health are gender blind, while studies which include gender analysis tend to be race blind. White cultural stereotypes about what constitutes 'normal' behaviour for women, combined with the tendency of mental health professionals to ascribe pathological diagnoses to both black people and women give cause for concern. Cope's study does give some gender breakdown in her statistics (Cope, 1989). Her figures show that the high compulsory first admission rate for 'Afro-Caribbean' men as compared to white men is not nearly so pronounced for women, particularly in the younger age group, but she makes no comment on these gender differences. This suggests that there may well be significant gender differences in the compulsory detention rates that African-Caribbean people experience, and these may well be age-related.

Research indicates that many women in the prisons, but particularly women of African and Caribbean descent, are being defined and treated as mentally ill, and incarcerated in psychiatric wings under heavy medication (see Mama, Mars and Stephens, 1986). The continuing pathologization of black women in and outside the prison system urgently demands attention, as does the identification and support of those black people who are experiencing mental disturbances.

The evidence suggests a growing encroachment of psychiatric expertise into the prisons and courtrooms along race and gender lines. Magistrates more frequently demand psychiatric reports for black (particularly African and Caribbean) defendants. Apart from the fact that people of African descent are disproportionately represented among the involun-tary hospital population being given psychiatric treatment, undergoing treatment may also be made a condition of probation or eligibility for parole for those in the prisons. The social services also utilize psychiatric reports on black mothers in child custody cases, while housing departments often require social reports. Psychiatric expertise can be a basis not only for imprisonment or compulsory confinement in hospitals, but also for either forced repatriation or refusal of entry (over a hundred each year). Both are indeed used by the immigration department, but it seems that significant numbers of Caribbean people are 'encouraged' to return to their places of origin because they are suffering from mental illness. This practice is considered entirely acceptable by eminent psychiatrists, who merely note the need for caution about how to ensure that repatriation is the best prescription (Rack, 1982). This particular form of 'treatment' is not applied to white Britons, and seems to be based on myths about large extended families and places in the sun. It ignores the problems that face black British people returning to the countries and rapidly changing cultures and underdeveloped economies that they left many years ago to seek a better life. Another more remote influence may be Britain's long tradition of deporting 'undesirable' members of the population to the colonies.

There is now evidence that people deported or otherwise encouraged to return to the Caribbean on the basis of mental disturbance end up in mental hospitals there. Burke (1973) found 8 per cent of all the patients in Jamaica's Bellevue hospital to be returned immigrants, while in Barbados Mahy (1976) found 52 per cent of his sample to have been advised to return there from Britain, many receiving state assistance to do so. Two thirds of these expressed strong regrets and would have liked to return to the UK. Further research is needed to examine whether there are gender differentials.

The use of medical 'expertise' at ports of entry and for repatriations and deportations of black people is a manifestation of a complex and manipulative relationship between the state and black people which often invokes negative and pathogenic judgements about 'Other' cultures.

In this context is seems that psychiatry plays a particular role, since psychiatric 'expertise' is being called in and acted upon by both welfare and policing structures such as the immigration department and the social services. The relation of psychiatry to black women is mediated by the dimensions of race and gender, but there is clearly a need for further research in this area.

Black women, police and prisons

In the 1970s and early-1980s race analyses of the repressive state structures of the criminal justice system have focused on black men or been gender blind (Hall *et al*., 1978; Gutzmore, 1975; Sivanandan, 1976; Solomos *et al*., 1982). Perhaps the analysis of police racism initially concentrated on the experience of black men because it is young African-Caribbean men who have tragically died in police custody and detention centres: Richard 'Cartoon' Campbell, Winston Rose, Colin Roach. However, by the end of the 1980s the fact that black women are also subjected to coercion, violence and abuse by the repressive state apparatuses could no longer be ignored. In 1985 two cases shocked the public. Cherry Groce was shot in the back and left paralysed from the waist down, and Cynthia Jarret died of heart failure, both during police raids on their respective homes in Brixton and Tottenham.

The prison research (Mama, Mars and Stevens, 1986) also found ample evidence of police and immigration departments' malpractice towards black women. For example, in one incident a young African woman student was subjected to anal intercourse by a police officer, who threatened her with deportation because her residence permit had expired (*The Guardian*, 26 October, 1981). Over two years of protracted legal battles later the woman was paid a ridiculously low sum in compensation and then deported, while the officer was found to be guilty of the charges.

More recently, the domestic violence study (Mama, 1989b) looked at police responses to domestic violence in the black communities and identified three areas of concern:[3]

(a) the reluctance of black women to call in the police even when serious, if not life-threatening, violent crimes are being committed against them;
(b) the reluctance of the police to enforce the law in the interests of the black women when they are called in to do so; and, most disturbingly,
(c) the evidence that the police themselves perpetrate crimes against black women.

The findings of this research indicated that when called (whether by neighbours, or by the woman being assaulted), police often failed to follow proper procedures, sometimes preferring to turn the affair into an immigration inquiry or seizing the opportunity to assault the black man in question. In one particularly disturbing case, an African woman who was being beaten by her husband was arrested by the police, subjected to racial and sexual ridicule and kicked down the stairs of the police station before being locked in a cell for the night (see Mama, 1989b, Chapter 6). Another finding of the same research concerned the manner in which both statutory and even some voluntary agencies pressure women to involve the police by demanding police reports before considering them for housing and other forms of support. In some instances this had extremely negative consequences for the women concerned, not least in terms of exacerbating the danger they already faced from their assailant.

The prison report also indicated the widespread imprisonment of African and Caribbean women for 'socioeconomic crime', namely non-payment of fines, shoplifting of petty items and small-time fraud (see Mama, Mars and Stevens, 1986). The evidence suggests that women from these groups have higher rates of apprehension by store detectives and police officers, and that once in court, are more likely to be harshly sentenced. In the case of violent crimes, although women commit very few, they are generally more harshly sentenced than men, and black women serve the longest sentences for both violent crime and drug smuggling. Feminist criminologists have argued that women are given stiffer sentences for crimes of violence because these involve them deviating from dominant notions of 'femininity'. In the case of black women (of African-Caribbean descent) who are given even stiffer sentences for violent crimes, the race and gender norms are themselves contradictory. The black woman who commits violence is on the one hand conforming to racist notions of black (particularly Caribbean) people as violent, but on the other hand, deviating from dominant notions of femininity. Since women of African descent are stereotyped as being strong and aggressive (and therefore more likely to be violent than white women), then the stiff sentences they receive cannot be explained in the way that has been suggested for white women.

Development and impact of the black women's movement

A major objective of future work must be to move beyond critique to develop appropriate concepts and theory which must be based on clear understanding of the economic, socio-political and cultural conditions of black women's lives. For activists there is the additional concern that this work must contribute to improving the situation by challenging and subverting oppressive social relations, institutions, ideologies and practices, rather than reinforcing and reproducing them uncritically.

There are new cultural and political forms evolving out of black British women's diverse historical experience, and these are textured by contemporary forms of racial, class and sexual oppression, and the corresponding patterns of rebellion and resistance (see Brixton Black Women's Group, 1984). Black feminism in Britain seeks to address and positively value the diversity of origin and variation in geographical, historical and cultural reference points. The priority given to 'Afro-Asian unity' by women's organizations such as OWAAD in the late 1970s and early 1980s, was a fundamental aspect of the then growing awareness of the need for a united front at a time when the British state was intensifying its discriminatory practices against black people in general and impacting on black women in ways that both male-dominated black organizations and the white-dominated women's movement have continued to have difficulty in recognizing and incorporating into their political analyses and practices.

Black feminism has emerged as a collective political perspective that demands a coherent and coordinated rebellion against the varied manifestations of class, race and gender oppression. Black feminism has continued to develop and to diversify, both as a basis for political organizing, and as a basis for theory and analysis. Black women's organizations initially developed autonomously in the various communities. However, towards the end of the 1980s a number of these were state-funded projects, constituted along the ethnically specific lines that gained ascendance under the contradictory conditions of Thatcherism and municipal socialism. This change reflected the growing focus on identity and a new competitive cultural politics that gained ascendance and replaced the 1970s/early 1980s notions of black unity and wider anti-imperialist and black liberation struggles. Small but significant numbers of black women (some of whom had been voluntary activists) became employed in welfare projects focusing on particular issues. For example, the Black Female Prisoners Scheme was established to address the conditions of black (particularly African and Caribbean) women in prisons, and Asian women's refuges were set up to address the problem of domestic violence. Most of these projects continue to be poorly resourced, even when compared to other (also under resourced) feminist projects and women's centres.

Black feminism has had impact on both race and gender politics in Britain. Within black politics it is apparent that feminist ideas have clearly had some impact, with sexual politics and gender relations becoming an acknowledged site of struggle within black communities. This is evidenced in the willingness of at least some organizations to begin to discuss issues like domestic violence and sexual harassment in black communities and homes.

Within the women's movement, it appears that black feminism forced debates on race and feminism. We have since seen a proliferation of feminist theoretical discourses on 'difference' and 'identity' in the literature, but at the more practical level race is not sufficiently taken on in feminist political practice. Instead, black women are still, after over a decade of struggle, frequently a last-minute or tokenistic addendum to conference programmes, and in women's projects resource considerations are still too often used to explain away the subversion and rejection of antiracist practice.[4]

Conclusion

Several important points emerge from the race and gender analysis conducted. Black women's experience indicates that the British state is composed of a complex of alienating and unsupportive agencies. The complexity and multiplicity of relations between black people and the British state is also striking. In part a result of the historical and contemporary diversity of 'black people', this complexity is also a result of the changing and complex nature of the late capitalist state. The inter-action between immigration, health and welfare services impacts on black women in ways that alienate, intimidate and further oppress them. Added to the increased policing of services, these processes operate to selectively exclude them and limit their access.

The growing influence of psychiatric 'professional expertise' into the courts, schools and prisons suggests that psychiatry plays a role in this process. Particular race and gender groups are more likely to be diagnosed as having psychiatric disorders in the course of their relations with the various welfare and policing agencies.

This evidence supports the argument that by focusing on a monolithic state structure and analysing relations between the state and black people in a gender blind way, much of the complexity of the processes of racial repression, containment and control by the increasingly interlinked and corporate arms of the state have been obscured. Not only are the police, criminal justice, immigration and prison departments coercive in their practice towards black people, but black women's experience of the Welfare State suggests that this also functions in coercive and repressive ways, often in collaboration with the police and immigration departments.

The economic crisis of the 1980s has been effectively exploited by governments committed to eroding the Welfare State. Discourses priorit-izing control of state expenditure have gained dominance over concern with people's health, education, housing and standard of living. These major changes in the British body politic have particularly affected black women, through their situations as single parents, as exploited, un-employed or underemployed and underpaid workers, as women and as black people.

The above analysis has gone beyond the hierarchy of oppressions approach, by placing the collective realities of black women at the centre of the analysis. Class, race and gender dynamics manifest concretely in the experience of black women and cannot be usefully disentangled or separated out since they constitute a whole reality and act simultaneously in a given moment.

For the black woman worker, as for other workers, the right to earn a living is being seriously undermined by the high levels of unemployment resulting from economic decline and industrial atrophy. Strategies being employed ostensibly to remedy this are particularly exacerbating the labour market situation of black women, as the case of women working in the health service demonstrates. The quantity and quality of work available to black women, already severely limited by historical and contemporary racial and sexual division of the labour market, is further deteriorating as a result of the economic situation and the strategies that have been developed in its wake.

Black women can draw courage from the fact that the historical evidence indicates ways that have been found to survive and resist the forces of class, racial and sexual oppression. The situation demands that we evolve new strategies, organize more effectively, consolidate the benefits of collective experience, and emerge into the 1990s stronger and more united, locally, nationally and internationally.

Notes

1 A similar pressure to identify within the categories of oppressed led some women to identify as 'political lesbians' and to a bizarre scorecard identity politics which led people to assert the various dimensions e.g. 'I am a black, lesbian, disabled, etc . . .' in order to appeal to an imaginary 'rainbow constituency'.

2 The *Social Trends* figures relate to academic qualifications. Brown (1984) examined vocational qualifications and found that in the age group 16–44 West Indian women were far more likely than all other groups to possess higher professional or clerical qualifications.

3 Police responses to abused women in general have already been criticized in detail (Edwards, 1986), but the research referred to here examined police responses to black women in particular.

4 For example, in women's aid and advice centres, workers are indeed overstretched and frequently exhausted and underpaid, but poor race relations in the collectives and workplaces also sap energy and political will. The guilt and anxiety that the subject of race arouses in most white women continues to block discussion and so preclude change, often merely further problematizing the situation of black women who seek to challenge the status quo (see Mama 1989b, Chapter 11 for a race analysis of the women's refuge movement).

References

Ahmed, S., Cheetham, J. and Small, J. (eds) (1987) *Social Work with Black Children and their Families*, London, Batsford.

Allen, I. (1988) *Any Room at the Top*, London, PSI.

Black Patients and Health Workers Group (1983) 'Psychiatry and corporate state', *Race and Class*, 25(2), pp. 49–65.

Brixton Black Women's Group (1979–1985) *Speak Out*, newsletter.

Broverman, G. *et al.* (1970) 'Sex role stereotypes and clinical judgements of mental health', *Journal of Consulting and Clinical Psychology* 34(1), pp. 1–7.

Brown, C. (1984) *Black and White in Britain, The Third PSI Study*, Aldershot, Gower/PSI.

Brown, G. and Harris, T. (1981) *The Social Origins of Depression*, London, Tavistock.

Bruegel, I. (1989) 'Sex and race in the labour market', *Feminist Review*, 32, pp.49–69.

Burke, A. (1973) 'The consequences of unplanned repatriation', *British Journal of Psychiatry*, **123**, pp. 109–11.

Carothers, J. C. (1953) *The African Mind in Health and Disease: a study in ethnopsychiatry*, WHO monograph, series no. 17, WHO, Geneva.

Cope, R. (1989) 'The compulsory detention of Afro-Caribbeans under the Mental Health Act', *New Community*, **15**(3), pp. 343–56.

Davis, A. (1981) *Women, Race and Class*, London, The Women's Press.

Dominelli, L. (1989) 'An uncaring profession? An examination of racism in social work', *New Community* **15**(3), pp. 391–404.

Doyal, L., Hunt, G. and Mellor J. (1981) 'Your life in their hands: migrant workers in the National Health Service', *Critical Social Policy*, **1**(2), pp. 54–71.

Edwards, S. (1986) *Police Responses to Domestic Violence in London*, Polytechnic of Central London.

Ellis, J. (ed.) (1978) *West African Families in Britain*, London, Routledge and Kegan Paul.

Foner, N. (1976) 'Women, work and migration: Jamaicans in London', *New Community*, **5**(1–2), pp. 195–202.

Gilroy, P. (1987) *There Ain't No Black in the Union Jack*, London, Hutchinson.

Glendinning, C. (1987) 'Impoverishing women' in Walker, A. and Walker, C. (eds) *The Growing Divide: a social audit 1979–1987*, London, CPAG.

Goody, E. (1978) 'Delegation of parental roles in West Africa and the West Indies' in Shimkin, D. B. *et al.* (eds) *The Extended Family in Black Societies*, New York, Morton.

Gutzmore, C. (1975) 'Imperialism and racism: the crisis of the British capitalist economy and the black masses in Britain', *The Black Liberator*, **2**(4).

Hall, S. *et al.* (1978) *Policing the Crisis: mugging, the state and law and order*, London, Macmillan.

Harrison, G. *et al.* (1989) 'A prospective study of severe mental disorder in Afro-Caribbean patients', *Psychological Medicine*, **18**(11), pp. 643–57.

Hernes, H. M. (1987) *Welfare State and Woman Power: essays in state feminism*, Oslo, Norwegian University Press.

Jacobs, S. (1985) 'Race, empire and the Welfare State: council housing and racism', *Critical Social Policy*, **13**, pp. 6–28.

Littlewood, R. and Lipsedge, M. (1982) *The Aliens and the Alienists: ethnic minorities and psychiatry*, Harmondsworth, Penguin.

Mahy, G. (1976) 'The West Indian psychotic returns from England', International Congress of Transcultural Psychiatry, Bradford (see Rack, 1982).

Mama, A. (1984) 'Black women, the economic crisis and the British state', *Feminist Review*, **17**, pp. 21–36.

Mama, A. (1989a) 'Violence against black women: gender, race and state responses', *Feminist Review*, **32**, pp. 30–48.

Mama, A. (1989b) *The Hidden Struggle: statutory and voluntary sector responses to violence against black women in the home*, London, Race and Housing Research Unit/Runnymede Trust.

Mama, A., Mars, M. and Stevens, P. (1986) *Breaking the Silence: Women's Imprisonment*, LSPU/WEG.

Modood, T. (1988) 'Black, racial equality and Asian identity', *New Community*, **14**(3), pp. 397–404.

Peach, C. (1972) *West Indian Migration to Britain*, Oxford, Institute of Race Relations.

Philips (1975) 'The black masses and the political economy of Manchester', *Journal of Black Liberation*, **2**(4).

Phizacklea, A. (1983) (ed.) *One Way Ticket: migration and female labour*, London, Routledge and Kegan Paul.

Rack, P. (1982) *Race, Culture and Mental Disorder*, London, Tavistock.

Radical Statistics Health Group (1987) *Facing the figures: what really is happening to the National Health Service?* London, Radical Statistics Health Group.

Rogers, J. (1945) *Sex and Race: Negro-Caucasian mixing in all ages and all lands*, New York, J. A. Rogers.

Runnymede Trust Statistics and Race Group (1982) *Britain's Black Population*, London, Heinemann.

Showstack-Sasoon, A. (ed.) (1987) *Women and the State*, London, Hutchinson.

Shyllon, F. (1974) *Black Slaves in Britain*, Oxford, Institute of Race Relations.

Sivanandan, A. (1976) 'Race, class and the state: the black experience in Britain', *Race and Class*, **17**(4), pp. 347–68.

Solomos, J. *et al.* (1982) *The Organic Crisis of British Capitalism and Race: the experience of the 70s*, Centre for Contemporary Cultural Studies, Race and Politics Group.

Thomas and Sillen (1972) *Racism and Psychiatry*, Bruner Mazel.

Thorogood, N. (1989) 'Afro-Caribbean women's experience of the Health Service', *New Community*, **15**(3), pp. 319–34.

Townsend, P. and Davidson, N. (1982) *Inequalities in Health*, Harmondsworth, Penguin.

Whitehead, M. (1987) *The Health Divide*, London, Health Education Council.

Williams, E. (1944) *Capitalism and Slavery*, London, André Deutsch.

Wright, G. (ed.) (1989) *The ABC of Thatcherism 1979–1989*, London, Fabian Society.

PART 2

INSTITUTIONAL RACISM

INTRODUCTION

To group together articles about racism or racial inequality in Britain, in housing, the labour market, the careers service, the criminal law and social work, indicates at least that black people fare less well than they should in all these areas – not just as job applicants, but as users of services, as seekers of resources, and so on. We do not encompass inequalities in education because these are addressed in our companion volume, *Racism and Education*, and space precludes including articles on other sectors like the health service, but the basic point is clear enough.

However, this alone does not tell us much about the nature of the racism that faces black people. In an earlier era our articles would, doubtless, have focused on direct, intentional racial discrimination as practised by a variety of gatekeepers. The most blatant examples of this were advertisements for accommodation – long since illegal – saying 'no coloureds'. In other spheres, notably in the search for employment, black applicants typically encountered a range of barriers which excluded them altogether, or confined them to specific occupations, grades or departments and, in summary, largely restricted them to less desirable forms of employment.

Some of these practices were designed to keep black people out completely and others sought merely to impose a 'black quota', and some were readily apparent while others were harder to detect. What they all shared was that they were knowingly and deliberately applied. Actually, it might be better to say that what they all shared was that they *appeared* to be knowingly and deliberately applied. Where a private landlord advertised a room saying 'no coloureds need apply' the case is clear enough. But in other instances matters may be less clear. There are, nevertheless, well established research techniques designed to uncover the existence of direct discrimination in such circumstances. Such techniques have been most widely deployed in measuring the incidence of discrimination in applications for private accommodation and applications for both blue-collar and white-collar employment. By using matched applicants, one white, one black, or matched application forms, identical except in so far as one is obviously from a black applicant and the other from a white applicant, discrimination that might easily be hidden from an individual black applicant is revealed. However, to establish that discrimination has taken place is not to put the large organization in the same position as the individual discriminator. Large organizations have better defences against the outsider than do individuals: policy in these matters may be decided behind closed doors and set down in restricted memos or merely enshrined in custom and practice. Even if direct discrimination is established it may remain difficult to discover whether it originated at senior level, whether it originated elsewhere but senior managers tolerated it, or whether it was unknown to senior management. Thus, if a suitably qualified black applicant is found to have been turned away by a junior employee at the factory gate or by someone in personnel, this could be explained as an error of judgement or simply disowned by senior management.

By grouping together these articles under the title 'Institutional racism' we approach discrimination in its covert, indirect and often unintentional forms. As has been said very often, overt and direct discrimination may not be apparent to the recipient even though it is obvious to those who mete out the unequal treatment; to be told that a flat is let or a job filled when it is not, can be an effective rebuff for, though crude, it may still be difficult to unmask it for what it is. How much more elusive then is the situation where discrimination is unintentional, is not – or need not be – apparent to the perpetrator, or where there is no perpetrator as such?

It is clear that by widening understanding of discrimination to encompass indirect or 'institutional' racism we are likely to have a much better understanding of the barriers that black people in Britain face. Though the impact of direct discrimination continues to be considerable, the imposition of a range of rules, regulations and procedures that though they are not *formulated* to diminish the opportunities for black people nevertheless have this effect is of great importance. But in saying this we come immediately to a problem at the heart of institutional racism, a concept that Norman Ginsburg explores in 'Racism and housing'. He argues that such racism can take many forms and that it cannot be fully understood solely by examining formal policy and procedures. Nor should the term institutional racism be used as if it is self-evident that all institutions are uniformly racist. Even if the proportion of black people employed in, serviced by, or incarcerated in a given institution does not reflect the ratio of black people to white in the local or national population, we should not simply say there is 'institutional racism'. To use the concept in this way is to diminish its value to the point where 'institutional racism' is little more than a slogan. What is required is first to decide what sort of evidence indicates that black people are being treated less equally than their circumstances justify, and then to explore the ways in which this happens, dividing them into the two categories corresponding to (a) deliberate and direct discrimination, and (b) indirect discrimination, the latter encompassing the sorts of practices that unintentionally disadvantage black people. Almost by definition, it follows that this second category will include a wide range of practices – rules, regulations, criteria, customs and so on – and that whereas in some cases the implications that these practices have for equal opportunity (or, conversely, for patterns of racial inequality) are readily apparent, in other cases they are much less so and might even be quite unexpected. John Wrench's article, 'New vocationalism, old racism and the careers service' helps to illustrate some of these points. In Wrench's view, the growing importance of the careers service in the youth labour market during the

1980s has increased its centrality to issues of equal opportunity. But this is not a straightforward process, rather it depends on the prevailing ethos of the service – which changed from an insistence on 'colour blindness' to an awareness of multiculturalism, and then to an emphasis on anti-racism – and, in no small measure, on external factors, notably government initiatives and legislation.

By choosing a number of examples from different spheres, we can illustrate the ways in which policies which seem to have been constructed without reference to 'race' may have disproportionate consequences for black people. For instance, the decision taken in 1991 to curb excess demand by restricting entry to solicitors' final examination courses to those who had been offered articles was described as introducing an 'unnoticed colour bar'. This was said to amplify existing racial discrimination in the profession because the only firms offering articles sufficiently far ahead were those that were the least likely to offer them to ethnic minority candidates (*The Independent*, 3 May 1991). Or take the use of psychometric tests by London Underground in 1988 to help to decide on selection for a large number of managerial posts: the CRE found that such tests particularly disadvantaged candidates of Afro-Caribbean origin. More widely, the CRE has found that the widespread reliance by employers on 'word of mouth' recruitment for many routine jobs has adverse consequences for black workers who tend to be more reliant on job centres and advertising in their search for employment. And in their study of access to apprenticeships in Birmingham, Lee and Wrench (1983) found that firms located in predominantly white areas expressed a preference for 'local lads', whereas those in inner city areas where most blacks lived pointed to the efficiency of public transport as an explanation for having a city-wide recruitment policy.

Though the most common feature of definitions of institutional racism is the discriminatory impact of administrative procedures and the key element therein is the emphasis on disproportionate adverse effect *rather than* intentional exclusion, the above examples should make us realize that in practice things are not so simple. The explanations given for following different policies by the firms studied by Lee and Wrench – each of which disadvantaged black applicants – are open to question; the consequences of relying on word-of-mouth recruitment for the racial balance of a workforce are by now quite well established; the differential impact of supposedly neutral tests are also beginning to become apparent; and the extent to which large law firms discriminated against ethnic minority candidates had previously been a cause for concern for the Law Society. Thus in the last resort the distinctions between unintentional and intentional, knowing and unknowing are, or may become, porous. We can see this in Richard Jenkins' article, 'Black workers in the labour market: the price of recession'. As Jenkins shows, the way in which many managers characterized 'acceptability' in workers has had important consequences for black employees. Yet, as he also shows, the way in which different groups of workers depended on different information networks to obtain employment may also put black workers at a disadvantage.

What we *can say* is that given that discrimination cannot be deduced from unequal outcomes, much less the nature of the discrimination involved, the presence of such inequality merely indicates a need for specific investigation of the kind that each of the authors in this section conducts. Thus in 'Black people and the criminal law: rhetoric and reality', Paul Gordon examines the way in which a number of factors – the lack of multiracial juries, the extent to which black defendants are less likely than their white counterparts to be granted bail, statistical anomalies in sentencing, and so on – served to criminalize black people in Britain during the 1970s and 1980s, despite the widespread assumption that the judicial process is impartial. And in 'An uncaring profession? An examination of racism in social work', Lena Dominelli argues that whether they enter the arena of social work as clients or as employees, black people experience negative treatment. Dominelli suggests that the failure to meet the needs of black people reflects the way three types of racism – personal, institutional and cultural – are rooted in the everyday routine of social work policy and practice. Though her article concerns black people, Dominelli believes that the deficiencies that she discerns can also be seen to reinforce inadequate social work practice towards *white* people. This is an important point that should be borne in mind when reading these articles: we should not neglect the extent to which the kind of procedures – whether 'colour blind' or not – that disadvantage black people *also* disadvantage other groups.

Reference

Lee, G. and Wrench, J. (1983) *Skill Seekers – Black Youth, Apprenticeships and Disadvantage*, Leicester, National Youth Bureau.

6 RACISM AND HOUSING

CONCEPTS AND REALITY

NORMAN GINSBURG

In analysing racism in housing policy and administration it is useful to distinguish three kinds of process, which often combine to produce the manifest racial inequalities in housing in contemporary Britain.[1] First, there is overt racial prejudice and discrimination by key individuals. This has influence over housing, particularly in the private sector among vendors, landlords, landladies and estate agents. Racial harassment in and around the home is the sharp end of racism, which also has a direct impact on the housing situation of black people.[2] Such person-to-person forms of racism may be described as *subjective racism*, and this is the only widely accepted definition of racism in British society. The 1976 Race Relations Act embodies official attempts to eliminate subjective racism. Secondly, there are policy and administrative processes in local housing agencies, particularly local authority housing departments, building societies and estate agents, which have resulted in adverse treatment of black people compared to white people. Such processes are not explained by subjective racism amongst the staff of such institutions, but are frequently legitimated by stereotyping black and white clients and/or simply by a failure to recognize the particular housing needs of black people. Evidence of racial inequalities in housing linked to local institutional practices suggests the presence of *institutional racism*. Finally, there are aspects of national and international processes that have an indirect but fundamental impact on black people's housing situation, notably government immigration and housing policies, the structure and workings of the labour market, and the interactions between 'race' and other major lines of stratification, particularly class and gender. These processes may be described as manifesting *structural racism*, because they are not tangibly institutionalized in the local housing scene; they are institutionalized in the socio-economic structure beyond immediate housing institutions.

These kinds of distinctions are useful for several reasons. First, there is the continual need to renew the challenge to those who would confine the notion of racism to overt subjectivist forms or to explicitly conspiratorial concepts of institutional racism. Secondly, it is important to beware of the fundamentalism inherent in structural approaches, which may implicitly devalue local resistance to institutionally racist processes. This is not to argue that institutionally racist processes are not of paramount significance in understanding and thus defeating racism in housing. We are only dealing here with analytical tools with which to order an understanding of racial inequalities in housing. In reality, subjective, institutional and structural processes are operating together, and resistance to an example of one kind usually involves challenging all three forms. 'Common sense racism' (see Lawrence, 1982), as articulated, for example, by Norman Tebbit during 1990 concerning the exclusion of the Hong Kong Chinese from the UK, has a widespread, perhaps predominant resonance among the British people, which is far from prosecutable and operates at all levels of civil society and the state. Thus, a vendor of a house or an estate agent on their behalf can attempt informally to exclude black buyers from a neighbourhood; a local authority housing department may feel obliged informally to take account of what they perceive as hostility among white tenants to having black neighbours on certain estates; and a national housing policy of expenditure cuts and council house sales could exclude black people in particular from affordable rented housing. These and other instances are frequently informed by a common-sense racism, which, to be blunt, puts white people first. In the end, the attitudes of individuals, as betrayed by the ideology of common-sense racism, nourish institutional and structural racism through political and bureaucratic processes. Nevertheless there has been, and continues to be, powerful resistance to these processes manifested, for example, in the community struggles against racial harassment, the pressure for anti-racist local authority housing allocation and investment policies, and the lobbying for central government funding for rented housing. This article will focus on elucidating aspects of subjective, institutional and structural racism applied to the 'race' and housing question in Britain. We begin with institutional racism in order to emphasize its central significance in this field. This is followed by a discussion of aspects of structural racism, and the article ends by examining racial harassment as an aspect of subjective racism affecting housing, which is frequently not conceptualized as such.

Institutional racism

The origins of the concept 'institutional racism' are traced by Williams (1985) to the Black Power movement in the US in the 1960s. Stokely Carmichael and Charles V. Hamilton in their book *Black Power* began by confronting the difference between individual (or subjective) and institutional racism. The latter

is less overt, far more subtle, less identifiable in terms of *specific* individuals committing the acts ... [it] originates in the operation of established forces in the society, and thus receives far less public condemnation ... But it is institutional racism that keeps black people locked in dilapidated slum tenements, subject to the daily prey of exploitative landlords, merchants, loan sharks and discriminatory real estate agents.

(Carmichael and Hamilton, 1969, p. 20)

The concept was then taken up by a number of social scientists, so that institutional racism came to be identified by two principal features: first, the production of racial inequalities by normal bureaucratic and pro-fessional administrative processes, and secondly, the irrelevance of the subjective consciousness of the individual officials, professionals and politicians involved. In other words institutional racism is in evidence where a public or private agency is presiding over long-established racial inequalities, the reasonable assumption being that the agency must in some way be held responsible for such an outcome, no matter how limited its resources and well-meaning its staff. The emphasis on its identification with outcomes may obscure an understanding of the complex reasons for those outcomes, buried in long-established, local political assumptions, for example. Hence a racism awareness programme for personnel involved in the day-to-day implementation of policy might be quite inappropriate if senior management or clients are not appraised of what is going on. To confront institutional racism effectively is often to take on an entrenched power structure, which has been legitimated by common-sense racism and sustained by structural processes.

Williams and Carter have described the problems of an uncritical application of the concept of institutional racism to educational processes and anti-racist strategies for education. They suggest that current use of the concept 'collapses into a profoundly reformist vision of inequality' (Williams and Carter, 1985, p. 7) by focusing on local practice in schools and ignoring wider, structural processes. It is therefore vital to emphasize that the concept of institutional racism has to be deployed alongside the concepts of structural and subjective racism. In fact institutional racism has rarely been used to analyse racialized housing processes in Britain. More attention has been focused on the process of racial residential segregation (Smith, 1989), on black people as a housing class (Rex and Moore, 1967) or on 'exclusionary social closure' (Sarre *et al.*, 1989). Yet there is now a large number of research studies of what can only be described as institutionally racist processes in housing, particularly in local authority housing departments and building society branches. These studies may be used to examine how institutional racism actually works.

Council housing and institutional racism

During the 1970s and 1980s research studies on 'race' and council housing were conducted in a number of local authority housing departments including Nottingham, Liverpool, Hackney, Tower Hamlets, Bedford and Birmingham. They mostly document institutional processes whereby black applicants for council housing waited longer than white people, and once rehoused received inferior accommodation to white people. In each study some difficulty was found in pinpointing the forms of institutional racism at work. Simpson (1981) studied Nottingham in the mid-1970s using the housing department's records which, unusually, had recorded the ethnic origin of new and transferred tenants since 1968. He identified two key aspects of the process. First, on average black families were larger in size and required larger properties than white families. The council did not have many larger properties to offer and those it did have were in a dilapidated state in the inner city area. Black families therefore had to wait considerably longer for housing or rehousing from over-crowded accommodation. Hence the city's housing stock was more poorly matched to the needs of black people than white people on this key parameter of number of bedrooms. This is a particular form of insti-tutional racism that is common to many local housing authorities. It also reflects traditional views about the size of council houses going back decades. Local authorities have never provided sufficient three, four and five bedroom dwellings because to do so was considered to be encouraging large families and the poverty commonly associated with large working-class families. Large families have traditionally always been seen as 'less deserving'. Secondly, Simpson found that black people were more likely to be allocated to complexes of flats rather than houses. This 'arose because housing department officials were more inclined to offer such poorer properties to black applicants in the first instance than they were to white ones' (Simpson, 1981, p. 257). Simpson was not able to ascertain whether this was done with conscious racist intent because he had little access to the actual workings of the allocation process but he certainly suggests that officers exerted negative discretion against black applicants.

The study of Liverpool by the Commission for Racial Equality (CRE, 1986) consisted of an analysis of lettings records in the late 1970s and a sample survey of tenants. This clearly reveals allocation to black people of the less desirable estates. The responses of black tenants suggested that housing officers believed they only wanted to live in one area and should not be offered as good accommodation as white people, and that the officers offered inferior information to black applicants. The pressure on officers to let properties quickly and the pressure of racial harassment on certain estates were recognized by the interviewees as non-subjective, institution-alized processes which contributed to the situation. A follow-up study by the CRE in Liverpool in the mid-1980s found direct racial discrimination 'in that black applicants nominated by the Council to housing association property were treated less favourably than white applicants in relation to the quality of property they obtained' (CRE, 1989, p. 47). This suggests subjective racism by officials. There was also further evidence of indirect, institutional discrimination in the allocation of council housing in the city.

The major study by the CRE (1984) of Hackney's allocation of council housing covered the period 1978–79. It used interviews with officers and tenants as well as departmental records. They found evidence of indirect discrimination and this led to the issue of a 'non-discrimination notice' under the Race Relations Act, 1976 in June 1983. Hackney was seen as a test case by the CRE and the report was widely publicized and discussed in local housing departments because, by implication, similar situations obtained in most urban local housing authorities. Unfortunately the report is less than explicit about the actual processes at work in Hackney. Factors such as shortage of appropriately sized accommodation and different levels of rent arrears among different ethnic groups were not found to be relevant. Other factors such as inferior allocations given to one parent families or cohabitees, or the indirect impact of racial harassment are not mentioned. The assessment and grading of applicants by housing visitors was identified as an area where subjective and institutional racism seemed to operate. The report considered that

> the difference in assessment, with whites doing better than blacks, reflected part of a (possibly unconscious) stereotyping process . . . housing officers may have been more willing to encourage and 'push' for white applicants as epitomised by their positive recommendations.
> (CRE, 1984, p. 74)

However, in fact 'there was not usually a strong relationship between the relative gradings and the actual allocation of property' (ibid.). The report found that 'expressed preference areas, and the offer and refusal systems, do not explain the different patterns of allocation between blacks and whites' (ibid., p. 77). Little insight is offered into the work of housing visitors and more senior housing officers in reaching final allocation decisions. The report leaves largely undisclosed the real reasons for the racialized allocation policies. There are strong hints, however, that a combination of the subjective racism of some officials and institutionalized managerial assumptions about area preference and racial harassment played a major part. The wide areas of discretion administered by housing officers appear to have prevented the researchers from establishing any clear parameters of institutional racism such as those suggested by Simpson. Nevertheless, the report implies that the processes of institutional racism in council house allocation are more complex and various than suggested by Simpson.

More insight into the inner processes of institutional racism is given by both Phillips (1986) and Forman (1989) in their analyses of the Greater London Council's (GLC) council house allocation policies in Tower Hamlets. Here the Bengali community had long experienced ghetto-ization in deck-access flats in Spitalfields, virtual exclusion from new GLC housing in the area and severe racial harassment as the GLC tried to 'disperse' them to estates beyond Spitalfields. Phillips found that official judgements 'must have been made about the suitability of Asians and non-Asians for particular vacancies on the basis of assumptions about group preferences and stereotypes of the groups themselves' (Phillips, 1986, p. 27). She suggests that:

> the reasons for this discretionary matching relate at least in part to management pressure to fill vacancies quickly and reflect the perceived difficulty of managing multi-racial estates in hostile white areas. It would also seem to reflect some assessment of applicant worth and the types of offer he/she deserves.
>
> (ibid., pp. 27–8)

So here we have at least three forms of institutional racism at work – pressure to fill vacancies and therefore match properties to tenants, housing officers' anticipation of racial harassment by established white tenants on better estates, and judgements by officers of deserving or undeserving status. These processes in general are in fact as long established as council housing management itself and have adversely affected Irish people, single mothers, unemployed people and so on (Jacobs, 1985, pp. 22–3). They were already at hand as tried and tested management techniques of municipal landlordism before the arrival of black tenants on a large scale. Hence

> the view that all social security and black tenants should be put together on certain estates was expressed to the researcher on several occasions by different officers . . . certain estates have been regarded as unsuitable for black tenants mainly, it seems, because of white tenants' objections to cooking smells . . . some Council employees may have been prepared to let white tenants dictate the pattern of housing allocation.
>
> (Phillips, 1986, p. 34)

Here is where subjective racism and institutional racism meet head on, though it is clearly not essential to a racist outcome for officers doing a tough job with low social status to be subjectively prejudiced themselves. As Phillips (1986, p. 37) points out 'it seems quite logical that, at present, it is in the interests of the estate officer to discriminate against those he/she perceives as a threat to the smooth running of the estate' in several formal and informal ways. The institutionalized acceptance of racial harassment, or the threat of it, is therefore routine in the absence of effective political opposition. Nevertheless, to some extent, by the mid-1980s the Bengali community had been successful in transforming the GLC and Tower Hamlets allocation and dispersal policies, so that there was a much stronger and more securely housed community in the East End, (see Forman, 1989, Chapter 10). It might be argued that Tower Hamlets is a special, atypical case because of the hard core and long history of working-class racism in the area. The otherwise inadequately explained evidence of similar official assumptions about applicants' area preferences in Nottingham, Liverpool, Bedford (Sarre *et al.*, 1989) and Hackney suggests, however, that Tower Hamlets is only an acute case of a very widespread phenomenon, as black tenants have long testified.

Henderson and Karn (1987) conducted an extensive study of racism and council housing policy and practice in Birmingham during the 1970s. They extended the various methodological approaches of the studies mentioned so far by surveying tenants and applicants, analysing department records and, most significantly perhaps, through the use of an 'ethnographic' study of the day-to-day work of housing officers at the various stages of the allocation process, including key discretionary decision-making. They found many forms of institutional racism at work. First, there were six policies of the department which clearly disadvant-aged Afro-Caribbean and Asian applicants for council housing and transfer:

1 The requirement for applicants to be resident in the city for at least five years, reduced to two years in 1977;

2 The disqualification of applications from owner-occupiers;

3 The disqualification of applications from single people of most ages;

4 The disqualification of applications from unmarried couples unless cohabitation had lasted five years for childless couples and two years for couples with children;

5 Rejection of applications from joint families;

6 The policy of dispersing black families within the housing stock operating from 1969 to 1975.

It is quite fruitless to unravel whether conscious, racist motivations prompted these policies. With the exception of the dispersal policy, they were no doubt legitimated with ostensibly benign intentions to support the conventional family and to give priority to the deserving. The latter were traditionally considered to be married couples expecting or already having children, living in rented accommodation or with parents, and long established in the white working-class community. The exclusion of owner-occupiers discriminates against all black people, and particularly Asians, who are much more likely than white people to be in low-cost owner-occupation. Lengthy residence requirements and the exclusion of single people obviously discriminated against relative newcomers to the city, amongst whom black people were strongly represented, at least up to the early 1970s. The exclusion of unmarried cohabitees has particularly affected Afro-Caribbean people, among whom such relationships are more common than among white people. The splitting of joint families particularly deterred Asian people, among whom such households are much more common. Birmingham City Council, like many others, did not recognize the needs of many black people for large accommodation for joint families and for larger than average numbers of children. The explicit dispersal policy seems to have been confined to a few housing departments such as Birmingham, Walsall and Lewisham. In Birmingham between 1969 and 1975 'the five properties on either side of one allocated to a black tenant were to be reserved automatically for whites' (Henderson and Karn, 1987, p. 128). This meant that quite quickly after its implementation black applicants and transfer applicants had to wait longer for accommodation. In practice there has been fairly explicit racial segregation of tenants in Birmingham before and since 1975, with black people increasingly confined to the inner areas and white people to the suburbs. The city council justified the dispersal policy as a means of preventing concentrations of black tenants in the inner city and to encourage black tenancies in the suburbs, the precise opposite of its effect in practice! According to Henderson and Karn (1987, p. 128) the introduction of the policy coincided with a threatened rent strike by white tenants on one estate objecting to the allocation of a property to a black family. Hence it was really a simple device for accommodating racist pressure, legitimated with a spurious liberal veneer about promoting racial harmony. The policy was dropped in 1975 as it became clear that it would be illegal under the Race Relations Act, 1976. Most of these six policies were not formally voted on or pronounced by the council, but they were well-known to everyone. This is a familiar policy making process in local and central government which enables discriminatory, controversial policies to be cloaked in the mysteries of administrative discretion, thereby allowing politicians to keep their hands clean should an effective political or legal challenge be mounted. In a brief postscript at the end of Henderson and Karn's book, a senior housing officer in Birmingham writing in January 1986 suggested that most of these policies had been abandoned, but it is not clear how well this has been publicized. The effects of the old policies could be felt for several generations by confining black people to less attractive, less marketable council housing or by excluding them from local authority housing altogether.

In addition to these formal policies, the use of more informal administrative discretion by housing officers is examined by Henderson and Karn. Like the CRE (1984) Hackney report and Phillips (1986) they confirm that discretion is used at all levels of authority in ways which, intentionally and unintentionally, disadvantage black people. The foremost priority of municipal landlords is to let properties quickly and to anticipate and prevent tension between tenants and between tenant and landlord. Hence 'the strong preference of whites for the suburbs produced a tendency for inner city vacancies to be offered to West Indians and Asians because housing officers expected white applicants to reject such property' (Henderson and Karn, 1987, p. 273). We do not know to what extent the preferences of white people were shaped by their attitudes to having black neighbours, nor to what extent officers' attitudes were influenced by anticipated or actual threats of racial harassment. Meeting applicants in their homes, housing visitors' 'perceptions of applicants were structured not only along race and class-cultural lines, but also according to their view of the principal women in the household' (ibid., p. 204). The alleged quality of women's domestic labour was judged very sharply.

Later in the area offices, decisions, for example, about accepting applications from owner-occupiers or single people were inconsistent and often adversely affected black people. It was found that 'some white tenants who had been owner-occupiers had managed to enter council housing as special cases, but Asians and West Indians had not' (ibid., p. 272). Final allocation was done centrally using computer coding, matching property to applicants, but

> it was the concern with lost rent that took priority in the matching process and led logically to pressure for rapid lettings. This inevitably led to the matching of applicants assumed to be 'disreputable' to properties considered to be 'unpopular'.
>
> (ibid., p. 226)

The allocation process is a complex web of discretionary decision-making. Such a process reflects long-established management philosophy in municipal landlordism going back to its nineteenth-century origins (Ginsburg, 1979, pp. 156–68). Applied in a racialized context it almost inevitably sharpens racial divisions:

> Area officers developed an image of applicants which implicitly located them on a respectable – disreputable working class continuum. This imagery was then applied to the vacant property in order to assess whether the applicant was likely to accept the property, but more importantly to assess whether that applicant, once he or she became a tenant in that particular street, was likely to create 'management problems' for the area officer and/or his colleagues.
>
> (Henderson and Karn 1987, p. 269)

Such decision-making seems to lie at the heart of the conventional council house allocation process, making it almost impossible to unravel explicit from unconscious racialized attitudes, and class prejudices from racial and gender stereotypes among the housing officers. This form of institutional racism is therefore embedded in the general form of managerial landlordism.

Three different forms of institutional racism in the provision of council housing are suggested by the studies we have examined:

1 Relative inadequacy in the physical standards of dwellings in relation to black applicants' needs, particularly the numbers of bedrooms, due to a failure to take into account the specific needs of black applicants in the house construction and acquisition programmes of the past.

2 Formal local policies creating differential access for black applicants such as dispersal policies. This must also include slum clearance and comprehensive housing rehabilitation programmes which, as Jacobs (1985, p. 20) points out, often seem to bypass black communities.

3 Managerial landlordism involving racialized assessment of the respectability and deserving status of applicants, assumptions about preferred areas of residence for different racial groups and about the threat of racial harassment by white people causing avoidable trouble for managers.

All these decisions have political origins. Ultimately it is elected councillors who have decided not to build enough four bedroomed accommodation, who approve formal local policies and who oversee the deployment of administrative discretion in the form of managerial landlordism. As we have shown, none of these forms of institutional racism depends on explicit, subjective racism among staff and politicians. Such attitudes are rarely expressed publicly; they are more likely to exert their influence quietly and routinely.

Institutional racism and owner-occupation

Either by choice or by denial of access to decent council housing, many black and ethnic minority people sought low-cost owner-occupied housing as the long-term alternative to initial settlement in rented lodgings. In this sector too, there is evidence of institutionalized, informal processes operating, not unlike those evident in the allocation of council housing. Relatively little research has been done in this field, which by its nature is private and politically inaccessible. From the late 1950s to the mid-1970s many black people bought cheap houses in neighbourhoods blighted by redevelopment or slum clearance plans that had been shelved. The mainstream building societies and banks would not lend on properties in areas that they regarded as a bad investment. A practice known as 'redlining' developed, the drawing of a red line round a mortgage exclusion zone on the map, often coinciding with the areas where black people could afford to buy (Sarre et al., 1989, p. 281). Thus the transactions were often managed and financed informally within ethnic minority communities, without involvement with white-dominated institutions. In some parts of the country this process developed into the establishment of black-owned businesses providing loan finance, estate agency, legal and surveying services. In other places, white entrepreneurs exploited the demand for mortgages from ethnic minorities, by offering more expensive (and more profitable) loans of one kind or another. The process is described by Sarre et al. (1989, pp. 276–81) in Bedford and by Karn et al. (1985) in Liverpool and Birmingham.

From the late 1960s, some of the mainstream lending institutions gradually began to relax discriminatory policies in order to cash in on the boom in low cost owner-occupation among the working class. By the 1970s in Bedford, prompted by local employers the London Brick Company, the

Abbey National Building Society were actively courting Italian and Asian customers. In general, however, banks and building societies had high refusal rates for black applicants in black neighbourhoods and, in the era when mortgages were rationed, were using less stringent status criteria for white applicants, Karn (1983, pp. 174–9). Lenders' 'stereotyping of preferences sustains the expectation that Asians and West Indians will only want to buy in areas where their community is concentrated, and that no whites will want to buy there or remain living there' (Karn, 1983, p. 178), which mirrors similar processes in the allocation of council housing. In Bedford Sarre *et al.* found a status hierarchy in the institutionalized stereotyping of mortgage applicants by building society managers, with Italian and Asian people viewed favourably but Afro-Caribbean people extremely unfavourably. The latter were stereotyped as 'unreliable and disorganised, as having a cavalier or irresponsible attitude to finance ... they are judged to have failed to display the thrift and resourcefulness so highly valued by the building society movement' (Sarre *et al.*, 1989, p. 289). In the early 1980s in Rochdale, the CRE (1985) found that some building societies, by refusing to lend on certain properties, such as those without front gardens, those below a certain value or those in inner city areas, were indirectly discriminating against Asian buyers.

In the autumn of 1988 the CRE investigated an estate agent in Oldham, issuing a non-discrimination notice against Norman Lester and Co. in June 1989. The subsequent CRE (1990) report showed that the firm tended to recommend white areas to prospective white purchasers and Asian areas to prospective Asian purchasers, to accept instructions from white vendors to deter prospective Asian purchasers and to offer mortgage facilities only to white clients. Two other Oldham estate agents were practising in similar ways, but this changed when the CRE challenged them informally. The CRE believe that such 'discrimination by estate agents may not be uncommon' (1990, p. 5), this being the third non-discrimination notice issued against an intransigent firm. Estate agents, solicitors and surveyors, frequently operating in coordination with each other and the local building society managers, often share such institutionally racist practices.

Institutional racism in the owner-occupied sector, as in the public sector, is the result of a blend of common-sense subjective racism and structural factors. The exclusion of certain areas, properties or people with low or insecure incomes has a common-sense financial and administrative legitimation, to the extent that a building society manager can claim that lending on such properties or to such people is too risky. Given that black people on average have lower incomes than white people, a feature of structural racism, it might be argued that the apparent institutional racism is merely a reflection of social structural factors for which local institutions cannot be held responsible. Yet it is quite apparent that the policies we have reviewed above cannot be legitimated in such terms, because black people with incomes the same as or higher than white people can still receive different treatment. This is best documented in the CRE (1985) study of Rochdale, where it is quite apparent that racial stereotyping by lenders was relatively autonomous from any structural, financial considerations. Repossessions among low income Asian mortgagors were no greater than those in the white community. It might be argued alternatively that the institutional racism we have described is essentially the product of subjective racism on the part of building society managers, estate agents and so on, as made clear by their explicit racial stereotyping. Fundamentally this is perhaps true but it is built into the managerial sub-culture, just as it is in municipal landlordism, so that individuals can argue that they are just pursuing prudent professional practices. Racial stereotyping is a means of handling the common-sense racism of civil society in a day-to-day context. Estate agents and building societies want to keep their white clients happy, just as local authority housing managers want to avoid hassle from white tenants. The usefulness of the concept of institutional racism is that it exposes such practices as routine and normal, without the exceptionalism associated with explicit subjective racism.

Government housing policies and structural racism

Obviously racial inequalities in housing cannot be fully explained in terms of institutionally racist processes. Government housing policies have played a structurally racist role in orchestrating the institutional environment in which housing is consumed. It is also true to say that the effects of some government policies have contradicted this general tendency, by encouraging housing opportunities for some sections of the black communities. Labour and Conservative government policies since at least 1977 have rested on two planks, active support for home ownership and withdrawal of support from council housing and council tenants. Government support for home ownership has many facets including housing improvement grants, capital gains tax exemption, the ending of major slum clearance, building society deregulation, council house sales and above all mortgage tax relief. Given that many black people chose or were forced into low-cost owner-occupation, it might be argued that such government policies have been of great benefit to them, but it is unlikely that this is in fact the case. Housing improvement grants, mortgage tax relief and capital gains tax exemption are strongly regressive; they have differentially benefited higher income groups, among whom there are very few black people in Britain. Mortgage tax relief, which was by far the most significant form of government financial assistance for housing in the 1980s, has not always benefited black people. Those black homeowners, especially in the 1950s and 1960s who were unable to get mainstream mortgages, relied on informal or fringe bank loans which did not attract tax relief.[3] Deregulation of mortgage finance and of the building societies during the 1980s has ended mortgage rationing, thereby breaking down some of the institutional racism legitimated by traditional financial conservatism. On the other hand the possible contribution of deregulation to raising mortgage interest rates through increased demand can hardly be said to have benefited low income households.

The promotion of council house sales since the 1980 Housing Act has without question had important structural racist effects. Over 1.25 million local authority dwellings have been sold since the Act, subsidized by discounts averaging over a billion pounds a year in total in the mid-1980s. The homes sold have very largely been those houses with gardens on attractive, suburban estates. These estates are populated mostly by white working-class households who benefited from the racialized allocation policies of the previous decades. Thus local institutional racism of the past combined with contemporary central government policy produce a powerful inegalitarian effect.

The sale of council houses is linked also to the second plank of government policies, that is the withdrawal of financial investment in council housing. Public expenditure on housing, which used to be dominated by the construction and maintenance of council housing and council rent subsidies, has suffered greater cuts in real spending than any other public expenditure programme over the years since 1976 (Flynn, 1988). According to the Chancellor's 1988 Autumn Statement, public expenditure on housing was cut by 79 per cent *in real terms* between 1979 and 1988. Yet there is a vital and growing need among black people in particular for reasonably priced, rented accommodation. The restraint in spending on council housing allied with council house sales has solidified and extended the racial inequalities already existing in the mid-1970s. The coincidence of increased housing needs, expressed politically by black people, and less public resources devoted to public investment in bricks and mortar is a sharply focused example of structural racism, or if you prefer, institutional racism at central government level. It is significant that there have been virtually no parliamentary or government policy documents addressing the 'race' and housing issue over the past decade. Lord Scarman's 1981 report on the 'Brixton Disorders' had little to say about housing except that

> council housing allocation policies must be seen to be fair . . . There is a strong case . . . for local authorities reviewing their housing policies – particularly their criteria and procedures for the allocation and transfer of council houses – in order to ensure that they do not, wittingly or unwittingly, discriminate against minority groups.
>
> (Scarman, 1982, p. 163)

The implication is that institutional racism probably does exist in this area, and this is echoed in several other parliamentary and government documents of the 1970s, but there have been no national policy initiatives whatsoever. Parliament and central government have washed their hands of the issue.

The structurally racist strand of central government housing policy continued with the Housing Act, 1988 and the Local Government and Housing Act, 1989. The intention of this legislation was to increase the pressure on local authorities and tenants to privatize council housing by a variety of techniques including the ending of local rent subsidies and incentives for private landlords to take over council estates. Unsubsidized rents and privatization of finance in the housing association sector is also being phased in with this legislation. The structurally racist effects are that black people's access to decent council housing to buy or to rent will be further eroded, while the move to unsubsidized rents will particularly affect low-income housholds, of whom a disproportionate number are black. The continued erosion of housing benefit enhances this process. The implementation of all these measures has been resisted fiercely by tenants up and down the country, led in part by black tenants (Ginsburg, 1989b).

Unquestionably the growth of homelessness in the 1980s particularly affected black people, both families and young single people. A survey in Brent by Bonnerjea and Lawton (1987) found that the proportion of Afro-Caribbean people officially accepted as homeless was twice that for Asian people and three times that for white people. The burden of homelessness is falling increasingly on black women, 46 per cent of Brent's official homeless were single mothers in the Brent survey. Bonnerjea and Lawton found 'not so much that black families were treated less favourably than average, but that white families were sometimes treated more favourably than average' (1987, p. 65). Thus, for example, white families tended to be in better temporary accommodation in hostels and hotels. Brent like almost all local authorities does not effectively monitor its policy practices on such criteria. A survey by Single Homelessness in London (SHIL, 1989), found that only three London boroughs monitored single homeless applicants by ethnic origin, and in these boroughs young black people suffered a greater degree of official homelessness than young white people. There is a growing but unknown number of single people, particularly Afro-Caribbean young people, who form the hidden homeless, sleeping rough or on floors and moving around (O'Mahony, 1988, Chapter 5). Either rejected by or rejecting the labour market, their families and official agencies, they form a new urban underclass, whose plight has been exacerbated by withdrawal of Income Support to the under-18s and the introduction of the poll tax in England and Wales in 1990.

Processes of overt institutional racism affecting homeless Bangladeshis in Tower Hamlets emerge from a CRE study covering the period 1984/5. They found 'significant differences' in the time spent in temporary accommodation by Bangladeshi families compared to white people (CRE,

1988, p. 10). This was not explained, as the council claimed, by differences in family structure between the two groups. There was also evidence that Bangladeshis were offered inferior temporary accommodation, for example, over thirty miles distant in Southend. The Home Affairs Committee of the House of Commons noted in a report in 1987 that for the homeless Bangladeshis in Tower Hamlets 'conditions in bed and breakfast hotels were often appalling, with severe overcrowding, lack of basic amenities . . . insect infestation and fire and safety hazards' (Home Affairs Committee, 1987, p. ix). The CRE concluded that Tower Hamlets had contravened the Race Relations Act in four respects and a non-discrimination notice was issued against the council in November 1987 with an extensive range of policy recommendations. In April 1987 Tower Hamlets adopted a much tougher policy on intentional homelessness. This included the cancellation of hotel bookings for ninety homeless applicants, most of whom were Bangladeshis, whose families were waiting in Bangladesh for entry into the UK. As the CRE explained 'the council declared them intentionally homeless on the grounds that they had accommodation in Bangladesh which was "available for occupation" and which it was "reasonable to continue to occupy"' (CRE, 1988, p. 55). An appeal against this decision was finally rejected by the Court of Appeal in April 1988, despite the fact the appellants had lived and worked in the UK for between 16 and 28 years. The CRE concluded that:

> the outcome of the Tower Hamlets cases is clearly very important and will have a significant impact on the housing opportunity of Bangladeshi separated families who, because of their pattern of immigration and settlement, are more likely to be declared intentionally homeless.
> (CRE, 1988, p. 56)

Indeed this decision affects all such families, most of whom are black. This is one key example of a wider process of tightening eligibility for accommodation and the definition of intentional homelessness under the Homeless Persons Act which has institutionally racist effects.

Racial harassment: subjective racism and housing

Racial inequalities in housing cannot be explained solely in terms of processes of institutional and structural racism as described so far. Subjective racism on the part of individuals in the housing consumption process, including vendors, private landlords, estate agents and housing department officials, is also significant, though its precise influence is hard to assess. Occasionally the CRE launches local investigations into such cases, presumably with the hope of having a deterrent effect. The most significant impact of subjective racism on housing takes the form of racial harassment in and around the home. From the studies of racialized allocation of council housing mentioned above, it becomes quite clear that racial violence and harassment in and around the home are very important factors sustaining racial inequalities in housing. The fear of possible anti-black racial violence is a factor that often motivates housing managers and black prospective tenants in allocating and choosing tenancies. From a survey of local authority housing departments, the CRE concluded that:

> there are many, effectively 'no-go' areas which have acquired a 'name' for racial harassment and where members of ethnic minorities are afraid to accept offers of homes, should they even be offered them. We have examples of this from throughout the country . . . Far too often we hear of an 'outer-city ring' or whole sections of a local authority area where housing officers say they are reluctant to make offers to black people because of potential harassment. These areas may often also contain good quality housing.
> (CRE, 1987, p. 20)

Racial attacks, racial harassment and the threat of them at home are thus very significant in perpetuating racism and racial inequalities in housing in contemporary Britain. Unfortunately, by 1990 there has been no published systematic monitoring of the implementation of policies to prevent harassment, few legal cases against perpetrators and apparently limited preventive work by welfare agencies. There is undoubtedly a tendency to avoid the issue on the part of managers, politicians and housing commentators because it is seen as too intimidating, too intractable a problem or simply as a policing problem. For local authority housing departments, the key policy issues are the transfer of victims and the eviction of perpetrators. The former is clearly the norm and the latter extremely rare. From a detailed study of the London Borough of Brent, Bonnerjea and Lawton (1988, p. 60) concluded that 'racial harassment equals transfers'. Like several local authorities with substantial black communities, Brent adopted a policy on racial harassment in the early 1980s covering victim support, prevention and action against perpetrators, but in reality as one housing officer put it 'the policy is to transfer, the practice is to offer bed and breakfast' (Bonnerjea and Lawton, 1988, p. 9). In other words, victims are encouraged to stay-put by the deterrent offer of alternative accommodation in bed and breakfast. For transfer to another home, victims have to wait between three months and a year. Bonnerjea and Lawton suggest that in Brent 'there is considerable under-reporting of racial harassment and that if more accurate reporting took place, then the entire transfer system would collapse . . . the racial harassment equals transfer policy only works within a housing system which is unaware of the problem' (1988, p. 27). They concluded that amongst the housing officers in Brent:

> there is little evidence of active deterrence [of harassment, and] . . . a total lack of a feeling of responsibility. Treatment of the problem has been made into a form-filling procedure, which is followed without conviction or interest.
>
> (Bonnerjea and Lawton, 1988, pp. 59–60)

This is clear evidence of an institutionally racist response to tenant harassment. The CRE (1987) report says that the number of victim transfers in their survey was 'significant', though precise figures were often unavailable from local authorities. Without action against perpetrators, victim transfers, or 'management transfers' as they are often called, may be urgent and vital, but they seal a victory for the perpetrators. Victim transfer is disastrous as a long-term solution, yet it is being widely implemented.

Action against perpetrators of racial harassment by housing departments is rare. Under pressure from the black community for more than a decade in an area notorious for white racist violence, the London Borough of Newham has developed a detailed and comprehensive set of procedures (Newham Monitoring Project, 1990). However, only two or three perpetrators were evicted annually in the late 1980s, compared with between 21 and 67 victim households rehoused out of several hundred cases reported each year. There is an impressive array of legal powers which the police, local authorities and the CRE can call upon in order to take action against perpetrators (Forbes, 1988). The failure to take up these powers seems to reflect technical inadequacies in the law and institutionalized resistance to using it. Undoubtedly local authorities fear provoking a white racist reaction by well publicized use of their powers. Therefore the resistance of local black communities, supported by groups such as the Newham Monitoring Project, the Southall Monitoring Project and Leicester Racial Attacks Monitoring Project, continues to bear the brunt of the struggle against racial harassment.

Obviously legal remedies on their own are of limited value, and it is clear that 'test cases' depend on community action both to initiate them and to ensure positive, long-term outcomes. As Forbes (1988, p. 5) says 'if legal action is combined effectively with work by community groups in the locality, the message conveyed to the perpetrator and others is that racial harassment is unacceptable and will not be tolerated'. But what does 'work by community groups' mean in this context? This perhaps gets to the nub of the issue. Certainly it means organization and collective resistance among black communities, but it also means antiracist activity with and by white tenants. Official reports all talk of policies being 'communicated' downwards to tenants in a somewhat bureaucratic, patronizing manner. The CRE found that 32 per cent of local authorities who said they had a racial harassment policy, had not communicated this to their tenants as a whole:

> In many cases where tenants had been informed of the policy this appeared to have been done in a minimal way, for example by just including it as part of a tenants' handbook, or through the conditions of tenancy arrangements.
> (CRE, 1987, p. 34)

Very few councils have energetically gone out to talk to tenants about their policies, even to tenants' associations.

Very little is known or recorded about the activities and attitudes of tenants' associations up and down the country. Over the past twenty years organized pressure from council tenants seems to have gone into decline. It is sometimes alleged that many tenants' associations are often influenced by racist attitudes. According to the CRE (1987, p. 33) 'many local black organizations and Community Relations Councils accuse tenants' associations of being, to all intents and purposes, racist'. Certainly where a tenants' association attempts to develop an anti-racist strategy, it may be blamed by police and tenants for 'inflaming the situation'. This occurred in Kentish Town, leading Gregg (1987, p. 14) to conclude that 'it is never a good idea to underestimate the strength of reaction of white tenants and white-dominated tenants' associations'. In the long term a key part of the solution must be to respond to such white attitudes condoning racial harassment in a way which constructively changes them. Local authorities surely have a major responsibility to initiate a process of undermining confused, individual prejudices, even if they may not be best equipped to provide it directly themselves. A rare insight into white and black attitudes is offered in an unusual booklet called *Tenants Tackle Racism* (Dame Colet House, undated). This is a verbatim report of seven antiracist workshop discussions in Tower Hamlets involving black and white tenants. The 'confused prejudices' of many white tenants are prominent, but equally there are also strong antiracist statements from both black people and some white people. The booklet concludes that at the workshops:

> a great deal of 'factual' misinformation (mainly media-inspired) was corrected . . . what came across repeatedly was white resentment to the imposition of anti-racist edicts and policies from the authorities and voluntary agencies . . . Alongside this was a continual criticism of the public landlord's inability to fulfil even the most basic of its duties towards tenants . . . Housing authorities cannot expect
> tenants to behave as 'good' tenants unless and until they themselves behave as 'good' landlords.
> (Dame Colet House, undated, p. 53)

Not surprisingly, the booklet concludes that local authority investment of time, money and energy into antiracist tenants' activity as well as concrete housing improvement measures are the long-term solution.

Policy responses and strategies for change

The local policy responses to the evidence of institutional racism in both the public and the private sectors have been fairly uniform, mirroring the CRE's requirements of Hackney council, (CRE, 1985, pp. 144–5). The CRE measures included record keeping and ethnic monitoring of applicants and transfer applicants; review of allocation procedures and practices; staff training in race relations and the appointment of senior race specialist officers (Domfe, 1985). Even these modest policy proposals were rejected by the left wing council in Liverpool according to Quarless (1985, p. 141) where the Labour group 'had an apparent fear of moving away from their mode of utilizing class as the barometer for policy development in terms of the provision of services'. Soon after the policy changes were publicly announced in Hackney in the autumn of 1984 there were strong protests from some white tenants' associations in the borough with accusations of reverse discrimination being made as well as threats of harassment against rehoused black tenants. Unfortunately, by 1990, there has been no published assessment of the effectiveness of the new policies in Hackney or elsewhere. It is therefore impossible to gauge to what extent the so-called white backlash combined with rate capping have restricted councillors' room for manoeuvre.

Jacobs (1985, p. 24) is strongly dismissive of the CRE's Hackney policies describing them as 'familiar, well-worn proposals for minor adminis-trative reform ... at best, irrelevant, likely to help no more than a handful of Black applicants and then only at the expense of equally badly housed whites'. Henderson and Karn (1987) also recognize that real change will only occur when the prevailing social climate which nourishes racism is altered. Yet they suggest that explicit antiracist policies in housing allocation can be an effective part of changing the climate and creating more political space for black people to press their housing needs. Henderson and Karn (1987, pp. 279–84) spell out in more radical detail than the CRE the management, monitoring, staffing, equal opportunities, training, disciplinary and other processes which could be developed to create real change in housing departments. Ideally such measures should also be taken up by housing agencies in the private sector. Unsurprisingly perhaps, Henderson and Karn's report met with a 'hostile reception' from the Birmingham Housing Department which initially sought to deny the existence of institutional racism in their work. More modest CRE style

rms were adopted by Birmingham some years later according to a
se Appendix to the book from a senior officer, but there is no published
account of the success or otherwise of their implementation.

Effective action against subjective racism in housing, particularly racial
harassment, also necessitates activity by local authorities and housing
associations. Paul Gilroy (1987, p. 14) has strongly criticized the various
activists who 'share a statist conception of anti-racism . . . in making the
local state the main vehicle for advancing anti-racist politics they have
actively confused and confounded the black community's capacity for
autonomous self-organization'. The danger of this happening cannot be
too strongly highlighted. This article may put too much emphasis on local
state action, but in the housing field, unlike other areas perhaps, the
limits of 'autonomous self-organization' are quite tightly drawn in the
current context. Black housing cooperatives are the nearest approxi-
mation to permanent, autonomous organizations, but they are to some
extent dependent on state support from the Housing Corporation and the
local authorities. The future withdrawal of some of this financial support
in the wake of the 1988 Housing Act is causing great anxiety about the
future of black housing associations and cooperatives (Grant, 1988).
Autonomous organizations do not, of course, have immunity from racial
attack, and have to consider actions not dissimilar to those which
municipal landlords must face.

Nevertheless it is true that direct interventions by local authorities are
often counter-productive. What is required is indirect support for community and voluntary initiatives, which does not undermine or coopt
them, combined with official policies and attitudes which are developed by
prior consultation and are fully accountable to the communities affected.
This already happens to some extent, of course, but much more activity in
four key areas is required: victim support; action aginst perpetrators;
antiracist communication and dialogue with tenants; and housing improvement and investment for all tenants in inadequate accommodation
and for the homeless. Local authorities and housing associations are
directly responsible and accountable as landlords, but they are also
responsible as guardians of the community in general. This is spelt out in
Section 71 of the 1976 Race Relations Act which places a duty on local
authorities to ensure that their various functions are carried out with due
regard to the need '(a) to eliminate unlawful discrimination; and (b) to
promote equality of opportunity, and good relations between persons of
different racial groups'. These obligations have been extended under the
1988 Housing Act to the Housing Corporation and Housing for Wales
which govern the activities of housing associations in England and Wales.
In a handful of cases local authorities have been formally challenged on
their performance under this Section, for example, as part of the CRE's
action against Hackney over the allocation of council housing, CRE
(1984). Certainly on the question of action against racial harassment,
there has been no such formal challenge up to 1990 under this Section, yet

surely there is plenty of evidence of inadequate performance by local authorities in this area.

All the measures discussed above ought to become key planks of local housing policy, attracting financial assistance to local authorities and housing associations from central government and the Housing Corporation. It is very striking that no official reports touch on this point about the role of central funding and policy initiation. The Racial Attacks Group (1989) report, for example, makes no mention of any role for central government departments and finance at all. Yet it is signed by ministers from six spending departments, whose foreword makes it quite clear that they have completely washed their hands of the issue. None of the seventy five main conclusions and recommendations of the report refers to central departments and their roles. In the context of the severe restraints on local agencies' expenditure, it will be a struggle to get spending on anti-racial harassment measures seen as a serious priority.

Of course, the hesitancy and inadequacy of local official responses to racial violence and harassment reflect local and national political priorities, but these are not totally determined. The 79 per cent real cut in public housing expenditure between 1979 and 1988 is not entirely unconnected with the growth of racist violence on council estates. It is hardly surprising that poor white people divert their resentment against the local authority about their deteriorating housing and local environment into hostility to antiracist policies. The challenge to change such thinking, following the drift of national housing policy in the late 1980s, is daunting but vital.

Conclusion

This review of the question of racism and housing suggests that successful antiracist strategy must be multi-faceted, aimed at turning the tides of subjective, institutional and structural racism. In Tower Hamlets the GLC, belatedly in the very last year of its existence, began to implement the kind of policy initiatives against institutional racism suggested by Phillips (1987) and by Henderson and Karn (1987). The radical commitment of the GLC to antiracist activity took a long time to come to any fruition in Tower Hamlets and has since been put into abeyance by the GLC's demise in 1986 (Phillips, 1987). As Phillips says:

radical policy statements do not in themselves bring about changes
in attitudes, working practices or housing opportunities for the
minorities. The evidence suggests that the variable commitment to
the race equality policy at all levels has hampered its
implementation.
(Phillips, 1986, p. 46)

Ouseley points out that the antiracist programmes 'were additional to the mainstream activities of the GLC'. Hence their influence in the mainstream areas like housing was often:

> superficial and cosmetic. In reality nothing changed. The mainstream institution was largely run by the bureaucrats and professionals who had always run it. It remained riddled with racism and sexism, even though on the surface there was a multi-ethnic veneer.
> (Ouseley, 1988, p. 87)

He therefore concludes that 'institutional racism cannot be eliminated without major surgery' (ibid., p. 88). This might involve: legal and disciplinary action against subjective racism among staff; radical restructuring of formal, institutionally racist, housing development and management policies; implementation of measures to undermine informal institutional racism exercised through managerial landlordism as detailed by Henderson and Karn; and finally and most importantly, community-based legal, security and propaganda initiatives by housing departments to counter racial harassment.

Countering the overwhelming effects of structural racism, particularly the effects of government policies, is an equally formidable task. The labour movement of the 1990s seems both ill-equipped and unwilling to take it on. Until and unless there emerges a national, political movement seriously committed to antiracist welfare policies, local progress will probably be sporadic and vulnerable. Effective antiracist strategy must seek both fundamental, structural change and gradualist, piecemeal changes within institutions. These are not alternatives, they must if possible go hand in hand, but in the absence of structural change, local antiracist policies can achieve some positive change.

Notes

This article is a revised and extended version of material included in Ginsburg (1989a) and Ginsburg (1989c).

1 This article takes these inequalities as a given, see Brown (1984), London Housing Forum (1988), Luthera (1988).

2 In this article the phrase 'black people' refers to people of Afro-Caribbean, African and Asian origin, who are commonly racialized as 'black' in contemporary Britain.

3 Sarre *et al.* (1989) incidentally suggest that Asian and Italian people's hostility to personal debt leads many of them to pay off their mortgages as quickly as possible, thereby limiting the benefits of tax relief.

References

Bonnerjea, L. and Lawton, J. (1987) *Homelessness in Brent*, London, Policy Studies Institute.

Bonnerjea, L. and Lawton, J. (1988) *No Racial Harassment This Week*, London, Policy Studies Institute.

Brown, C. (1984) *Black and White Britain: the third PSI survey*, London, Heinemann.

Carmichael, S. and Hamilton, C. (1969) *Black Power: the politics of liberation in America*, Harmondsworth, Penguin.

CRE (1984) *Race and Council Housing in Hackney: report of a formal investigation*, London, Commission for Racial Equality.

CRE (1985) *Race and Mortgage Lending: report of a formal investigation*, London, Commission for Racial Equality.

CRE (1986) *Race and Housing in Liverpool*, 2nd edition, London, Commission for Racial Equality.

CRE (1987) *Living in Terror: a report on racial violence and harassment in housing*, London, Commission for Racial Equality.

CRE (1988) *Homelessness and Discrimination*, London, Commission for Racial Equality.

CRE (1989) *Racial Discrimination in Liverpool City Council: report of a formal investigation into the housing department*, London, Commission for Racial Equality.

CRE (1990) *Racial Discrimination in an Oldham Estate Agency*, London, Commission for Racial Equality.

Dame Colet House (undated) *Tenants Tackle Racism*, Dame Colet House, Ben Jonson Road, London E1.

Domfe, W. (1985) 'Hackney's policy to comply with the CRE non-discrimination notice', *Housing Review*, **34**(4), pp. 139–40.

Flynn, R. (1988) 'Political acquiescence, privatisation and residualisation in British housing policy', *Journal of Social Policy*, **17**(3), pp. 289–312.

Forbes, D. (1988) *Action on Racial Harassment: legal remedies and local authorities*, London, Legal Action Group.

Forman, C. (1989) *Spitalfields: a battle for land*, London, Hilary Shipman.

Gilroy, P. (1987) *Problems in Anti-Racist Strategy*, London, Runnymede Trust.

Ginsburg, N. (1979) *Class, Capital and Social Policy*, Basingstoke, Macmillan.

Ginsburg, N. (1989a) 'Institutional racism and local authority housing', *Critical Social Policy* (24), pp. 4–19.

Ginsburg, N. (1989b) 'The Housing Act, 1988 and its policy context', *Critical Social Policy* (25), pp. 56–81.

Ginsburg, N. (1989c) 'Racial harassment policy and practice: the denial of citizenship', *Critical Social Policy* (26), pp. 66–81.

Grant, C. (1988) 'Raising the stakes', *Roof*, November-December, pp. 30–3.

Gregg, A. (1987) 'Tenants tackle racial harassment', *Roof*, September-October, pp. 14–15.

Henderson, J. and Karn, V. (1987) *Race, Class and State Housing*, Aldershot, Gower Press.

Home Affairs Committee (1987) *Bangladeshis in Britain: First Report from the House of Commons Home Affairs Committee 1986–7*, Volume 1, London, HMSO.

Jacobs, S. (1985) 'Race, empire and the welfare state', *Critical Social Policy* (13), pp. 6–28.

Karn, V. (1983) 'Race and housing in Britain: the role of major institutions' in Glazer, N. and Young, K. (eds) *Ethnic Pluralism and Public Policy*, London, Heinemann.

Karn, V., Kemeny, J. and Williams, P. (1985) *Home Ownership in the Inner City*, Aldershot, Gower Press.

Lawrence, E. (1982) 'Just plain common sense: the "roots" of racism' in Centre for Contemporary Cultural Studies, *The Empire Strikes Back*, London, Hutchinson.

London Housing Forum (1988) *Speaking Out: report of the London housing enquiry*, London Housing Forum.

Luthera, M. (1988) 'Race, community, housing and the state' in Bhat, A., Carr-Hill, R. and Ohri, S. (eds) *Britain's Black Population: a new perspective*, Aldershot, Gower Press.

Newham Monitoring Project (1990) *Annual Report 1989: ten years of Newham Monitoring Project*, London E7 8NW.

O'Mahony, B. (1988) *A Capital Offence: the plight of the young, single, homeless on the streets of London*, Ilford, Dr Barnardo's.

Ouseley, H. (1988) 'Equal opportunities lost: the case of education', *Race and Class*, **24**(4), pp. 84–91.

Phillips, D. (1986) *What Price Equality?: report on the allocation of GLC housing in Tower Hamlets*, London, Greater London Council.

Phillips, D. (1987) 'The rhetoric of anti-racism in public housing allocation' in Jackson, P. (ed.) *Race and Racism. Essays in Social Geography*, London, Allen and Unwin.

Quarless, R. (1985) 'Race and housing in Liverpool', *Housing Review*, **34**(4).

Racial Attacks Group (1989) *The Response to Racial Attacks and Harassment: guidance for the statutory agencies*, London, Home Office.

Rex, J. and Moore, R. (1967) *Race, Community and Conflict*, Oxford, Oxford University Press.

Sarre, P., Phillips, D. and Skellington, R. (1989) *Ethnic Minority Housing: explanations and policies*, Aldershot, Avebury.

Scarman, L. (1982) *The Scarman Report: the Brixton disorders*, Harmondsworth, Penguin.

SHIL (1989) *Single Homelessness Among Black and Other Ethnic Minorities*, London, Single Homelessness in London (SHIL) Anti-Racist Sub-Group.

Simpson, A. (1981) *Stacking the Decks: a study of race, inequality and council housing in Nottingham*, Nottingham, Nottingham Community Relations Council.

Smith, S. (1989) *The Politics of 'Race' and Residence*, Cambridge, Polity Press.

Williams, J. (1985) 'Redefining institutional racism', *Ethnic and Racial Studies*, **8**(3), pp. 323–48.

Williams, J. and Carter, B. (1985) '"Institutional racism": new orthodoxy, old ideas', *Multiracial Education*, **13**(1), pp. 4–8.

7 NEW VOCATIONALISM, OLD RACISM AND THE CAREERS SERVICE

JOHN WRENCH

In all the changes which have been wrought by government on the educational system over the last ten years the desire to get education to service the needs of industry and commerce has been paramount. The 1980s have intensified the 'new vocationalism'; an ideology '. . . in which the liberal humanist goals of social justice and personal development have been severely attenuated in favour of those emphasising vocational preparation and a technically-oriented curriculum, especially for "low attainers"' (Esland and Cathcart, 1984, p. 5, quoted in Finn, 1987, p. 168). As Bash puts it, 'The *market* is now a dominant theme in the formulation of UK educational policy' (1989, p. 19). The state is no longer seen as a potential agent for engineering greater social equality. The free market approach to education means that schools are seen to have two separate preparatory functions: 'the inculcation of appropriate attitudes to economic life, and acquaintance with the skills and knowledge required for the world of work' (Bash, 1989, p. 25).

There has been much concern over the implications of the new direction of government educational policies for ethnic minorities, both in the overall context of the 'new vocationalism' and in the specific manifestation of the Education Reform Act (ERA). Questions are being raised as to the implications for the black communities of the national curriculum, the new tests and records of achievement, the role of governors, local financial management, and the 'opting out' of schools from local authority control. As for antiracist work within schools, Ball and Troyna conclude 'there seems to be general agreement from those involved in anti-racist educational initiatives that the ERA will threaten the progress already made' (1989, p. 28). These educational changes take place in the context of the Conservative government's strident opposition to equal opportunity initiatives associated with Labour-controlled local authorities (Coulby, 1989, pp. 10–17).

This article will focus on the effects of this ideological assault, not on schools and colleges, but on another organization found within local education authorities, the careers service. The article draws on research carried out between the years 1983–87 on equal opportunities in the youth labour market, the role of the careers service and the operation of racial discrimination by employers (Wrench, 1987, 1990; Cross, Wrench and Barnett, 1990).

The primary role of the careers service is to offer advice and information to young people of school-leaving age about the careers and openings available to them. In 1988 the service carried out about a million individual careers guidance interviews and placed about 312,000 young people in jobs or on the Youth Training Scheme (YTS) (*Careers Service Bulletin*, Spring 1989). In its location as a free standing body between schools and employers the British careers service is different from its equivalents in many other countries, which are based either within the arenas of work or education (Maguire and Ashton, 1983). Although the local careers services are located within each local education authority, the service is the responsibility of a minister in the Department of Employment. In its dual role as both a provider of vocational guidance and a labour market placement agency, the careers service will inevitably feel the effects of the 'new vocationalism'.

One consequence of their intermediate location has always been the often contradictory pressures experienced by the careers service from the different interests it is supposed to serve. As one Midlands careers officer put it 'We are wearing too many hats and I am not too sure which hat you are supposed to be wearing more . . . The biggest paranoiacs in the world are careers officers.' Careers officers have become used to pleasing no-one in their work. They are criticized by employers for not knowing enough about industry, for not having enough time and resources to give proper information to the youngsters, for not keeping up with changes in the world of work, and for supplying employers with the wrong type of recruits (Lee and Wrench, 1983, pp. 37–8). At the same time young people do not always rate their experiences with the careers service positively (Sillitoe and Meltzer, 1985; Cockburn, 1987; YETRU, 1986).

Traditionally many employers have regarded the careers service as peripheral to their recruitment strategies. A study of the recruitment of apprentices by employers in the late 1970s (Lee and Wrench, 1983) found that many of the larger employers rarely used the careers service, whilst others would turn to it only to make up a last minute shortfall in their annual quota. Some even saw use of the service to be tinged with inferiority: 'Generally the careers service lads are problem lads' (Lee and Wrench, 1983, p. 37). However, with the reduction in the numbers of conventional apprenticeships and the introduction of YTS in 1983 the perceived importance of the careers service changed. The Manpower Services Commission (MSC) saw it as central to the operation of YTS. In 1987 around 75 per cent of YTS recruitment took place via the service; in 1988 it was nearly 90 per cent (*Careers Service Bulletin*, Spring 1988; Spring 1989). The government reflected this greater interest through a 1987 joint initiative by the Department of Employment, the Department of Education and Science and the Welsh Office – *Working Together for a*

Better Future – in which every local education authority was asked to review and improve its existing careers education and guidance.

Equal opportunities

Within its overall plans for employment generally, and the careers service and YTS in particular, the government has been careful to mention the importance of equal opportunities. The 1988 white paper *Employment for the 1990s*, which set out the government's priorities for the next decade, stressed in the preface by Norman Fowler, former Secretary of State for Employment:

> We must prevent discrimination in recruitment and employment on grounds of race, sex, disability or age, which hinders the best use of the country's human resources at a time when the population of working age is hardly growing. We must tap the energies and develop the talents of people who live in our inner cities.

Similarly *Working Together for a Better Future* (paragraph 29) contains a resolution on 'the particular needs of ethnic minorities':

> . . . The unfortunate consequences of prejudice and discrimination must also be faced: the careers service must ensure that ethnic minority young people are treated fairly in recruitment to jobs or YTS. Careers education and guidance programmes must be sensitive to these points to be credible to minority groups.

However, at the same time the government is engaged in policies which are likely to undermine efforts by the service to reduce the inequality of experience suffered by ethnic minority young people when leaving school and seeking work.

If the careers service is becoming more central to the operation of the youth labour market, and figures more importantly in the government's plans for training and employment, then in theory it is correspondingly elevated to a more crucial role in the sphere of equal opportunities. In fact even before YTS it could be argued that the careers service had a particularly significant role for ethnic minority young people, who, when seeking work, have been more reliant on the use of the careers service than their white counterparts (Brooks and Singh, 1978; Lee and Wrench, 1983; Sillitoe and Meltzer, 1985; Verma and Darby, 1987). At the same time, the careers service has not always been aware of its possibly disproportionate impact on the futures of ethnic minority young people, and of the need for good equal opportunity practice. Careers officers have sometimes been shown to be 'colour blind' – not admitting there are any special circumstances relevant to their work with ethnic minority young people (Eggleston *et al.*, 1986), or to be affected by stereotypes in their judgements of ethnic minority clients (Brown, 1985; Sillitoe and Meltzer, 1985).

Having said this, there is evidence that in recent years the issue of equal opportunities has been raised higher on the careers service agenda, with new guidelines from the Department of Employment Careers Service Branch on work with ethnic minorities, prepared in consultation with the Commission for Racial Equality (CRE). The number of individual local services which have been active in their concern for properly organized and implemented equal opportunities work seems to have been increasing over recent years, with a growing awareness that the stance of 'colour blindness' is no longer acceptable. However, one problem remaining for those who are concerned with galvanizing the service into greater equal opportunities consciousness and action is that it is made up of relatively autonomous local services, each with different practices, different policy and training emphases and different priorities. Furthermore, careers officers themselves work very much as individuals in one-to-one relationships with their clients, so it is often difficult to see whether unprofessional practices or stereotyped judgements are in fact operating to disadvantage ethnic minority clients.

Research findings

It was partly because of these difficulties that research became necessary. One major project covered nine different careers services in multi-ethnic areas of the North, Midlands and South of the country (Cross, Wrench and Barnett, 1990). Fieldwork began in late 1985: a sample was taken from careers services' files of 2,923 young people, including data on their ethnic background and educational attainment. Careers officers were asked to fill in questionnaires relating to a sub-sample of about 900 of these young people, providing further information relating to their occupational aspirations and aptitudes. Finally, 88 careers staff were individually tape recorded in interviews which explored their work with ethnic minority young people, their understanding of equal opportunity issues, and their response to racial inequality in the labour market.

The research highlighted a number of issues of racial inequality for the service. For one thing it confirmed previous evidence on the low participation in YTS of some ethnic minority young people (Baqi, 1987), with Asian young people significantly under-represented on the scheme. This was not true for Afro-Caribbean youngsters, particularly boys, who were proportionately *over*-represented on YTS – yet Afro-Caribbean boys were virtually absent from the most desirable employer-based schemes and did not appear to get beyond private training agencies or their equivalents *regardless of how well they performed educationally* (Cross, Wrench and Barnett, 1990, p. 52).

The perpetuation of racial inequality on YTS was a well established fact described in earlier research (Fenton *et al.*, 1984; Pollert, 1985; Cross and Smith, 1987). This issue was explored further in tape recorded interviews with 88 careers staff who were asked to describe the various factors which in their experience operated to bring about unequal distribution within YTS. It was clear that one major factor at work here was racial discrimination. About half of careers officers interviewed expressed the view that racial discrimination in the wider labour market operated to reduce the chances of ethnic minority school leavers. Many of these could describe examples which had been thrown up during the course of their work, or that of their colleagues. Two examples are quoted here from many that were related to the interviewer:

> About a year ago a colleague in this office had a girl who was right for a retail vacancy; phoned up the employer, said 'I've got a girl who would do', and the employer happened to say 'Oh, by the way, she isn't black is she?' He said 'Do you realise you are breaking the law by just asking me that?' The employer said that they were a fairly high class store and it may affect the selling – he eventually said 'I didn't say anything, thank you very much' and put the phone down.

> We had one last week where we sent a youngster for a vacancy and he was told that there was no vacancy. We had checked an hour before that there was a vacancy and we sent him down. The poor little soul came back out of the snow and said 'Excuse me, have you sent me to the right firm, because they told me that there were no vacancies?' So I rang them up and I said 'Have you interviewed this boy?' and they said 'We took his name and address'. I said 'Did you tell him that there were no vacancies?' and they said, 'Oh, just a minute, I will have to refer you to somebody else' and that virtually went on all day, backwards and forwards. But that has gone out of my hands now, and we are not putting that back up as a vacancy . . . because I think that is direct discrimination.

(quotes taken from Wrench, 1990)

Roughly one quarter of respondents were of the view that racial discrimination was operating in YTS in access to schemes and work placements, and could quote tangible reasons for their suspicions. Employers would say things like 'I'd like to take him, but what would my customers think?' Often, managing agents would report to careers staff their difficulties in placing black trainees with work experience providers, who would stipulate that they only wanted a white trainee, or would refuse to interview a youngster with an Asian name (Cross, Wrench and Barnett, 1990, p. 66).

The way in which careers staff respond to racial discrimination, whether blatant or merely suspected, was examined. Although careers staff were emphatic that they would not condone blatant racism, some conceded that there was a possibility that they may remain passive in the face of suspicions that an employer is being 'selective' – that they might just be 'letting things go'. Some conceded that they indulged in 'protective channelling', directing ethnic minority young people away from firms and schemes where they suspect they will be rejected, so as not to cause them unnecessary disappointment (Cross, Wrench and Barnett, 1990, p. 69). A Midlands careers officer stated 'it might be that this place has got a history of taking whites only. Rather than disappoint the kid – going for an interview that's a waste of time – you don't send him to that scheme.' A Northern officer explained 'As a service we are fairly protective about these kids you know – we don't like to give them to people who perhaps won't take them anyway.' Some talked of the pressures on careers staff which lay behind 'protective channelling'; 'It might be that you want to make sure that they get accepted. There's a lot of pressure on us to get kids into schemes.' Others referred to the more passive sin of failing to challenge a young person's under-aspirations or stereotyped choices in regard to YTS schemes (Cross, Wrench and Barnett, 1990, p. 69).

The next important question is the extent to which more *positive* responses to discrimination in the labour market occur within the service. There appeared to be great variety between local services: in some, staff were well rehearsed in the procedures of response to incidents of discrimination, and seemed prepared to challenge racist instructions from employers. However, it was clear that in a number of services, action was not as common as it might be. Some staff seemed afraid to challenge racist instructions from employers and were reluctant to report a case of infringement of the Race Relations Act to the CRE. Others simply pretended that there was 'no racial discrimination around here'. Many careers staff appeared quite unfamiliar with the official guidelines on the correct procedures to follow in the case of suspected incidents of racial discrimination (Cross, Wrench and Barnett, 1990, p. 71).

One syndrome encountered was that of 'fatalism' amongst careers staff, where inactivity in the face of suspected racial discrimination was related to a feeling of resignation that the service was powerless when jobs were scarce and 'proof' was difficult. A number of careers staff conceded that the fear of losing a scarce vacancy might well enter their thoughts in any potential confrontation with an employer: 'In training days, that's what I've picked up generally – "try not to lose the vacancy; try to be as tactful as possible".' Some officers complained about the lack of support from senior management in a potential confrontation of racist employers. 'The boss we have has been so hot on relationships with employers and getting vacancies that when you get a vacancy you are very reluctant to do anything that might mean you might lose it, because they are very hard to come by.' The result was that this careers service manager was visibly reluctant to pursue even blatant cases of racial discrimination by employers, a fact which was then reflected in the passivity of careers officers themselves within that service (Cross, Wrench and Barnett, 1990, p. 75). Careers officers argue that they have very little power – that if they refuse to take on a vacancy the employer can simply fill it elsewhere.

Clearly, one major reason why ethnic minority school leavers do not get the most desirable jobs and YTS places is the operation of racial discrimination by employers and placement providers. Yet there exists a great variety between local services in their response to racial discrimination, and there is evidence that in its many, sometimes subtle, forms it is not always 'noticed' or confronted. Although a growing number of services throughout the 1980s adopted what might be called a 'multi-cultural' perspective (for example, training sessions on the avoidance of cultural stereotypes, outreach and community work to establish links with different ethnic community groups, the translation of careers literature into different languages), an *antiracist* perspective was less common. Thus it is possible to conceive of a situation where 'equality' existed in the fair and professional treatment of ethnic minority clients by the careers officers in their guidance and counselling, without any change being effected in outcome in terms of labour market success because of a reluctance to challenge racist employers.

Professional ideology of the careers service

It is not enough to explain an unreadiness to confront racial discrimination in the labour market as simply a function of the attitudes of the careers officers themselves. This has to be seen in the historical context of the development of the professional philosophy of the careers service, and in the contradictions which stem from its structural location within society, as well as the more recent pressure on the service from wider political developments.

Davies (1985) writes that the guiding professional philosophy of the careers service has for a long time been influenced by 'developmental theory': the view that young people require expert guidance and counselling in order to help them make the right decision. Davies writes that the restructuring of local government in 1973/4 gave the service an opportunity to justify professional status, developing a range of guidance techniques – counselling, non-directive interviewing, psychometric testing – to enable them to come to the appropriate recommendation to the young person.

However, the developments of the 1980s produced something of a crisis with the growth of youth unemployment, the introduction of YTS and the new pressures on the service from government and the MSC/Training Agency. Maguire and Ashton noted that the new demands were leading to a realization that 'greater emphasis needed to be placed on the importance of employer liaison', thus challenging the earlier philosophy which many people in the service had held (1983, p. 89). Correspondingly they argue that many careers officers were having to re-assess their own role, moving them away from that of professional counsellor and towards employer liaison work, 'requiring them to adopt a quasi-selling role in their work with employers' (1983, p. 90).

Others have described how the changes of the 1980s produced a loss of confidence by careers officers in their work. Davies argues this was not just because of unemployment but because the original 'developmental' model was wrong. For him, the careers service had 'adopted a theoretical model of dubious relevance'. In reality, careers officers did not have much effect on the formation of a young person's occupational aspirations. Their contact with the young person was too short and too late. The developmental model assumed that young peoples' occupations were determined by choice – thus they needed professional guidance so as to help them make the best choice. This model neglects the fact that peoples' aspirations and opportunities are influenced and constrained by the limitations of opportunities in the local labour market, and by factors such as social class, education, peer groups, or gender (and in this case, race). However, Davies sees many within the service as reluctant to underplay this professional counselling role because it allows a claim to professional status which helps the service to increase its autonomy and 'fend off' external agencies such as the MSC/Training Agency (Davies, 1985, p. 17).

Davies argues that careers officers became disillusioned. Some within the service felt that in the new circumstances they should become a political pressure group acting on behalf of young people to challenge government policy on youth unemployment. This radical position was attacked by Peter Morrison, Minister of State for Employment, addressing the 1983 Annual Conference of the Institute of Careers Officers. He warned that many in authority had come to regard the careers service as dangerous social engineers who were unwilling to help employers by encouraging people to take up places on YTS. He made it clear that the future of the service depended on how they handled YTS (*Times Educational Supplement*, 7 October, 1983). The Minister warned that the Rayner Review into the operational efficiency of the careers service would be particularly interested in its contribution to the YTS. He suggested the careers service should pay less attention to occupational guidance and more to placing young people into schemes (*Careers Bulletin* 1983, pp. 20–21; Davies, 1985, p. 20).

The years of economic, political and professional change have produced a diversity of responses. Davies concludes that by the mid 1980s there were three stands of opinion in the careers service. One was the radical approach advocating withdrawal of co-operation in YTS and a challenge to government policies on youth unemployment. Another consisted of those resigned to co-operating with YTS and amending careers service procedures accordingly. The third was a tendency 'held by many less vocal careers officers' who felt that it was best to carry on with the same policies and procedures as before in the hope that things would get better.

Thus, as far as equal opportunities goes, we have something of a paradox. In the 1970s there was evidence that racism and equal opportunities were simply not being addressed as issues by the service. This 'blindness' would not have been put under challenge by the flawed 'developmental' model and the professional ideology of the service. It would seem that some careers officers were unwilling to admit to the existence of forces such as racism which determine a client's future not on the basis of individual capacities and achievements, but on ascribed characteristics, thus rendering the professional guidance role less relevant. For those officers who were happy to pretend that racism didn't happen, the 'developmental' model was quite consistent with an interpretation of inequality in labour market success as rooted in personal and individual factors within the client.

In the 1980s, from within the service itself, there arose questioning of the 'developmental' view and of the corresponding emphasis on interviewing and counselling skills still predominant in professional training. However, at the same time that the old professional model was being questioned from within, external pressures were already beginning to force the service into a role of servicing employers as a labour market placement agency. Yet this model, too, has implications which are not conducive to the active confrontation of employer racism, albeit now for different reasons.

Satisfying employers

The new 'employer emphasis' sits uneasily with the desire by many careers staff to address more forcefully the issue of racial discrimination in the labour market. A range of pressures now conspire to limit antiracist activity – and this is not simply the overt political pressure to serve employers. A classic way to limit equal opportunity activity in any organization is to limit the resources necessary for such activity. Equal opportunity initiatives cost time and money. For example, to produce change within a service, all levels of staff will need further training, including that on how to recognize discrimination and deal with pressure to discriminate by employers. A system of ethnic monitoring will need to be implemented in order to obtain a measure of the problem. The careers service has had to cope with an enhanced role under two year YTS without the corresponding enhancement of resources. Careers officers themselves argued that they were already fully stretched by the scheme, and were in some places finding difficulty in providing vocational guidance to school pupils. 'They . . . cannot see how they could undertake the detailed assessment of 500,000 YTS entrants without considerable expansion of the service' (*Times Educational Supplement*, 12 July 1985).

There is constant pressure on staff to get YTS places filled quickly, which leads to a tendency not to 'notice' possible infringements of the Race Relations Act. The fact that senior staff in particular are told to get YTS employers satisfied quickly means that often junior staff are not encouraged to tackle 'pressure to discriminate' cases, or are not properly supported when they do. This can lead to a syndrome of passivity and fatalism by some staff in the face of suspected racial discrimination by employers. The paucity of resources is mirrored by those of the CRE. Legal remedies for racial discrimination are very weak in Britain (see Lustgarten, 1987; Lustgarten and Edwards in this volume). As it is, careers staff, who have endured the extra work and stresses as a key witness in the prosecution of a racist employer, are not particularly encouraged to report further infringements of the Race Relations Act to the CRE when they see how little is likely to come out of the prosecution itself.

Various rationalizations for passivity emerge within the service. Not prosecuting racist employers may be justified by senior staff by the argument that they need to 'educate' and maintain 'good will'. This stance was regarded somewhat cynically by one CRE official: 'Some careers officers are so worried about the relationship with the employer that when they say "I don't want any blacks" they try to educate them, back politely out of the door and contact them again later.' Similarly, a Northern careers officer saw the 'educate the employer' argument as a rationalization for an easy way out, 'because it is long term, because it isn't immediate it doesn't put any immediate demands on time and personal effort and so on. So you've got to question why they are saying that.'

More recently an area of potential for anti-racism has been further undermined by the Local Government Act. In theory a careers service staffed by people who are aware and concerned about racial inequality could play a major role in tackling labour market racism, simply through their unique knowledge of local employers. This point is best made by an employment officer with the CRE in an interview with the author:

> When you look at it the careers service is in a key position in the labour market. It has got the 'street wisdom' about racism that is going on today in the local youth labour market. They know where the racist employers are, they know where the racist schemes are, they've got that information. People are just beginning to get clued in to the fact that they have got an awful lot of information in their heads. They can actually provide quite damning evidence against a lot of big names.

The service therefore would have been ideally placed as an agency for channelling information to a local authority contract compliance unit. Indeed there were some in the CRE and the careers service who were anticipating such a role until the government introduced the 1988 Local Government Act. The Act will prohibit 'non-commercial' considerations in the granting of contracts, and will allow only the very limited operation of contract compliance on race, and none at all on sex.
[. . .]

The labour market of the future

The injustices of systematic racial discrimination in recruitment are often only revealed through research. These have brought to light the operation of stereotypes in recruitment decisions and the use of quiet methods of exclusion, such as the selective use of white catchment areas and word of mouth and family recruitment (Lee and Wrench, 1983; Jenkins, 1986) or covert tests which have shown how the simple knowledge that an applicant is not white will severely reduce his or her chances of being called for an interview (Hubbuck and Carter, 1980). Now, with the increasing insertion of a third party – the careers service – between employer and school-leaver the preferences of employers become more visible, particularly to any local careers service which uses a system of ethnic monitoring of the success rate of applications, and which is staffed by people with the motivation to watch over racial injustice. However, under YTS – unlike its predecessor, YOP – recruitment does not have to be done through placing agencies but can be carried out directly by an employer. This has been one factor contributing to the segmentation within YTS. Although the careers service is now more centrally involved in the youth labour market and the placing of most young people on YTS, it is not involved in the filling of a significant minority of places. Knowing that the employer can always go elsewhere for recruits has meant that careers officers are in a less strong position to monitor employers' activities and to press for change in their recruitment practices.

It is perhaps not surprising that many of the larger employers do their own recruiting. A study of recruitment to YTS in the early years found that large numbers were still not using the careers service, and concluded that 'rather than due to any failure by the careers service in coming up with suitable candidates for YTS places, Mode A sponsors used other recruitment methods more out of a disinclination to use the careers service in the first place' (Risk, 1987, p. 14). From the beginning there emerged a 'dualism' within YTS (Cross, 1987; Finn, 1987) with a 'YTS aristocracy' for the fortunate minority of trainees. The future decentralization and handing over of YTS to employers, and the further throwing open of training to the free market will simply increase the segmentation and undermine attempts for equal opportunity and a broader access to quality training. Some high quality training opportunities for school leavers will exist outside YTS; other employers within the scheme will impart genuine transferable skills and promise long term employment, whilst controlling their own recruitment and remaining highly selective. The larger part of YTS will remain of questionable value, providing a rather low-level socialization for work and serving primarily to keep young people off the unemployment register and lower their expectations of wages and future employment. By far the majority of these will be placed by the careers service.

There is the added factor of the sharp reduction in the numbers of young people coming on to the labour market. *Employment for the 1990s* reports that the numbers aged 16–19 in the population will have fallen by over one million between 1983 and 1993. This means a shortage of trainees for YTS. By November 1989 it was reported that numbers on YTS had been falling throughout the year – 'nobody can be sure how much of the drop is due to a fall in the size of the age groups, and how much to the greater availability of jobs' (*Times Educational Supplement*, 24 November, 1989). According to a survey in September 1989, 43 per cent of firms which in 1989 turned to YTS for their more routine jobs could not fill all their vacancies, and 75 per cent of firms reported problems recruiting skilled manual workers (*The Guardian*, 11 September, 1989).

Some commentators see this as a force for greater equality of opportunity for ethnic minority school leavers in the future. The labour force will contain more people from ethnic minorities, with the most significant increase amongst school leavers. In a speech in September 1988 to the Institute of Careers Officers (reported in *Careers Service Bulletin*, Autumn 1988), employment minister John Cope stated:

> The demographic time bomb means that many employers will need to make radical changes to their recruitment patterns as the number of young people falls. . . . Employers must tap the talent, often unused or undervalued, amongst long term unemployed people, amongst women and ethnic minorities.

However, the danger is that otherwise unemployed ethnic minority young people will get less desirable schemes and jobs, often below their capabilities. This has already been demonstrated in the case of Afro-Caribbean boys in YTS by Cross, Wrench and Barnett (1990).

It is true that there has always been a body of opinion in the service that has regarded education in schools as too academic and not vocational enough for many of the lower attaining pupils. However, this is not the same thing as saying that careers officers will therefore automatically embrace all that goes along with the 'new vocationalism'. Nor do careers officers see their role as simply one of providing whatever employers want. In recent years many within the service have recognized the importance of adopting equal opportunity policies and fighting racial discrimination on behalf of their young clients. The government-level pronouncements quoted earlier appear to support a concern for equal opportunity issues. Similarly, the 1985 Careers Service Annual Report voices a particular concern over what could be done to get larger numbers of ethnic minorities into employer-led YTS. Many services have now abandoned the earlier position of colour blindness and are training staff on cultural sensitivities, forming stronger links with communities, and taking other initiatives such as holding open evenings in temples, mosques and community clubs (*Careers Bulletin*, Spring 1986). If the lower participation on YTS is seen as a result of ignorance and a lack of communication with ethnic minority communities, then this sort of activity by a service might be appropriate. However, some careers officers feel that one reason for the low participation of ethnic minorities in YTS is a rational anticipation by young people of unfair treatment and less likelihood of a job at the end (Cross, Wrench and Barnett, 1990). Ethnic minority young people do not want equality of access to low paid schemes offering little more than low-level work socialization. The thing that will be most likely to convince them is a visible change in access to prestigious schemes offering decent training, and equality in access to employment afterwards. [. . .]

Conclusion

[. . .]

The careers service enters the 1990s in a different state of awareness than when it entered the 1980s. Although there are still local services where race and equal opportunities consciousness remains as dormant as it was before, more people within the service have become aware of their role in relation to ethnic minority clients. Furthermore, there has been a growing realization by many that multiculturalism is not enough, and that antiracism is a necessary part of their activity. At the same time, there are now many ways in which the wider environment is less friendly to antiracist emphases in careers work. But there are also contradictory developments which will allow a raised consciousness within the service to be put to some practical effect. The changed demographic balance and shortage of young people entering the labour market have allowed many within the service to open dialogues with employers on equal opportunity which were not possible before. The change in the labour market has swung some of the balance of power back to the careers service, which can now exert some influence to see that the improved opportunity for school leavers to find employment does not simply mean that black young people end up once more in the least desirable jobs.

The alleged 'powerlessness' of the service can be overstated by careers staff, and can be rationalization for doing nothing. There are a number of measures which should form a starting point for action. Each careers service should produce an equal opportunity statement which includes details of its monitoring strategy, training aims, and guidelines for dealing with employers who infringe the Race Relations Act. Ethnic monitoring is essential to demonstrate patterns of submission, acceptance, rejection and final destination of young people. Such statistics will show whether young people from particular ethnic groups are being disproportionately channelled into certain sectors, or receive unequal treatment by employers. Employers can be visited to discuss the reasons for recruitment imbalances as shown by these statistics. Training programmes can be initiated to sensitize staff to the various forms of racial discrimination, and train them in the procedures to follow when 'pressure to discriminate' occurs. This should co-exist with a readiness to consult with the CRE and ultimately forward cases of discrimination for prosecution. Such things will cause extra problems and work for local services, and there will continue to be a need for the momentum to be maintained by committed individuals. There are many things within the climate of 'new vocationalism' which have made things less easy. In a climate where the 'new vocationalism' is added to the old racism, the danger is that it will be seized upon by some as a new rationalization for the old passivity.

References

Ball, W. and Troyna, B. (1989) 'The Dawn of a New ERA? The Education Reform Act, "RACE" and LEAs', *Educational Management and Administration*, **17**.

Baqi, L. (1987) *Too Little, Too Late*, London, London Conference of Indian Organisations.

Bash, L. (1989) 'Education goes to market' in Bash L. and Coulby, D. (eds), *The Education Reform Act*, London, Cassell.

Brooks, D. and Singh, K. (1978) *Aspirations versus Opportunities*, London, Commission for Racial Equality.

Brown, K. M. (1985) '"Turning a blind eye": racial oppression and the unintended consequences of white "non-racism"', *Sociological Review* **33**(4).

Cockburn, C. (1987) *Two Track Training: sex inequalities and the YTS*, Houndmills, Macmillan.

Coulby, D. (1989) 'From educational partnership to central control' in Bash, L. and Coulby, D. (eds), *The Education Reform Act*, London, Cassell.

Cross, M. (1987) '"Equality of opportunity" and inequality of outcome: the MSC, ethnic minorities and training policy' in Jenkins, R. and Solomos, J. (eds), *Racism and Equal Opportunity Policies in the 1980s*, Cambridge, Cambridge University Press.

Cross, M. and Smith, D. (eds) (1987) *Black Youth Futures: ethnic minorities and the Youth Training Scheme*, Leicester, National Youth Bureau.

Cross, M., Wrench J. and Barnett, S. (1990) *Ethnic Minorities and the Careers Service: an investigation into processes of assessment and placement*, Department of Employment, Research Paper No. 73, London, HMSO.

Davies, C. P. (1985) *A Study of the Factors Involved in the Occupational Aspirations of Fifth Year Secondary School Pupils*, MPhil, University of Aston in Birmingham, May 1985.

Department of Education and Science, Department of Employment, Welsh Office (1987) *Working Together for a Better Future*, London; Central Office of Information.

Department of Employment (1988) *Employment for the 1990s*, Cm 450, London, HMSO.

Eggleston, S. J., Dunn, D. K. and Anjali, M. with Wright, C. (1986) *Education for Some: the educational and vocational experiences of 15–18 year old young people of minority ethnic groups*, Stoke-on-Trent, Trentham Books.

Esland, G. and Cathcart, H. (1984) 'The compliant creative worker: the ideological reconstruction of the school leaver', *Proceedings of the Standing Conference on the Sociology of Further Education*, Paper No. 84/22e, Blagdon, Coombe Lodge.

Fenton, S., Davies, T., Means, R. and Burton, P. (1984) *Ethnic Minorities and the Youth Training Scheme*, MSC Research and Development Paper No. 20, Sheffield.

Finn, D. (1987) *Training Without Jobs: new deals and broken promises*, Houndmills, Macmillan Education.

Hubbuck, J. and Carter, S. (1980) *Half a Chance? A Report on Job Discrimination against Young Blacks in Nottingham*, London, Commission for Racial Equality.

Jenkins, R. (1986) *Racism and Recruitment: managers, organisations and equal opportunity in the labour market*, Cambridge, Cambridge University Press.

Lee, G. and Wrench, J. (1983) *Skill Seekers – Black Youth, Apprenticeships and Disadvantage*, Leicester, National Youth Bureau.

Lustgarten, L. (1987) 'Racial inequality and the limits of law' in Jenkins, R. and Solomos, J. (eds), *Racism and Equal Opportunity Policies in the 1980s*, Cambridge, Cambridge University Press.

Maguire, M. J. and Ashton, D. N. (1983) 'Changing face of the careers service', *Employment Gazette*, March.

Pollert, A. (1985) *Unequal Opportunities: racial discrimination and the Youth Training Scheme*, Birmingham, Birmingham Trade Union Resource Centre.

Risk, J. (1987) 'Opportunities for the 16-year-old school leaver', *Careers Bulletin*, Spring.

Sillitoe, K. and Meltzer, H. (1985) *The West Indian School Leaver*, Vol. 1, London, OPCS/HMSO.

Verma, G. K. and Darby, D. S. (1987) *Race, Training and Employment*, Basingstoke, Falmer.

Wrench, J. (1987) 'The unfinished bridge: YTS and black youth' in Troyna, B. (ed.), *Racial Inequality in Education*, London, Tavistock.

Wrench, J. (1991) 'Gatekeepers in the urban labour market: constraining or constrained?' in Cross, M. and Payne, G. (eds), *Social Work and the Enterprise Culture*, Basingstoke, Falmer.

YETRU (1986) *'They Must Think We're Stupid': the experiences of young people on the Youth Training Scheme*, Birmingham, Youth Employment and Training Resource Unit/Trade Union Resource Centre.

Source: Wrench, J. (1990) 'New vocationalism, old racism and the careers service', *New Community*, **16**(3), pp. 425–40.

8 BLACK WORKERS IN THE LABOUR MARKET
THE PRICE OF RECESSION
RICHARD JENKINS

It is perhaps ironic, although certainly not accidental, that the current high level of sociological interest in labour-market issues has only developed at a time when the market for labour is in a state of crisis, if not quite imminent collapse. I shall take the existence of a crisis in the labour market, manifest in particular by high levels of unemployment nationally, the collapse of the 'traditional' manufacturing sector and disproportionately high levels of youth unemployment, for granted. Instead, I shall explore the impact of that crisis upon one group, namely black workers. I shall also take for granted the undisputed facts of ethnic disadvantage in the labour market; black workers have been disproportionately hard hit by unemployment, and black youth in particular is increasingly being pushed to the margins of paid employment (Smith, 1981; Troyna and Smith, 1983). In order to place the discussion in its appropriate context, it is necessary to discuss the organizational framework of the labour market outcomes of black workers, in particular, selection criteria and the recruitment process.

The study which is briefly documented here was carried out between 1980 and 1983 whilst the author was employed at the SSRC (now ESRC) Research Unit on Ethnic Relations at the University of Aston in Birmingham.[1] The major focus of the research project was upon discrimination against black workers in recruitment to manual and routine non-manual jobs. From the beginning, it was conceived as both a study of racist discrimination, on the one hand, and the processes of the labour market, on the other. As a consequence, it is hoped that the results will speak to two distinct academic interest groups, i.e. sociologists of race relations and students of the labour market.

The core method used in this project was a long, semi-structured ethnographic interview with managers who were reponsible for recruiting manual and routine non-manual labour. A total of forty organizations agreed to co-operate with the research: fifteen manufacturing companies, fourteen public sector organizations and eleven retailing firms. In as much as the management structure of all of these organizations was sufficiently specialized to support a personnel function, they may all be thought of as being in the 'medium-to-large' size bracket. They were all situated in the West Midlands Metropolitan County area.

Although documentary material relating to the organizations was collected, the main source of data was the interview. All told, 172 managers were interviewed: 69 personnel specialist and 103 line managers. Case-studies were made of two of the organizations, one in manufacturing (27 interviews: 10 personnel specialists and 17 line managers) and one in the public sector (38 interviews: 4 personnel specialists and 34 line managers). Trade unionists in these two organizations were also interviewed, as were some local full-time officials.

Selection criteria: the importance of being acceptable

The analysis of selection criteria starts off from the proposal that selection criteria tend to be of two sorts: functionally specific criteria of *suitability*, which relate to competence of *ability* to do the job in question, and functionally non-specific criteria of acceptability, which relate to wider organizational matters such as 'stability', 'reliability', and 'predictability', in short, the degree to which the worker is habituated to employment or otherwise organizationally acceptable. Claus Offe has drawn a similar distinction between 'functional' and 'extra-functional' characteristics (1976, pp. 47–99), and David Gordon's concepts of 'quantative efficiency' and 'qualitative efficiency' also appear to have much in common with what I am saying here (1976, pp. 22–6). Both sorts of criteria come into play in recruitment; in this research, however, I decided to concentrate on acceptability, since there are no indications that black workers are primarily disadvantaged in the market because of their inability to pass over the relatively low thresholds of suitability attached to most manual or routine non-manual jobs (Daniel, 1968; Dex, 1982; Smith, 1981).[2]

The major criteria of acceptability were divided up into three categories, *primary*, *secondary* and *tertiary* criteria, according to the frequency with which they were mentioned by the managers interviewed. Primary criteria were 'appearance', 'manner and attitude' and 'maturity'; secondary criteria were the interviewer's 'gut feeling', the applicant's labour market history (i.e. periods of unemployment and number of jobs), speech style, 'relevant experience', age and marital status (for male workers), literacy, and 'personality and the ability to fit in'; the tertiary criteria were English language competence and references from past employers. Two important further dimensions of acceptability which shortage of space prevents me from discussing here, are *non-verbal communication* in the selection interview and *gender*.

Presented in this fashion, these criteria are somewhat enigmatic. Elsewhere the meanings of these criteria for recruiters have been explored using extensive ethnographic quotations (Jenkins, 1982). It is clear from the data that there are differences in the criteria which are used in the recruitment of manual and non-manual workers, and in the manufacturing, retailing and public sectors. There are also differences in the pattern of criteria used by personnel and line managers which I shall not, however, discuss here, for reasons of space.

Looking at the recruitment of manual workers, managers are most concerned about 'appearance', followed by 'maturity', 'manner and attitude', labour market history and 'age and marital status'. Less important are 'relevant experience', 'gut feeling', references and speech style. Looking at those managers recruiting non-manual workers, however, the pattern is as follows: of most apparent importance are 'appearance', 'manner and attitude', and 'gut feeling', followed by speech style, labour market history, 'maturity', 'personality and the ability to fit in' and 'relevant experience'. Of lesser importance are literacy, references and the candidate's competence in spoken English. Thus while 'appearance' and 'manner and attitude' are very important for all workers, 'maturity', labour market history and age and marital status (for males) are more important for manual workers, 'gut feeling' on the manager's part playing a greater role for their non-manual counterparts.

If, however, we look at the differences between the public, manufacturing and retailing sectors then a different pattern emerges. In manufacturing the three most important criteria are 'maturity', labour market history and 'gut feeling'. These are followed by 'manner and attitude', age and marital status, literacy, 'appearance', English language competence, 'relevant experience', 'personality and the ability to fit in', and references.

By contrast, in the public sector organizations, 'appearance', 'manner and attitude' and 'maturity' were the criteria most often mentioned by managers. Mentioned less frequently were 'gut feeling', 'personality and the ability to fit in', speech style, 'relevant experience', labour market history, and competence in the English language.

Finally, coming to the retailing sector, there are five criteria which appear to be of major importance: 'appearance', 'manner and attitude', speech style, literacy and 'gut feeling'. Lower down the order of priorities are competence in English, 'maturity', relevant experience, and references.

Thus it is clear that there is a pattern of differences in the attributes relating to acceptability which are sought by recruiters in the organizations in the three industrial sectors in question. The sources of these differences are probably the differences between the three with respect to formal organizational 'structure' and the social organization of the labour process.

One thing which all of these organizations and employment sectors do have in common, however, is the close relationship between selection criteria of acceptability and managerial control of the workplace. In attempting to recruit acceptable workers employers are trying to avoid managerial problems in the future, and to maintain their control of the workplace and the daily routines of organizational life. There are at least three important aspects to this. First, there is the quest for the habituated 'responsible' worker, someone who will be able to manage him- or herself in the particular work context (or, at worst, will not create any major problems). Most of the criteria which are used to judge these attributes are, to say the very least, 'unscientific', depending as much on the recruiter's hunch as anything else. Secondly, there is the desire to prevent problems arising with the existing workforce as a result of hiring new workers who may be unacceptable to them. Thirdly, there is the basic aim of recruiting a workforce who can understand and obey spoken and written orders. There are, therefore, three sides to acceptability: the recruitment of manageable workers, the avoidance of industrial relations problems, and the maintenance of communication at the workplace. All are essentially about the control of the workforce and the labour process.

The differing versions of the notion of acceptability can also have their consequences – typically detrimental – for black job-seekers. The first point to bear in mind here is the routine ethnocentricity of many of these ideas of acceptability. 'Appearance', 'manner and attitude', 'speech style', and the manager's 'gut feeling', for example, are all criteria which depend to a greater or lesser degree upon shared cultural competences. This is all the more so considering the importance of non-verbal communication in the assessment of these attributes by the manager. Thus a white recruiter may choose to interpret an avoidance of direct eye contact by an applicant as indicating anything from a lack of self-confidence to 'shiftiness'. However, for many job-seekers whose cultural background lies in the Indian sub-continent, the refusal of eye contact may be a respectful attempt to avoid impoliteness. For many of the managers I interviewed, such behaviour in an interview would be an indicator of unacceptability.[3]

Another example of the potential power of ethnocentricity is the criterion of 'age and marital status'. Basically this refers to the notion that, if there is an 'ideal' employee, *he* is a 'married-man-with-two-kids-and-a-mortgage', an idea which has been reported elsewhere (Blackburn and Mann, 1979, p. 105; Nichols and Beynon, 1977, pp. 97, 199). This rests upon two assumptions: one, that this is the 'normal', 'respectable' household type, and two, that a worker in this position is so burdened down by responsibilities that he *has* to come to work whether he wants to or not. Quite apart from the explicit sexism of this criterion (both in its content and its likely consequences), this is an extremely culturally specific model of the 'normal' family. Cultural differences with respect to the norms of kinship, marriage and residence being what they are, there is no doubt that the household arrangements of proportionately more black than white workers will fall beyond this pale of normality.

A second problem with criteria of acceptability concerns the new recruit's need to 'fit in' with the existing workforce. That this can be a source of discrimination was shown by the Commission for Racial Equality's formal investigation into BL's Castle Bromwich plant (1981). Thirdly, the fact that so many criteria of acceptability operate tacitly and implicitly not only makes research difficult for the social scientist, it also renders the selection process mysterious and opaque. This makes the investigation of complaints of discrimination more difficult than it might otherwise be, and helps to create the organizational space wherein racism can flourish.

Coming to criteria such as competence in spoken English or literacy, here there are also difficulties for black job-seekers. In the case of literacy, the major problem is the employer who sets unrealistically high literacy requirements for unskilled jobs. Looking at competence in English, however, the situation is more complex, in as much as it appears not to be formally tested for in the same way as literacy, assessment depending largely upon the subjective judgements of recruiters. Once again, this allows ethnocentricity and racism a route into the selection process. Finally, in that black workers appear to be more likely to suffer from involuntary redundancy, dismissal and unemployment (Dex, 1982, pp. 18–25, 40–9; Smith, 1981, pp. 67–93), they are less likely to have acceptable labour market histories in the eyes of many recruiters, thus setting up a vicious circle of disadvantage.

These are some of the implications which the notion of 'acceptability' may have for black job-seekers. It remains, however, to briefly explore one other area, the relationship between *stereotypes of acceptability* and the *ethnic stereotypes* of black workers held by managers. Many of these ethnic stereotypes (such as 'West Indians are lazy, happy-go-lucky or slow', or 'Asians are clannish and don't mix') fly in the face of the ideas bound up in the notion of acceptability.[4] To make matters worse, many of these interviewees see the employment of black workers as creating managerial problems which would not arise with an all-white workforce. This too is a further dimension of the unacceptability of black workers for white managers.

In this section I have outlined some of the meanings of worker acceptability in the eyes of the managers interviewed in this research project. Following from this, the consequences for black workers of the importance of acceptability were outlined. In the next section, I shall discuss the recruitment processes which provide the organizational settings for selection decision-making.

Recruitment processes: formality, informality and 'word of mouth'

The recruitment process can be divided up into three elements: *recruitment channels*, organizational *recruitment procedures*, and the selection *interview*. Looking at channels of recruitment there are differences between industrial sectors, on the one hand, and occupational categories (i.e. manual, skilled manual and routine non-manual) on the other.

In manufacturing, employers typically look within their own organization first before going elsewhere. The medium most commonly employed is the internal advertisement, although non-competitive promotion and the straightforward redisposition of labour are also important. A small number of firms routinely approach the public Employment Services first, while one manufacturing organization did not advertise at all (internally or externally), relying wholly on unsolicited applications and 'word of mouth'. If internal search fails to produce an acceptable candidate, the most popular recruitment channels are 'word of mouth', the Employment Services and newspaper advertisements, in that order.

By contrast, in the public sector, although internal recruitment wherever possible is similarly important, there is a greater subsequent use of newspaper advertisements. In some organizations, the formal policy is that canvassing disqualifies the applicant. Despite this, 'word of mouth' is the next most popular recruitment channel, followed closely by the Employment Services. Equally noteworthy is the very low first preference usage of the Employment Services, and the complete non-usage of private agencies.

Coming to the retailing organizations, the most characteristic feature is a much less definite pattern of preferred recruitment channels. There is a striking diversity in the alternatives which are used by these recruiters, particularly for non-skilled manual jobs (mainly shop assistants). However, 'word of mouth' is the channel which finds some use by most employers. In addition, all of the following have some significance: consulting files of previous applicants, unsolicited applications and casual callers, and public noticeboards. Many organizations use the Employment Services once their original recruitment channel has failed them.

Looked at with reference to occupational categories and the kinds of jobs which are being filled, there are further differences in the recruitment channels employed. Private employment agencies, for example, are exclusively used to recruit non-manual workers; unsolicited applications and casual callers are primarily a source of recruits to manual jobs. 'Word of mouth' is very important for all categories of vacancy, while internal search is the preferred channel of recruitment for everything except shop assistants. The Employment Services are more or less equally significant for all jobs in the categories under consideration, although there is some variation between sectors.

It is important to note that two of these recruitment channels, internal search and 'word of mouth', overlap to a considerable degree. This is because employers may use their workforce as a means of contacting potential applicants, and, even where this is not the case, existing employees will communicate information about vacancies to their families and friends. The widespread use of 'word of mouth' contacts in recruitment may be thought of as extending the scope of the internal labour market outside the formal boundaries of the organization.

This brings us to organizational recruitment procedures, the procedures for processing applications and taking applicants through the stages of recruitment. There are, once again, important differences between industries. In manufacturing, the personnel function typically screens applicants before passing them on for a decision to line management. In the public sector there are two characteristic procedures: in the first, line management is responsible for the entire process; in the second, there are selection panels but line management makes the final decision. In retailing, however, one recruitment procedure characterizes this area of employment: personnel specialists are responsible for all aspects of recruitment.

Looked at with respect to occupational categories, there are also some contrasting patterns. The only situation, outside retailing, in which personnel handles every aspect of recruitment involves non-skilled manual vacancies. Within the public sector, however, the influence of personnel specialists is greater in the recruitment of non-manual employees. Similarly, in manufacturing, panel interviewing becomes more important as the vacancy rises up the manual/non-manual hierarchy.

There are two conclusions to be drawn: (a) the internal market, and its extension via 'word of mouth', is the most important arena of search for employers, and (b) generally speaking, allowing for the small size of the retailing sector (relative to manufacturing or the public sector), personnel managers have only slight decision-making powers in recruitment.[5]

For reasons of space I shall not discuss the selection interview here, except to characterize it as typically a highly informal affair, both in its conduct and in the specification of job requirements. Looking at interviewing in internal recruitment and promotion, it is clear that it is likely to be even more informal than external recruitment interviewing, largely because so much is already known about the candidates.

One major aspect of this research into recruitment processes was the examination of 'word of mouth' recruitment. When asked for their reasons for using this channel, the recruiters interviewed gave the following most frequently: the reputation of the recommender serves to predict the reliability of the new recruit; the presence of the recommender in the workplace may guarantee the new recruit's 'good' behaviour; it is part of the 'family firm' ethos; 'word of mouth' is good for industrial relations; it is cheap and easy, particularly with so many job-seekers in the market; and finally, it is a good source of extra general information about the applicant. Thus, 'word of mouth' is at least three things at once: an industrial relations strategy, an efficient recruitment channel, and a criterion of acceptability in its own right. These results compare well with earlier research in the United States (Rees, 1966).

It is possible to discern in these patterns of recruitment procedures certain consequences for the black job-seeker. Given its importance as a channel of recruitment, 'word of mouth' is an ideal place to start the discussion. In the first place, particularly in organizations with small numbers of black employees or most of their black employees in low-status jobs, 'word of mouth' may result in the reproduction of the hierarchical *status quo* within the organization. White workers will tend to have better access to job information – both in quantitative and qualitative terms – than their black peers. At the extreme, an all-white workplace with a heavy reliance on informal social networks as a source of recruits will be almost certain to remain an all-white workplace. Secondly, as 'word of mouth' is an informal process, unrecorded and largely unaccountable for, the enabling conditions for the operation of racist discrimination are created. Finally, the issue of acceptability is also of some significance. If it is important for the recommender or mediator to be acceptable, then, bearing in mind the previous section's argument about the comparative acceptability of black workers, black workers may not be influential as pivots in the chain of recommendation, certainly for jobs other than those which are seen to be appropriate for them. Once again there is the reproduction of the current labour-market disadvantage of black workers.

The general emphasis on internal search as a first channel of recruitment also has its disadvantages for black job-seekers. Internal search tends to close off the initial availability of job information to those in the organization, or in 'the know'. If black workers were evenly distributed throughout occupations or organizations then this would not be a problem for them. As it is, however, they are *not* evenly distributed and it *is* a problem. It is a problem, what is more, which is compounded by the greater informality which characterizes much internal recruitment, since informality, as I have already argued, is an enabling condition of racism.

The relative lack of influence of the personnel function may also put black workers at something of a disadvantage. As the professional people involved in recruitment they are, to some degree, the 'natural' custodians of meritocratic recruitment, fair treatment and equal opportunities. Nor is this a caricature of the personnel role: many of the personnel specialists I interviewed took this view of the personnel profession. However, the weak place of the personnel function within the political hierarchies of most organizations ensures that they rarely have the opportunity to actually practise their professional responsibilities.

Recruitment channels acquire a further significance if they are examined in the context of the job-search patterns of black workers. Looking at adult workers first, it appears from the most recent pieces of research (Courtenay, n.d., pp. 15–22; Smith, 1981, pp. 98–103), that there are only minor differences in job-search patterns between white and West Indian workers. There may be a tendency for white workers to use newspaper advertisements more often as a source of information, but informal kinship and friendship networks seem to be important for both. The main differences are between white and West Indian workers, on the one hand, and Asian workers, on the other, regardless of gender. The latter appear to rely more on 'word of mouth' or direct approaches to employers; they are less likely to use the state Employment Services. According to the evidence from this study, direct approaches from job-seekers are primarily a source of applicants to manual jobs. The heavy reliance of all groups of workers upon 'word of mouth', and other informal job-acquisition strategies, limits the job-seeker to the fund of contacts which are available to his/her immediate social group by virtue of their work histories and present employment status. Because of the place of black workers in the labour market and their stereotyping by white managers, these resources may well restrict the scope of 'word of mouth' contacts to providing 'more of the same', at best. Asian workers, therefore, as a result of their concentration upon 'word of mouth' contacts and direct approaches to employers, may be limiting the effective scope of their job-search to manual jobs at the bottom end of the labour market.

The pattern for young workers, however, is different. One of the earliest pieces of research (Beetham, 1967) concluded that black school-leavers were more likely to use the Employment Services (the Youth Employment Service, at that time) to find work. The situation has not changed much, if more recent studies are anything to go by (Anwar, 1982, p. 19; Commission for Racial Equality, 1978, pp. 8–9; Dex, 1982; Lee and Wrench, 1983, pp. 60–1). Black school-leavers and young workers still rely heavily on the Careers Service and the Job Centres for vacancy information and job placement.

As a corollary, there are differences in the pattern of use of 'word of mouth': for apprenticeships for example, white school-leavers use kinship and friendship networks to a greater extent than their black peers and do so more successfully. More generally it appears that Asians use social networks more than whites, who, in turn, use them more than West Indian youth. There are also some gender differences, white girls being more likely to use newspaper advertisements than their West Indian peers. Finally, Asian youth are much more likely to use a direct approach to employers than either whites or West Indians.[6]

The importance of the Employment Services for young blacks has implications for their likelihood of finding employment, and for the type of job they may be offered. As we have seen, this research indicates that internal search and 'word of mouth' are the most important recruitment channels for employers. When jobs do come on to the open market, internal candidates will have been taken up wherever possible and they are likely to be relatively low-status, 'port of entry' jobs, at best. These will typically be the jobs which go to the Job Centres. To illustrate the nature of the problem, only seven of the organizations examined (17 per cent of the total) normally notified the Employment Services of all of their routine non-manual vacancies. Evidence from other studies suggests that the Employment Services are seen by many employers as a last-resort source of 'low grade' labour (Carter, 1966, p. 147; Keil, 1976, pp. 17–19). Despite high levels of unemployment, many of the managers in this study made disparaging remarks about the Employment Services during the interview. It seems safe to assume, therefore, that the reliance by young black workers on the Employment Services may serve to further handicap them in the labour market.

However, this discussion of job-search strategies and recruitment channels is *not* another exercise in 'blaming the victim'. Job-search behaviour cannot be understood in isolation; it is heavily dependent upon the recruitment channels used by employers. Job seekers can only take advantage of the recruitment channels which are effectively open to them; many jobs are found, not deliberately sought out. Thus the differing opportunity structures for black and white workers have an important effect. All workers, for example, may use 'word of mouth'; that is not to say, however, that this strategy gives all workers access to similar jobs. It clearly does not. Secondly, black job seekers, inasmuch as they face substantial discrimination, are engaged in a more difficult endeavour than their white peers. High levels of discrimination in recruitment have been convincingly demonstrated by well-documented situation testing in 1966 and 1973–4 (Daniel, 1968, pp. 76–9; Smith, 1977, pp. 105–26). More recently, similar research has argued that the level of discrimination may actually have increased (Hubbuck and Carter, 1980).

Neither is there any suggestion from existing research that the disadvantaged position of black job-seekers is a reflection of differing persistence in the job-search. In fact, in response to discrimination, black workers are *more* persistent in applying for jobs, making many more applications per job obtained than white workers (Commission for Racial Equality, 1978, pp. 8–9; Smith, 1974, p. 33). Remaining with the response to racism, Shirley Dex has recently argued that the concentration upon Job Centres by West Indian youth, and their turning away from kinship and friendship networks as a source of labour market information, is a rational attempt to avoid jobs such as those held by their parents (Dex, 1982, p. 20). In no sense, therefore, should my appraisal of the relative utility of particular job-search strategies for black workers be interpreted as blaming them for their own labour market disadvantage. Their behaviour may – as with all social actors in all contexts – contribute to the production and reproduction of their situation. However, due to a history of discrimination and domination, black workers have less power to make their actions count in producing labour-market outcomes than do white workers or managers. In this sense, therefore, it is perhaps most appropriate to view their job-search behaviour as a rational response to a situation over which they have little control.

Changes in the labour market:
the implications for black workers[7]

Perhaps one of the most interesting results of this research is the importance which is currently attached to internal search, the internal labour market (ILM), as an arena of recruitment. Over two-thirds of the manufacturing and public sector organizations tried to recruit through the ILM first for manual, skilled manual and routine non-manual vacancies. For the other organizations in these sectors, the ILM was typically used simultaneously with external search; even in these cases it has an important role.

Of greater interest, perhaps, is the evidence that there has been an increase in the use of internal search recently. This trend is already discernible if one compares studies carried out early in the 1970s (Courtenay and Hedges, 1977; Dunnell and Head, 1973). Of the organizations in this study, 73 per cent of the manufacturing firms, 43 per cent of the public sector organizations and 18 per cent of the retailing companies reported that the present recession had led to some increase in their use of internal search, including 'word of mouth' recruitment. Although it is not easy to disentangle from other ILM procedures such as the use of internal vacancy notices, 'word of mouth' recruitment appears to be more significant than previously. An important implication of this trend is that the state Employment Services may be notified of fewer vacancies. Furthermore, if the arguments earlier in this chapter are correct, there will also be a tendency for those vacancies which are notified to be increasingly 'lower-level' jobs.

Why this increased reliance on internal search and recruitment? In the first place, it reflects the problem posed for organizations by redundancy. An organization which finds itself having to shed labour will seek to fill whatever 'normal' vacancies may arise – and they do arise from time to time – from among its outgoing workers. Such a strategy avoids the need to pay those workers redundancy payments, and in as much it allows part of the burden of redundancy to be offset, helps to smooth over the potentially disturbed waters of industrial relations. In some cases, in fact, this recruitment strategy is as much the result of trade union pressure as anything else. The use of internal search may vary, from simply pinning notices on internal notice-boards to the regular preparation of a central consolidated vacancy sheet by the headquarters of a manufacturing group or a public authority. This approach can also be seen as extending the boundaries of the ILM outside the immediate limits of the workplace or the enterprise.

However, simply reducing the *number* of workers employed is frequently only of secondary importance to the *restructuring* of the labour process; in the words of one interviewee, 'It's a question of moving people from nonessential to essential jobs.' As a result of pressures of this kind, mobility agreements are increasingly becoming a part of the industrial relations accommodation which is being reached in many workplaces between profitability and some sort of fragile job security. Within this kind of context the traditional rules governing redundancy may become an embarrassment for both management and unions. When the shared goal is the retention of the most 'flexible', 'reliable' or potentially retrainable sections of the workforce, ideas such as 'last in–first out' are, by tacit agreement, laid to one side; the redundancy exercise becomes more selective than it might otherwise have been.

Another reason for turning to the internal market is because it is both cheaper and easier. A newspaper advertisement or a card in the local Job Centre might result in a deluge of applicants. 'Word of mouth' is important in this respect, vacancy information passing out of the gates only via the network of existing employees. Some of the organizations in the study consciously encourage this process, in order to limit the number of applications they receive.

Cheapness, convenience and the problems of redundancy and restructuring are not the only, or even the main, reasons for the increased concentration upon the internal recruitment arena, however. The evidence from this study is clear: employers are using recruitment strategies of this kind for two other reasons.

In the first place, they are hoping to retain or recruit a more acceptable 'class' of worker. Keenly aware that they are, for the first time in a long time, in a buyer's market for labour, they are intent on capitalizing upon that enviable position. This also affects their industrial relations stance; many employers are relishing a rediscovered militancy. Returning to the point about the selectivity of redundancy, a production manager at a metalwork plant admitted, for example, that, 'There were a few dead legs but we got rid of them, with redundancies and early retirements . . . and giving them the sack.'

The process is not always this overt; in some places union militancy has survived the recession and can still make its presence felt. The recruiters who were interviewed, however, agreed that internal candidates are much easier to evaluate with respect to their acceptability, in that they are a known quantity. In this process it is not difficult to select out the 'unreliable' worker or the 'troublemaker'. People with these kinds of reputation do poorly in internal procedures; their redundancy money may be considered a small enough price for getting rid of them. Finally, it should not be forgotten that 'word of mouth' is also centrally concerned with the recruitment or promotion of habituated, acceptable workers.

However, it is not *just* a question of worker acceptability. There is a second discernible managerial goal here: internal, or informal external, recruitment may be a more or less conscious control strategy, at both the individual and the organizational levels. As the quest is for habituated, 'reliable' workers, this is an obvious statement; however, it is also true in other respects. For example, workers, particularly young workers recruited through informal social networks, can to some extent be controlled indirectly through the mediator or wider peer-group pressure. Furthermore, if 'word of mouth' is an aspect of the 'family firm', then, paternalism being a particular approach to industrial relations, it is seen to be part of a wider control strategy, the workforce being allowed to participate in recruitment in return for co-operation and 'reliability'.

Returning to the ILM, increased managerial control is also to be seen here. As the procedure is typically more informal than external recruitment, outcomes can be more easily secured. Competitive procedures may, for example, be ignored and the acceptable person simply given the vacant job. A greater degree of control is also being exercised over manpower planning. In most organizations the managerial level at which authorization to fill a vacancy must be sought has risen; what is more, vacancies are more likely to be approved if they are to be filled internally. This ensures that if the organization does have to go outside for recruits, it will only be at the lowest level.

These then are some of the changes in labour market processes which have resulted from financial constraints within work organizations, on the one hand, and high levels of unemployment, on the other. I shall briefly discuss the consequences of these labour-market changes for black workers.

First, the shift to the internal market and 'word of mouth' means that established workers, in the sense of those who are in work at all, and *particularly* those who are in stable, 'established' jobs,[8] and the members of their social networks, are likely to have better access to job information. 'Established workers', in the sense that I am using the expression here, are disproportionately more likely to be white than black; black workers are, perhaps, increasingly only going to hear about 'black jobs' or 'shit work'. It is ironic that those black youngsters who, as Shirley Dex suggests, are deliberately moving away from their parents' information networks in order to prevent this from happening, and using the public Employment Services, are, if the arguments of this paper are correct, possibly *increasing* their chances of being offered jobs at the bottom of the market. That is, of course, if they are lucky enough to be offered any jobs at all.

Apart from the fact that 'word of mouth' serves to reproduce the occupational *status quo*, there are other problems with this kind of recruitment. Not the least of these is its informality, which may allow scope for discrimination to operate. Similarly, as argued earlier, given that recruiters can be selective about whose recommendation to accept, there is always the possibility that black workers will not be able to introduce applicants as successfully as their white colleagues. For similar reasons, the apparent rise in the levels of acceptability which employers are looking for is a further cause for concern. Given that we live in a society which has yet to accord legitimacy to the presence of large numbers of black people, there is good reason to suspect, and the data from this study bears this out, that they are regarded as undesirable aliens by many white employers and workers. In the tight labour market of earlier and economically better days, black labour was necessary, if not desirable or acceptable. Now it is no longer even necessary. There is some evidence from this study which shows that, in some organizations, trade unionists are more concerned to protect the jobs of their white, rather than their black, comrades.

It is not, however, simply a matter of discrimination in recruitment; as I have already argued, selection for redundancy or other forms of severance may be equally discriminatory. Returning briefly to the research findings, 'the need to maintain a racial balance' is a problem with which many managers see themselves confronted in the multi-ethnic workplace. What 'balance' actually means, however, is a majority of white workers. It is clear from the interview material that 'balance' may also mean keeping black workers in their place, that is, in unskilled or otherwise undesirable jobs. There is additional indirect evidence that some managers have used a redundancy situation to remedy the matter and restore a 'balance'. A central strand in this concern with 'balance' is the reassertion of managerial control, which is seen to be undermined by the presence of too many black workers, who 'form cliques' and 'stick to themselves'. In this light, it is interesting that the trade unions are often as keen as management on the notion of 'balance'.

Finally, a further consequence of the recession has been to diminish managerial interest in the introduction of equal opportunity policies within organizations. There are a number of reasons for this: in a buyer's market, there is no longer the pressure on organizations to present themselves as 'good employers'; policy formulation and organizational change can be expensive; with the change of government in 1979, the state policy climate in the race relations area has changed; given the present levels of unemployment there may be active hostility from unions and white workers to the notion; and, finally, many employers, in their new-found militancy, are inclined to resist any interference in their affairs, which is what they may perceive the race relations legislation to be. All of these factors come together to create a climate which is hostile to the active pursuit of equal opportunities.

I have very briefly explored some of the changes which are taking place in the social processes of the labour market. Many of these changes have definitely detrimental consequences for black workers. Caught between their disadvantaged position in the information networks of the labour market, the subtle, or not so subtle, racist discrimination of employers in selecting for redundancy or employment, increased attempts by manage- ment to reassert control at the workplace, and a changing climate with respect to equal opportunity initiatives, it is little wonder that black workers have been so disproportionately affected by the current recession. It remains to be seen whether their position will achieve some sort of precarious stability, or deteriorate even further.

Notes

1 This research has been written up as a final report for the Unit, 'Racism and recruitment: managers, organisations and equal opportunity in the labour market', which was published by Cambridge University Press in 1986. The Unit has now changed its name to the Centre for Research in Ethnic Relations, and moved to the University of Warwick.

2 For a further discussion of the argument that black workers are not discriminated against because they are unsuitable, see Jenkins and Troyna (1983).

3 For a specific example of just such a case, see 'Seeing error of their ways', *The Guardian*, 7 January 1983.

4 It should, perhaps, be pointed out here that there is little evidence of consensus among these managers as a group with respect to the ethnic stereotypes they hold, although there are well-defined clusters of shared stereotypes.

5 The relatively weak position of personnel management within organizations is discussed by Watson (1977).

6 The sources of the assertions in this paragraph are Commission for Racial Equality (1978, p. 8–9), Dex (1978–9, p. 364; 1982, pp. 42–3) and Lee and Wrench (1983, *passim*).

7 Much of the argument in this section derives from an earlier paper jointly written with Alan Bryman, Janet Ford, Teresa Keil and Alan Beardsworth of Loughborough University (Jenkins *et al.*, 1983). I am grateful to them for their considerable contribution to that argument and their permission to use the material here.

8 To avoid misunderstanding, I am not here proposing a 'dual labour market' model.

References

Anwar, M. (1982) *Young People and the Job Market – A Survey*, Commission for Racial Equality.

Beetham, D. (1967) *Immigrant School Leavers and the Youth Employment Service*, Institute of Race Relations.

Blackburn, R. M. and Mann, M. (1979) *The Working Class in the Labour Market*, Macmillan.

Carter, M. (1986) *Into Work*, Pelican.

Courtenay, G. (n.d.) *Local Labour Force Survey*, Social and Community Planning Research.

Courtenay, G. and Hedges, G. (1977) *A Survey of Employers' Recruitment Practices*, Social and Community Planning Research.

Commission for Racial Equality (1978) *Looking for Work: black and white school leavers in Lewisham*, CRE.

Commission For Racial Equality (1981) *B L Cars Ltd . . . Report of a Formal Investigation*, CRE.

Daniel, W. W. (1968) *Racial Discrimination in England*, Pelican.

Dex, S. (1978–9) 'Job-search methods and ethnic discrimination', *New Community*, **7**(1), pp. 31–9.

Dex, S. (1982) *Black and White School-leavers: the first five years of work*, Research Paper no. 33. Dept of Employment.

Dunnell, K. and Head, E. (1973) *Employers and Employment Services*, Office of Population Censuses and Surveys.

Gordon, D. M. (1976) 'Capitalist efficiency and socialist efficiency', *Monthly Review*, **28**(3), pp. 19–39.

Hubbuck, J. and Carter, S. (1980) *Half a Chance? A Report on Job Discrimination Against Young Blacks in Nottingham*, Commission for Racial Equality.

Jenkins, R. (1982) *Managers, Recruitment Procedures and Black Workers*, Working Papers in Ethnic Relations no. 18. Research Unit on Ethnic Relations.

Jenkins, R., Bryman, A., Ford, J., Keil, T. and Beardsworth, A. (1983) 'Information in the labour market: the impact of recession', *Sociology*, **17**, pp. 260–7.

Jenkins, R. and Troyna, B. (1983) 'Educational myths, labour market realities' in Troyna, B. and Smith, D. I. (eds), *Racism, School and the Labour Market*, National Youth Bureau, pp. 5–16.

Keil, T. (1976) *Becoming a Worker*, Leicestershire Committee for Education and Training/ Training Services Agency.

Lee, G. and Wrench, J. (1983) *Skill Seekers – Black Youth, Apprenticeships and Disadvantage*, National Youth Bureau.

Nichols, T. and Beynon, H. (1977) *Living with Capitalism: class relations and the modern factory*, Routledge and Kegan Paul.

Offe, C. (1976) *Industry and Inequality*, Edward Arnold.

Rees, A. (1966) 'Information networks in labour markets', *American Economic Review*, **56**, pp. 559–66.

Smith, D. J. (1974) *Racial Disadvantage in Employment*, Broadsheet no. 544, Political and Economic Planning.

Smith, D. J. (1977) *Racial Disadvantage in Britain*, Pelican.

Smith, D. J. (1981) *Unemployment And Racial Minorities*, No. 594, Policy Studies Institute.

Troyna, B. and Smith, D. I. (eds) (1983) *Racism, School and the Labour Market*, National Youth Bureau.

Watson, T. J. (1977) *The Personnel Managers*, Routledge and Kegan Paul.

Source: Roberts, B., Finnegan, R. and Gallie, D. (eds) (1985) *New Approaches to Economic Life*, Manchester, Manchester University Press.

9 AN UNCARING PROFESSION?

AN EXAMINATION OF RACISM IN SOCIAL WORK

LENA DOMINELLI

Social work purports to be the profession that cares for the welfare of its clients and aspires to meet their material and emotional needs (Compton and Galaway, 1975). To what extent can black people, i.e. people of Afro-Caribbean and Asian origins, expect this axiom to apply to them and their needs when they approach the personal social services or come into contact with the criminal justice system? This article considers this question in terms of the services white social workers working in predominantly white institutions provide for black clients, the position of black social workers as employees, and training provisions for black students. Unfortunately, the answer to this question is that white practitioners, educators and their departments have served the interests of black populations badly (ADSS/CRE, 1978; Taylor, 1981; Rooney, 1980; Small, 1984; Sewell, 1985; Devine, 1983; Tipler, 1986; Dominelli, 1988; Williams, 1987). Moreover, this situation has persisted despite various attempts which have been made to counter it since the mid-1970s (Rooney, 1987). Why has social work been unable to respond to the needs of black people? What role have white workers had in perpetuating this state of affairs? And how can they be empowered to serve the needs of black people as black people? This article explores these questions by examining the impact of racism in social work and then considering what action white people can take to tackle it.

Racism in social work

Much has been written about the failure of social workers to meet the needs of any client group which comes into contact with them. For example, social work has been criticized for failing to meet the needs of working-class clients (Corrigan and Leonard, 1979); women (Brook and Davis, 1985); sexually abused children and their parents (Bell, 1988). Therefore, the argument goes, as social work has not succeeded in meeting its objectives whatever client category is examined, black people endure the same failures as other groups. On one level, this contention contains an element of truth. All social work clients suffer from having to seek resources and support from workers and departments which are overstretched, under-resourced, under-staffed and operating on the basis of competing demands for their services. However, I would argue that the position of black people is qualitatively and structurally different from that of white client groups. For besides being denied services for the organizational reasons described above, black people have to contend with the impact of racism and the way in which its dynamics affect service delivery, training provisions and the employment opportunities available to them. White people do not have to face the implications of being at the receiving end of racist social dynamics.

Lorde defines racism as 'the belief in the inherent superiority of one race over all others and thereby the right to dominance' (1984, p. 115). Bromley and Longino (1972) identify three forms of racism, each interacting with and reinforcing each other; individual racism, institutional racism, and cultural racism. Individual racism comprises those personal attitudes and behaviours which individuals use to prejudge racial groups negatively. Without institutional backing, these rest at the level of prejudice. Institutional racism draws on the public legitimation of prejudice, i.e. the institutionalized exercise of power to exclude groups which are defined as racially inferior from having access to society's resources and power and pathologize or blame those so excluded for their predicament. Cultural racism consists of the values, beliefs and ideas, usually embedded in our 'common sense', which endorse the superiority of white culture over others (Barker, 1981). In other words, cultural racism becomes an ideology with a structure and a practice. The interconnections between these three types of racism make racism present in the day-to-day routines and minutiae of life, thereby enabling it to transcend the overt forms of racist behaviour white people associate with supporters of the National Front (Dominelli, 1988). It is the subtle presence of racism in our normal activities, coupled with our failure to make the connections between the personal, institutional and cultural levels of racism, which make it so hard for white people to recognize its existence in *their* particular behaviour and combat it effectively. Thus racism permeates social work interactions unless we take specific steps to counter it.

The existence of racism in social work has already been amply documented (ADSS/CRE, 1978; Gitterman and Schaeffer, 1972; Banks, 1971; Kent, 1972; Small 1984; Sewell, 1985; Fletchman-Smith, 1984). But its impact has not been simply one of excluding black people from service provisions or employment opportunities. It has also operated in ways which have resulted in the over-representation of black people in its more punitive institutions. In other words, racism in social work operates through two channels which shape client–worker interactions: the exclusive channel and the inclusive one. The dynamics inherent in the racially exclusive tendency result in black people having limited access to the 'goodies' or caring services provided through social work intervention. For example, black elders have not received their share of home-helps, meals-on-wheels, and are under-represented in sheltered accommodation schemes (Bhalla and Blakemore, 1981; Farrah, 1986); black women leaving violent homes have found few refuges dedicated to meeting their specific needs (Guru, 1987); black social workers are scarce in most social work departments, and when they are employed, they tend to be located in the lower echelons of the labour hierarchy (Rooney, 1982, 1987).

The dynamics which form an integral part of the inclusive tendency have produced a situation in which black people are over-represented in those social work institutions which provide services. These are considered less desirable and at the sharp end of social work practice because they are more directly engaged in controlling people's behaviour by reinforcing the socialization processes which social workers deem lacking in the client's life, e.g. schools for the educationally subnormal (Coard, 1971); penal institutions (Home Office, 1986); and the higher echelons of the tariff system (Dominelli, 1983).

The two channels through which racism makes its presence felt in social work practice mark social work's contradictory relationship to black people. The contradiction between excluding black people from welfare services and including them in provisions oriented around social work's social control function can be explained in terms of the impact of racism in its three forms on the different relationships white social workers have with different client groups within the black population. In other words, those black client groups which white social workers consider 'deserving' of services, but whose needs are deemed to be catered for through black self-help groups, and community and kinship networks, are shunted off through the exclusive channel. Meanwhile, those black client groups which white social workers see as deviating from acceptable white social norms are considered potentially threatening and in need of control to ensure that their socialization takes place in accordance with white middle-class expectations. Therefore, they are responded to through the inclusive channel. The racist dynamics responsible for the inclusive tendency rely on pathologizing black people, the relationships they develop with each other, and their cultural norms. The racist dynamics reproduced through the exclusive channel rely on stereotyping black culture as being able to 'care for its own' while the detrimental effects of racism on the development of black cultural forms are either ignored or denied. This happens, for example, when the British Immigration laws which divide black families (Gordon, 1985; Plummer, 1978) and make it impossible for them to reconstruct helping relationships between extended and joint family members are discounted in social work intervention with black people.

These two trends are the product of strategies which white people use to deny, ignore and minimize the presence of racism in their own institutions, culture and personal behaviour. These strategies can interact with each other and the boundaries between them can be blurred, but they include: denial strategies, colour-blind strategies, patronizing strategies, omission strategies, decontextualization strategies, and avoidance strategies (Dominelli, 1988). These may be defined as follows:

* *Denial strategies* are based on the idea that there is no such thing as cultural and institutional racism, only personal prejudice in its crude manifestations.

* *Colour-blind strategies* focus on the notion that all people are the same – members of one race with similar problems, needs and objectives.

* *Patronizing approaches* operate on the basis of a false acceptance of equality between black and white people and their lifestyles. But, when the final evaluation between them is made, white people and their lifestyles always come out superior.

* *Dumping strategies* rely on placing the responsibility for eliminating racism on black people's shoulders.

* *Omission strategies* rest on the view that racism is not an important part of social interaction, and can be safely ignored in most situations.

* *Decontextualization strategies* acknowledge the presence of racism in general terms, but fail to do so in specific instances involving daily routines and interactions.

* *Avoidance strategies* are predicated on accepting that racism exists, but denying the particular responsibility of the individual to do something about it.

The following case-study reveals how these strategies are manifested when white social workers intervene in black people's lives.

Racism in service provision and delivery: case-study[1]

Permjit Kaur was a 75-year-old Sikh woman who lived on her own in an inner city area which had a high proportion of black people. She came to the notice of the social services department when a woman friend suggested she go to them for help with her housing needs after her husband died. She spoke little English and was terrified at the thought of facing an official body, but agreed to go when her friend promised to accompany her. The two of them walked the one-and-a-half miles to the district office as money was short. But because both of them had arthritis in their feet and Permjit had asthma and angina, it took them a long time to reach their destination. When they got there, although the door was open,

the social workers were nowhere to be seen. There was a sign in
English saying to ring the bell for attention. But since neither
woman read English, it was lost on them. They felt that since it was
too far to return home without seeing anyone, they would wait until
someone turned up. As there was only one chair in the entrance hall,
they agreed to take turns sitting on it. They had waited for over an
hour when a harassed white worker rushed into the building, took
one look at them and went through the door marked 'Staff Only'.
About half an hour later, the same worker came out, and noticing
the women were still there asked if they were waiting for their
husbands. Permjit explained in her broken English that she wanted
to see a social worker. When asked if she had telephoned first to
make an appointment, she replied in the negative, saying she didn't
know she needed one. The worker, looking somewhat embarrassed,
informed her that as the sign (in English) by the door proclaimed,
she did, but that she should ring the bell and hope that someone
could come to attend to her. 'They are all very busy in the back', he
said, 'And I must dash out to an important meeting.' By this time,
Permjit felt like going home, but her friend insisted they should
persist with their objective and ring the bell. This they did and
moments later, a (white) worker opened the door slightly and said,
'Someone will see you in a minute', and disappeared. It was another
20 minutes before another (white) person attended to them. Permjit
explained what she wanted and was told that they would have to
wait a bit longer for someone to interview them. Half an hour passed
before a young white male worker invited them into an interview
room. When they went into the room, the walls were covered with
posters of white people – young and old, telling them of the services
which were on offer to them. Ironically, one displayed white elders
enjoying the amenities of sheltered housing. The worker sat them
down and proceeded to ask them some questions. Permjit was
getting very embarrassed by the questions he asked which were to
do with where her relatives and family were, not with her need to
get accommodation that didn't require her to climb stairs now that
her arthritis and angina were so bad. She tried to explain that the
suggestion for rehousing originated with her GP who felt that her
having to climb five flights of stairs to get into the flat she had
shared with her husband was getting beyond her physical
capabilities. But the social worker either did not understand this or
pretended not to hear. He kept asking her where her extended
family was and why they weren't taking care of her. She didn't
understand his line of reasoning at all. Neither did her friend. The
worker began feeling frustrated at his failure to communicate
effectively with Permjit and eventually decided to inform her that he
was unable to offer her anything, but that she and her friend could
try the housing department and see if any help were available
through that agency. Permjit and her companion left the district

office feeling totally defeated. As they slowly and painfully made their way across the car park, the harassed worker they had first encountered came out of the office, dashed past them, got into his car and drove off.

Analysis

There are many points at which the practice evident in this case could be subjected to critical scrutiny from an antiracist perspective, but I shall focus only on the main ones. To begin with, this case is one which highlights the exclusive tendency at work and illustrates all three forms of racism. Personal racism is particularly evident in the failure of the young white male worker who interviews Permjit to take on board the fact that he is relating to an Asian woman and to deal specifically with her needs and sensibilities as such. Institutional racism is manifest in the failure of the office to have signs translated into languages other than English, to provide interpreters for clients whose English is a second language, to employ black social workers, and to supply black people who live in its catchment area with information on the services it has available and how they can gain access to them. Cultural racism is apparent in the way the young white male worker assumes that Permjit has an extended family and that it will take care of her. It is also present in the absence of positive images of black people to which black clients can relate.

The strategies which the white social workers have used in avoiding the issue of 'race' in the interaction with the two Asian women are:

Decontextualization: This they enact by ignoring the fact that they are dealing with black women and not ensuring that they provide the facilities they require to make an adequate assessment of Permjit's needs.

Omission: The white workers do not recognize that racism permeates the whole of the women's encounter with them and their department, from the moment the two of them walk in the door until the moment they leave.

Colour-blindness: The white workers assume that the services which are available for dealing with white people are sufficient for black people, i.e. everyone is treated the same, as if their needs were the same. For example, one sign in English explaining how to get in touch with the duty worker is considered sufficient to meet the needs of whoever comes through the door.

Denial: The white workers have failed to make the connection between their racist responses and the institutional racism being perpetrated by the department, and with which they are colluding, e.g. not ensuring they are able to undertake an adequate assessment of Permjit's needs, not treating her as someone who has come into the office for help in her own right rather than as an appendage to her male relatives. At this point, the white male social worker's thinking indicates a combination of sexist as well as racist dynamics.

Patronage: The white social workers' reactions to the two women are of patronizing tolerance, making their intervention a waste of the two women's time and energies.

Avoidance: The two social workers recognize the inadequacy of their department's response to the two black women, but decide to ignore it and carry on with their work as usual.

Dumping: The young white male social worker is dumping the responsibility of providing for this woman's needs on the black community via her (non-existent) extended family.

The case demonstrates poor social work practice in general affecting both white and black clients, e.g. the way in which workers fail to control the stress in their work and allow their being overworked to interfere with their responses to clients and the unwelcoming arrangements in the entrance hall. Their racist practice affecting black people, only some of which has been highlighted in the analysis given above, compounds the more general aspects of their poor practice. Moreover, if the white social workers had picked up on the evidence indicative of inadequate practice on all counts, they could have improved both the facilities for and the services available to white as well as black clients. For example, making the entrance hall more comfortable for people who have to wait for attention; not treating clients' time as less valuable than their own, not using being overworked to legitimate inadequate assessments of clients' situations. All of these issues should be seen not only as examples of poor individual practice, but also as inadequate organizational policy and practice. Although structural deficiencies have a profound effect on individual practice, social workers should not be held personally accountable for their presence, e.g. being under-resourced and overworked. Dealing directly with these is the responsibility of management. Nevertheless, individual social workers have the duty of letting their seniors know how structural deficiencies affect their particular caseload and working collectively through various organizations, e.g. trade unions, support groups and networks, towards their elimination. Therefore, individual social workers should not be scapegoated for structural inadequacies. Rectifying these requires political resolve as well as individual commitment to pressing for improvements. But in addition to tackling the structural dimension through political and collective action, there is the personal dimension which social workers should recognize and take on board both individually and collectively when combating racism. Thus, to eliminate racism, social workers must engage individually and collectively in changing policy and practice at the personal, organizational and societal levels, often simultaneously.

White social workers are frightened to confront the issues of racism directly (Rooney, 1982; Fletchman-Smith, 1984; Stubbs, 1985). This is partly due to their ignorance about racism as a social force and their lack of understanding of black people's life experiences as they are mediated by and through racism (Kadushin, 1972; Mizio, 1972; Kent, 1972). This fear and ignorance can be partially explained by inadequate training, which mirrors the inadequate attention society pays to the issue of racism. Training does not equip white social workers with antiracist theory or practices with which to embark on their professional careers.

Professional ideology and ethics in social work militate against white social workers being able to handle racism in their practice because these individualize the worker and the relationship that is established with the client, thereby ensuring that the privileged and powerful group position of the former and the unprivileged and powerless group position of the latter are not acknowledged in their work (Kadushin, 1972; Mizio, 1972; Banks, 1971; Fletchman-Smith, 1984). Professionalism also ends up encouraging white social workers to see the client–worker relationship as occurring in a vacuum (Corrigan and Leonard, 1979), isolated from the impact of various social forces, including racism. Because of their impact on decontextualizing individual black clients and black groups from their social context, the ideology and methodology of the profession with its emphasis on casework, professional autonomy, and individual intervention do not easily lend themselves to antiracist practice (Dominelli, 1988).

In addition, white social workers who have tried to work in antiracist ways with black people and have failed to do it successfully have become paralysed by their failure; while others have become daunted by the enormity of the task before them (Stubbs, 1985). Some white social workers become so incapacitated by their anxieties over handling 'race', that everything becomes entangled within it, and they become unable to separate out issues other than those related to racism, e.g. not acknowledging adolescent conflicts between black parents and their children (Ahmed, 1984). In such situations, white social workers interpret differences between children and their parents as the predictable outcome of black family dynamics which indicate that they are unable to cope (Ahmed, 1978). Moreover, white social workers fail to recognize the connections between racism and other forms of social divisions, e.g. sexism, ageism, classism, as the case study described above indicates.

Racism in the employment of black social workers

With the exception of a few London boroughs such as Hackney which have established antiracist policies aimed at ensuring that the employment of black people in the social services department reflects their composition in the local population, the presence of black workers in social services departments is limited (ADSS/CRE, 1978; ABSWAP, 1981; BICSG, 1984; Stubbs, 1985). Within mainstream provisions, black workers tend to be concentrated in volunteer posts, temporary posts, and residential posts, which carry low salary levels, poor prospects of career advancement and promotion, and few opportunities for exercising their professional discretion (Rooney, 1982). Probation services have also been slow in appointing black probation officers, particularly at senior levels (Taylor, 1981). This has meant that black people have had to rely on the voluntary sector, particularly that initiated by black people themselves for employment opportunities in the welfare arena, and for the provision of the social work experience which would eventually entitle them to undertake one-year training courses.

Departments, including those which have begun to employ black workers in significant numbers, have failed to ensure equality of treatment and opportunities to employees (Rooney, 1982, 1987). Many social services and probation departments have sought to deal with the issue of racism by employing black social workers, but have ended up dumping the responsibility of eradicating racism on their shoulders, and thereby failing to engage their white social workers in this task (Stubbs, 1985). Once employed in social work, black workers have been used in a variety of ways. One method has been what I have called the 'Opening the Door Model' under which social services departments have interpreted the employment of black people as simply having them in the office to encourage black clients to make use of their existing provisions. This has often resulted in the black social worker being seen as the person who would work exclusively with black clients (Rooney, 1982). Work under the 'Opening the Door Model' has usually been constrained by black social workers having to work with black clients in the same way as white workers work with white clients – by providing a generic service utilizing the casework approach (Rooney, 1980), despite this approach often having been criticized or being inappropriate for the needs of black people (Stubbs, 1985; Rooney, 1980, 1987; Dominelli, 1988). For example, white social workers and their managers have been worried about black social workers 'over-identifying' with black clients and have expressed the concern that this would lead to a lack of 'confidentiality' in their work. This they have felt is particularly apparent when black social workers discuss the problems of black clients in the presence of community members, friends and relatives who accompany them. Or, as Rooney (1980, p. 47) puts it:

[black] workers who may have been employed to provide new skill, new knowledge, to be an additional resource, are ground into performing work within normal priorities. Remember it is those normal priorities which were found wanting as far as service to the black community was concerned.

Meanwhile, white workers continue working as usual with white clients showing little interest in learning how to work effectively with black clients (Rooney, 1980, 1987). In these situations, white social workers and their managers usually do not deem it important to establish a climate in which both white workers and white clients can display confidence in the work of black social workers and in their presence in authoritative positions in the office.

Another model which is used in the employment of black social workers is what I have called the 'Black Specialist Model'. Under this model, black workers are appointed as specialist workers in special units aimed at responding primarily to the needs of black clients. These posts are usually Section 11 appointments which carry with them another set of problems which also reinforce racism. These problems have included: the ghetto-izing of services for black people in some outpost of the department (Rooney, 1982); the failure of departments to provide mainstream career opportunities for black workers appointed under Section 11 contracts (Dominelli, 1988); the inappropriate use of Section 11 money to appoint white people to provide services for white clients (Duffield, 1985); and the overburdening of individual black workers with the amount of work they are expected to undertake (Rooney, 1987).

Black workers have been unhappy about their exploitation under Section 11 contracts, but at the same time they have acknowledged that the opportunities for employment in social work would have been much diminished without Section 11 funding (Stubbs, 1985). Moreover, without Section 11 funding, a number of very imaginative and worthwhile schemes operating in the interests of the black community would have never got off the ground.

Black social workers risk being abused and exploited by having the responsibility of eradicating racism fall primarily on their shoulders through either the 'Opening the Door Model' or the 'Black Specialist Model'. In order to avoid this, white social workers and managers have to accept the challenges black social workers offer to their ways of working and to the white supremacist ideologies which infuse their work. They must become committed to transforming their practice in accordance with antiracist norms across the range of client groups and work with black colleagues in egalitarian ways.

Racism in social work education and training

Social work education and training lies firmly in the hands of white educators and practitioners. Collectively and individually, they have failed to address adequately the issue of racism in either social work theories or practice (Dominelli, 1988). Early attempts to deal with the issue of 'race' have not succeeded in meeting the needs of black people. For example, Cheetham's *Social Work with Immigrants* (1972) highlights the importance of working with black people, but does so in the context of their being immigrants whose problems, can be directly related to their experience as such. Thus they are seen as being responsible for their own predicament. While these issues do merit some consideration in their own right, their being used as the sole determinants of black people's position in Britain has meant that black people are being blamed for the problems foisted on them by racism (Gilroy, 1987). In other words, Cheetham's work defines the problem as black people's inability to cope with being in Britain rather than that of racism blocking their every attempt to improve their standard of living and carve out a life on terms acceptable to them. Such an approach has also contributed towards the institutional-ization of the image of black people as 'immigrants' (first, second and third generation), that is, people whose stay in Britain is temporary, a prelude to returning to their countries of origin. It also endorses white people's perception of black people as persons from foreign cultures who have quaint customs which are interesting in a folksey way, but which impede their progress in white British society. Such analyses end up pathologiz-ing black cultures and life styles. Other books have continued this line of argument and treat black people and their cultures as the problem that needs to be addressed. Ely and Denney's *Social Work in a Multi-racial Society* (1987) is one of the latest in a long line of such texts. Like its antecedents, this book has failed to come to grips with racism and focuses on getting (white) social workers to understand cultural differences between black and white people rather than tackling racism as the problem requiring attention.

Radical white social work theorists and practitioners have also failed to address the issue of racism in their work in any substantial way. For example, Corrigan and Leonard's *Social Work under Capitalism* (1979) highlights the working class client's experience of social work. But without saying so, it is very clearly a book about the experience of the white working class. Brook and Davis' book, *Women, the Family and Social Work* (1985), focuses on white women's experience of sexism. Beaumont and Walker's book *Working with Young Offenders* (1985) hardly mentions the needs of black offenders or their treatment in the criminal justice system.

It has been black people, writing from a black perspective rooted in their experience of racism in Britain, that have begun to shift the eyes of white academics and social workers towards racism as a structural phenomenon which permeates every aspect of social work intervention and is reflected in all white social workers' individual practice. For example, Small's, *The Crisis in Adoption* (1984) has revealed the theoretical and moral bankruptcy behind white practitioners' work with black children in care when their identity needs as *black* children are ignored. The findings of the Lambeth Black Families Unit, which John Small was instrumental in creating, has shocked white opinion when it challenged fostering practice and revealed that potential black foster parents were being excluded from fostering children by criteria that could be met largely by white middle-class two-parent families. It has also demonstrated that black workers are in a better position to identify and respond to the needs of black families. Working on another line of enquiry, black feminists, e.g. Bryan *et al.*, in *The Heart of the Race* (1985), have highlighted the destruction both racism and sexism wreak on black women's lives. Similarly, it has been black people who have exposed the discriminatory treatment young blacks endure at the hands of the police and the courts, e.g. Gilroy (1982) and John (1978).

Black people have also found it hard to get into predominantly white training and educational establishments either as students aiming to obtain the qualifications which are necessary for them to enter the social work arena as practitioners (CCETSW, 1985), or to acquire posts as teachers. The relative exclusion of black people as both students and employees has made the relationship between black people and training courses an unhappy one.

Black people applying to courses have found themselves excluded by admissions requirements which have been based on a white experience of education. In the first instance, the admissions criteria ignore the discrimination which initially prevents black people from reaching the higher echelons of the education hierarchy. But, even black people who have succeeded in obtaining undergraduate degrees have found entry to postgraduate social work courses elusive because their practice experience has been found wanting. As much of their practical work has been acquired in black community settings which do not fit easily with their white interviewer's ideas about what constitutes (mainstream) social work, their experience has been discounted for the purposes of securing a place on a course. As Rooney (1980, p. 44) says:

> when it comes to interviews, there's an almost irresistible impulse to be sensitive to those qualities in people which mirror our own. A natural predilection for the conventional leaves us susceptible to the flattery of those who appear to agree with us.

But even when they manage to obtain places on courses, black students have found their struggles far from over. Very rarely do they find black tutors employed in a full-time capacity on their courses. This means that there are few positive role models for them to emulate and little possibility of their finding someone to discuss how to survive the racism which features so strongly on courses and in their daily lives. In addition, white tutors and students use black students as the 'race' experts and place them in positions of doing the teaching on 'race' without their receiving either recognition or reward for doing such work. The lack of black practitioners on placements has meant that black students are not getting support in this arena either. In fact, when it comes to the assessment process, black students have found themselves failing both the written and the practical work in disproportionate numbers (Willis, 1987). Thus, white social work educators need to ensure that they both attract black students to their courses and provide the conditions under which their educational experience is a healthy and non-discriminatory one by having the black staff and support networks required to make this possible.

But, while black students are let down by the racist nature of their courses, so too are white students. White students also suffer the frustration of wanting to be taught how to work in antiracist ways in both their academic work and fieldwork when they discover that the resources and instruction necessary for such teaching to take place are lacking on their courses. The employment of black tutors in permanent mainstream capacities can pick up on some of these points, but white staff also need to shoulder their responsibilities in this matter and may require substantial retraining to make this possible. Otherwise, the employment of black social work educators becomes another site at which white people dump the responsibility of dealing with racism on the shoulders of black people. It also means that white institutions have got to take their obligations to provide black teachers with the resources they need to undertake their work in a non-tokenistic way and to foster the support networks black people want to establish for themselves. Thus, change in academic institutions must also encompass the personal, organizational and cultural levels.

Conclusion

The evidence in this article has demonstrated that the claims of social work as a caring profession aimed at helping people meet their needs are not fulfilled in its relationships with black people, whether they are clients, workers, or students. Black clients miss out through the lack of provisions aimed specifically at meeting their needs as black people (i.e. as people whose lives are shaped by their experience of racism). Black social workers find that their needs as black workers are ignored and that it is extremely difficult for them to initiate changes which will endorse the acquisition of new skills and new knowledge in the provision of services for black and white clients. Black students find that if they undertake social work training, the lack of resources to meet their specific needs as black students can lead to their being set up for failure. Finally, it is clear that racism not only produces poor practice vis-à-vis black people, it also reinforces inadequate practice towards white people. In order to ensure that good practice which fosters an antiracist perspective becomes the order of the day for the benefit of all social work clients, white practitioners, educators, trainers and managers need to embark on a process which transforms social work as we currently know it. Achieving such a transformation requires personal, organizational and societal changes which must be supported at the political, social, economic, ideological and individual levels.

Note

1 The material in the case study was obtained by the author when interviewing practitioners.

References

Ahmed, S. (1978) 'Asian girls and culture conflicts', *Social Work Today*, **9**(47), August, pp. 14–16.

Ahmed, S. (1984) 'Social Work with Ethnic Minorities', Paper given at the British Association of Social Workers Annual Conference at Nene College, Northampton, April.

Association of Black Social Workers and Allied Professionals (1981) *Black Children in Care: Evidence Submitted to the Select Committee on Child Care*, London: ABSWAP.

Association of Directors of Social Services and Commission for Racial Equality (1978) *Multiracial Britain: The Social Services Response*, London: ADSS/CRE.

Banks, G. (1971) 'The effects of race on one-to-one helping interviews', *Social Service Review*, **45**, June, pp. 137–146.

Barker, M. (1981) *The New Racism: Conservatives and the Ideology of the Tribe*, London, Junction Books.

Bell, S. (1988) *When Salem Came to the 'Boro*, London: Pan Books.

Beaumont, B. and Walker, H. (1985) *Working with Young Offenders*, London: Macmillan.

Bhalla, A. and Blakemore, K. (1981) *Elders of the Ethnic Minority Groups*, Birmingham, All Faiths for One Race.

Black and In Care Steering Group (1984) *Black and in Care: Conference Report*, London, Blackrose Press.

Bromley, D. and Longino, C. F. Jnr. (1972) *White Racism and Black Americans*, Cambridge, Mass., Schenkman Publishing Co.

Brook, E. and Davis, A. (1985) *Women, the Family and Social Work*, London, Tavistock.

Bryan, B., Dadzie, S. and Scafe, S. (1985) *The Heart of the Race: Black Women's Lives in Britain*, London, Virago.

Central Council for Education and Training in Social Work (1985) *Ethnic Minorities and Social Work Training*, Paper 21.1, London, CCETSW.

Cheetham, J. (1972) *Social Work with Immigrants*, London, Routledge and Kegan Paul.

Coard, B. (1971) *How West Indian Children are made Educationally Subnormal*, London, New Beacon.

Compton, B. and Galaway, B. (1975) *Social Work Processes*, Homewood, Illinois, The Dorsey Press.

Corrigan, P. and Leonard, P. (1979) *Social Work under Capitalism*, London, Macmillan.

Devine, D. (1983) 'Defective, hypocritical and patronising research', *Caribbean Times*, 4 March, p. 4.

Dominelli, L. (1983) *Women in Focus: community service orders and female offenders*, A Research Report for the Nuffield Foundation, Coventry, Warwick University.

Dominelli, L. (1988) *Anti-Racist Social Work*, London, BASW/Macmillan.

Duffield, M. (1985) 'Challenge to city on section II money', *Social Work Today*, **16**(3), 1 April: p. 5.

Ely, P. and Denney, D. (1987) *Social Work in a Multi-racial Society*, London, Gower.

Farrah, M. (1986) *Black Elders in Leicester*, Leicester Social Services Department Report, Leicester, SSD.

Fletchman-Smith, B. (1984) 'Effects of race on adoption and fostering', *International Journal of Social Psychiatry*, **30**, pp. 121–8.

Gilroy, P. (1982) 'Police and thieves' in Centre for Contemporary Cultural Studies, *The Empire Strikes Back: race and racism in 1970's Britain*, London, Hutchinson.

Gilroy, P. (1987) *There Ain't No Black in the Union Jack*, London, Hutchinson.

Gitterman, A. and Schaeffer, A. (1972) 'The white professional and the black client', *Social Casework*, May, pp. 280–91.

Gordon, P. (1985) *Policing Immigration: Britain's internal controls*, London, Pluto Press.

Guru, S. (1987) 'An Asian women's refuge', in Ahmed, S., Cheetham, J. and Small, J. (eds), *Social Work with Black Children and their Families*, London, Batsford.

Home Office (1986) *Ethnic Minorities, Crime and Policing*, London, HMSO.

John, G. (1978) *Black People*, Milton Keynes, Open University, Unit 23.

Kadushin, L. (1972) 'The racial factor in the interview', *Social Work*, **17**(3), pp. 88–99.

Kent, B. (1972) 'The social worker's cultural pattern as it affects casework with immigrants', in Triseliotis, J. (ed.), *Social Work with Coloured Immigrants and their Families*, London, Institute of Race Relations for Oxford University Press.

Lorde, A. (1984) *Sister Outsider*, New York, The Crossing Press.

Mizio, E. (1972) 'White Worker – Minority Client', *Social Work*, **17**(3), May, pp. 82–7.

Plummer, J. (1978) *Divide and Deprive*, London, Joint Council for the Welfare of Immigrants.

Rooney, B. (1980) 'Active mistakes – a grass roots report', *Multi-racial Social Work*, **1**, pp. 43–54.

Rooney, B. (1982) 'Black social workers in white departments', in Cheetham, J. (ed.), *Social Work and Ethnicity*, London: George Allen and Unwin.

Rooney, B. (1987) *Resistance to Change*, Liverpool University Project Report.

Sewell, T. (1985) 'The black child in danger', *The Voice*, 7 September, p. 14.

Small, J. (1984) 'The crisis in adoption', *The International Journal of Psychiatry*, **30**, Spring, pp. 129–41.

Stubbs, P. (1985) 'The employment of black social workers: from "ethnic sensitivity" to anti-racism', *Critical Social Policy*, **12**, Spring, pp. 6–27.

Taylor, W. (1981) *Probation and After-care in a Multi-racial Society*, London, Commission for Racial Equality.

Tipler, J. (1986) *Is Justice Colour Blind? A Study of The Impact of Race in the Juvenile Justice System in Hackney*, London, Hackney Social Services Department Research Paper No. 6.

Williams, F. (1987) 'Racism and the discipline of social policy: a critique of welfare theory', *Critical Social Policy*, **20**, September, pp. 4–59.

Willis, M. (1987) 'Report on handling "race" issues at Birmingham Polytechnic', unpublished paper.

Source: Dominelli, L. (1989) 'An uncaring profession? An examination of racism in social work', *New Community*, **15**(3).

10 BLACK PEOPLE AND THE CRIMINAL LAW
RHETORIC AND REALITY
PAUL GORDON

Introduction

Discussions of the criminalization of black people in Britain[1] have so far been confined to accounts of relations between the police and black people. The evidence of the innumerable studies which have been carried out is incontrovertible and supports the conclusion offered by Stuart Hall nearly a decade ago that 'the police have undertaken, whether willingly or not, to constrain by means which would not long stand up to inspection within the rule of law, an alienated black population and thereby, to police the social crisis of the cities' (Hall, 1979, p. 13). Yet, it is as if policing was an end, rather than a beginning; a beginning of a *process of criminalization* which continues from the point of arrest through the courts and beyond (Gordon, 1983). Our knowledge of this process to which the black community in Britain has been subjected remains partial. We know comparatively little, for instance, about what happens after the point of arrest by the police. We know little, too, about the decision to prosecute black people, the kinds of charges brought, the granting or refusal of bail; we have little hard evidence about the treatment of black people in the courts, about the conduct of trials, the behaviour and attitudes of court personnel including magistrates and judges, the sentencing process, the probation and after-care services, and so on.

At the same time we *do* know of the suspicion with which many black people regard the agencies of the criminal justice system. As a black youth put it to one of the few researchers who has bothered to look at this issue:

> Goin' to court is frightenin' 'cos you know you're not goin' to get justice, no chance. We're black . . . and that's enough to put you down. It's nothin' for the police; they come round here givin' us trouble, arresting us and draggin' us off to court, they just see it as a job but we see it different. We know that they're all in it together coppers, probation officers, solicitors, magistrates the lot.

(Hil, 1980, p. 173)

We know too, if we care to remember, of the many major trials during the 1970s and 1980s which form part of the history of black people in Britain, of racism and of resistance. Our knowledge is partial, but is nevertheless considerable. This article, which is based on reports of major trials involving black defendants since the early 1970s, and on research of a more academic nature, attempts to examine the meaning of the 'rule of law' for black people, to assess the rhetoric of the law – that justice is not only blind but colour-blind, undiscriminating in its application – against the reality of the black experience of the British criminal justice system.

The criminalization process

At least since the early 1970s black people have faced serious criminal charges and what they have alleged is discriminatory treatment at the hands of the criminal law and the criminal process in Britain. In 1971, for instance, serious charges of incitement to riot and affray were brought against eight men and women following a demonstration against police harassment in the Notting Hill area of west London. Although the incitement charges were rejected by magistrates at committal hearings, new charges of riotous assembly were brought the following day. These were also rejected, but the charges of affray were allowed to stand and when the cases came to court in 1972, new charges of riot were brought by a special procedure which circumvented the normal committal process through the bringing of charges against a ninth defendant. Eventually, however, the nine defendants were acquitted of the riot charges and only two of the affray charges were upheld. Undeterred by the collapse of this case, the public prosecution authorities the same year brought serious charges of affray against several black defendants who had been arrested during a police raid on a black youth club, the Metro in Notting Hill in London. Again, however, the prosecution case collapsed and none of the charges of affray, causing grievous bodily harm or possession of offensive weapons was upheld. Three years later in 1975, charges of affray, along with other serious charges were brought against 12 black people who had been arrested following another raid on a club, this time the Carib club in Cricklewood, but again all the defendants were acquitted, nine at the trial itself, one after a re-trial and two on appeal. The following year, charges of affray were again brought against black defendants, this time against people arrested during disturbances which followed police intervention at the Bonfire Night celebrations in Chapeltown, Leeds. Although the prosecution this time secured three convictions, 21 of the 24 charges brought were dismissed.

In addition to having faced serious public order charges, black people have also been the subject of serious conspiracy charges which, until the law was changed in 1977, carried more severe penalties than specific offences.

Such charges were also more easily proved since they required less by way of evidence than substantive charges and could be brought even where no evidence of the actual offence has been obtained. Such conspiracy charges had long been favoured charges of the state in political cases and the cases of black defendants joined those of, for instance, the editors of the underground magazine *Oz* in 1971, the Angry Brigade and anti-apartheid campaigner, Peter Hain, in 1973, the Shrewsbury pickets and the editors of *International Times* in 1973, and the British Withdrawal from Northern Ireland Campaign in 1975 (Spicer, 1981).

In the 1972 case of Kamara, for instance, which was brought after students had occupied the High Commission of Sierra Leone in London, the defendants were convicted not just of unlawful assembly but of conspiracy to trespass. The students' appeal that such an offence was not known to English law because there was at the time no criminal offence of trespass, was rejected. Conspiracy charges were also used against the Islington 18, black youths who were arrested following the Notting Hill Carnival in 1976 which had ended in street fighting between carnival goers and the police. After jury deliberations lasting 170 hours, then the longest in the history of the Central Criminal Court, and a case costing some £250,000 of public money, all the conspiracy charges were dismissed although some charges of theft and robbery were upheld. The year after the trial of the Islington 18, 19 black youths, the Lewisham 19, were convicted of charges of conspiracy to rob after a jury was shown secretly taken video film. In 1982, 12 black youths in Bradford, were acquitted of charges of conspiracy to damage property and to endanger the lives of others and of conspiracy to cause grievous bodily harm. The 12 had all been involved in the making of petrol bombs which, they argued and the jury accepted, had been done solely to protect themselves and their community against an attack by fascists which they believed to be imminent. The collapse of the case against the Bradford 12 did not, however, deter the prosecution authorities from bringing conspiracy charges the following year in another case involving the right of the black community to defend itself against racial violence.

In all these cases it would seem, the use of conspiracy charges was a clear attempt not just to criminalize black protest and black people, but to maximize the chances of the police and prosecution in securing convictions in the absence of hard evidence. They were attempts to ensure that the defendants, if convicted, received heavy sentences. That they did not always succeed was frequently due to juries who were prepared to make up their own minds as to the evidence. Indeed, the failure of these and other conspiracy cases led directly to attacks on the jury system and calls for restrictions on the right to jury trial, a point to which I return later. In addition, such conspiracy cases were being widely seen as clearly political and became the focus for high profile, community-based defence campaigns. As such, it seems resonable to surmise, they were seen by the prosecuting authorities as counter-productive and the year after the

Bradford 12 trial, another case involving the issue of community self-defence against racial violence illustrated the changing prosecution practice. In 1983, charges of conspiracy to assault persons unknown were brought against eight Asians in east London, the Newham 8. The charges were brought after the formation of a self-defence group following a series of attacks on Asian school pupils. These conspiracy charges were later changed to charges of affray, of which four of the eight were convicted. The dropping of the conspiracy charges was significant for it indicated that the prosecution authorities had learned, albeit belatedly, the lesson of the previous conspiracy trials. Instead of risking another unsuccessful and embarrassing prosecution, they substituted charges which were less likely to be seen as political. Not only that, but the prosecution chose to use a charge, that of affray, which would be unlikely to fail. Since there had been fighting between the defendants (or some of them) and the police, then there had been an affray, and those involved were inevitably guilty.

'Riot trials'

Any account of the criminalization of black people by the criminal law and the criminal justice system must also look at the trials which have followed major demonstrations or civil disturbances which have occurred in Britain since the late 1970s and which are usually referred to as riots. It must be emphasized, however, that none of the instances discussed below was 'racial' in the sense of involving only black people: they were clearly multiracial, involving black people of both Afro-Caribbean and Asian origin and white people. Nevertheless, each instance was seen at the time as 'racial' and has been remembered as such.
[...]

After the Bristol riot of 1980, the first of what was to become a series of major confrontations between the police and black (and white) people in Britain's inner cities, more than 100 people were charged with offences such as theft, threatening behaviour and possession of offensive weapons. As happened after Southall, most of these charges were heard by magistrates and most of the defendants were convicted and fined heavily. But three months after the disturbances, 16 people had the charges against them changed to the serious offences of riotous assembly, charges which were described by one defence lawyer as 'intensely speculative' but which were defended by the Director of Public Prosecutions. Despite this, charges against four of the defendants were dismissed at committal stage, three defendants were acquitted on the directions of the judge and the jury acquitted five others. Charges against the other four were dropped when the jury failed to agree (Joshua et al., 1983).

The behaviour of the magistrates in the cases which followed the Bristol 'riot' was a sign of how magistrates would respond to other civil disturbances. In 1981, it is clear that magistrates responded with considerable haste and panic to the events of April and July. Bail was frequently denied to people arrested during the disturbances. For instance only 35 per cent of those arrested in Brixton, south London, were granted bail with conditions attached and only 17 per cent given unconditional bail. In Nottingham only 16 per cent of those charged were granted bail on their first appearance in court, in Leeds the figure was only 4 per cent. Where bail was granted it was generally subject to strict conditions including curfews and the requirement of substantial monetary sureties.

By July 1982, three-quarters of those who had been dealt with had been convicted. The police had clearly learned the lesson of the Bristol riot trial and had pursued lesser charges against those arrested so that they could not be tried in front of juries. The policy appeared to pay off in that the overriding tendency appeared to be for magistrates to accept the evidence of police officers and reject the testimonies of defendants even when these were convincing. Particularly in the early cases, many of those convicted were sent to prison, even where they had no previous convictions. Overall, 40 per cent of those convicted of the more serious offences were sentenced to terms of imprisonment, while only 20 per cent of those convicted of summary offence were sent to prison. Those who were unemployed were more likely to be sent to prison than those in work, 46 per cent compared to 29 per cent. Those described as 'West Indian/African' by police were more likely than whites to be sent to prison, 38 per cent compared to 34 per cent. Asians, however, were less likely than either to be sent to prison, 23 per cent (Home Office, 1982).
[...]

The trials of those involved in the civil disturbances since 1979 illustrate not just the degree of panic which overtook the criminal justice system, but show too the extent to which the state, by means of the criminal justice system, is prepared to go to abandon normality and adopt 'special measures' in its efforts to restore 'law and order'. The parallels here with the situation which has pertained in Northern Ireland, which has been government by 'emergency' measures since the late 1960s, are considerable, as are those with the treatment of miners and their supporters arrested during the 1984/85 miners' strike. That it could do so and come up against very little political opposition indeed is a point to which I return in the conclusion.

Bail and remand

In theory, people facing criminal charges are presumed to have a right to be freed on bail pending trial. In practice, the presumption is easy to rebut and even where bail is granted it may be subject to stringent conditions laid down by the court. In the 1977 case of the Islington 18 who were arrested following the 'riot' at the Notting Hill Carnival, for instance, eight of the defendants were still in prison when their cases came to trial eight months after their arrest. The others had been released on bail only in the face of determined policy opposition and claims that witnesses would be intimidated, that the accused would abscond and that the accused had previous convictions. (In one case, the previous conviction in question was of theft of a sandwich some four years previously.) One of the accused was required to find a surety of £3000, all had to report to the police daily – one 14-year-old had to report twice daily – and virtually all had curfews imposed.

Even more stringent conditions were imposed in the case of the Bradford 12 some years later. Initially, all of the accused were refused bail and some were held in prison for three months. When they were released, sureties of up to £20,000 were demanded, passports had to be surrendered, a curfew from 10 p.m. to 7 a.m. was imposed, and daily reporting to the police was required. In addition, the defendants were prohibited from meeting one another except in the presence of a solicitor and were banned from taking part in any political activity, conditions which were clearly aimed at weakening the formation of a united defence campaign which was gaining widespread local and national support. These were clearly exceptional cases but they reflect the daily imposition of bail conditions on black defendants, conditions which can include curfews, geographical restrictions, sureties and so on. In any case, black people seem less likely than whites to be granted bail in the first place. Home Office figures show that black people, particularly those of Afro-Caribbean origin are over-represented in the remand prisoner population. Thus, the proportion of Afro-Caribbeans among untried males in prison was 7 to 10 per cent, somewhat higher than among the males received into prison under sentence, 6 to 7 per cent. (Both these figures are, of course, considerably higher than the proportion of Afro-Caribbeans in the population as a whole which is about 1 per cent for men aged 14 to 64.) The Home Office explains this by arguing that it is due in part to the higher proportion of those of Afro-Caribbean origin among untried prisoners in custody who were known later to have been found not guilty. But this does not explain why so many black people are being remanded into custody in the first place, particularly when so many are either acquitted in court or not proceeded against (17 per cent of Afro-Caribbeans, 3 per cent of Asians) and particularly when the proportions of those acquitted or not proceeded against is considerably higher than among whites, 6.5 per cent of Afro-Caribbeans, 5 per cent of Asians but only 3 per cent of whites (Home Office, 1986). Although there have been no studies of the effect of race on bail decisions (other than these bare figures) research has shown that the most significant factor in the courts' decision to grant bail or to remand in custody before trial is the decision by the *police* whether to grant bail or to hold in custody before appearance in court. This factor is followed by the nature of the offence and court policy (Jones, 1985). In other words, a decision by the police to refuse release influences the court in its decision whether to grant bail and if the police are exercising their discretion in a racist manner this will be further compounded, rather than alleviated, by the decision of the court.

Juries

Black people have continually had to fight for any right to be tried by a jury of their peers which has for so long been supposed to be right for all people in Britain. In 1969, for instance, the black political activist Michael X objected to being tried by an all-white jury but the court usher, when asked by the judge to find any black people in the court, could find only one man who had been called for jury service. In this case, the judge at least seemed prepared to acknowledge the unfairness of the situation to the defendant, but only a few months later the same judge refused to allow defence objections to an all-white jury. Similarly, in 1971 defence applications by barristers acting for people in the Mangrove trial for black people to serve on the jury were rejected and it was only through extensive use of the challenge by the nine defendants that two black men were called as jurors (Gordon, 1983).

As a result of such cases and the unwillingness of the courts to ensure that juries were genuinely multiracial, black defendants resorted to the use of the peremptory challenge to try to ensure that at least some jury members were black. In the trial which followed the 1980 Bristol riot, for instance, challenges were used to ensure that the defendants, all of whom were black, had their case heard by a jury which included a number of black people. All the defendants were either acquitted or had the charges against them dropped, but the case elicited a reaction from the judiciary and politicians which questioned the very idea of trial by jury and the right of defendants to challenge potential jurors. Conservative Member of Parliament Alan Clark (now a government minister), for instance, claimed that the proceedings showed that 'black jurors, whether out of racial loyalty, fear of intimidation or a combination of both, are highly unlikely to convict accused black persons of offences connected with civil disturbance' (*Hansard*, 19 May 1981) and only a few months later Lord Denning, then Master of the Rolls, told an audience of judges that the 'abuse of the right of challenge' by the defence at Bristol had been used to get a 'jury of their own choice or at any rate a jury on which there would be disagreement by more than two'. Conviction could therefore be avoided. The following year, Denning took the attack further, directly questioning the fitness of black people to serve as jurors. In his book, *What Next in the Law?*, Denning said that the English were no longer a 'homogenous race':

They are white and black, coloured and brown . . . some of them come from countries where bribery and graft are accepted ... and where stealing is a virtue so long as you are not found out. They no longer share the same code of morals or religious beliefs.

Using the Bristol trials as example of what he called 'jury packing', Denning claimed that not all British citizens were suitable to sit as jurors and that 'black, coloured and brown people do not have the same standards of conduct as whites'. In the face of the furore which followed the reporting of these passages and the threat of legal action from two of the black jurors in the Bristol trial, Denning's book was withdrawn and amended. In addition, Denning announced his retirement.
[...]

Sentencing

Many people have pointed to the disproportionate numbers of black people, especially those of Afro-Caribbean origin, in prisons, borstals and detention centres. The first results of the Prison Department's monitoring of the ethnic origin of prisoners were published in June 1986 (Home Office, 1986) and showed that:

about 8 per cent of the male prison population and 12 per cent of the female prison population were of West Indian or African origin, whereas they made up only between 1 and 2 per cent of the general population. They accounted for about 10 per cent of the male remand population, 7 per cent of the adult male sentenced population and 8.5 per cent of sentenced male young offenders.
... the proportion of prisoners of Asian origin was similar to or lower than their proportion in the general population. Overall they accounted for about 2.5 per cent of the male prison population and 2 per cent of the female prison population compared with about 3 per cent of the population as a whole.
... in the case of prisoners under sentence the disproportions were even greater. Thus black people made up 12 per cent of young offenders and 11.5 per cent of adult prisoners, but only 6 and 5 per cent respectively in the comparable age groups in the general population. For women, the corresponding proportions were 12 and 16 per cent compared with 6 and 5 per cent respectively for the comparable age groups.
... the average sentence length of black prisoners was also longer than that of white prisoners. In the case of under 21-year-olds, the average sentence of white prisoners was nine months, but for those of West Indian/African origin it was 12 months and for those of Asian origin it was 11 months. In the case of those prisoners over

the age of 21, the average sentence length for white prisoners was 13 months, but for those of West Indian/African origin it was 16.5 months and for those of Asian origin it was 26 months.

. . . black prisoners, whether of West Indian/African or of Asian origin had fewer convictions than white people sentenced for the same type of offence. For example, 38 per cent of whites had 11 or more previous convictions compared with 22 per cent of West Indian/ African origin prisoners and only 8 per cent of Asians; 62 per cent of whites had six or more convictions, but only 48 per cent of West Indian/African originating prisoners and 20 per cent of prisoners of Asian origin.

The first thing to be said about these figures is that they confirmed what black people and prisoners' groups (such as the National Prisoners Movement, PROP) had been saying for a long time: that black people were grossly over-represented in the prison population. These claims had always been denied by the prison authorities. That said, what conclusions can be drawn from these bare statistics about the operation of the criminal law and the criminal process in relation to black people? The answer must be very little. For instance, there is little information about the seriousness of the offences for which people have been sentenced, so it is not possible to know why black people are serving longer sentences than whites, other than that a high proportion of black people are convicted of offences involving illegal drugs which tend to carry higher than average sentences. In addition, it is known that a higher proportion of black people are either tried or sentenced in Crown Court which has greater sentencing powers than the lower magistrates courts. This may reflect differences within each offence group of the seriousness of the offences involved. It may also reflect differences in the proportion opting for trial in the Crown Court for offences which can be tried in either the magistrates court or the Crown Court, or the decisions made by magistrates courts in deciding whether an offence is more suitable for trial at a magistrates court or the Crown Court. In other words, black people may be facing more serious charges which can only be dealt with at Crown Court, or they are electing trial at Crown Court, perhaps in the belief that they will get a fairer trial there, or they are being sent to Crown Court by magistrates who feel their own powers are insufficient to deal with them.

Few studies have looked at the sentencing process and black people, and those that have are open to criticism on a number of grounds. Fludger, for instance, in his study of black people in borstal between 1974 and 1976, found that black inmates had fewer convictions than their white counterparts. They had, he said, arrived in borstal 'at an earlier stage in their criminal careers'. This could not be explained by their having been convicted of more serious offences but no alternative explanation was offered (Fludger, 1981). Since then only three studies have looked at the sentencing process in relation to black defendants. In the first study,

McConville and Baldwin, using data gathered for other studies in Birmingham in 1975 and 1976 and London in 1978 and 1979, looked at just under 1,400 contested and guilty plea cases in Crown Courts, including 339 cases involving black defendants. Matching the black and white defendants as closely as possible according to age, sex, criminal record and previous sentence, the authors concluded that 'there appears to be no evidence, of direct, systematic bias on racial lines in sentencing in the Crown Courts'. This finding, the authors described as 'tentative, but important' (McConville and Baldwin, 1982). This research, however, is open to criticism on a number of grounds. First, the research data had been gathered some years previously and for a different purpose. Second, the research looked only at Crown Courts and not at magistrates courts where most criminal cases are heard. Third, and most important, the study did not look at whether the criteria used to match the defendants were themselves influenced by race. For example, it might be the case that the black defendants had more previous convictions as a result of police harassment. There was a danger, one anonymous critic said at the time, that the findings would 'achieve a publicity they do not deserve'.

The second study, by Crow and Cove, did look at magistrates courts, examining 668 cases, including those of just over 100 black defendants. The authors concluded that there was no basis for concluding that 'non-Whites' were likely to receive different sentences than 'Whites'. In criminal justice terms, they said, the cases of the different ethnic groups in the sample were handled 'in similar ways and the sentences they are given are similar'. But unlike McConville and Baldwin, who had at least stated that their findings were tentative, Crowe and Cove concluded their article with a claim, certainly not justified by such a small piece of research, that their findings 'may serve to contribute to the development of confidence in the court system among ethnic minorities' (Crowe and Cove, 1984, p. 417).

A third, even smaller study was that carried out by Mair as a pilot study for a more detailed piece of research. Mair collected data in two magistrates courts in Leeds and Bradford, covering 1,173 cases, but including only 123 black defendants. Mair found no significant differences in the sentencing of black and white defendants except that black people were considerably less likely than whites to be given probation orders and more likely to be given community service orders. He also found that Asian defendants were less likely than whites to be referred for social inquiry reports before sentence, while defendants of Afro-Caribbean origin were more likely to be so referred. This is a point of some importance to which I return later. Mair concluded that although it was difficult to draw any firm conclusions, the evidence did not support the 'more optimistic assessment' made by Crowe and Cove (Mair, 1986, p. 134).

The evidence on the sentencing of black people, such as it is, raises more questions than it answers. Above all, what none of the studies has been able to explain is the disproportionate number of black people in the prisons and other penal establishments. This has implications for future research, a point to which I return at the conclusion of this article.

Probation

One area of possible differential treatment which might result in black people running a higher risk than white defendants of being sentenced to imprisonment is that of probation. As mentioned above, for example. Mair (1986) found in his small sentencing survey that black people were less likely to be given probation than white defendants, while an earlier study of the West Midlands showed that black adults were significantly under-represented on probation, but that children and young people were over-represented on supervision. In addition, black people were, in general, significantly more likely to be under supervision after release from imprisonment or detention, but less likely to be on supervision before release (Taylor, 1981). A few small studies illustrate some of the reasons for these findings.

For example, one study of probation officers' perceptions concluded that probation staff lacked an adequate understanding of Rastafarianism, seeing it either in psychological terms as a form of deviance which stemmed from 'inadequate socialisation', or in sociological terms seeing it as an ethnic solution to a supposed 'identity crisis'. Hardly any officers even considered the possibility that black people might adhere to Rastafarianism because of their material situation, while most saw it as an individual, psychologically-determined phenomenon. It was hardly surprising that all the probation staff interviewed said they had encountered 'problems' in their dealings with Rastas. Not surprisingly either, only 1 of 15 social enquiry reports examined in this study recommended that the subject be placed on probation (Carrington and Denney, 1981).

Other studies, albeit also on a small scale, have looked at the social enquiry reports prepared for courts by probation officers. One such study found that a number of reports included a range of racist attitudes and sentiments. One report looked at, for example, spoke of the subject's 'mild paranoid attitude which I believe to be part of a cultural more [sic] associated with his ethnic propensities' (Whitehouse, 1983). The potential effect of such remarks is considerable and could well result in black defendants being more likely to be given a custodial sentence.

A more recent study, again carried out in the West Midlands, found that black defendants were more likely than whites to be given an immediate custodial sentence, 35 per cent compared to 21 per cent, and that considerably fewer black defendants received community service orders, although again this was a small scale study covering 222 cases, a quarter of them involving black defendants. An analysis of the social enquiry reports concluded that reports on black defendants were more likely to include negative comments. These, the report noted, were often the result of attempts to describe clients objectively but such attempts were based on implicit assumptions of normality and which ignored the consequences of structural inequality, for instance, that black people were more likely than their white counterparts to be unemployed or homeless. In addition, many of the reports made unnecessary references to the subject's mental state. Although recommendations for non-custodial sentences were made in 90 per cent of the reports on black defendants compared with 88 per cent of the reports on white defendants, the courts were less likely to follow the recommendations on black defendants than on whites. The courts accepted the probation workers recommendations in 43 per cent of the cases involving black defendants and in 58 per cent of the cases involving white defendants. Where the recommendation was not followed, black defendants were more likely to receive a custodial sentence, 50 per cent of such cases compared with 35 per cent of white defendants. This difference could not be explained by black defendants having been convicted of more serious offences. If anything, the report said, it was the white defendants who had been convicted of proportionately more serious offences (Pymm and Lines, 1987).

Through a combination of overt racism, a patronizing attempt to 'understand' black clients and a failure to understand the material situation of black defendants, the probation service has not only failed defendants but has put them at risk and contributed to their criminalization by the courts.

[. . .]

Conclusion

Black people's experience of the British criminal justice system shows clearly that the rhetoric of the law does not accord with the reality of its practice. The law is not colour-blind, but a means by which black people have been subject to a process of criminalization. Yet, this process has gone largely unrecognized and undocumented by organizations supposedly concerned with the advancement of civil liberties, the protection of rights and the achievement of justice. Black people have been invisible in their work. At the same time, the 'race relations industry' must itself be indicted in this respect as must academics and other researchers who have, with few exceptions, failed to investigate the many issues which the black experience has thrown up and the many problems this has posed for liberal democratic theory of the rule of law and an impartial judiciary.[2]

Two particular issues stand out. First, throughout the 1970s and early 1980s, black activists (and some white prison campaigners such as those in PROP, the National Prisoners Movement) pointed to the growing numbers of black people in British prisons, borstals and detention centres and at the racist treatment of black people in prisons. Yet there was little recognition indeed of this issue outside the black community itself. Secondly, we might note the failure – by academics, civil liberties groups, race relations organizations or whatever – to monitor the treatment by the criminal justice system of those arrested and charged after the urban disturbances in 1981 and 1985 and thereby call power to account. In both cases, the concerns of black people went unheeded. (None of this is to suggest that black people have been alone in their experience of the reality of the criminal law. The 'rule of law' has been rather less than reality for numerous other groups in society. It is to emphasize the particular black experience and to offer a corrective to accounts – even critical ones – which would ignore it.)

Since the 1981 urban riots, of course, this lack of interest in black people appears to have changed as organizations (and some academics) have fallen over themselves in a rush to 'take race seriously'. Yet, appearances can be, and often are, deceptive. The dominant response in recent years to the interaction of race and the criminal justice system has mirrored that adopted by many other professions in Britain. This is an approach which is best described as 'multicultural' in which the 'answer' is seen to lie in greater 'sensitivity' towards black people, greater understanding of their cultures and lifestyles, and so on – usually to be achieved through multifarious forms of 'training' combined with 'equal opportunity' policies and the recruitment of more black personnel, whether as lawyers, probation officers, magistrates or whatever. Such an approach ignores the central question of racism, the institutional practices of a society based on unequal social, economic and power relations. It avoids the fundamental issue of the political economy of black labour in Britain in the late 1980s.

This political economy sought the presence of black workers from the colonies and former colonies for the purposes of post-war economic reconstruction, as units of labour which would depart when their labour was no longer needed. But when it became clear that the new immigrants would not simply lift up their tools and go, their presence was defined as a problem in successive immigration laws. These both defined black people as a problem whose numbers therefore had to be controlled and erected barriers in the way of family reunification, thus encouraging the depar- ture of those already here (Sivanandan, 1982). At the same time, the enforcement of the law turned increasingly inwards, redefining breaches of the law and leading to increasing numbers of deportations and removals, and challenging the rights of those settled here to welfare benefits and other services (Gordon, 1985).

Just as immigration law defined black people as a problem whose numbers had to be controlled, so black people already settled in Britain (and determined to stay here) were increasingly seen as a problem, particularly by the police who imposed their own definition – of a 'law and order' problem. Black people, particularly but not exclusively black youth, were portrayed as openly disorderly and criminal, as requiring special policing practices and as deserving the treatment they received in the rest of the criminal justice system. The police, as Stuart Hall has said in the quotation at the start of this article, have undertaken to police the 'social crisis of the cities', a social crisis in which there is no place for black labour, especially that of black youth, and little pretence that black people are here on anything but sufferance and on condition that they accept their subordinate status in British society without complaint. At the end of a long line of agencies and programmes aimed at the forceable assimilation, containment and control of black people – from schools to Manpower Servicedom to urban programmes – stand the police and behind them the force of the criminal law and the criminal justice system. Black people, it seems, must be disciplined and punished if they will not be contained.

At the same time, the association of black people with crime so firmly made by the police and sections of the mass media and the criminalization of black people by the agencies of the criminal justice system have become central to racist ideology. Criminality and disorder took the place of disease, sexuality and miscegenation which had previously been the central themes in public discussion of race in Britain: these supposed features have increasingly been identified as essential parts of black culture, emphasizing the supposed 'otherness' of blacks in Britain, and serving as common-sense explanations for national crisis and decline (Gilroy, 1987; Hall *et al.*, 1978).

It is always tempting to conclude accounts of this nature by calling for further research and study. Those of us involved in research have a tendency (to put it mildly) always to be looking for new areas of work. Yet, in this case, there *is* a need for further research, for further knowledge. How, for instance, do the courts deal with black defendants before them, not just in the major trials of the kind described in this article but, equally important, on a day-to-day basis? Why are there many more black people in prison than might be deduced from their numbers in the population as a whole? How do the courts respond to serious urban disturbances? These are all important questions to which we have only the most partial answers. Such research should not be considered an end in itself, nor should it be allowed to be a means of assisting the management of the 'black problem', as most race relations research has been (Bourne, 1980). It can be, and needs to be, seen as a means of understanding the parameters of contemporary racism, a racism which has been central to the movement towards authoritarianism in Britain at least since the late 1960s. In so doing it can also be a means of empowering black people in their struggles against criminalization.

Notes

1 I use the word 'black' throughout this article to mean people of Afro-Caribbean *or* Asian origin, the predominant use in Britain, particularly by black people themselves. Where a particular report or document uses other terminology I have followed this, even though it makes for some inconsistency.

2 In this respect it is a matter of some regret that a major research project on black people and the criminal justice system, to have been carried out by Maureen Cain, failed to secure the necessary funding.

References

Bourne, J. (1980) 'Cheerleaders and ombudsmen: the sociology of race relations in Britain, *Race and Class*, **21**(4).

Carrington, B. and Denney, D. (1981) 'Young Rastafarians and the probation service', *Probation Journal*, **28**(4).

Crowe, I. and Cove, J. (1984) 'Ethnic minorities and the courts', *Criminal Law Review*, July 1984.

Denning, Lord (1982) *What Next in the Law?* London, Butterworth.

Fludger, N. (1981) *Ethnic Minorities in Borstal*, London, Home Office Prison Department.

Gilroy, P. (1987) *There Ain't No Black in the Union Jack: the cultural politics of race and nation*, London, Hutchinson.

Gordon, P. (1983) *White Law: racism in the police, courts and prisons*, London, Pluto Press.

Gordon, P. (1985) *Policing Immigration: Britain's internal controls*, London, Pluto Press.

Hall, S. (1979) *Drifting into a Law and Order Society*, London, Cobden Trust.

Hall, S. *et al.* (1978) *Policing the Crisis: mugging, the state and law and order*. London, Macmillan.

Hil, R. (1980) 'Black kids, white justice', *New Society*, 24 January 1980.

Home Office (1982) *The Outcome of Arrests during the Serious Incidents of Public Disorder in July and August*, London, Home Office.

Home Office (1986) *The Ethnic Origins of Prisoners: the prison population on 30 June 1985 and persons received, July 1984–March 1985*, London, Home Office.

Jones, P. (1985) 'Remand decisions at magistrates courts', in Moxon, D. (ed.), *Managing Criminal Justice: a collection of papers*, London, HMSO.

Joshua, H. *et al.* (1983) *To Ride the Storm: the 1980 Bristol 'riot' trial and the state*, London, Heinemann.

McConville, M. and Baldwin, J. (1982) 'The influence of race on sentencing in England', *Criminal Law Review*, October 1982.

Mair, G. (1986) 'Ethnic minorities, probation and the magistrates' courts', *British Journal of Criminology*, **26**(2).

Pymm, L. and Lines, P. (1987) *Report on the Birmingham Court Social Enquiry Report Monitoring Exercise*, Birmingham, West Midlands Probation Service.

Sivanandan, A. (1982) *A Different Hunger: writings on black resistance*, London, Pluto Press.

Spicer, R. (1981) *Conspiracy: law, class and society*, London, Lawrence and Wishart.

Taylor, W. (1981) *Probation and After-Care in a Multi-Racial Society*, London, Commission for Racial Equality.

Whitehouse, P. (1983) 'Race, bias and social enquiry reports', *Probation Journal*, **30**(2).

Source: Gordon, P. (1988) 'Black people and the criminal law: rhetoric and reality', *International Journal of the Sociology of Law*, **16**(3).

PART 3

RACISM AND EQUAL OPPORTUNITY POLICY

INTRODUCTION

As a matter of course we need to take care that in using a given concept, there is agreement about what it means. And failing that we need to ensure that disagreements are at least openly discussed. This is particularly so in the case of 'equal opportunity', for, as Nick Jewson and David Mason show in 'The theory and practice of equal opportunities policies: liberal and radical approaches', not only are there two quite different concepts of equal opportunity policy, but we find that among its analysts and practitioners it is widely assumed that the concept is straighforward and self-evident. Not surprisingly, perhaps, what the concept entails in practice is often the subject of considerable disagreement. In part this confusion can be ascribed to a failure to examine adequately the assumptions upon which views about equal opportunity are based and in part it reflects a difference between radical and less-radical approaches to the subject.

At first sight it seems quite simple to provide a general formulation that encapsulates the principles of equal opportunity. To borrow from a landmark US Supreme Court judgment we can speak of 'the removal of artificial, arbitrary and unnecessary barriers to employment when the barriers operate to discriminate on the basis of racial and other impermissible classification.' And we can easily encompass the question of institutional or indirect racism if we specify that this applies both to overt discrimination and to practices which, though they are equal in application, discriminate in their effect. Such a formulation is at the heart, not only of equal opportunity, but also of the overlapping concept of meritocracy. According to the former 'no-one is denied training or job for reasons that have nothing to do with their competence or capacity' (Seear, 1981, p. 295) and according to the latter achievement is and should be increasingly based on education, qualifications, skills and experience and decreasingly based on ascriptive factors of birth, rank and so on. Put in these terms it seems unexceptional to say that it will be to the benefit of both employers and employees if these concepts secure general acceptance: applicants for jobs will be chosen on merit and employers will have the widest choicc of personnel. In 'Equal opportunities policy and race equality', Peter Gibbon explores the idea that equal opportunity policies – by introducing rationalized bureaucratic procedures to the selection of personnel – may seem equally attractive to capitalist enterprises and to disadvantaged groups alike. Such a view accords with the idea that there are qualitative differences between employees that can be objectively identified and, once identified, can be used as the basis for selection, access to training, promotion and so on.

If qualifications are seen as the essential defence for black workers against discrimination in the labour market we may assume that even when black applicants possess seemingly appropriate qualifications, if they do not obtain jobs as readily as their white counterparts then it is merely because the principle of equal opportunity has not yet been as widely accepted as that of meritocracy. Yet, drawing on his research in Sheffield, Gibbon found that neither the *existence* of an equal opportunity policy, nor even its *implementation* seemed to produce any change in employment outcomes. If this is so, how do we account for it? Like Jewson and Mason, Gibbon ascribes some importance to a confusion between different interpretations of equal opportunity policies and different expectations of what is to be gained from their introduction. However, the degree of discrimination against black applicants should not lead us to take a complacent view of how the labour market operates in practice: that is, to make the assumption that it is fair for everyone *except* for blacks or women – in fact the only groups for whom 'fair equality of opportunity' is legally enshrined. On the contrary, as Offe (1976) has argued persuasively, the identification by employers of qualitative differences between job applicants is less an objective process conducted along meritocractic lines than a legitimation of employer authority and control which, because of its very imprecision, permits the continued widespread use of ascriptive labels, supposedly a thing of the past.

No doubt black applicants with given qualifications are more likely to be labelled as unsuitable, and conversely less likely to be regarded as employable, than equally qualified whites, but the labels 'suitable' and 'unsuitable' are hardly objective, or certainly not as objective as widely assumed. But even were they objective, and if employers took a 'colour-blind' approach to recruitment, the outcome might still be seen as racist even if the intention was otherwise. We can see this by using the concept of '"discrimination *before* the market" [which] denies those who are discriminated against the same opportunities as others have to develop their capability' (Phelps-Brown, 1977, p. 145). Thus inequalities in housing, in the provision of social services and, above all, in education, handicap job applicants at a later date. The 1976 Race Relations Act widened the legal definition of discrimination to include policies which, irrespective of intention, have the effect of disproportionately excluding black people from access to housing, employment and other spheres. But this is far from being a simple extension of the concept, its application or its implications. If one takes equal opportunity in employment as a case in point, the complexities grow larger as the notion of discrimination is extended. For example, we might anticipate that attention is paid not only to barriers to entry into different occupational categories, firms or industries, but also to barriers facing those already on the bottom rung in these locations and to access to training programmes which may facilitate promotion. But is it enough to ensure that equality of opportunity prevails from now on if the disproportions of staff resulting from previous inequalities remain? If not, then is 'compensation' to be extracted only from succeeding generations of applicants and those at junior job levels while those who have reached senior job levels in part by the exclusion of black competitors, remain unaffected?

These questions may be in advance of what the law is prepared to contemplate. For, as Lord Scarman remarked, the idea of the 'statutory black man' remains unacceptable. Nevertheless, as Lustgarten and Edwards make clear in their article 'Racial inequality and the limits of the law', which has been extensively revised and updated for this volume, *what* the law is prepared to contemplate is at the heart of the issue. In this sense, to take a particular stance towards reverse discrimination, contract compliance, the possibility of class action, and the scale of damages that might influence the conduct of employers, should perhaps be subsumed under the more general issue of whether the law can be seen as a means of achieving social policy and, indeed, of what that social policy is.

The importance of these questions, particularly of those that relate closely to the urgency with which employers approach the issue of equal opportunity, becomes clearer if we consider some of the reasons why – when we examine the effectiveness of equal opportunity policies at a general level – the *appearance* of change may be greater than the *reality* of change. In the first place, introducing change into complex, formal organizations is a complicated matter. It therefore should come as no surprise that there is a wide gap between formal commitments on equal opportunity and developing a strategy of implementation that may prove capable of transforming decision-making with regard to recruitment, promotion and so on. In addition to this, as we have already suggested, it is much too simplistic to assume that all that is needed is to develop explicit criteria and clear procedures for judging applicants. The increased formalization of employment procedures can provide an organizational smokescreen for discrimination, contrary to their presumed purpose. It is for this reason that in assessing the 'life chances' of equal opportunity policies we must pay particular attention to organizational politics, to who are the natural custodians of equal opportunity policies, to the leverage they exert and to the assumptions that they and others bring to the subject. Ken Young in his article 'Approaches to policy development in the field of equal opportunities' takes these issues further in respect of local authority policy and practice. In particular, he is concerned with the ways in which formal and informal structures of power, authority and influence – and the means by which these are expressed – serve to undermine equal opportunity strategies undertaken by local authorities. Though Young centres his analysis on organizational possibilities and constraints, nevertheless he acknowledges the wider context of inflated expectations about what local authorities could achieve, of the extent to which many local councillors and officials wait patiently for the concern with racial equality to diminish, and other influences. This wider context is the subject of Gideon Ben-Tovim *et al.*'s article, 'A political analysis of local struggles for racial equality'. Here Ben-Tovim and his colleagues explore what they describe as the politics of racial inequality and the role of various political forces in maintaining or reducing these inequalities. In particular, they emphasize that the most common sign of a determination to resist the claims of racial equality is not merely a general refusal to acknowledge the consequences of racism, but a specific insistence on pursuing 'colour blind' policies.

References

Offe, C. (1976) *Industry and Inequality*, London, Edward Arnold.

Phelps-Brown (1977) *The Inequality of Pay*, London, Oxford University Press.

Seear, N. (1981) 'The management of equal opportunity' in Braham, P., Rhodes, E. and Pearn, M. (eds) *Discrimination and Disadvantage in Employment: the experience of Black workers*, London, Harper and Row.

11 A POLITICAL ANALYSIS OF LOCAL STRUGGLES FOR RACIAL EQUALITY

GIDEON BEN-TOVIM, JOHN GABRIEL,
IAN LAW, KATHLEEN STREDDER

Introduction

The analysis of local politics and struggles for racial equality which makes up this article has been developed on the basis of our involvement in local politics. The raw data of our political experience have been accumulated through our participation in and contact with local organizations (e.g. community relations councils, antiracist groups and the Labour Party), our contact with local officers and politicians, including our roles as members of formal local committees, and our involvement in local campaigns. Our research has been carried out in Liverpool and Wolverhampton over a six-year period, although our involvement in local politics in both areas dates back considerably beyond this. More specifically, our work has included campaigns to secure and implement an equal opportunity policy with Liverpool City Council and to alter racist housing allocations and management structures in the Council and major local housing associations; in Wolverhampton it has included race-related political interventions in the fields of education and youth provision.
[. . .]

The study of race itself has thrown up a variety of perspectives. Each develops its own analysis in terms of a particular conception of race and of the nature and source of racial inequality. In contrast to many positions, we choose to focus on the politics of racial inequality and on the role played by political forces in both reinforcing those inequalities on the one hand and seeking to reduce them on the other. We are not concerned, therefore, with exploring race relations in terms of culture or in terms of biological differences where those are said to manifest themselves in intelligence or (in the case of sociobiology) in innate tendencies to compete and discriminate on racial grounds. Nor do we wish to explain race relations or racialized labour in terms of class inequalities, capital accumulation and patterns of migration. This is not to suggest that race does not have a cultural or class dimension or even a symbolic significance

attached to biological 'differences' (e.g. colour). Our concern with these perspectives is the secondary role assigned by them to the analysis of politics and political intervention. At most, politics becomes a kind of residue, or what is left (for manoeuvrability) once the determining factors, i.e. culture, biology or the economy, have exerted their influence.
[...]

The economy does have a place in the political analysis of race, but its role should not usurp the significance of the political processes to which it is subject, i.e. as an arena of struggle in which policies and practices with regard to investment, employment and management that serve to reinforce racial inequalities can be set against forces within the labour movement or the antiracist movement which seek to redress them.

Our conception of politics therefore is not restricted to formal governmental institutions but refers to a mode of analysing institutional structures and relations in general. Within these institutional contexts, it focuses on sites of struggle and conflict, the outcome of which cannot be predicted. [...] In this article therefore we shall conceive race policy initiatives neither as necessarily tokenistic nor as correct solutions to problems but rather as resources whose outcomes depend on the mobilization of forces for and against racial equality.
[...]

Our analysis begins with a consideration of one overriding experience of local governments from the standpoint of local organizations. This experience can be encapsulated in the notion of marginalization. The means by which the process of marginalization operates is linked to those conditions referred to above which in turn provide the basis for the exercise of power. We consider examples of these conditions in the second part of the article. We have also argued in this Introduction that those conditions are in part defined through and as a result of struggle. The role of antiracist forces in helping to contain and redefine those conditions through pressure for political including policy reforms will be considered in the third part of this article.

Local politics and struggles for racial equality in Liverpool and Wolverhampton

The process of marginalization

One primary and pervasive experience of local organizations which take up the issues of racism and racial equality with local government is that of marginalization. One effect of this experience is to push antiracist forces away from the centre, towards the periphery of local politics (cf. Ouseley,

1984). Not surprisingly, then, struggles against racism have become struggles within and against marginalization. The process of marginalization can be identified by a close examination of three forms of relation between local government and local organizations.

Marginalization through consultation

Governments, both central and local, of all political complexions have attached, at least nominally, some significance to the involvement of local communities in local decision-making. Race-related policies and policy documents have, albeit sometimes ambiguously, laid stress on the need to consult minority communities. The reality of consultation, however, in our view can hardly be said to represent a significant advance in terms of an extension of local democracy. On the contrary, and almost without exception, the variety of consultative measures in which we have been involved or which we have observed close at hand have served to emphasize inequalities between consultors and consulted. This has been the case irrespective of the particular form of consultative measure.

Committees, located within local government structures, have become an increasingly popular form of local consultation. These sometimes have statutory status, as do the Race Relations Committees in both Wolverhampton and Liverpool. At other times they are created in response to a particular issue or crisis, have only informal links with the existing committee structure and thus take on a semi-statutory status. In each of these cases, however, elected representatives, sometimes attended by local officers, sit alongside representatives of local organizations, and overall the committee has a brief or remit.

Although statutory and semi-statutory committees would appear to provide the 'best' opportunity for consultation to involve serious dialogue and responsible action on the part of local city councils, the experience of local organizations on Liverpool's Race Relations Liaison Committee demonstrates the circumstances of community powerlessness even at this level. Devoid of any rights or sanctions, the Black Caucus of the Race Relations Liaison Committee has witnessed formal decisions regularly ignored, or directly opposed, in the Policy and Finance Committee or, in some cases, in the leadership caucus of the Party Group, from which the Black Caucus is excluded.

This process, which included the rejection of a million-pound DoE grant-aided sheltered housing scheme for the ethnic elderly, culminated in the appointment by the Labour Group of a Principal Race Relations Adviser despite massive objections by the black representatives on the appointment committee. These objections were based on the appointee's total lack of relevant qualifications and experience and on his stance on racial inequality which he subordinated to the more general issue of urban deprivation and class inequality. The ensuing boycott of this appointment by local authority unions and black organizations led to the suspension of the Race Relations Liaison Committee and the previously legitimated black representatives and groups were branded by the Labour leadership as an 'unrepresentative faction' (*Black Linx*, 1984).

A second form of consultation is the variety of one-off public meetings organized by local authorities in response to the increasing demands by community groups over the last decade. These include day conferences, seminars, workshops and exhibitions on a range of issues (e.g. mother-tongue teaching or policing practices) and are viewed by members and officers of the local authority as consultative exercises, in so far as they are concerned with community-linked issues. The fact is, however, that most often they fail to provide the opportunity for the exchange and development of ideas, let alone for the making of policy. On the contrary, they are more likely to create a false consensus and a context in which dissension and conflict are covertly, if not openly, discouraged; and recommendations, statements of intent and even written reports which emerge from them are likely to be disregarded.

A third form of local consultation is the *ad hoc* meeting which involves politicians and officers on the one hand and representatives of local organizations on the other. This obviously differs from the committee in that it has no statutory status and therefore is subject not only to termination at the discretion of the elected representatives but also to their whim and will for the nature, aim and action of the meeting. Consultations in Wolverhampton with the local Council for Community Relations [WCCR] over funding arrangements under Section 11 provide a clear example of the problems encountered here. The differences in power between the political and officer leadership on the one hand and WCCR on the other manifested themselves in such things as control over the agenda and the direction of the discussion; control over the information that was to be made available; control over those decisions that are negotiable and those that are not; and, ultimately, the power of veto.

Antiracism as extremism

The absence of any genuine forms of participatory machinery has encouraged alternative kinds of community response to emerge. In Wolverhampton, for instance, the absence of adequate forms of consultation over Section 11 provoked black organizations to write a letter of complaint to the Home Office, to threaten a boycott of local elections, and in one instance to stand an independent candidate against the incumbent Labour Party member. Such actions were dismissed as naïve and extreme by local Labour politicians, although they were nevertheless predictable given the failure of local organizations to have any effect on the Local Authority.

In the case of the appointment of the Principal Race Relations Adviser in Liverpool, black groups were forced to undertake a variety of protests (a sit-in, a disruption of a council meeting, a march and a regular vigil outside the municipal offices). These actions were used by the Labour Group to label, isolate and undermine the opposition that was mounted in this way, through slurs of 'self-appointed leaders', using 'alien' methods of protest, encouraging 'violent' activities and 'dividing the working class'.

It is not only the various kinds of reaction described above which attract labels of extremism and fanaticism. Equally unacceptable is the content of antiracist arguments, which is often dismissed as hysterical, outrageous or pure fanaticism. Antiracist arguments are described in these ways because they fall outside local bureaucratic definitions and interpretations of race problems (e.g. those which explain race problems in terms of cultural differences). These official definitions, articulated by principal officers and administrators, have become deeply embedded in professional policy and practice. Their respectability and apparent neutrality often serve both directly and indirectly to legitimate local popular racist opinion.

Antiracism, since it challenges the prevailing norms inherent in institutional policy and practice, is thus inevitably regarded as extreme. This is particularly the case in so far as local organizations are encouraged to resort to direct action, protest, accusation and demonstration. In our experience there is a tendency for politicians and professionals to capitalize on the extremities of antiracism and to use them as a pretext for inaction rather than responding systematically to the principles underpinning antiracism and the struggle for racial equality.

[...]

Funding cultural initiatives

There is a tendency on the part of local authorities to restrict race relations initiatives to one-off, high-profile measures rather than to develop a sustained, mainstream-oriented programme of action. This tendency is in part a reflection of trends within central government philosophy and funding policies. In particular, inner city initiatives including the Urban Programme and *Policy for the Inner Cities* (Cmnd 6845) have provided a framework within which funds have, somewhat ambiguously, been made available for meeting the special needs of minority groups. The term 'ethnic group' becomes significant in this political context, since resources are thus linked to ethnic (or cultural) differences or needs (cf. Stewart and Whitting, 1983).

Inner city policies have been directed on a selective basis to those geographical areas of highest social need, including both Liverpool and Wolverhampton. Resources have thus been allocated to fund a range of local centres and projects for Afro-Caribbean, Asian and Chinese communities. In general, the funding of these centres and other limited project iniatives provides confirmation that measures are being taken by the two local authorities, a fact which may be expedient in the aftermath of street conflicts or 'riots'. At the same time such funding can serve to divert attention away from racial inequalities which are institutionally generated and/or maintained through mainstream provision. The failure to link these *ad hoc* cultural initiatives to any kind of participation in formal political processes has further served to immunize local organizations and groups. Not only are cultural initiatives expedient, visible and non-threatening through their isolation. They are also relatively cheap, particularly for local authorities who are able to claim approximately 75 per cent of the total cost of their programmes etc. from central government.

[...]

Conditions which serve to marginalize antiracist forces

Local political ideologies

We have suggested above that power in social relations could be analysed in the first instance in terms of those conditions which create the potential for its effective exercise. In this section we shall identify a number of such conditions, the first of which has been the prevalence of a particular form of racial ideology, which has been referred to elsewhere as 'colour-blindness' (Ouseley, 1982b), so called because it fails to acknowledge the specific dimension of racism and racial inequality and consequently resists any attempt to tackle racism independently of the patterns of urban deprivation or class inequality. Its strength lies in its compatibility with various shades of political opinion and its consequent accommodation within certain brands of liberalism, conservatism and socialism as well as the universalistic ('a-political') ideologies and practices of public administration and its practitioners. Each of these broader ideologies in turn is able to justify action, or more strictly in the case of colour-blindness inaction, through a defence of the supremacy of individual rights, national interest or class struggle over the needs, disadvantages and rights of racially defined groups.

What binds the threads of colour-blind ideologies therefore is the absence of racism (except when it is defined in the very narrow sense of overt and conscious discrimination). What varies is the justification for the absence which may in our experience be anticipated in various ways, including assertions that to raise the question of racism is divisive, an incitement to racial discord or an invitation for a 'white backlash', or that the problems attributed to black people are shared with the white population, the working-class, or all in the inner cities.

This failure to acknowledge the specific dimensions of racism is linked in terms of its policy implications to various forms of resistance to positive action: thus special provision, e.g. for ethnic elders or Asian girls, has at times been opposed in the name of a commitment to integrated facilities, despite the exclusion of black people from such provision or its unsuitability for particular minorities. Positive action has also been dismissed on the basis of opposition to 'preferential treatment', however much existing practices are shown to favour the indigenous white population.

Thus the whole spectrum of political ideologies may each appeal to conventional forms of reason and morality which in so far as they continue to prevail serve to undermine the force and credibility of antiracist politics. The latter has thus the formidable task of forging links with positions which appear broadly incompatible at one level (e.g. conservatism, liberalism, socialism) but which converge in the common refusal to acknowledge the specific character of racism and racial inequality along with the policy implications which follow from this acknowledgement.

Legislation and central policy initiatives

The relationship between those conditions which serve to marginalize antiracist forces can be regarded as both mutually supportive and at times inconsistent. In other words, we do not regard them as some kind of chain of cause and effect; nor do we regard one condition as more significant than the others. Central policy initiatives, including legislation, can under certain conditions be used both in support of and in opposition to political ideologies, such as colour-blindness, operating at a local level.

In general, central policy initiatives add up to a patchy, somewhat inconsistent framework comprising laws, policy statements, directives, circulars, reports, regulations and consultative machinery. In so far as race has become an issue centrally, it has been confined to a number of special policies which have served to reinforce overtly negative (as far as black people are concerned) formulations of the race problem (e.g. policies on immigration and policing). It has also provided an extremely loose, permissive and ambiguous framework within which positive policies need or need not be developed locally (e.g. the Urban Programme or the Race Relations Act with its non-directive support for 'positive action' initiatives). Finally, the 'special' nature of these intiatives has left a whole range of policy fields untouched in terms of providing directives, regulations and terms of enforcement for the development of positive initiatives at a local level.

Section 11 of the 1966 Local Government Act exemplifies all three of the above characteristics. Section 11 was not in terms of its inception a measure designed to redress racial injustices or to promote racial equality. It was more a form of financial compensation paid by central government to certain local authorities for (staffing) expenses arising from the settlement of immigrants and from associated 'problems' within their local areas (Young, 1983). In this sense then Section 11 serves to reinforce negative views of black people and to make understandable and legitimate local hostility at their presence. The absence of any positive framework for the specific allocation of the monies available allowed local authorities to claim funding for staff salaries without developing special job responsibilities or even, for the most part, identifying holders of Section 11 posts. Finally, even if Section 11 had been used positively, it would have always remained a 'special measure' and its central administrative location within the Home Office would have prevented it from providing a means for a fundamental rethinking of mainstream policy within local education authorities, social services and other departments.

Local bureaucratic control of policy-making and administration

It is not only political representatives who are resistant to pressure from below which seeks to challenge prevalent ideologies, policies and practices. Senior officers, administrators and public practitioners (e.g. teachers) have all developed strategies which can be used to inhibit initiatives aimed at promoting racial equality (cf. Young and Connelly, 1981).

[. . .]

Financial constraints inhibiting redistribution

Cut-backs in central government's financial support to local authorities, alongside increased controls on how local government allocates its resources, can provide strong additional arguments for resisting positive change. What is perhaps more revealing is the consistency with which positive action has been resisted over the past twenty years irrespective of changes in the levels and form of financial control by central and local government. In our view, economic austerity and growing central control over local budgeting are not as significant in themselves as they are in terms of the pretexts they have provided for further inaction.

In our experience many local organizational proposals aimed at eliminating institutional racism have at best entailed no additional cost and at worst required the redistribution of current expenditure. The expansion of the black workforce within the local public sector, the attachment of equal opportunity conditions to public contracts with the private sector, the creation of participatory structures within local government involving black organizations and parents in the running of public services, the expansion of a youth counselling service at the expense of traditional youth club provision, and the allocation of black applicants to council properties on an equal basis to whites are all possible within both the limits imposed by central government and local pressure to minimize rate increases.

In conclusion to this section we would therefore argue that there exist strong forces within local government which can serve and, in our experience, have served to militate against the use of the local public sector as an instrument of positive social change in the pursuit of racial equality. Deep-seated cultural traditions within the Town Hall foster political styles of rhetoric, posturing and megalomania among politicians which not only serve to alienate the vast majority of apolitical constituents but also have a wearing effect on those committed to positive social change. These traditions can thus serve to reinforce the strength of bureaucratic tradition which has little to challenge it from above. Such effective control is thus exercised both defensively and self-interestedly and is invariably justified in the name of administrative neutrality. What is perhaps most disturbing of all, in our expeience, is the extent to which both politicians and officers have joined forces in the face of pressure from antiracist forces from outside the Town Hall. In the course of their active conscious collusion, which we have witnessed directly in the context of consultation, they have employed with considerable sophistication the clichéd practices of gerrymandering and filibustering in order to withstand the pressure from representatives of the community.

Forms of antiracist struggle

The marginalization of antiracist forces and the conditions which make marginalization possible have been the focus of the first part of our analysis. The purpose so far has been to establish the context in which racism is challenged and racial equality pursued. In what remains of this article we examine three different forms of struggle, each of which offers its own particular challenge to racial inequalities.

The three forms of struggle, i.e. spontaneous protest, pressure for community resources and planned political struggle, reflect a variety of responses to the problem of racial inequality. Although all three are committed to challenging racism, some are more explicit and specific than others in defining their objectives. Strategies correspondingly vary, according to stated (or unstated) objectives, since each form of struggle has its own priorities and its own understanding of how best these might be achieved (cf. Ben-Tovim et al., 1982b).

The effects or consequences of struggle may be quite concrete, e.g. a positive redistribution of resources, or more abstract and less tangible, e.g. an acknowledgement of the role of institutionalized forms of racism in creating and maintaining racial inequality. Race-related reforms can thus be seen to represent the more tangible effects of struggle. In common with other effects these reforms help to redefine the conditions of future struggle and hence should in our view play an integral role in the development of antiracist strategy. The significance which we attach to calculation of this kind is responsible for the emphasis we place on planned political struggle. Overall our assessment of change vis-à-vis racial inequality, which we take to be the focus of our analysis, is thus based on, and will vary according to, those conditions analysed in the previous section and the particular forms of antiracist struggle which we discuss below.

'Riots' as an issue in local politics

Spontaneous street protests are significant not only because they have proved important catalysts for reform but also for the way in which they have become issues in local politics.

[. . .]

Our experience here reveals that whatever the insurrectionary nature of street conflict, its major impact (ironically, probably, for many of its advocates and participants) can only be described as reformist. In many respects, disturbances or the threat of them have been a more effective lever and instrument in local reform, notably resource allocation (e.g. in terms of funding for an Afro-Caribbean Cultural Centre in Wolverhampton or the Liverpool 8 Law Centre in Liverpool), than those political forces for whom such change constitutes an integral part of their political practice.

The form of response on the part of local statutory bodies to periodic street conflicts or the threat of them has, however, remained consistently *ad hoc* and gestural. That responses are invariably made *in the wake of* these 'crises' and not as a matter of principle or for that matter in response to formal and informal pressure through conventional political channels must encourage a cynical view of local policy development (cf. Edwards and Batley, 1978). Whether these 'panic' responses take the form of one-off projects or of impromptu meetings of national or local politicians with community leaders, they are rarely followed up. Furthermore, such responses have consistently marked an absence of political will on the part of statutory agencies to tackle in any kind of sustained way the problems of racism and racial disadvantage.

Pressure for community resources

Community and project work, which incorporates explicit commitment to racial equality, varies considerably in the range of its activities. Supplementary schools, projects for young offenders, and the provision of welfare rights counselling are examples of the various forms it can take. Across this broad spectrum of activities, community and project work seeks to meet the perceived needs of the community through the making of provision which either supplements or represents an alternative to mainstream provision. In principle, this kind of activity brings organizations into direct daily contact with members of the community who seek help on an individual basis or through group activity. Hence casework and

project development have become important features of community work organizations.
[...]

The outcome of any community work initiative will appear piecemeal and minimal given the potency and prevalence of racial inequality. The establishment of a supplementary school may benefit its own pupils but will not necessarily affect the vast majority of black children in mainstream education. Welfare rights counselling may benefit a minority of individual claimants, in contrast to a change in policy and/or the law which may affect claimants as a whole. The significance of community work organizations therefore may lie in their identification of community needs and their highlighting of deficiencies in mainstream provision. Unless these needs are pursued, however, in the context of struggles for institutional change, their impact will be correspondingly limited. In so far as institutional deficiencies are tackled in this broader context, community work activity gives way to planned political struggle.

Planned political struggle: challenging local policy and the policy-making framework

Our third form of intervention may be distinguished from spontaneous protest because of its planned characteristics and from resource-bidding because of the breadth and scope of its target: i.e. it seeks to challenge policy and the existing policy-making framework.
[...]

Below we identify some of the characteristic features of political activities with which we have been directly associated. These characteristics, it should be noted, reflect a series of challenges to those conditions described above which serve to marginalize antiracist political forces. Throughout this article we have stressed the contingency of those conditions, i.e. with respect to the possibility of predicting their realization with any certainty. This contingency results precisely from political struggle, which in turn depends on the nature and characteristics of antiracist forces. Overall, our experience once again makes us cautious in our appraisal of these struggles. Apparent breakthroughs often turn out to be momentary and fleeting, victories somewhat hollow, concessions gestural and reforms less consequential than they at first appear, with advance subsequently turning into retreat. What follows then are some of the characteristics of antiracist struggle, each of which seeks to redress racial inequality by challenging those conditions which serve to reinforce it.

(a) Redefining the problem

A major undertaking of antiracist organizations has been to argue the case for positive action, supported by evidence of institutionalized racism and resulting inequalities. We have already noted the strength of colour-blind ideologies in local politics and the ways in which they act as a strong force of resistance to positive programmes for racial equality. Antiracist forces have thus sought to provide evidence of inequalities on the one hand and of the compatibility of positive action with the broader political objectives of socialism on the other.

In Liverpool, the production of a profile of opprtunities in the city included evidence of the disproportionately low number of black workers in the City Council (Ben-Tovim *et al.*, 1980; Ben-Tovim, 1983), while a survey of council housing proved the discrepancies in the quality and location of housing allocated to black and white tenants (Commission for Racial Equality, 1984). Similarly, in Wolverhampton the inadequacy of youth facilities for groups of young people of Afro-Caribbean and Asian descent, cases of alleged police harassment, evidence of disproportionate numbers of expulsions from school, and the disproportionately low numbers of black school governors are just some examples from a flow of evidence of racism and inequality (Gabriel and Stredder, 1981 unpublished paper).

At the heart of these debates is the question of where responsibility lies. The argument underlying positive action places that responsibility unequivocally on the institution. The absence of black people from employment in the Town Hall, of Asian girls from youth facilities in Wolverhampton, of black people from desirable council property in Liverpool or of Asian languages from schools in Wolverhampton must be considered in terms of institutional failure to redefine job responsibilities, to develop appropriate criteria for selection and to devise recruitment procedures which ensure greater proportions of black employees and to develop provision which is attractive to young Asian women. Redefining the problem thus becomes challenging assumptions which attribute the above problems to the lack of qualified applicants, to cultural conflict within the Asian community, to community housing preferences or to the failure of black people to integrate with or assimilate to Western culture.

The implications of relocating the problem in these terms point unambiguously towards some kind of positive action, which may have been argued for in consultative meetings, in the local press, in Labour Party meetings and in *ad hoc* deputations to civic leaders and others. The ever-present danger is that a concession to positive action might mask a cynical lack of commitment to act on its implications. Moreover, politicians and officers by virtue of their political position and their control over administration are able to ignore sporadic pressure from consultative procedures, etc.

(b) Building alliances

Those engaged in political struggle have sought in varying degrees to embrace as wide a spectrum as possible of concerned groups and organizations from within the community in order to pre-empt attempts to dismiss antiracism as unrepresentative of community demands (Ohri and Donnelly, 1982; Ouseley, 1982a). In Liverpool, the equal opportunity campaign included a broad range of community representation, co-ordinated through the Merseyside Community Relations Council, which enabled a variety of forms of pressure to be exerted at different points and in a united manner within the apparatus of local government (Ben-Tovim *et al.*, 1981, 1982a).

Nevertheless, our organizational experience has repeatedly confirmed to us the fragility of alliances. They invariably rely on a base of active support which is in reality quite narrow, however representative the views of the community spokespeople. The breadth of organizational support often masks a core of individuals working simultaneously in a number of organizations. The departure or withdrawal of a key indivi-dual, therefore, can often threaten the survival of a seemingly broad-based alliance. Collaboration between organizations, if it succeeds at all, may only do so for the lifetime of a particular issue. Invariably, struggles crystallize around a set of concrete demands; in the unlikely event of their acceptance, the disbanding of the alliance structure may follow. Despite the crucial significance of the next stage of policy implementation, this political reality combines with the disproportionate responsibilities which fall to a few under-resourced organizations and over-committed activists (together with effective manoeuvring, delaying and dividing on the part of politicians and officers alike) to weaken the long-term thrust of collective community pressures.

(c) Breaking down resistance

A priority in antiracist struggle is the identification of crucial points of potential institutional resistance and the attempt to neutralize these, if not to win them over. The significance of gaining trade union support for the principle of an equal opportunity policy in Liverpool became clear at the campaign's earliest stages. Trade unions not only represented one source of official opposition, which had to be negotiated. They were, perhaps more significantly, regarded as crucial in terms of the policy's implementation. The campaign therefore undertook various activities to persuade the Liverpool Trades Council and later local trade unions to join the call for an equal opportunity policy within the authority. This ultimately proved decisive in the campaign's success, given the marked tendency on the part of local governments to respect the views of local trade unions in so far as the latter appear resistant to the principle of positive action. In Liverpool's case, trade union support thus effectively challenged institutional recalcitrance, a condition which was only realized through the development of links between trade unions, antiracist groups and other community organizations.

(d) Using central initiatives in support of antiracist struggles

The relative ease with which local authorities have been able to resist pressure for positive action is in part made possible by the failure of

l government to take a strong and effective positive lead on racism
cial equality. On the contrary, local authorities have invariably
used central policies for legitimating inaction. Overall the onus remains
heavily on local organizations to maximize the scope and use of central
policy initiatives. The context provided by central government, however,
is one of remoteness from local struggle. It rarely provides sustained and
co-ordinated support for local struggle, and in some situations it works as
much against as for local struggle.

For example, during the equal opportunity campaign in Liverpool the
Commission for Racial Equality made a general promotional visit to the
city in order to gain local council support for a positive policy in line with
the 1976 Race Relations Act. Unfortunately, poor organization on the part
of the Commission for Racial Equality on this occasion, including a lack of
co-ordination with the local Community Relations Council, seemed to do
little to alter local official attitudes. Similarly, in Wolverhampton, local
organizations planned to take advantage of a visitation from the Home
Office to press the case against the local authority's misuse of Section 11
funds, but effective stage-management on the part of the authority
combined with selective listening and adept manoeuvring on the part of
the Home Office team to silence would-be opposition.

Our overriding experience of central initiatives should not, however, lead
us to ignore the way in which local struggles have effectively appealed to
and utilized the centre both in specific instances and in a more general
sense. In Liverpool, campaign activists made use of the 1976 Race
Relations Act, and in particular of Section 71's general exhortations to
local authorities to promote equal opportunities. Similarly, in Wolverhampton, Home Office revisions to the administrative guidelines governing Section 11 funding were used to encourage the local authority to
provide more information and to involve communities in submissions for
funding.

(e) Lobbying local politicians and officials

Because political struggles against racism invariably take place at the
margins of local government, the struggles often never reach the formal
agendas of local decision-making machinery. In so far as they do, a
successful outcome clearly depends on the support of local politicians and
officers for specific demands. Hence, in the case of Liverpool's equal
opportunity campaign, much lobbying and canvassing was carried out in
the build-up to the committee meeting at which the issue was ultimately
debated and accepted. This included meetings with the leaders of all
parties, discussions with key officers, submission of written material to all
Councillors, co-ordination with trade unions and ensuring a substantial
and visible minority presence at the meeting itself.

The eventual adoption by the City Council of an equal opportunity policy
statement was, then, the culmination of nearly two years' sustained and

co-ordinated campaigning by an alliance of local organizations. This resulted in a complete about-turn in the way the politicians and officials had traditionally regarded issues of race in the city. But, as the Home Office was quick to acknowledge, this grassroots achievement in Liverpool was unique. Elsewhere, in our experience, continuity of effort is often broken down by institutional forces of resistance. Conditions which make for the marginalization of antiracist forces realize themselves despite pressure from below. Even in Liverpool, the successful conclusion to the campaign must be set against subsequent events. In other words, even a policy decision as significant as that promoting equal opportunity can only ever be regarded as a stage in a process of struggle which is ongoing and within which there may be setbacks. In the case of Liverpool, the Labour leadership has since fought and won back its control over the appointment of the Principal Race Relations Adviser. There has also been, of course, the subsequent suspension of the Race Relations Liaison Committee which was set up to oversee the equal opportunity policy.

Conclusions

Our analysis of political struggles for racial equality in local government has confirmed the integral role of organizations and of policies in those struggles, both of which are frequently overlooked in social science literature including Marxism. Political struggle, in our experience, is marked by movements of advance and retreat which are invariably slow, sometimes imperceptible, but never predictable. Of course we can say that the forces of resistance to racial equality within local government can be formidable, particularly the prevalence of racial ideologies. The most common of these 'attitudes' in our experience is characterized by a refusal to acknowledge racism and relatedly to pursue any of the steps necessary to redress it. The continuing prevalence of colour-blind ideologies within local government is made possible through the realization of other conditions: the ambiguity and permissiveness of central policy initiatives, the control exercized at the local officer level over information as well as policy implementation and administration, and the compatibility of colour-blindness with a broad range of mainstream political ideologies.

We have argued that the above conditions are not fixed. Their realization depends in part on the strength of the challenge from antiracist forces, which have challenged institutional resistance through spontaneous protest, bidding for resources and planned political struggle. The last of these, of which we have most direct experience, has sought to challenge those conditions referred to above in the most specific and direct ways. That is to say, it has engaged in struggle over conflicting definitions of the problem, it has attempted to pre-empt charges of extremism through the building of alliances, to break down resistance through negotiation and representation and to turn central resources from negative obstacles into positive initiatives in support of antiracist struggles.

Reforms and policy initiatives which result in part from these struggles over conditions help define future conditions of struggle. For this reason alone, planned struggle cannot afford to ignore or to dismiss as divisive or gestural reforms, such as equal opportunity policies, specialist race staff, new committees and units, and monitoring; instead it must acknowledge them as integral parts of the conditions of struggle. To argue this is not to deny the fragility of advances secured through struggle; nor is it to underestimate the attack on a reform's potential through the reassertion of those forces of resistance described above. The weaknesses of antiracist forces cannot, regrettably, be ignored in this analysis. They invariably operate within a narrow conception of what is regarded as politically legitimate, so that the task facing local organizations in the struggle against marginalization, pseudo-forms of consultation and charges of extremism is indeed immense.

[. . .]

References

Ben-Tovim, G. S. (ed.) (1983) *Equal Opportunities and the Employment of Black People and Ethnic Minorities on Merseyside*, Liverpool, Merseyside Association for Racial Equality in Employment.

Ben-Tovim, G. S., Brown, V., Clay, D., Law, I., Loy, L., Torkington, P. (1980) *Racial Disadvantage in Liverpool – An Area Profile*, Liverpool, Merseyside Area Profile Group.

Ben-Tovim, G. S., Gabriel, J. G., Law, I., Stredder, K. (1981) 'The Equal Opportunity Campaign in Liverpool' in Cheetham, J. *et al.* (eds), *Social and Community Work in a Multi-Racial Society*, New York, Harper and Row.

Ben-Tovim, G. S., Gabriel, J. G., Law, I., Stredder, K. (1982a) 'Race politics and campaign activity – a comparative study in Liverpool and Wolverhampton' in Craig, G. *et al.* (eds), *Community Work and the State*, London, Routledge and Kegan Paul.

Ben-Tovim, G. S., Gabriel, J. G., Law, I., Stredder, K. (1982b) 'A political analysis of race in the 1980s' in Husband, C. (ed.), *'Race' in Britain*, London, Hutchinson.

Black Linx (1984) Merseyside Community Relations Council Newsletter (December).

Commission for Racial Equality (1984) *Race and Housing in Liverpool – A Research Report*, London, CRE.

Edwards, J. and Batley, R. (1978) *The Politics of Positive Discrimination*, London, Tavistock.

Ohri, A. and Donnelly, L. (1982) 'Alliances and coalitions in the struggle for racial equality' in Ohri, A. *et al.* (eds), *Community Work and Racism*, London, Routledge and Kegan Paul.

Ouseley, H. (1982a) 'A local black alliance' in Ohri, A. *et al.* (eds), *Community Work and Racism*, London, Routledge and Kegan Paul.

Ouseley, H. (1982b) *The System*, London, Runnymede Trust.

Ouseley, H. (1984) 'Local authority race initiatives' in Boddy, M. and Fudge, C. (eds), *Local Socialism?*, London, Macmillan.

Stewart, M. and Whitting, G. (1983) *Ethnic Minorities and the Urban Programme*, Bristol, University of Bristol, School for Advanced Urban Studies.

Young, K. (1983) 'Ethnic pluralism and the policy agenda in Britain' in Glazer N. and Young, K. (eds), *Ethnic Pluralism and Public Policy*, London, Heniemann.

Young, K. and Connelly, N. (1981) *Policy and Practice in the Multi-Racial City*, London, Policy Studies Institute.

Source: Mason, D. and Rex, J. (eds) (1986) *Theories of Race and Ethnic Relations*, Cambridge, Cambridge University Press.

12 THE THEORY AND PRACTICE OF EQUAL OPPORTUNITIES POLICIES

LIBERAL AND RADICAL APPROACHES

NICK JEWSON AND DAVID MASON

Introduction

Mapping philosophical assumptions, formulating analytical distinctions and disentangling disparate arguments are all routine aspects of intellectual craftsmanship. Generally speaking, cognitive skills of this kind are not highly regarded outside the walls of institutions of higher education, and are commonly derided as 'of academic interest only'. This article is an exploration, in one particular social context, of some of the causes and consequences of the neglect of these skills. The article is concerned with the development of equal opportunities policies at the workplace.[1] It suggests that the confused and contradictory deployment of different conceptions of equal opportunity policies can constitute an important aspect of the struggle for control of resources, deference and legitimacy at work.

In the course of research on the development of equal opportunities policies in a manufacturing company and in a local authority [North County Council], it rapidly became obvious to us that the various participants in the policy-making process were using terms and concepts in a confused, arbitrary and contradictory manner (cf. Young and Connelly, 1981). Sometimes this appeared to be a product of muddle and misunderstanding; on other occasions it appeared to be the result of more conscious and deliberate attempts to mislead and mystify opponents and outsiders. Furthermore, we soon discovered that much of the advisory literature in this field, emanating from statutory and voluntary bodies, also falls into the conceptual traps and errors with which we had become familiar at our research sites. In order to clarify our own thoughts, therefore, we found it useful to make a simple but basic distinction between two different conceptions of equal opportunities policies. These two conceptions we call the liberal and the radical views.

The theoretical distinction between liberal and radical conceptions is by no means a novel one (see for example, Rae *et al.*, 1981: esp. pp. 64–82).[2] They draw upon quite different notions of society, of the individual and of the role of the state. Moreover, they derive from quite different intellectual pedigrees. (See for example, Dunleavy, 1981; Held, 1984.) Indeed, in the context of intellectual debate, most people have little difficulty in telling one from the other. However, *in practice* – that is in making relationships with others in specific social contexts – confusion between the two stubbornly holds sway. At our reserach sites we frequently came across individuals and groups who invoked various aspects of both conceptions, depending upon the time, the circumstances and their needs. Policy makers thus evolved their beliefs and negotiating stances out of a fluid and paradoxical amalgamation of philosophically antithetical positions. As a consequence we repeatedly observed situations in which participants in the policy-making process were unaware that other groups and individuals drew unintended, and often hostile, conclusions and implications from their statements and utterances.

Our objective in this paper is to demonstrate some of the functions and consequences of these misunderstandings. In our research we observed that participants in the policy-making process often found it convenient or expedient to ignore or neglect the differences between liberal and radical conceptions. On occasion their conflation enabled disparate groups, with irreconcilable objectives, to be drawn into debate or negotiation with one another. It also enabled offers of support or resources made in one context to be withdrawn or withheld in another. In short, conceptual confusion facilitated both social ambiguity and social ambivalence. However, the benefits of such expedients were often short lived. Generally their long term effect was to generate disappointment with, and distrust of, equal opportunities policies. Thus, for example, a policy might initially provide an arena for negotiation and a source of goodwill between parties at the workplace. Nevertheless a policy based on mutual misunderstandings might eventually become the focal point of accusations, from all sides, of treachery, betrayal and bad faith.
[. . .]

Elements of equal opportunities policies

Figure 1 sets out the main dimensions of the contrast between the liberal and radical approaches.

In an earlier paper, in the context of a discussion of monitoring, we have

Elements of equal opportunities policies	Conceptions of equal opportunities	
	Liberal	Radical
Principles	Fair procedures	Fair distribution of rewards
Implementation	Bureaucratization of decision making (e.g. training)	Politicization of decision making
Effectiveness	Positive action	Positive discrimination
Perceptions	Justice seen to be done	Consciousness raising (e.g. training)

Figure 1   Elements of liberal and radical conceptions of equal opportunities policies

identified four elements or dimensions of equal opportunities policies (Jewson and Mason, 1984/5). These elements of equal opportunities policy constitute the vertical axis of Figure 1. They are as follows.

1 *Principles of equal opportunities policies*
Refers to the notions of fairness and justice which are, explicitly or implicitly, enshrined in the detailed rules and regulations of the formal policy.
2 *Implementation of equal opportunities policies*
Refers to the social mechanisms or devices which enable principles of equity and fairness to be put into operation or translated into day to day routines. In other words, the means by which principle is translated into practice.
3 *Effectiveness of equal opportunities policies*
Refers to the consequences of implementation for patterns of social life within the institution or enterprise. It is concerned with the results of the, more or less adequate, realization of the principles of the policy: has implementation actually brought about fairness and justice?
4 *Perceptions of equal opportunities policies*
Refer to thoughts and feelings about the policy by the various participants in the policy-making process. It is concerned, then, with the extent to which the policy is *believed* to be fair, to have been implemented and to be effective.

In the remainder of the article we will compare liberal and radical conceptions of equal opportunities policies with respect to each of these dimensions, identifying some of the prominent confusions between these two approaches.

Principles of equal opportunities policies

The liberal conception argues that, in principle, equality of opportunity exists when all individuals are enabled freely and equally to compete for social rewards. The role of policy maker is seen as analogous to that of an umpire or referee. Policy makers are required to ensure that the rules of competition are not discriminatory and that they are fairly enforced on all. It is not their job to determine who are the winners and losers, but to ensure only that the social mechanisms by which winners and losers select themselves are based on principles of fairness and justice. It follows that the function of equal opportunities policy is to devise fair procedures, such as those designed according to principles of rational-legality and bureaucratic impartiality. They scrupulously avoid both direct and indirect forms of discrimination.[3] Thus for those subscribing to the liberal view, the principles embodied in equal opportunities policies are procedural ones.

This conception of the principles of equal opportunity policies has its roots in theories of classical liberalism or liberal democracy (Arblaster, 1984; Salvadori, 1977). Contemporary representatives of this position are distributed widely across the political spectrum, from Keynesianism to Thatcherism (see for example, Walton, 1984). However, liberals of all shades share an abhorrence of traditional privilege, self-perpetuating elites and arbitrary social restraints. Typically they believe that natural ability and talent are randomly distributed throughout the population and are not the preserve of an hereditary estate. It is also characteristic of all brands of liberalism that they assert the necessity of some degree of state regulation of society in order to obtain the maximum possible levels of freedom and liberty for all. (The main differences among liberals concern the extent and type of minimal state intervention necessary, not the need for a strong and resolute state machine as such (cf. Neuman, 1964).)

Liberalism, however, differs from the radical perspective, to be discussed in a moment, in a number of critical ways. First, liberals conceive of talent and ability as *individual* attributes. They assume that the removal of collective barriers to the expression of individual talent will enable the best person to win and, more generally, permit all individuals to make the best of themselves. This view ignores, or has great difficulty in accommodating, the structural sources of social capacities and skills – and, hence, the structural sources of social inequality. Secondly, the liberal view asserts that equality of opportunity is to be guaranteed by maximizing the economic and political liberty of the citizen. State intervention must not exceed the barest minimum necessary to secure individual liberty. Thus in economic life the unfettered operation of a perfect market in labour is typically regarded as ethically ideal. Discrimination in employment is one example of the distortions of free competition which liberals abhor. Discrimination is not, then, regarded as intrinsic to the operation of capitalist labour markets but as a blemish upon them, derived from the persistence of backward or traditional cultural practices and values (cf. Hutt, 1964). Hence it is assumed that the 'normal' operation of the labour market will generate a random distribution of ethnic and other groups within the occupational hierarchy (see, for example, Powell, quoted in Foot, 1969, p. 129). A variant of this thesis asserts that citizenship rights provide that irreducible minimum of social equality from which all individuals may compete on a fair basis (cf. Marshall, 1963; Crosland, 1956 and 1974; Tawney, 1964; Rawls, 1972).

To summarize, then, the aim of liberal equal opportunities policies is the removal of unfair distortions to the operation of the labour market by means of institutionalizing fair procedures in every aspect of work and employment.

The radical approach is very different. It seeks to intervene directly in workplace practices in order to achieve a fair distribution of rewards among employees, as measured by some criterion of moral value and worth. Thus the radical view is concerned primarily with the outcome of the contest rather than with the rules of the game, with the fairness of the distribution of rewards rather than the fairness of procedures. Discrimination, it is conceded, affects individuals but it is argued that it can only be identified at the level of the group: '. . . it is not possible for a society to determine whether or not it is an equal opportunity society without collecting and analysing economic data on groups' (Schmid, 1984, p. 265). In this view, since it is manifestly the case on a priori grounds that women and black people are the equals of men and whites, the actual distribution of occupational rewards should be made to reflect this fact. 'Equal opportunities' cannot be said to exist until the representation of black people and women in the various divisions of the labour force reflects their presence in society as a whole.[4] The absence of a fair distribution is, *ipso facto*, evidence of unfair discrimination. It should be clear that the radical view places no particular store by the outcome of free market processes. Rather it is believed that there are independent standards of human dignity and moral worth which must take precedence. These may be derived from ideologies such as marxism, feminism or 'black power'.

There is, however, a further point to be made. The radical perspective entails a, more or less explicit, attack upon the concept of ability or talent that is embraced by the liberal view. First, it is asserted that the terms 'ability' and 'talent' are not the politically or morally neutral ones that they purport to be. Rather, it is suggested, they contain and conceal a series of value judgements (see, for example, Rose and Rose, 1979). It is argued that those behaviours and skills which are classified as 'abilities' are invariably those of the ruling class or ruling elite. Those in positions of power define *desirable* knowledges and skills; their acolytes such as teachers and examiners institutionalize these conceptions of 'ability' in educational curricula and in measures of educational attainment (cf. Young, 1971; Bowles and Gintis, 1976). Secondly, the radical perspective is not only conscious of the social definition of ability but also its social transmission. It is thus sympathetic to work in the sociology of education concerned with both the transmission of 'cultural capital' across the generations and the relationship between cultural reproduction and social reproduction (cf. Bourdieu, 1971a,b; 1973; Bourdieu and Passeron, 1977; Althusser, 1972). In this analysis, then, 'ability' and 'talent' cannot be conceived as individual attributes. Thirdly, the radical view questions whether educational and technical qualifications, which are conventionally taken as evidence of individual ability, are actually a functional necessity for the performance of many or most modern occupations. It is pointed out that, following upon the deskilling of work in capitalist societies, the tasks entailed in a great many occupations do not require any significant level of technical competence or knowledge (cf. Braverman, 1974; Zimbalist, 1979; Wood, 1982; Thompson, 1983). This is, arguably, the case in the vast majority of semi-skilled and unskilled manual occupations as well as many routine white-collar occupations. Moreover it is pointed out that, in the case of middle-class occupations, the character of the educational qualifications demanded as entry requirements bear little relation to the tasks actually performed. In this instance, educational qualifications are seen as screening devices intended to help preserve the most desirable areas of the labour market for the sons and daughters of the bourgeoisie (cf. Maguire and Ashton, 1981; Ashton *et al.*, 1982; Berg, 1970).[5]

For all these reasons radicals feel justified in setting aside, when necessary, the judgements of the market place. Indeed the liberal concept of 'the meritocratic rise of the talented' is characterized as an ideology which legitimizes existing social inequalities whilst concealing their true determinants (cf. Bowles and Gintis, 1976; Flude, 1974; Sharp and Green, 1975). From the radical viewpoint, therefore, it is perfectly legitimate selectively to waive requirements for formal entry qualifications in order to ensure that categories or groups of deprived people gain access.
[. . .]

Implementation of equal opportunities policies

Implementation entails different activities for the two conceptions of equal opportunities policies. In the liberal view, implementation requires

the bureaucratization of procedures. For radicals it requires the politicization of decision making.

For liberals, the problems of implementation are those of devising fair
procedures. Liberal approaches, therefore, normally entail the bureaucratization of more and more aspects of work life. The remnants of
tradition, custom, charisma and personal patronage in employment
practice are subordinated to the disciplines of formal rules and regulations.

This approach to implementation is characterized by a number of
difficulties and limitations which can lead to disappointment with, as well
as misunderstandings about, liberal policies. First, formalization may
damage existing informal channels of communication valued by the
disadvantaged population. The abandonment of such informal channels
may be interpreted as a shift towards practices that are more racist and
sexist rather than less. [. . .] Secondly, the implementation of formal
procedures does not guarantee their practical effectiveness. This may be
due to circumvention by neglect; that is, formal procedures being
permitted to atrophy (see, for example, Torrington, 1982; Snell *et al.*,
1981). Alternatively it may be due to circumvention by manipulation;
that is, procedures may be followed in the letter but contravened in the
spirit (Jewson and Mason, 1984/5). For example, jobs and vacancies may
be internally advertised but such an idiosyncratic set of qualifications
may be specified that the post is effectively ear-marked for a particular
individual or small group. [. . .]

In combating circumvention by neglect and by manipulation, liberals
place great faith in training, primarily conceived as instruction in the
requirements of the law and the details of formal procedures. There may
also be training directed towards increasing understanding of other
cultures (see Peppard, 1980; Shaw, 1981/2). However, whilst such
training may be an essential aspect of a successful policy, instruction in
the operation of procedures can, of course, facilitate their evasion as well
as their implementation.

Leaving aside the detailed problematics of training, there are yet more
critical aspects of the implementation of the liberal conception of policy to
which radicals draw attention. There are major aspects of work life that
can never be bureaucratized or subject to regulation by formal rules. A
considerable body of literature suggests that informal norms and codes of
conduct are always present even in the most authoritarian or formal of
institutions (see, for example, Blau, 1963; Gouldner, 1954; Goffman,
1968). Moreover, it is impossible, even within a limited area of social
activity, to specify a set of rules which can unequivocally respond to every
contingency or situation. Consequently there are always major areas of
social life which escape bureaucratic control and thus cannot be made
'fair' by invoking formal procedures. For example, it is well known that
some important aspects of business, managerial and professional careers

are conducted in leisure settings or other informal non-work contexts. Black and female employees require equal access to these relationships as well as the more formal processes of decision making. Such access cannot be guaranteed, however, by bureaucratic procedures.

These problems make liberal policies vulnerable to accusations of promising more than they can deliver and of raising expectations that cannot easily be satisfied within the terms of the procedural approach. We shall argue in the next section that the social pressures thereby generated in the implementation of liberal policies can easily tempt policy makers to employ radical legitimizations of the effectiveness of policy. None of this should be taken as a justification for not devising formal procedures whenever possible. It does, however, lead us to a consideration of the somewhat wider notion of implementation contained in the radical perspective.

It is the claim of radicals that the limitations of scope encountered in the bureaucratization of procedures can be transcended by the strategy of politicization of all aspects of work life. Politicization implies that decisions within an enterprise or institution are not made according to technical or bureaucratic criteria of rationality but rather in terms of the prosecution of a struggle for power and influence on the part of specific subordinate groups. Decision making is not guided primarily by procedural detail, historical precedent or legal technicalities. Instead it is interpreted as an opportunity to advance the sectional interests of the oppressed. This criterion for action is urged upon all personnel in all social contexts, both formal and informal. All relationships and activities are to be harnessed to the struggle for radical principles of equality. Thus officers of the organization are urged to aid, advance or favour members of disadvantaged groups wherever possible. In addition they are required to consider the implications for black people and women of all decisions of whatever kind.

Such a strategy does not necessarily entail bureaucratization, although it certainly does not exclude the possibility of procedural reform. A major vehicle of this approach to implementation is the promotion of correct ideological consciousness. The selection of decision makers is also likely to be made on political criteria. Thus political views and attitudes of members of the organization will be monitored while appointments and promotions will be decided on the basis of ideological zeal and soundness. Such appointments may be made independently, or even irrespective, of technical or educational qualifications. Some of the most extreme examples of these practices were to be found in the bureaucracies of Nazi Germany, Maoist China and Stalinist Russia. In the last, of course, even matters of biological theory and agricultural technique were decided by reference to the politically correct line (Medvedev, 1968; Joravsky, 1970; Lecourt, 1977). In contemporary Western capitalist societies politicization does not reach such levels. It is not, however, wholly absent. [. . .]

Whilst, as already noted, politicization can take place in concert with bureaucratization, the radical conception of implementation may be pursued with such a degree of indifference to the demands of bureaucratic functioning that the entire equal opportunities policy can be placed in jeopardy. [. . .]

Frequently it is such apparent indifference to procedural consistency that alarms those who subscribe to a liberal position and which is highlighted by those who are opposed to the whole project of equal opportunities policy. Thus radical policy makers, albeit in a different fashion to liberals, also face resistance, dismay and disappointment when implementing their programmes. This brings us to the kernel of our argument. It is our contention that the various practical difficulties of managing implementation constitute a powerful incentive for policy makers to conflate liberal and radical measures of, and justifications for, the effectiveness of policy.

Effectiveness of equal opportunities policies

In order to secure the maximum effectiveness of equal opportunities policies, liberals and radicals propose similarly named, but in fact dramatically different, practices. These are respectively 'positive action' and 'positive discrimination'.

As with many other aspects of equal opportunities policy and policy making, the meanings of these two terms are variously defined and frequently confused. (Compare, for example, Bindman 1980a,b; CRE, 1980; Dworkin, 1981; Glazer, 1975; Jain and Pettman, 1976; Kilson, 1983; Prashar, 1984; Scarman, 1981; Welch, 1981.) In this article, however, we shall take positive action to refer to efforts to remove obstacles to the free operation of the labour market. The aim of positive action is to promote free and equal competition among individuals. Included under this rubric might be crèche facilities at the workplace, language training, extended leave arrangements and advertising campaigns designed to reassure candidates from disadvantaged groups that their applications will be judged on their merits. Positive action stops short of tampering with the decision-making process itself. Thus, for example, selection for posts remains based on individual attainment or technical qualification. Positive action is intended solely to enable more individuals to enter the competition free of 'artificial' and functionally irrelevant disabilities.

Positive discrimination, in contrast, entails the deliberate manipulation of employment practices so as to obtain a fair distribution of the deprived or disadvantaged population within the workforce. This may take the form of the imposition of quotas or the operation of multi-tier entry requirements (cf. the Bakke case and the DeFunis case in the USA; see Bindman, 1980a; Dworkin, 1981). Examples of such arrangements in the UK include the requirement that companies employ a minimum percentage of registered disabled people. Positive discrimination, then, seeks to promote the achievement of disadvantaged groups by directly intervening in the assessment or evaluation of individuals.

It can be seen that, in spite of frequent confusion of terminology, two quite different principles are at stake. We are readily convinced by those who argue that, if the objective is to obtain a representative distribution of black people and women in the labour force, positive discrimination is likely to be more effective than positive action. However, whilst positive discrimination is not outlawed in all fields of social policy, it is unequivocally illegal in respect of race and sex. Radicals are, therefore, thwarted by the law in deploying their most effective mechanism of social reconstruction. In these circumstances it is tempting for them covertly to pursue a policy of positive discrimination whilst claiming to be engaged in positive action or procedural reform. In other words, a radical policy may masquerade as a liberal one. This confusion may be a product of either deliberate subterfuge or self-deception.
[. . .]

Radicals may, then, disguise themselves in liberal clothing. In other circumstances, however, liberals may repay the compliment. When under pressure to justify the effectiveness of procedural reforms, for example, liberals very often succumb to the temptation of providing radical legitimations for liberal policy actions. Thus it is common for liberals to defend the fairness of procedures by reference to an actual or expected increase in the representativeness of the distribution of black people and women in the workforce. When, for well known structural reasons, this does not occur it is frequently assumed that yet further innovations in procedural fairness are the solution to the problem. In addition, more sophisticated forms of implementation may be sought, together with assertions about the need for monitoring. However, as we have argued elsewhere (Jewson and Mason, 1984/5), the concept of monitoring is not free of the confusions identified here.
[. . .]

What we are arguing, then, is that at the heart of the confusion of the two perspectives is the assumption that fair procedures (in the liberal sense) lead to fair outcomes (in the radical sense). Both liberals and radicals are led, by quite different routes, to make this assertion. Liberals do so in order to justify confining their policy actions to procedural reforms; radicals in order to foster the belief that those policy actions which are legal can create, or at least contribute to, a fundamental transformation in the distribution of occupational rewards. In point of fact this linking of liberal procedure to radical outcome is not *necessarily* entailed in either perspective. Furthermore there are good sociological reasons to doubt its veracity. Nevertheless, liberals and radicals are led to assert this position by the practical exigencies of defending and advancing their respective policies.[6]

Perceptions of equal opportunities policies

For liberals, perceptions of equal opportunities policies are concerned with whether justice is seen to be done, i.e. whether the workforce has accurately perceived the fairness of procedures. The aim is for everything to be seen to be above board. If a disadvantaged group persists in suspicion and resentment, even after an effective policy has been implemented, increased publicity and greater openness of procedure may well be recommended. Within the liberal conception, then, the massaging of perceptions is essentially a task of public relations; that is, it entails eliciting approval without challenging or disturbing existing values and beliefs.

Liberals are concerned to ensure that discriminatory motives are not imputed where none really exists. Thus liberals may be particularly anxious to ensure that members of the work-force differentiate between racial/sexual discrimination and other social processes at work in the enterprise. [. . .]

Radicals analyse, and react to, perceptions of policies in a somewhat different fashion. For radicals the promulgation of policy is an opportunity for consciousness raising, an occasion to urge the deprived and exploited to consider their condition and its remedies. In responding to, and manipulating, perceptions of equal opportunities policy, collective aware-ness and solidarity may be increased, false consciousness may be confronted and dispelled, and the contradictions and broken promises of ruling ideologies may be exposed. In addition, the monitoring of perceptions of equal opportunities policies may become a forum in which racists and sexists are encouraged to admit the error of their ways. This may take the form of public confessions of past misdemeanours, the resocialization of the ideologically unsound, or the exemplary punishment of incorrigible transgressors. The aim is not simply to gain approval for a specific set of procedures but rather to manufacture and manipulate moral sensibilities on a wide range of social issues.

All this implies that radicals do not regard the monitoring of perceptions as the conclusion or completion of the policy-making process. The raising of collective consciousness is conceived as an integral part of a long and enduring struggle. Indeed radicals may regard this as the most fruitful contribution that the policy can make to the attainment of 'equal opportunities'. With their awareness of the structural determinants of social inequality, radicals do not usually expect limited workplace programmes to make a substantial impact on the overall distribution of rewards and resources in a society. However, such programmes may be supported for the sake of raising aspirations and fostering expectations that fuel demands for more general social change.

It is in this context that the radical attitude to training is best comprehended. For radicals, the primary function of training is not that of procedural instruction. Rather it is regarded as the principal vehicle of the consciousness raising exercise, a programme of moral purging and political re-education. This was evident at the local authority which we studied. Much of the training programme organized at North Country Council took the form of racism- and sexism-awareness courses, attendance at which was mandatory for Heads of Departments and other senior officers. These courses appear to have taken a didactic form in which lecturers forcefully drew attention to many forms of conscious and unconscious prejudice and discrimination. Some officers to whom we have spoken felt as if they were 'in the dock'. Needless to say, whether or not accusations of racism and sexism were justified, they did little to endear the equal opportunities policy to officials. Their resentment was directed not only at the contents of the courses but also at the fact that an educational setting could be used for this kind of activity. This indignation added force to existing suspicions, harboured by some officials, that councillors intended the equal opportunities policy to say one thing and do another – in effect to appear to be liberal and actually be radical. Thus their belief that the policy was an exercise in bad faith was reinforced. For councillors, this reaction confirmed *their* suspicions that many officers were covert racists and sexists.

Conclusion

We have argued that conceptual confusions and misunderstanding are a ubiquitous feature of the practice of equal opportunities policies. Perhaps all social relationships are based, to some degree, upon mutual misapprehensions. However, we have suggested that a systematic pattern of muddle and deception can be identified which is an intrinsic feature of the social relationships that constitute equal opportunities policies. At our research sites, mistaken interpretations of the nature and purpose of policy were inextricably bound up with the strategies and tactics pursued by various policy makers and the shifting patterns of conflict and co-operation characteristic of the policy making process. The implications are that conceptions of equal opportunities policies cannot be understood simply as organizational blueprints and that the conceptions of fairness which they embody cannot be comprehended simply as bodies of knowledge or belief. Instead they must be seen as social practices, i.e. social activities which engage groups and individuals in a dynamic structure of intended and unintended actions in relation to others.

Our characterizations of liberals and radicals are, it should be clear, themselves ideal-types. The individuals and groups whom we have discussed in terms of these labels were rarely theoretically or logically consistent in either their actions or utterances and, within groups, there were clearly differences of emphasis. In part, this lack of consistency was a consequence of a failure to think through the implications of objectives and policies. More importantly, however, the lack of consistency and the confusions to which it gave rise were a result of the fact that groups formulating and implementing policies do so in social contexts character-ized by struggles for power. These struggles for power are themselves historically contextual and are, thus, concerned as much with the general structure of the organization as they are with the specific detail or objective of particular policies. In these circumstances, confusions may be either the unintended consequences of power struggles and negotiation or the outcome of deliberate attempts to manipulate situations and percep-tions. Confusion may then be both a result of power struggles and a tool in their prosecution.

If the participants in these power struggles are not always consistent, however, the ideas which they manipulate may be said to have a certain internal logic. (The discomfort of Conservative supporters of free market principles when faced with the essentially anarchic proposals of the Libertarian Alliance is illustrative of the effects of such a logic.) The expedient, or accidental, adoption of items of an opponent's or a critic's conceptual armoury may lead one along a logical road quite divergent from the straight and narrow path of one's own preferred principles. In these circumstances both liberals and radicals may simultaneously be cynical manipulators and confused victims of their own manipulation.

Notes

1 Legislation (such as the Equal Pay Act, 1970; Sex Discrimination Act, 1975 and the Race Relations Act, 1976) has made the issues of racial and sexual discrimination at work a matter of practical managerial responsibility. The legislation does not require an employer to develop a formal equal opportunities policy, and indeed research has shown that only a small proportion of even 'leading' employers have done so (EOC, 1978). Nevertheless, a growing number of companies have found such a policy legally, politically and, indeed, managerially expedient. (See, for example, Torrington, 1982; CRE, 1983). The existence of a policy may, in certain circumstances, assist an employer in defending a tribunal case. The Codes of Practice issued by the CRE and the EOC recommend the formulation of such policies and compliance with them may also serve as one aspect of a defence against a claim of race and sex discrimination (see, for example, EOC, 1982: para 32).

2 Thus, for example, liberal conceptions of equal opportunities policy may be said to advocate a form of 'contest mobility' while radical views may be characterized as a version of 'sponsored mobility' (Turner, 1960). (For reviews of debates conducted during the 1950s and 1960s, concerning the meaning of the term 'equality of educational opportunity' see Coleman (1968) and Rogoff (1961).) The distinction, however, has more ancient origins

than these. Two thousand years ago Aristotle distinguished *arithmetic* and *proportional* equality, 'the former meaning that everyone is treated the same while the latter requires that people receive things in proportion to desert, i.e. equal treatment in the same circumstances where the circumstances can vary among individuals and groups. Some people in some places may be recognized as more deserving than others' (Smith, 1979, p. 40).

3 Although in widespread use, the terms 'direct discrimination' and 'indirect discrimination' are not to be found in the legislation. Nevertheless, both of these forms of discrimination are prohibited by the Sex Discrimination Act and the Race Relations Act. Direct discrimination, in essence, consists of treating an individual, on the grounds of race or sex, less favourably than others are or would be in the same circumstances. Indirect discrimination refers to a situation where rules or standards are applied equally to all, but the requirements or conditions demanded are such that a substantial number of one sex or ethnic group has little or no chance of qualifying (see, for example, CBI, 1981; Wainwright, 1979; Bindman, 1979).

4 An additional source of uncertainty in some radical policies is a lack of clarity as to the boundaries of the relevant deprived population. For example, should the proportion of black people in skilled grades be the same as that in the plant, the Company as a whole, the local community, or the nation as a whole? (cf. Lundahl and Wadensjo, 1984, pp. 271–2).

5 A further point concerning radical views of ability and talent is that, when it comes to the assessment or evaluation of skills, radicals tend to discount intellectually acquired knowledge in favour of the wisdom of personal experience. It is sometimes argued that only the insights and experiences of the oppressed are valid and reliable forms of knowledge. Thus, for example, white males can know nothing of racism or sexism.

6 One of the consequences of assuming that liberal procedures lead to radical outcomes is to divert criticism from the effectiveness of policy to its implementation. Thus the typical liberal response to a perceived failure to obtain fair outcomes is yet further formalization of procedures. Radicals, in contrast, perceive such a result as a product of a lack of political will on behalf of those who manage the policy and insist, therefore, upon greater politicization of decision-making. In both cases, then, the necessity to re-examine basic assumptions is avoided and confusions and misunderstandings are deliberately or accidentally perpetuated.

References

Althusser, L. (1972) 'Ideology and ideological state apparatus' in Cosin, B.R. (ed.) *Education: Structure and Society*, Harmondsworth, Penguin.

Arblaster, A. (1984) *The Rise and Decline of Western Liberalism*, Oxford, Blackwell.

Ashton, D.N. *et al.* (1982) *Youth in the Labour Market*, Research Paper no. 34, Department of Employment.

Berg, I. (1970) *Education for Jobs: the great training robbery*, Harmondsworth, Penguin.

Bindman, G. (1979) 'Indirect discrimination and the Race Relations Act', *New Law Journal*, 26 April.

Bindman, G. (1980a) 'Positive action', *New Community*, Winter, 8(3).

Bindman, G. (1980b), 'The law, equal opportunity and affirmative action', *New Community*, 8(3).

Blau, P.M. (1963) *The Dynamics of Bureaucracy*, 2nd edn, Chicago, University of Chicago Press.

Bourdieu, P. (1971a) 'Intellectual field and creative project' in Young, M.F.D. (ed.) *Knowledge and Control*, London, Collier-Macmillan.

Bourdieu, P. (1971b), 'Systems of education and systems of thought' in Young, M.F.D. (ed.) *Knowledge and Control*, London, Collier-Macmillan.

Bourdieu, P. (1973) 'Cultural reproduction and social reproduction' in Brown, R. (ed.) *Knowledge, Education and Cultural Change*, London, Tavistock.

Bourdieu, P. and Passeron, J.-C. (1977) *Reproduction in Education, Society and Culture*, London, Sage.

Bowles, S. and Gintis, H. (1976) *Schooling in Capitalist America*, London, Routledge and Kegan Paul.

Braverman, H. (1974) *Labour and Monopoly Capital*, New York, Monthly Review Press.

CBI (1981) 'Statement' and 'Guide on general principles and practice' reprinted in Braham P. *et al.* (eds) *Discrimination and Disadvantage in Employment: the experience of black workers*, London, Harper & Row.

Coleman, J. (1968) 'The concept of equality of educational opportunity', *Harvard Educational Review*, special issue (Winter), **38**(1), pp. 7–22.

CRE (1980) *Equal Opportunity in Employment: why positive action?*, A Guidance Paper, London, CRE.

CRE (1983) *Implementing Equal Opportunity Policies*, London, CRE.

Crosland, C.A.R. (1956) *The Future of Socialism*, London, Jonathan Cape.

Crosland, C.A.R. (1974) *Socialism Now*, London, Jonathan Cape.

Dunleavy, P. (1981) 'Alternative theories of liberal democratic politics: the pluralist-Marxist debate in the 1980s' in Potter, D. *et al.* (eds) *Society and the Social Sciences*, London, Open University Press and Routledge and Kegan Paul.

Dworkin, R. (1981) 'Reverse discrimination' in Braham, P. *et al.* (eds) *Discrimination and Disadvantage in Employment: the experience of black workers*, London, Harper and Row.

EOC (1978) *Equality between the Sexes in Industry: how far have we come?*, Manchester, EOC.

EOC (1982) *Code of Practice: revised consultative draft*, Manchester, EOC.

Flude, M. (1974) 'Sociological accounts of differential educational attainment' in Flude, M. and Ahier, J. (eds), *Educability, Schools and Ideology*, London, Croom Helm.

Foot, P. (1969) *The Rise of Enoch Powell*, Harmondsworth, Penguin.

Glazer, N. (1975) *Affirmative Discrimination: ethnic inequality and public policy*, New York, Basic Books Inc.

Goffman, E. (1968) *Asylums*, Harmondsworth, Penguin.

Gouldner, A.W. (1954) *Patterns of Industrial Bureaucracy*, Glencoe, The Free Press.

Held, D. (1984) 'Central perspectives on the modern state' in McLennan, G. *et al.* (eds) *The Idea of the Modern State*, Milton Keynes, Open University Press.

Hutt, W.H. (1964) *The Economics of the Colour Bar*, London, Andre Deutsch.

Jain, H.C. and Pettman, B.O. (1976) 'The American anti-discrimination legislation and its impact on the utilization of blacks and women', *International Journal of Social Economics*, **3**, 109–34.

Jewson, N. and Mason, D. (1984/5) 'Equal opportunities policies at the workplace and the concept of monitoring', *New Community*, **12**(1).

Joravsky, D. (1970) *The Lysenko Affair*, Cambridge, Mass., Harvard University Press.

Kilson, M. (1983) 'In defence of affirmative action', *New Community*, **10**(3), pp. 464–9.

Lecourt, D. (1977) *Proletarian Science? The Case of Lysenko* (translated by Ben Brewster), London, New Left Books.

Lundahl, M. and Wadensjo, E. (1984) *Unequal Treatment: a study in the neo-classical theory of discrimination*, London, Croom Helm.

Maguire, M.J. and Ashton, D.N. (1981) 'Employer's perceptions and use of educational qualifications', *Educational Analysis*, 3(2).

Marshall, T.H. (1963) 'Citizenship and social class' in *Sociology at the Crossroads*, London, Heinemann. pp. 67–127.

Medvedev, Z.A. (1968) *The Rise and Fall of Lysenko* (translated by I.M. Lerner), London and New York, Columbia University Press.

Neuman, F. (1964) *The Democratic and Authoritarian State*, New York, Free Press.

Peppard, N. (1980) 'Towards effective race relations training', *New Community*, 8 (1 and 2), Spring/Summer, pp. 99–106.

Prashar, U. (1984) 'The need for positive action' in Benyon, J. (ed.) *Scarman and After*, London, Pergamon Press.

Rae, D. *et al.* (1981) *Equalities*, Cambridge, Mass., Harvard University Press.

Rawls, J. (1972) *A Theory of Justice*, Oxford, Oxford University Press.

Rogoff, N. (1961) 'American public schools and equality of opportunity' in Halsey, A.H. *et al.* (ed.) *Education, Economy and Society*, New York, The Free Press.

Rose, H. and Rose, S. (1979) 'The IQ Myth' in Rubenstein D. (ed.) *Education and Equality*, Harmondsworth, Penguin.

Salvadori, M. (1977) *The Liberal Heresy*, London, Macmillan.

Scarman, Lord (1981) *The Brixton Disorders, 10–12 April 1981* (Cmnd 8427), London, HMSO.

Schmid, G. (1984) 'The political economy of labour market discrimination: a theoretical and comparative analysis of sex discrimination' in Schmid, G. and Weitzel, R. (eds) *Sex Discrimination and Equal Opportunity: the labour market and employment policy*, Aldershot, Gower.

Sharp, R. and Green, A. (1975) *Education and Social Control*, London, Routledge and Kegan Paul.

Shaw, J. (1981/2) 'Training methods in race relations organizations', *New Community*, 9(3), Winter/Spring, pp. 437–46.

Smith, D.M. (1979) *Where the Grass is Greener: living in an unequal world*, Harmondsworth, Penguin.

Snell, W.P. *et al.* (1981) *Equal Pay and Opportunities*, Department of Employment, Research Paper No. 20.

Tawney, R.H. (1964) *Equality*, London, Allen and Unwin.

Thompson, P. (1983) *The Nature of Work: an introduction to debates on the labour process*, London, Macmillan.

Torrington, D. (1982) *Management and the Multi-racial Workforce*, Aldershot, Gower.

Turner, R.H. (1960) 'Sponsored and contest mobility and the school system', *American Sociological Review*, 25(5).

Wainwright, D. (1979) *Discrimination in Employment*, London, Associated Business Press.

Walton, T. (1984) 'Justifying the welfare state' in McLennan, G. *et al.* (eds) *The Idea of the Modern State*, Milton Keynes, Open University Press.

Welch, F. (1981) 'Affirmative action and its enforcement', *American Economic Review*, 71(2).

Wood, S. (1982) (ed.) *The Degradation of Work*, London, Hutchinson.

Young, K. and Connelly, N. (1981) *Policy and Practice in the Multi-Racial City*, London, Policy Studies Institute.

Young, M.F.D. (ed.) (1971) *Knowledge and Control*, London, Collier-Macmillan.

Zimbalist, A. (ed.) (1979) *Case Studies on the Labour Process*, London, Monthly Review Press.

Source: Jewson, N. and Mason, D. (1986) 'The theory and practice of equal opportunities policies: liberal and radical approaches', *Sociological Review*, 34(2).

13 EQUAL OPPORTUNITIES POLICY AND RACE EQUALITY

PETER GIBBON

EOPs – background, content and assumptions

'Equal opportunities policies' (EOPs) have been in fashion with a variety of institutional and business interests in the UK for most of the 1980s. In essence they amount to selling rationalized bureaucratic methods of selection and recruitment to capitalist enterprises and to disadvantaged groups in terms of their benefits to both sets of interests.

In the first instance it is useful to distinguish between factors involved in the promotion of EOPs and factors involved in their adoption.

The promotion of EOPs in. Britain may be seen as the product of coincidence of a number of trends. First, and most significantly, there is the increasing scale and volume of organized and semi-organized protest by groups excluded from or disadvantaged in the labour market. Most notable here has been protest and campaigning by black people (exemplified by the uprisings of the early 1980s) and by women. Protest and campaigning by the disabled, gays and lesbians and people on Economic League lists have also been increasingly evident. Secondly, there is the preference of Conservative Governments since 1979 for voluntaristic and business-led 'solutions' to problems of disadvantage, rather than compulsory and state-led ones. This is reflected positively in the ideology of 'active citizenship' and negatively in general governmental disparagement and undermining of the set of legal and institutional instruments for dealing with disadvantage established by Labour governments in the 1960s and 1970s. Thirdly, there are efforts by the Commission for Racial Equality (CRE) and Equal Opportunities Commission (EOC) to adapt to a basically unfavourable environment by shifting their emphasis from appeals for social justice and tougher legislation to forming a governmental-business consensus around the idea that being 'fair' to the disadvantaged (and everybody else) will benefit human resource optimization and organizational efficiency generally. Fourthly, there are efforts by specialists within enterprises to emphasize their own 'professionalism' and to define their organizational territory in a period where their traditional function of managing employee relations has been increasingly marginalized.

By 1989 a very large number of public and private sector enterprises were declaring themselves to be EOEs [Equal Opportunity Employers]. This was especially true of local authorities, most nationalized (or ex-nationalized) industries, large public companies and companies dependent wholly or partly on central or local government contracts. In addition there was a concentration of equal opportunity employers in the voluntary sector. In a summing-up of findings from the existing literature and from his own research, Jenkins (1986) lists as reasons for adoption by organizations:

- responses by some employers with multi-racial workforces to actual disputes on race-related issues arising within the workforce
- instruction to adopt or voluntary adoption following a tribunal hearing on race or gender-related matters. Alternatively, efforts to pre-empt tribunal cases arising[1]
- efforts to promote a progressive public image
- imposition by parent organization after takeover
- internal campaigning by activists (usually women or blacks in local authorities)[2]

A distinction is in order between what EOEs do and what the contents of EOPs are. Existing research (including that which I conducted) has found that there is no direct relation between declarations that an organization is an EOE and possessing a written EOP, let alone implementation of such an EOP. However, where written EOPs are present, the more comprehensive of them increasingly appear to lay down specific procedures for mainstream selection and recruitment. These are largely formal, rationalistic and bureaucratic, designating fixed regulations covering advertising, short-listing, interviewing and appointment, sometimes with training for those involved in these processes. These regulations involve drawing up objective descriptions of the job and type of person required to do it, as well as the objective assessment of the person most conforming to this description from a given field of applicants. EOPs also typically involve monitoring workforce composition by race and gender[3] and designate discrimination and/or harassment as disciplinary offences. Less typically they may include various forms of 'positive action' provision, which in the UK is legally confined to various types of targeted advertising, the provision of 'reserved' training courses and, very rarely, the reserving of particular jobs for members of particular races. An increasing number of employers also engage in employee relations practices which, while rarely included in formal EOPs, have the intention of promoting equality of opportunity. These include provision for extended leave, minority religious holidays/observance, job-share, movement between full and part-time work and (very occasionally) workplace nurseries.

EOPs may be said to embody two sorts of assumptions, although these are rarely if ever spelt out by their proponents or even their critics. One set of assumptions lies behind their promotion by organizations such as the CRE and EOC and concerns the economics of discrimination. The second lies behind their promotion by personnel specialists and concerns the economics of 'human resource management'.

CRE/EOC advocacy of model EOPs, including positive action provisions, implies a conception of employment discrimination with both 'supply' and 'demand' aspects. According to this conception, on the supply side there is a deficit of black people and women entering the labour market with levels of qualification allowing them to compete successfully for employment. On the demand side there are obstacles of irrationality and ignorance (including restrictive practices by trade unions) which distort demand from buyers away from black people and women.

Part of the solution to these problems is seen as supply-side positive action by employers, training-providers, etc., in order to upgrade the 'qualification deficit' suffered by women and black people, thereby allowing them to compete better in the labour market. The major part of the solution is seen as occurring on the demand side, however. The voluntary introduction of objective and unbiased recruitment and selection procedures will avoid irrational decisions based on prejudice and hence lead to the employment of increasing numbers of black people and women as well as enhancement of the occupational levels at which they are normally found.

The principal practical problem with this model becomes self-evident as soon as its assumptions are spelt out. This is that while the model presupposes both supply and demand-side action, its actual subjects – employers – by definition normally have little involvement with, control over or direct interest in supply-side issues. Any attenuation of discrimination by the elimination of irrational decisions on the employment demand side will be at best slight so long as the 'qualification deficit' of those subjected to discrimination is not eradicated. Power to effect this eradication is only marginally to be found in the hands of employers or voluntary agencies. In virtually all industrialized countries for the last century it has been in the hands of the state, in the shape of the education system and its adjuncts. In other words, removing discrimination in employment will be ineffective so long as racism and sexism continue to be perpetuated in the education system and in other state-led training provision. But of course acknowledging this clashes with the voluntaristic bent of the initiative.

In his seminal work on EOPs, Jenkins (1986) has elaborated some of the other, complementary sets of assumptions embodied in EOPs, namely those about human resource management. These assumptions are that for every job there will be a 'best person', that there are in principle accurate and reliable ways of determining who this 'best person' might be, and that the optimally functioning organization is that in which the 'best person' for any and every job actually occupies this job. Jenkins himself points out one major problem with this set of assumptions. It is that all employment is viewed through the prism of individualistic professional employment as requiring specific identifiable and possibly unusual qualities, for which there are corresponding measurable signs of merit or suitability (including formal qualifications). Of course all employment is not like this. Most jobs, as Jenkins observes, could be done equally well by anybody. Or as Andre Gorz (1985) has remarked, a majority of those employed use less 'skill' at work than they would driving a car to or from work. It could be added that even where specific identifiable qualities or qualifications are required for a particular (probably professional or skilled) job, the chances of any single individual alone unambiguously embodying these qualities is much less than the chances that none will or that more than one will. In the latter two cases the model becomes unworkable, since there will be no (single) best person.

More importantly it could also be added that the identification of all employment with individualistic professional employment, and the correspondent identification of the selection process as one of rewarding merit, itself embodies a bias toward those possessing formal qualifications and/or the ability to substitute for them verbally in socially acceptable ways. Just as bourgeois law and citizenship reproduces bourgeois class domination by treating persons with vastly discrepant economic resources as having equal rights to use their property as they see fit, so EOPs reproduce and even increase the employment prospects of the already formally qualified. They do this by treating persons with vastly different levels of formal qualification as having equal employment rights. In neither case does the 'right' confer equal chances to realize objectives; all it does is to legitimate as fair the realization of the interests of the already advantaged.[4]

The existing literature on EOPs

Apart from the work of Jenkins (see above) and certain other academic writers whose work will be described below, the bulk of the literature on EOPs can be described as coming from within the CRE/EOC consensus. By this is meant that it has tended to share the assumptions of these organizations about what EOPs can achieve in principle, although it is often negative about what they achieve in practice. The gap detected between promise and practice tends to be explained in terms of non-implementation rather than intrinsic deficiencies and limitations. While different conclusions are drawn from the phenomenon of non-implementation, none of these are developed into a critique of EOPs as such.

This literature's most recent expressions include studies by Stone (1988) of local authorities and Webb and Liff (1988) of a US university. While

Stone provides no data on the employment consequences of local authority EOPs, she shows that a large proportion of local authorities with EOPs have failed to establish clear executive responsibility for their implementation. Furthermore, even where such provision was made, there were many instances of the grade or location of the responsible individual or individuals being inappropriate with respect to the status necessary to influence the organization or even gain access to relevant information.

Webb and Liff show that despite an elaborate EOP, a US university failed to significantly change the gender balance of its employment outcomes over a prolonged period. Their argument is that the implementation of the formalized and bureaucratic practices which the EOP entailed was actively resisted and circumvented by those previously exercising 'discretion' in recruitment and selection.

This was partly because these individuals resented the removal of this discretion, with its attendant power, and partly because formalization and bureaucratization intensified administrative workloads to a point considered undesirable. Webb and Liff also acknowledge the role of low labour turnover in failing to generate changes of outcomes.

A major CRE-sponsored study of implementation conducted in 1987–8 is believed to come to similar conclusions to Stone's, although at the time of writing it remains unpublished.

The positions on EOPs occupied by Stone, Webb and Liff and the unpublished CRE study are themselves part of the subject investigated by the other branch of the existing literature, which mainly focuses on the organizational politics of EOPs in British local authorities.

It will be recalled that one of the sources of promotion of EOPs mentioned at the outset of this paper was efforts by personnel specialists within organizations to emphasize their own professionalism by introducing apparently rigorous recruitment and selection methods, and that one of the sources of their adoption listed by Jenkins was internal campaigning by activists (usually women or blacks in local authorities). According to Jewson and Mason (1986) and Young (1987), these contrasting sources of EOPs give rise within local authorities to different views of the role they should play. Personnel professionals tend to adopt a 'liberal individualist' (Jewson and Mason) or 'regulatory' (Young) approach to EOPs, emphasizing the elimination of direct and indirect discrimination by non-professional line managers, rather than the emergence of any particular sort of employment outcome.

By contrast, a critique of EOP implementation on the basis of apparently inadequate changes in employment outcomes is freqently part of the rhetoric of those emphasizing the 'radical-collectivist' (Jewson and Mason) or 'redistributive' (Young) approach to EOPs. This approach sees EOPs primarily as means of changing outcomes or shares of resources. It is occupied by activists who probably campaigned for the introduction of

EOPs and presumably also by the CRE and EOC themselves. Both Jewson and Mason and Young emphasize the typical confusion, part unintended and part deliberate, between these two interpretations of EOPs, particularly by politicians within local authorities.
[. . .]

On the one hand, those working within the framework of the CRE/EOC perspective have a demonstrable commitment to the promotion of equality of outcome, although this is marred by an inadequate under-standing of the real logic embodied in the assumptions of the EOP model. This perspective embodies an uncritical acceptance of the idea that if only the EOP model were implemented in reality as it is set down on paper, equality of outcome would be delivered (given a reasonable level of labour turnover).

On the other hand, those working within the framework of studying the organizational politics of EOPs tend to have a more sophisticated (though still usually incomplete) understanding of the assumptions logically entailed by EOPs. They are at least apparently aware that any EOP interpreted according to genuinely formalized and bureaucratic principles is unlikely to deliver equality of outcomes. The deficiency of their approach is that it evinces no particular interest in the promotion (if not by EOPs) of equality of outcome, i.e. in the interests of disadvantaged groups. Or at least, the question of how to seriously promote equality of outcome is missing from these writers' agendas. Instead there are simply academic-sounding warnings to avoid 'intellectual confusion'. The remainder of this paper seeks to develop the policy implications for promoting equality of outcome and employing EOPs which follow from a critical view of their real assumptions.

Some research findings from Sheffield

The purpose of the project conducted by the author in 1988 for Sheffield City Council and Sheffield Council for Racial Equality was to determine the precise relationship between employers' adoption of EOPs and employment outcomes for black people and women. For reasons of space and the limitations of the data generated, the following exposition will concentrate on outcomes to do with race. While the distribution of women's employment as a whole which was uncovered by the survey was quite different from that of black men and women considered together, and pursuit of equal outcomes for women will consequently have to chart a different tactical course than that for black people, the relationship between policy possession and outcomes was not dissimilar and the general strategic considerations which follow from this are probably identical.

Black employment in Sheffield and survey methodology

A few words of background will be provided about black employment/unemployment in Sheffield and about the survey itself, before the results of the latter are described.

In 1988 there were about 24,000 black people living in Sheffield, comprising about 4.5 per cent of its population of 530,000. On the basis of activity rate estimates in a detailed study of census data carried out by Bussue and Drew (1985), the economically active black population is estimated to have reached 5 per cent of all Sheffield's economically active by 1988. The three largest single employers of black labour in the city are (in rank order) the District Health Authority (between 600 and 700 black employees), the City Council (between 500 and 600) and South Yorkshire Transport (around 300).[5] Other large concentrations of black workers are found in the restaurant trade and in taxi-driving. (Of these organizations, only the City Council describes itself as an EOE and only it was included in the population sampled.) The latest reliable figure for black adult unemployment in the city dates from 1981, when it was 24 per cent (male) and 16.7 per cent (female) in Sheffield's seven central wards. The black male rate was a third higher, and the black female rate was double comparable rates for white males and females.

Recent reasonably reliable sectoral surveys of black employment have shown black people to comprise 1.2 per cent of the city centre retail workforce (1987), and 2.6 per cent of the engineering industry workforce (1988). [. . .] In October 1988 all employers stating they were equal opportunity employers in job adverts appearing over a fixed period in the *Sheffield Star* were sent a questionnaire. This asked them (inter alia) to state whether or not they possessed a written equal opportunity policy or statement, when it was introduced, what it involved, the systems of responsibility and reporting it embodied and the methods used in order to avoid discrimination in recruitment and selection. Employers were also asked to provide statistics on the composition of their workforce by race and gender.[6] Of 78 employers contacted, 58 responded (74 per cent), 52 by providing more or less usable replies (66.7 per cent) and six by refusing (7.6 per cent). Nineteen follow-up interviews were conducted with a structured sub-sample of the respondents. These included most of the organizations which reported crude black employment levels of above 3 per cent of their workforce and a number of those with negligible or very low levels of black employment. These interviews explored employers' perceived reasons for outcomes.

Equal opportunity policy provision and type of employer

The research found that by sector of employment, mainstream policy provision was commonest in the retail sector and in utilities and was found least in private sector manufacturing and the 'private sector miscellaneous'[7] category of organization. The retail sector and utility sector employers in the sample were distinguished from other responding employers mainly by the degree of organizational bureaucratization of their personnel function, while in relation to employers in the former sectors, those responding in the private sector manufacturing and 'private sector miscellaneous' categories could plausibly be described as 'under-bureaucratized'.

By geographical base of employer, it was found that Sheffield-based organizations were considerably less likely to have developed mainstream EOP provision than branches of national organizations operating in Sheffield. Moreover, the less mainstream EOP provisions were made by Sheffield-based employers, the more likely it was that these employers were small employers (insufficient information was available about the size of national organizations to draw any conclusions for organizations in this category).

A tentative association was thus established between degree of bureau-cratization, and perhaps size, and probability of possessing a developed policy. There were, however, some important exceptions to this possible association. For example, there was one very large (and bureaucratized) local employer whose 'policy' consisted of a five-line statement borrowed verbatim from another organization. Also, there was one distinct group of mainly small organizations (in the voluntary sector) which tended to have highly developed policies. These small voluntary sector employers were also the most likely in the sample to have adopted any form of positive action provision.

EOP implementation and type of employer

With regard to issues of implementation it was decided to use the indicators suggested in CRE and EOC publications and adopted by Stone (see above). Employers were asked about the presence/absence of dedicated resources to assist EOP implementation, and the presence/absence of a system of managerial reporting. A majority of nationally-based and an even larger majority of locally-based EOEs had no such dedicated resources. Dedicated resources in nationally-based organiza-tions were found most commonly in utilities and financial sector organizations.

The four organizations based in Sheffield with a dedicated budget or other resources to support implementation were all public sector organizations other than utilities. However, in all cases the resources dedicated tended to be fairly feeble in relation to total administrative budgets.

While over four-fifths of nationally-based policy-possessing EOEs with branches in Sheffield had a designated manager responsible for EOP implementation located at the point of recruitment, less than half of these reported specifically and regularly on equal opportunity issues to a higher manager or management body in the organization. In over a quarter of this group of respondents, no reporting on equal opportunity issues was ever requested or had ever occurred. A total of 14 out of 15 locally-based policy-possessing EOEs had designated managers or equivalents with equal opportunities responsibilities, but again only seven of these regularly reported to anybody. The organizations where regular reporting was occurring were concentrated in the 'other public sector' category and in the voluntary sector. Thus, just as there is arguably some sort of association between bureaucratization and policy possession, so too there seems to be a tentative positive association between bureaucratization and implementation. Once more, evidence that the highest degree of commitment to EOPs tended to be found in the voluntary sector cut across this finding.

From the findings described it can be concluded that policy management and implementation structures for the translation of policy into practice were a good deal less developed than policies themselves. Whereas over 70 per cent of responding organizations had undertaken some form of mainstream policy provision and about half had something resembling a developed policy, regular reporting was much less common and only a handful of organizations had dedicated specific resources to the issue. These findings broadly concur with those of Stone described above. They leave open the question of whether 'implementation' as defined here makes for any difference in practical outcomes, or whether it merely expresses something about how particular organizations function.

Employment outcomes

1 *General*

Turning to practical outcomes, the aggregate level of black employment among the 47 respondents sampled who provided detailed race monitoring information was 768 out of 43,672 employees (1.75 per cent). If the local authority is discounted, the aggregate level falls to 228 out of 15,226 employees (1.5 per cent). Only in manufacturing industry organizations and in voluntary sector organizations were 3 per cent or more of the workforce black. In financial sector organizations the proportion of black workers was less than 1 per cent, while in all other sectors described it was between 1 and 2 per cent. Almost two-thirds of all employers responding employed no black workers at all in supervisory, professionally-qualified or managerial (SPQ and M) grades. Black workers in these grades were almost always found only in organizations where concentration of black people occurred in lower grades – although the presence of black workers at lower grades was associated with their presence at higher grades in only 16 cases out of 24. (See Table 1.)

It was decided to approach the question of the relation between EOPs and black employment from the following direction: that of the employment record of partially matched groups of employers with and without developed EOPs (including developed implementation systems); that of the characteristics in EOP terms of partially matched groups of employers with high and low levels of black employment; and via interviews with employers with high levels of black employment.

2 Employers with and without EOPs

In order to achieve a partial matching, all organizations with less than 10 or more than 1,000 employees were excluded from the comparison; also excluded from consideration were those still at various stages of policy development and those organizations providing no monitoring information. The definition employed of 'developed' mainstream policy is that the organization concerned had adopted at least three of the following provisions: job descriptions and person specifications, selection tests, written recording of all decisions, provision of written instructions/

Table 1 Development of EOP/black employment record*

	A	B	C	D	E	F	G
Total organizations	4	11	5	16	6	8	4
Total monitored employment	364	1099	441	3030	905	1980	817
Total black employment	9	22	6	74	28	37	22
Total black employment (%)	(2.5%)	(2%)	(1.4%)	(2.4%)	(3%)	(1.9%)	(2.7%)
No. of organizations without black SPQ and M workers	4	7	4	5	4	2	0
No. of organizations with more than 3% SPQ and M workers black	0	2	1	5	1	2	2

* Excludes organizations for which race monitoring information unavailable.

Key to categories:
A — without statement or policy
B — mainstream policy only
C — 'developed' mainstream policy only
D — all taking positive action
E — three or more positive action measures
F — 'developed' mainstream policy + positive action
G — 'developed' mainstream policy + positive action + implementation

training for selectors, external advertising of all posts, procedures for dealing with harassment, and 'anti-racist training'. 'Implementation' in Column G in Table 1 refers to the presence of a designated person with overall responsibility plus a system of regular and specific reporting.

It would appear from Table 1 that making mainstream policy provisions (developed or not) or taking positive action (whether or not in the context of mainstream policy provision) has little or no apparent association with levels of gross black employment; it does not even seem to be associated with a smaller probability of having no black SPQ and M grade black workers.

The same seems to be the case when adequate implementation systems are present with other provisions and positive action, although the number of organizations with no black SPQ and M workers goes down to zero (in a group of four).

To determine whether the age of a policy was a distorting factor, the mean age of the policies of the four organizations in the column G was compared with the 11 organizations in the 'mainstream policy only' column (B). The former was 3 years (mean deviation 1.5 years); the latter was 2.6 years (mean deviation 1.8 years).

3 Employers with and without 'high' levels of black employment

Approaching the same issue by a different route it was decided to take the 10 organizations with nearest to 300 employees (the mean for the whole sample excepting the local authority) who employed no black workers and the 10 organizations nearest to 300 employers who employed more than 3 per cent black workers and compare which policies were present.

It seems from Table 2 that the main differences in policy terms between the 'best' and the 'worst' 10 employers was that while the 'worst' 10 were actually more likely to have developed mainstream policy provision than the 'best' 10, the 'best' 10 were more likely to have undertaken positive

Table 2   Black employment record ('best' and 'worst' recruiters of blacks)/ development of EOP

	A	B	C	D	E	F
'Best ten'	0	3	1	6	1	1
'Worst ten'	2	6	4	2	1	0

Key to categories:
A — without statement or policy
B — mainstream policy only
C — 'developed' mainstream policy only
D — taking positive action
E — 'developed' mainstream policy + positive action (PA)
F — 'developed' mainstream policy + (PA) + implementation

action of some sort. This is consistent with the slight improvement in gross employment of blacks when three or more forms of positive action are adopted evident from Table 1.

4 Origins of 'high' levels of black employment

The question of course is whether 'good' employers in the above sense are 'good' because they use positive action (it seems clear that they are unlikely to be good because of using mainstream policy) or whether they happen to have adopted positive action because they are 'good' employers. Furthermore, if the latter seems likely, then what exactly is it that produces a 'good' employer?

Six employers among those with the highest proportion of black people in their workforces were asked in interviews what they felt was responsible for these proportions. In the first case, a leisure-services organization in the public sector, the level of black employment reached had been attained as a result of 'a number of positive initiatives seeking to redress the ethnic balance', by a line manager 'without any push from our side' (i.e. senior management), before the formulation and adoption of a policy.

In the second and third cases (a manufacturing company and a training organization) senior managers felt that the levels of black employment attained had been the result of 'the genuine integration of equality of opportunity within the mainstream life of the organization'. In neither case had there been any particular intention to recruit black people. Actually, the intention in both cases was self-consciously to recruit from other targeted 'non-standard' sectors. The manufacturing company had a policy of employing every unemployed disabled person who was employable; the training organization had a policy of setting on every psychiatrically ill or formerly psychiatrically ill person who was employable.

In both cases, pursuit of equality of opportunity was at least on a par with business objectives, and acceptance of an ideology of avoiding and opposing stereotyping was a condition of employment for managers. The managers of both organizations appeared genuinely surprised when told that they employed black people in larger proportions than in the local population at large. Neither had operated with race-equality targets of any description. One organization had developed contacts with black community groups through its mainstream structure and work and notified these groups and others of vacancies and also used the ethnic minority press. Asked what 'making equal opportunities part of mainstream practice' meant in practical terms, the manager of the training organization stated:

[What's special about us is that] I think [management here's] constantly aware that people are discriminated against, without becoming paranoid about it. [We've] developed an ethics and an ideology which the people who work here [have to accept]. It's transmitted to them as part and parcel of being here. It's my ideology.

The three remaining cases were all housing associations. In the first (a nationally-based organization), the selection of a staff group with a black complement had been undertaken by a single manager (with head-quarters' support) before the opening of the Sheffield office. Among his appointees was a black personnel/employment officer who liberally applied positive action measures. These included setting on black professional trainees via the PATH[8] scheme and targeted advertising with community groups:

I went down to SADACCA.[9] They have public meetings once a week and they advertised that I'd be down there talking about a construction work apprenticeship scheme. SADACCA run a training programme for refurbishment. They had a list of youngsters and people over 18 who wanted to join their training scheme so I tapped into that and sent letters to them all inviting them to apply. I think one of the reasons why (we got so many replies) was that a black person was there promoting it. That encouraged them to apply. So did knowing that black people were working in a team here. If you're black and you look at an organization and there's no black people there, you just think 'Well I don't know, what's the point of applying?'

The employment officer was adamant that she would not 'positively discriminate' ('It's setting people up to fail'). On the other hand she was also adamant that more than a policy, an organizational *commitment* was required before reasonable numbers of black people could be recruited by an organization. Asked what type of equal opportunity policy she would advocate, she stated 'One that's short and to the point and states that the objective is to recruit more black people.' A 'short and to the point' policy had benefited her work, as had (in her view) the weakness rather than the strength of centralized control and reporting within the organization.

The fifth organization (and second housing association) had also recruited its high proportion of blacks before formally adopting a policy. One black person was not 'recruited' but a founder of the organization; the three others all joined as a result of positive action initiatives taken as the organization developed (advertisements for a bilingual secretary and for black trainees).

A manager of the sixth organization (and the third housing association) stated directly that the progress made in the area of employment had little to do with the organization's equal opportunity policy, which again postdated much of the recruitment of black workers:

[The problem with our equal opportunity policy] is that it quickly became something completely sacred. We put this thing in place which then became a tablet of stone . . . rather than a policy which helped this organization to get people in employment in pursuit of what we were doing as an organization. If somebody didn't follow the guidelines they were punished for it. It became something to beat each other with. I'd go so far as to say that there was confusion about what equal opportunities actually meant. Some people used the recruitment and selection policy as a way of absolving their own conscience. They didn't have to think about it anymore because we had this tablet of stone which said if you do this you're okay. In practice, all the other personnel issues went by the board. So all jobs were being advertised externally and there were people inside saying 'Well that's all well and good, but where's my opportunity?' That meant we had to start looking at how things fitted together. The conclusion was us acknowledging that we had a set of objectives as an organization. These don't include being fair to the whole world, they are about getting staff who can do a job that would produce this end product of good housing. Okay, if you've only got ad hoc policies around employment they can become very subjective and that can militate against all sorts of groups of people. But equally because you've got a tablet of stone the opposite isn't going to be true. We can end up with a situation where we've got a black person doing a temporary job and doing it well, who's not going to get that same job when it's advertised externally because there'll be a better qualified white for it. We have to get people to think 'what's this policy for?'

Summary

To sum up these research findings, there appears to be little or no relation between possession of even a developed and implemented EOP (although there are few enough instances of the latter) and stimulating change in employment outcomes, at least in the short-term. Where the latter had occurred to the advantage of black people, this was driven by political decisions within organizations to prioritize the equalization of outcomes, often in conscious distinction to 'being fair to everybody'. The meaning of positive action for employers who took these decisions was not as a supplement to 'being fair to everybody', but as a set of techniques enabling organizations which had decided to employ disadvantaged groups in greater numbers to conform to the letter of the law. It is possible, furthermore, that the factors making for adoption and implementation of EOPs and the factors making for the adoption of decisions facilitating equality of outcome are antithetical. On the whole, EOP development seems plausibly linked to bureaucratization, and possibly appeals to bureaucratic organizations or branches of organizations because of its formalizing qualities. Moreover, the more bureaucratic an organization is, the more it is arguably likely to pursue implementation seriously. The promotion of equality of outcome, by contrast, requires the suspension or sidelining of bureaucratic norms and procedures within an organization and (at least temporarily) the elevation of politics to a position of command.

The policy implications of a critical view of EOPs

If the arguments rehearsed and the research findings reported above undermine the apparent CRE/EOC priority of seeking to oblige all employers to adopt and 'genuinely implement' EOPs, they do not immediately suggest an alternative general strategy. One which they might suggest, namely explicitly attacking EOPs and calling for explicit political commitments to promoting equal outcomes, is probably just as one-sided and possibly more dangerous than the CRE/EOC line. This is because the realistic alternative to EOPs for 99 per cent of employers is not making a political commitment to promoting equal outcomes but retaining or reverting to essentially nepotistic forms of recruitment and selection. Equally, the tendency is for attacks from the left on the CRE, EOC and their projects to become appropriated by the right as evidence that 'nobody wants state intervention to reverse race and sex discrimination'. It is also worth pointing out that struggles for and around EOPs may have *indirectly* progressive effects not related to their effect on employment. For example, they have been known to serve both as objects and later as platforms for campaigns by blacks and/or women and/or other disadvantaged groups within organizations, which may not otherwise have occurred. EOPs may also confer a certain legitimacy upon the grievances raised by these groups in their consequent struggles. In at least two of the organizations examined in the survey described above such trends were evident. Finally, the idea of a single undifferentiated policy toward *all* employers is in any event unrealistic since employers are not only heterogeneous with regard to their present employment records, but also in their relations to the labour market and their vulnerability to different forms of pressure. A more sophisticated approach to promoting equality of outcomes might take this last observation as a cue, and firstly seek to classify British employers along the lines of divergence suggested above. [...]

Although other starting points for such a classification of employers may be equally useful, one beginning from characterstics of employers in different sectors of the economy will enable some of the findings of the research described above (and other earlier research) to be fed in. (Its deficiency, of course, is that this procedure fails to take account of differences between various sizes of employer, locally owned/branch enterprises, conditions obtaining in different regions, etc. within particular sectors.)

[. . .]

Notes

1 Since their adoption by parliament in 1984–5 the Codes of Practice on Employment drawn up by the CRE and the EOC have had the status of considerations which industrial tribunals have been bound to take into account when reaching decisions. In addition, under the Local Government Act 1988, local authorities may take an employer's possession of a Code of Practice covering race equality into account when awarding contracts. (The same legislation bans local authorities from using workforce composition as a disqualification.)

2 The criticisms of EOPs which follow are not intended to devalue the campaigning referred to here. While EOPs may not live up to expectations, such campaigning may have independently progressive effects. This issue is explored in a slightly different way in the section titled 'The policy implications of a critical view of EOPs'.

3 The monitoring of workforce composition by gender is in any event a legal requirement for the great majority of organizations, since crude information on gender must be provided for National Insurance, Census of Employment and other mandatory returns.

4 The issues of whether there really are accurate and reliable ways of determining who 'the best person' for a job might be, and of whether the optimally functioning organization is that where 'the best person' occupies each job cannot be discussed here. With regard to the second of these issues, suffice it to recall the political 'achievements' of Harold Wilson's Cabinet of the 1960s, which contained no fewer than eight Oxbridge first class degree holders.

5 1983 figure for South Yorkshire Transport.

6 In order that answering the questionnaire should not be too complex an operation for employers, respondents were asked to break down employees by race and gender separately, rather than to cross-tabulate this data. As a result it was impossible to generate separate information on black men and black women.

7 All those private sector organizations not involved in manufacturing, financial services, retail and training, and which were not utilities. Respondents included a construction company and two distributive organizations.

8 Acronym for Positive Action Training for Housing, a private sector black trainee scheme based in Leeds.

9 Acronym for Sheffield and District Afro-Caribbean Community Association.

References

Bussue, L. and Drew, D. (1985) *Ethnic Minorities in Sheffield: key facts*, Sheffield City Polytechnic, Department of Applied Statistics Research Report AS/5.

Gorz, A. (1985) *Pathways to Paradise*, London, Pluto.

Jenkins, R. (1986) *Racism and Recruitment: managers, organisations and equal opportunities in the labour market*, Cambridge, CUP [an extract from which appears in this volume].

Jewson, N. and Mason, D. (1986) 'The theory and practice of equal opportunity policies: Liberal and Radical approaches', *Sociological Review*, **34**(2) [an extract from which appears in this volume].

Stone, I. (1988) *Equal Opportunities in Local Authorities: development effective strategies for the implementation of policies for women*, London. HMSO.

Webb, T. and Liff, S. (1988) 'Play the white man: the social construction of fairness and competition in equal opportunity policies', *Sociological Review*, **38**(3).

Young, K. (1987) 'The space between words: local authorities and the concept of equal opportunities', in Jenkins, R. and Solomos, J. (eds) *Racism and Equal Opportunities in the 1980s*, Cambridge, CUP.

Source: Gibbon, P. (1990) 'Equal opportunities policy and race equality', *Critical Social Policy*, **10**(1), summer.

14 APPROACHES TO POLICY DEVELOPMENT IN THE FIELD OF EQUAL OPPORTUNITIES

KEN YOUNG

Introduction

The 1980s have been a decade of debate as regards the development of equality of opportunity in local government. It is of course too soon to attempt a definitive assessment of the achievements of that decade. The significance of the changes which have occurred, the distinction between rhetoric and reality, can be confidently judged only in a longer perspective. This article sets out to clear the ground for such an exercise, providing both a narrative account of the development of policy and an approach to the analysis of its implementation.

The first, descriptive, part of this article rehearses the recent history of British race relations policy, setting it in its governmental context and identifying three phases of development. The second, analytical, part explores the factors which underlie the 'implementation gap' or shortfall in achievement, and shows why attempts to secure real change in local authority practice are fraught with difficulty – possibly (and hence paradoxically) with greater difficulty than in most organizations of comparable size. The concluding part takes stock of the present and likely future situation, arguing that the most striking feature of the decade has not been the concrete activities and programmes that have flourished (and perhaps atrophied) but rather the spread of conceptual and linguistic conventions in the context of which they have been conceived.

1 Recent history

The development of local authority approaches

The extent to which local authorities now seem to occupy centre stage in the politics of race can distract attention from the recency of that interest. We have seen dramatic and sudden changes in the positions adopted by some authorities, often (but not always) in the wake of a change of political control. However, in taking stock of the local authority situation it is important to have regard to the roles of central government (variable, but with some continuing encouragement and pressure), of the Commission for Racial Equality and of local non-statutory groups and alliances. It is also wise to take a longer view of the many considerations which preoccupy local politicians and officials, a view which suggests that issues and causes may have a life-cycle of their own. Three distinct periods may be readily delineated.

Responding to immigration

The earliest responses of local government to ethnic minorities in Britain were shaped by a desire to incorporate newcomers into British society. Immigration from the West Indies began as early as 1948 and increased throughout the 1950s. It was followed by immigration from the Indian sub-continent, both flows being limited by the introduction of the first controls on entry in 1962, which were followed in turn by further and more stringent controls in 1968, 1972 and subsequently. Central government policy throughout this period was characterized by immigration control on the one hand and encouragement to the newcomers to 'assimilate' on the other. From 1965 this encouragement was reinforced by the first of a series of Acts prohibiting racial discrimination.

If central government was the effective gatekeeper, it fell to local authorities and to voluntary bodies to ease the transition of the settlers at the local level. Initially at least, groups of concerned citizens led the way in organizing inter-racial social events and challenging acts of racial discrimination (Hill and Issacharoff, 1971). These groups eventually took on a more formal aspect as Community Relations Councils, under the central tutelage of National Committee for Commonwealth Immigrants, and later the Community Relations Commission, receiving additional financial support from the local authorities. Thus began the curious arrangement whereby the lead role in race relations at the local level was taken by voluntary bodies, sometimes representative of the minority communities, sometimes not, and funded jointly by a national agency and by the local authorities. Local government was, however, the minor partner in this relationship. Very few local authorities gave more than token support for the administration of what were generally small and powerless organizations, and that often on the tacit understanding that they would refrain from criticizing their benefactor (Gay and Young, 1988).

By 1964 it was becoming apparent that anti-immigrant sentiment could be exploited for political ends, and the Labour Government, anxious to stem the potential for racial conflict, introduced a modest funding programme for localities with concentrations of immigrants from the 'New Commonwealth'. This funding became available to local authorities under Section 11 of the Local Government Act 1966. It took the form of grant in aid for the employment of additional local authority staff and was mainly used for the employment of teachers to reinforce English language teaching to Asian children in schools.

The second central government initiative in this period was the launch of what Prime Minister Harold Wilson termed 'a new urban programme'. This similarly provided grant aid to local authorities for a diversity of special projects and was again prompted by the desire to head off a possible mobilization of anti-immigrant sentiment by channelling funds towards areas of 'special social need', an elliptical reference to areas of immigrant concentration (Edwards and Batley, 1978).

A number of important points need to be made about policy developments in this first phase of local race relations. The first is the inexplicitness of both the Section 11 scheme and the urban programme. Originated by concern for race relations – in the proper sense of inter-community relations – neither source of funding was directly tied to the interests of the ethnic minority communities. Section 11 was a form of grant aid to local authorities, not to community groups, and was intended to ease the additional 'burden' occasioned by the presence of large numbers of immigrants. In practice, some at least of this assistance came to be seen simply as supplementary funding to schools.

While the Section 11 scheme remained an instrument – indeed, one might almost say the instrument of race relations policy – the urban programme cut loose almost immediately from its origins as a race-related programme. In neither case had it been seen as politically desirable to link the funding too directly to benefiting ethnic minorities; in both cases the ambiguity of intention was advantageous to government. But this inexplicitness sent no clear signals to local authorities, with whom the initiative to bid for funds remained. Nor did this inexplicitness make it any easier to monitor programme perfomance or even to address the issues raised by the particular circumstances of ethnic minorities in Britain (for a fuller discussion see Young, 1983).

The anodyne nature of race policy in the 1960s has been neatly caught in the titles of just two academic studies of that time: *Doing Good by Doing Little* (Kirp, 1979); and *Promoting Racial Harmony* (Banton, 1985). The assumptions – and the language – of the time constituted what Michael Banton has termed 'Britain's liberal hour'. The common thread was an indirect approach to race issues, tackling them obliquely while maintaining a low political temperature.

The final point concerns the flexibility and longevity of the two schemes developed in that period. Now some 20 years old, they remain the principal sources of funding for schemes targeted on the needs of the ethnic minority communities. Just as it was expedient to downplay these needs from the late 1960s to the late 1970s, so it became expedient to give them more attention in the 1980s, when the ambiguity of the programmes enabled a new drive and a new emphasis to be readily accommodated. It is their very inexplicitness and lack of specificity that enabled Section 11 and the urban programme to act as mirrors of larger political concerns. That these time-worn programmes continue to be significant – indeed, have an enhanced significance – is a measure of the greater political importance commanded by ethnic minority issues in Britain in the 1980s.

Tackling racial disadvantage

The next distinctive phase begins with the Race Relations Act 1976. This was a crucial departure in two senses. First, Section 71 of the Act laid upon local authorities for the first time a statutory duty to take steps to eliminate racial discrimination and disadvantage in the operation of their powers. It read:

> ... it shall be the duty of every local authority to make appropriate arrangements with a view to securing that their various functions are carried out with due regard to the need
> (a) to eliminate unlawful racial discrimination
> (b) to promote equality of opportunity, and good relations, between persons of different racial groups.

Local authorities henceforth became the local lead agencies in the pursuit of policy goals in respect of race, a status further symbolized by the similarity of the wording of this obligation and that placed upon the new national lead agency, the Commission for Racial Equality.

Secondly, the Act introduced for the first time a prohibition on indirect discrimination. The existing prohibition on direct discrimination – acting to exclude people on grounds of colour or race – was already well-understood, having been introduced in the 1965 Act and extended in 1968; but it was not clear that it had done much to advance the general well-being of ethnic minorities. There was now added to it a ban on excluding people from access to goods or services by means of requiring irrelevant conditions – for example linguistic skill in an employment setting where it was not required for job performance – which had the effect of discriminating against members of a group. For the first time, then, an 'effects test' could be levelled at local authority decisions. The intention of this new feature of the Act was therefore to tackle not only discriminatory behaviour as such, but the maintenance of practices which perpetuated what was now described as racial disadvantage. Not surprisingly, our review of local authority responses to the 1976 Act undertaken in 1979–81 concluded that the concept of indirect discrimination was shrouded in mystery and ill-understood (Young and Connelly, 1981).

These two legislative provisions – the conferment of a statutory duty and the broadening of the definition of unlawful discrimination – provided the

_r_ local authority policy development over the next twelve years.
_p_ace of that development was initially slow. By 1981 few local
_ie_s had reconsidered their practices, even though the 'effects test'
ment might be argued both to call for such a review, and to ensure
that _t_he voice of people affected by local authority decisions was given a
hearing (Young and Connelly, 1984). In a report commissioned by the
Home Office in 1979, Naomi Connelly and I commented on the need for a
determined promotion effort on the part of local authorities if the
intentions of the Race Relations Act were to be realized; a subsequent
paper spelled out what might be involved in such an approach (Young,
1982).

In the absence of a strong central lead, diversity of response prevailed. In
1983 we categorized the stance of the hundred or so local authorities
within whose areas substantial numbers of ethnic minority citizens lived
into four groups:

- those who were testing out the political and legal possibilities and
  developing approaches which aimed to give a fair deal to black people;
- those who were reviewing their policies and moving cautiously forward
  in a fairly conventional manner, but with some willingness to accept
  the need for change;
- those who were aware that a changed social, moral and legal climate
  presented a challenge to traditonal practices but were unsure as to
  what might be an appropriate response;
- those who as a matter of political preference set their faces against
  change and were prepared to ignore the requirements of their statutory
  duties.

It was a reasonable expectation at the time that experience would spread,
that good practice would be gradually disseminated, and that local
authorities would 'move up the learning curve' towards a greater
consistency of practice.

In the event, race policies developed rather differently. The most dramatic
impetus came from the urban conflicts of 1981. In the spring of 1981, a
senior civil servant explained to us the absence of any policy initiatives on
race from his department: race issues 'were on the back burner'. The
metaphor was grimly apt; within weeks violence had exploded on the
streets of Brixton, to spread rapidly to most large British cities.

Whatever the aetiology of the conflicts, of which those in Brixton and
Toxteth were the most severe, they were widely read as a demand on the
part of the ethnic minority communities – and young Afro-Caribbeans in
particular – for greater equality of treatment. Many local authorities,
shocked by the events, began to seriously consider their stance for the
first time. Elsewhere, the sense of imminent danger lent urgency to policy
review.

But the response came not only from the local authorities. The central departments and the Department of the Environment and the Home Office in particular, adopted a far more interventionist line, using the flexibility of the urban programme to redirect resources to multi-racial areas, seeking at the same time more immediate and demonstrable benefits to the minority communities. The Commission for Racial Equality and the Department of the Environment intensified their persuasive efforts; the latter gave a junior minister some co-ordinating responsibilities with respect to local authorities and race, and an inter-governmental working party on local authorities and race equality was established.

The Section 11 scheme has been in a state of continuous revision since then, with new guidelines emphasizing the need both for consultation with minority groups and more stringent deployment of staff. Central funding was provided to establish the Local Authorities Race Relations Information Exchange (LARRIE) as a clearing house for practice. If 'racial harmony' was the slogan of the earlier period, 'tackling racial disadvantage' might be fairly said to be that of the early 1980s (Young, 1985).

From consensus to conflict

While it would be an overstatement to describe the early 1980s as a period of consensus, it was at least one in which a new orthodoxy had emerged, around which Conservative ministers and local politicians of both parties could negotiate. That orthodoxy might be summarized in terms of an acceptance of racial disadvantage – the historic accretion of generations of discrimination – as a problem to be tackled by central and local govern-ment in partnership. Being explicit about race was seen as a necessary precondition for measures of 'positive action' – purposive interventions to ensure a fair share of goods and services as well as respect and prestige to the minority communities. And central government at least as active an architect of the new orthodoxy as were the local authorities.

At the time of writing the scene is one of confusion and acrimony. Political changes in some localities have produced a picture of even greater diversity in approach than that which prevailed 10 years ago. A concern for equality of opportunity has been eclipsed by a growing commitment to equality of outcome, a preoccupation which, I argue elsewhere, generates a far sharper conflict (Young, 1987). Indeed, the comfortable notion that equal opportunity (or fairness) would in itself lead inexorably to equal outcomes (or justice) is no longer so widely or confidently subscribed to. Similarly comfortable and even pleasurable notions of multiculturalism characterized local education policies for a period of more than ten years, only to be eclipsed by harder-edged notions of 'antiracist' education, which have in turn come under bitter attack as counter-productive. The so-recently-established orthodoxy has already given way to a plurality of antagonistic goals. The 'racialization' of policy debate has revealed its flaws and shortcomings. Something approaching an intellectual crisis has emerged at the centre for race policy in Britain.

There is a political crisis too. As local councillors have turned their attention to race issues, the working of their own local authorities – and the roles and relationships that underpin that working – has come under critical scrutiny. Local authority officers, as the continuing or permanent element in local administration, have in some cases become the scapegoats for years of political failure. Political demands are made in a spirit of impatience, demands which can be met in some cases only at some cost to the good government of the locality. The standard of administration and the quality of working relationships in some local authorities has fallen below any tolerable level, bringing deep discredit to local government and putting at risk what is left of central government's willingness to tolerate a measure of local authority discretion. This is not to say that race is the only issue to have had such an impact on local government; rather, it is one of a series of questions on which issues of power and responsibility have in the last five years come to turn.

In other localities recent developments have been in quite the opposite direction. Here the flirtation with race equality issues – or at least with their pursuit through the high-profile route of special committees and administrative units – has proved brief. There is an emerging view, openly put, that such overt gestures to the minority communities may incur heavier electoral costs than benefits. Today, the local politics of race has become polarized around a more intense espousal of race-specific measures on the one hand, and their more dismissive disavowal on the other.

A sober judgement must be that the movement towards adapting local authority practices to better meet the challenges of a multiracial society has reached a critical point. On the one hand there is a steadily spreading recognition among many of the less urban local authorities that past exclusionary practices must be dropped and steps taken to promote equality of opportunity. On the other hand, there is now markedly less confidence that an acceptable body of knowledge and practice exists which can be drawn upon by the 'learners'. On the one hand, more blatant forms of racism have been tempered. On the other, many local councillors and officials quietly wait for the concern with race equality to burn itself out.

2 Exploring the implementation of policy change

The feasibility analysis of organizational change

The recent history of approaches to equal opportunity in local government teaches some hard lessons. Unrealistic expectations, and a failure to understand the sheer intractability of large bureaucratic organizations have compounded the ever-present difficulties that stem from covert racial hositility or entrenched professional attitudes. This second part of the article explores some of the dynamics of organizational change and argues that while local authorities have readily declared themselves in favour of equal opportunities, their own internal processes are to a remarkable degree inimical to its achievement. Indicative rather than conclusive, the approach outlined here provides a set of concepts for exploring the implementation of policy change through the assessment of feasibility.

Any feasibility analysis must deal with two fundamental aspects of the situation that is under scrutiny; put simply, with what the relevant people believe and with the power relations between them. The two are of course not wholly independent dimensions: beliefs and values encompass issues of power and independence; formal relationships can underpin the way we see the world. Nevertheless, what I shall call the appreciative context and the organizational context of change have independent effects upon outcomes. I shall use the example of efforts to achieve equal opportunities in employment to illustrate the argument, parts of which are set out at greater length elsewhere (Young, 1987 and 1988).

The appreciative context of equal opportunity policies

By the appreciative context I mean that constellation of images, beliefs, judgements, values and perceptions that are to be found within any organization. They may be largely held in common, sufficiently shared and consistent enough to enable us to speak of the 'assumptive world' (Young, 1979) or 'culture' of the organization, or they may not. Professional world views or ideologies can play an important part in constituting the appreciative context of a public service agency, although there may be marked disparities between what is believed and valued by its managers and what is held to be so by those who deliver its services. Equally, different professions may construe common issues in radically divergent ways.

Appreciative gaps of this type are endemic in organizations, but a local authority presents the extreme case of multi-professional bureaucracy under the control of popularly-elected party politicians, among whom there may or may not be consistent assumptions about means, ends and actions. I want to deal here with the ways in which 'equal opportunity' is understood; with the scope and content accorded to the policy; with instrumentalities, or the processes by which it is thought to be carried forward; and with the implementation difficulties peculiar to the various constructions of equal opportunity.

The appreciative context of a local authority is specific to a particular policy area. Different policies mobilize different forces within the organization. Universalist policies designed to change behaviour within the organization as a whole at all levels – of which an equal opportunity policy is an example *par excellence* – are likely to face the most complex of problems in their implementation. This is because the issues which such a policy seeks to address – in this case recruitment to the organization – will be differently construed by people at different points in the organization.

Understandings of equal opportunity

There is a wide range of understandings of what an equal opportunity policy might entail, and different constructions of the purpose of a particular policy can coexist within a particular authority. Equal opportunity policies may be broad or narrow in their scope, and can espouse goals that range from marginal adjustment of the procedures of the authority to far-reaching changes in its patterns of recruitment. Given that such goals represent a range from the immediately achievable to the intrinsically difficult, it is a matter of some importance that a given policy commitment can be understood very differently by different people within the same authority. The appreciative context of equal opportunity policies is typically one of ambiguity, inexplicitness and confusion.

The first emphasizes procedures, and takes at least the initial aspiration of policy to be the reform of procedures and routines so as to (i) preclude the exercise of directly discriminatory judgements by recruiters, and (ii) to remove indirectly discriminatory barriers. Here the emphasis is on tackling practices and procedures that may have intended or unintended exclusionary consequences. Such an approach recognizes that managers exercise discretion and discrimination in the recruitment process; the aim is to ensure that such judgements are fair and lawful – that they are made on the basis of what the Institute of Personnel Management has called 'fair discrimination'. In so far as such a policy is concerned with equality, it seeks to ensure that candidates for employment are accorded equal treatment.

The aims of such a policy are regulatory rather than redistributive. They give prominence to those who will play a role in achieving greater systematization of procedures: personnel managers and race relations staff. In progressing such a policy of procedural change they may be involved at all stages in the recruitment process, from drawing up job descriptions and person specifications, through advertising and short-listing to selection and monitoring of the selection processes. Associated training programmes may cover any of these areas and include interviewing training for selectors. The criteria for the success of such a policy are generally implicit and the activity seen as self-justifying. This understanding of equal opportunity is principally concerned with fairness.

Different in its implications, although often proceeding in the same manner, is the understanding of equal opportunity as a redistribution of employment in favour of previously excluded groups. Such a policy goal is more explicit in its egalitarianism: it seeks what might be termed equal shares or equal outcomes. In practice, the achievement of equality is usually posited on some notion of ethnic representativeness, in which the ethnic composition of the local authority is seen as properly reflecting that of the community which it serves.

The programme inherent in such a policy position usually subsumes and transcends the concern to eliminate discrimination. It poses as the test of policy its success in changing the pattern of recruitment and, in the longer term, the composition of the authority's workforce. To that end it may support more positive measures to reach out and encourage recruitment from the minority communities. This position may be more common among councillors than among officers, although many officers also support it, some believing it to follow naturally as the consequence of the very procedural changes which they are attempting to effect. This second understanding of the nature of equal opportunity is principally concerned with justice.

Either understanding, if explicit and shared, can provide a coherent basis for policy. But such explicitness is rare, and the coexistence of contrasting understandings within the same organization more common. Inexplicitness about outcomes probably smooths the path for the adoption of an equal opportunities policy in some at least of these authorities. However, the effect of such ambiguity is to postpone conflict from the policy formulation stage to the point where concrete proposals are put forward for implementation.

The scope and content of equal opportunity policies

Not only do understandings of the meaning of equal opportunity vary between and within local authorities, the actual substance of policy is itself highly variable. The principal issue here might be posed in terms of 'equal opportunities for whom?'

The precise form which an equal opportunity policy takes may be shaped by the ethnic composition of the locality, the recruitment issues and efforts taking different forms according to the linguistic or other characteristics of the local communities. An equal opportunities policy might be explicitly geared to opening up blue collar employment; or it might concentrate (perhaps for reasons of internal political or administrative opportunism) on the white-collar grades; or it might cover both.

But local authorities also place quite different emphases on equal opportunities for ethnic minorities, for women, for disabled people or for gays and lesbians. The coverage of 'equal opportunity' is then a major facet of policy variation, and one which has direct implications for implementation. For example, measures to achieve greater consistency and fairness in recruitment procedures (through, for example, the redesigning of application forms) might be of benefit to black people and women in equal measure. The development of a training strategy might be seen as a vehicle for reducing the significance of race, sex or sexual orientation as a barrier to recruitment or advancement. Some changes in personnel policy aimed at achieving greater flexibility might particularly advantage women who are currently in the labour force. The establishment of equal opportunity units within the authority might have the inadvertent consequence of strengthening the competitive advantage of white women *vis-à-vis* black men.

There are few safe generalizations to be made. Local authorities equal opportunity policies are often additive in nature, the initial agreement that some characteristic – for example race – should not be a basis for adverse discrimination being readily followed by the specification of a (possibly extensive) list of characteristics the possession of which might similarly be or have been a basis of exclusion. It seems likely that in some authorities (but not in others) the linking of sex and race in an equal opportunities strategy can add impetus and aid agreement. Extending the coverage of equal opportunities to disability may have a similar effect. Extending it further to cover sexual orientation or spent criminal convictions may lead to resistance. That resistance may or may not then spill over to affect the prospects for implementation of earlier-agreed measures. These are dynamic relationships with unpredictable outcomes.

The instruments of policy

The third major source of variation in the appreciative context of equal opportunity relates to the processes by which it is expected change will come about. Some of the people concerned with progressing equal opportunity policies choose to emphasize procedures and the need for compliance with them. On such a view, equal opportunities are achieved by changing the rules and standard operating procedures of the organization and enforcing and policing their observance. Others emphasize the need to change appreciations through essentially declarative policies, through interventions to change the culture of a department, or through training strategies to enhance awareness – reflecting perceptions of power relations within the authority as well as perceptions of the change process itself.

Whatever the approach and the assumptions underlying it, it can only be carried into effect through the identification within the authority of those who are to act as the principal instruments of policy. Such a change in the organizational context of the authority in turn reflects notions of instrumentality; an equal opportunities policy may be seen as 'everyone's concern' or as the province of specialists. It may be seen as a management issue or as a matter of all staff. It may be led and monitored through the political structures – thus becoming a 'member's issue' – or it may be seen as something to be built into the mainstream of management practice.

Finally, its achievement may be seen as something to be sought through the absorption of a generalized moral concern into the normal run of decision-making or as something to be handled programmatically, through specified targets and action plans.

The nature of policy and implementation difficulties

Each of these three sets of issues – understandings of equal opportunity, the scope and coverage of the aspiration to equalize, the means by which such ends can be sought – bear in different ways upon the relative difficulty of implementation. Over time, the experience of attempting to implement a change in policy may itself feed back into the appreciative context of the authority, with failures and shortfalls fostering a sense of this type of change as 'too difficult', and with successes extending the sense of the possible.

The achievement of the limited aspiration to fairness or equal treatment lies more readily within reach than the more ambitious programme of achieving justice or equal outcomes. This is not to underestimate the practice and political difficulties of achieving such procedural changes. But in this case the goal is specified in terms of the arrangements of the authority itself and is not predicated on uncertain responses from the labour market. It enjoys a greater inherent feasibility.

Similarly, the achievement of the limited aspiration to equality (of whatever kind) for distinct and specified groups in the population lies more readily within reach than does the broader ambition of equality for everyone. Indeed, given the financial resource and internal labour market conditions of local authorities, the more broadly based equal opportunity policies run the risk of having no visible results to display to any one of the would-be beneficiary groups. Ultimately, all members of otherwise excluded social groups are in competition with one another for that scarce resource, employment.

Finally, the pursuit of equality (of whatever kind, for whomsoever) by means of purposive action, carefully delineated programmes and a clear designation of responsibilities maximizes the possibilities of achievement against the purely declarative policy which is not followed through. But while this is now increasingly conceded, any such approach must still be assessed in the light of, and tailored to the realities of, the organizational context within which policy is first proposed and then pursued.

The organizational context of equal opportunity policies

The organizational context comprises the formal and informal structures of power, authority and influence, and the procedures, controls incentives and sanctions through which they are expressed. In the case of change strategies which are led from the top, the organizational context of a particular institution may be favourable or unfavourable to a successful outcome, supportive or subversive of the desires of management. To some extent this is a matter of the formal characteristics of centralization and decentralization and the mechanisms of communication that sustain them, and to some extent a matter of traditions built up in the authority over a long period, perhaps since reorganization in 1965 or 1974. However, even where the formal authority of management may appear to sustain powerful interventions, the informal authority of lower participants, the operational discretion of middle management ('managers must manage'), or custom and practice in labour relations may effectively undercut and nullify it.

I want now to indicate some of the key sources of variation in the organizational context of the authorities, as they impinge upon the implementation of equal opportunity policies. These are, respectively, the problem of organizational scale; the range of local authority functions and the degree of differentiation stemming from it; the strength of 'central' integrating mechanisms; and the significance of informal power relations.

Points of entry: the problem of scale

The potential for exclusionary racial discrimination is inherent in the large organization. Every public service bureaucracy has a multitude of points of entry. Few of any size take all or even most of the decisions over appointment at a central point, although there is evidence that the personnel function is more dispersed in local authorities than elsewhere in the public sector. So the problem of the implementation of any change policy immediately arises. The greater the autonomy of lower level management to appoint, the greater the problem of securing consistency in practice.

The implications of this vertical division of power are most evident where the organization has a territorial locus, for the larger the territory the greater still the necessary decentralization. A large shire county may employ 30–50,000 people over a large territory, operating through area offices with substantial delegated authority. In terms of the difficulties facing those who seek to introduce an authority-wide employment policy, the difference between such an authority and a shire district employing perhaps a tenth of that number in a compact urban area is crucial.

The smallest and most compact local authorities have a sufficiently limited number of points of entry for the achievement of consistency in recruitment to be a feasible aim. In the medium sized but non-education authorities the number of points of entry might be around 3–400. In the shire counties it may be in excess of 3000. In practical terms, this precludes any possibility of the effective monitoring of recruitment processes, as distinct from recruitment outcomes.

Functional range and horizontal differentiation

Some public service agencies provide a single function or service. Local authorities, however, provide a range of services, leading to a departmental form of organization and the further lateral division of management responsibility. Indeed, local authorities are so sharply differentiated in this regard – having grown as semi-autonomous departments around separate statutory functions through the medium of distinct professions – that they might be fairly regarded as multi-organizations.

The degree of departmental differentiation is least in the shire districts. The London boroughs and metropolitan districts are more complex, with social services being an important department in both. The shire counties are more differentiated still, with education departments enjoying more apparent autonomy than in the metropolitan districts. The organizational context of pronounced vertical and lateral differentiation tends to militate against the implementation of any universalist policy, the more so where the central integrating functions – chief executive, personnel, management services – are weak or limited in their scope.

Integrating mechanisms

One popular route to non-exclusionary or antiracist practice is through the tightening of procedures to limit the discretion from which discrimination can flow. In the local authority case this often takes the form of some kind of reinforcement of central services. That may call for an expanded and more active personnel department. But there are few local authorities where the remit of personnel runs wide enough to act as a vehicle for such a policy. Education departments in particular may be effectively off-limits for central services.

Race relations units – or their equivalent – are a further form of integrating mechanism which may share or contest 'ownership' of an equal opportunities policy with the personnel department. In most instances, however, the central race function suffers even more severely than personnel from the absence of an effective organizational resource for challenging and intervening in the decisions of service-providing departments. Low status, and the inability to meet departmental chief officers 'eye to eye' hampers the performance of the integrating role. In the early stages of an equal opportunities policy, personnel and race relations staff may each be preoccupied with the need to gain organizational advantage over the other. The growing tendency to accord the heads of equal opportunity units chief officer status can be read as a deliberate attempt to overcome this difficulty.

The power and influence of personnel departments (or central personnel sections in chief executives' departments) varies widely. To some extent this reflects the type and size of the authority, the larger authorities tending to have a more developed departmental personnel function. However, in these cases the links between the centre and the departments are typically weak, personnel providing a support role to departmental staff and operating in an essentially reactive mode. Moreover, the scope of central personnel varies considerably even between authorities of similar size and type, largely for local and historical reasons. Where race units are established, their role is highly variable and in some cases is undergoing rapid change, as they seek to establish a strategic position within the authority, while their competitors seek to counter their power.

Informal organization

Informal power relations in practice pervade the formal organization. This is most particularly true for local authorities, where a pattern of political direction by elected members of the council is superimposed upon the conventional departmentalized bureaucracy. The responsiveness of the politicians to community, party or labour union groups who may have little contact with or visibility to managers can vastly complicate – or in some circumstances simplify– the implementation of an agreed policy line.

A nationally 'tight' organizational structure with apparently strong channels of central influence may be undercut by trade union power and networks of influence linking elected members and union officials. Such networks may cut across the authority not on a departmental basis but according to grade, where (for example) white-collar unions may be weak and blue collar powerful. The formal structures which underpin the personnel function – organization as a separate department rather than as a central services section, reporting lines to a full committee rather than to a sub-committee – seem to provide only approximate indicators of power. More important is the *derived power* that flows from the engagement in personnel issues of the authority's most senior politicians.

It is through informality also that the impediments posed by the organizational context so far described may be subverted. An authority which normally operates in a highly departmentalized manner in the delivery of services with weak central resources may be open to powerful issue-specific integrating leadership from political leaders whose influence runs throughout the authority. A race relations adviser occupying a relatively junior position in the formal hierarchy may have private and political channels of influence that count for more than grade when issues are in dispute. The formal aspects of the organizational context may be visible and stable; the informal aspects are not immediately apparent and are likely to change over time with shifts in the patterns of political influence and interest.

3 The next decade

Towards an assessment

Notwithstanding my initial disclaimers, it is appropriate at this point to attempt some provisional assessment of the significance of this past decade of policy development and to seek pointers to the next. The account given in the first part of this article lends little credence to the gradualist assumptions of epidemiological models of policy change. The analysis set out in the second part emphasizes that the outcomes of such change are indeterminate, contingent as they are upon a complex interplay of thought and language, process and power.

The predominant characteristic of that interplay is ambiguity – the ambiguities of language, and the ambiguities of power. Such ambiguity is the very stuff of taken-for-granted ideas undergoing transformation. These shifting ideas of rights and relationships that are encompassed in the term 'equal opportunity' are on a par (allegorically speaking) with the construction of such apparently diverse social phenomena as scientific orthodoxy, fashion, or popular rumour, for each is concerned with shifts in taken-for-granted assumptions. Each is a way of talking about and giving stability to uncertain realities, of fixing temporarily the flux of experience, of making sense of situations, vesting them with order and hope, replacing one plausible story with another.

Equal opportunity issues are highly charged, addressing as they do the boundaries of identity in the contained and constrained social order of the workplace. The burden of fear and uncertainty is eased by the collective adoption of safe ways of talking about them. To bring off that adoption is the essence of the political challenge, for politics is at root a linguistically constituted activity. Changes in modes of thought – even modish thoughts – should not be considered trivial or insubstantial. Rather, they provide the means of framing the issue, the better to address it. Thus the history of equal opportunity in this past decade may best be read as a history of what people have learned to say, rather than as a history of concrete accomplishment.

This is comforting, for at first sight the prospects of any further concrete accomplishment during the 1990s appear to be diminished. The current transformation in local authority powers, responsibilities and management practices actually removes from political control much of the scope for the decisions which those who represent or hope to advance ethnic minority interests might have hoped to influence, while the restriction of co-option and twin-tracking will take a significant number of them out of the political arena. Changes in housing (choice of landlord, House Action Trusts) and education (opting out, core curriculum, devolved management) together with the extension of compulsory competitive tendering to a wider range of services, are intended to diminish the role of local authorities as providers of services in favour of an as-yet vaguely-defined role as 'enablers' (Ridley, 1988; Stewart and Stoker, 1989). To the existing ambiguity of language will be added a new degree of ambiguity of power.

But these changes do not spell the end of the politics of equal opportunity. Rather, the coming decade promises to be every bit as fertile a period of political argument as was the last. For example, the simple concept of an identity of interest among all ethnic minority citizens, attributing to them a shared black experience regardless of their actual communal, religious or political affiliations is likely to continue to break down. The glib implications of the term 'racial disadvantage' may be increasingly challenged. The organizational practice of ethnic labelling will evoke continuing unease as to its meaningfulness, while prevailing notions of multiculturalism will be seen as failing to capture the dynamic and interactive processes by which human identity is managed over time. What will be at issue in the 1990s is the way in which we construe ethnicity itself. The more important manifestations of the politics of race in the 1990s are then likely to be less concerned with programmes than with language and concepts, as we struggle to find a mode of discourse that can do justice to the subtlety and variety of the influx of social experience.

References

Banton, M. (1985) *Promoting Racial Harmony*, Cambridge, Cambridge University Press.

Edwards, J. and Batley, R. (1978) *The Politics of Positive Discrimination*, London, Tavistock.

Gay, P. and Young, K. (1988) *Community Relations Councils: roles and objectives*, London, CRE.

Hill, M. and Issacharoff, R. (1971) *Community Action and Race Relations*, London, Oxford University Press.

Kirp, D. (1979) *Doing Good by Doing Little*, Berkeley, University of California Press.

Ridley, N. (1988) *The Local Right: enabling not providing*, London, Centre for Policy Studies.

Stewart, J. and Stoker, G. (eds) (1989) *The Future of Local Government*, London, Macmillan.

Young, K. (1979) 'Values in the policy process', in Pollitt, C., Negro, J., Lewis, L. and Patten, J. (eds) *Public Policy in Theory and Practice*, London, Hutchinson.

Young, K. (1982) 'An agenda for Sir George: local authorities and the promotion of racial equality', *Policy Studies*, 3(1), pp. 54–70.

Young, K. (1983) 'Ethnic pluralism and the policy agenda in Britain', in Glazer, N. and Young, K. (eds) *Ethnic Pluralism and Public Policy*, London, Heinemann.

Young, K. (1985) 'Racial disadvantage', in Ranson, S., Jones, G.W. and Walsh, K. (eds) *Between Centre and Locality*, London, Allen and Unwin.

Young, K. (1987) 'The space between words: local authorities and the concept of equal opportunities', in Jenkins, R. and Solomos, J. (eds) *Racism and Equal Opportunities in the 1980s*, Cambridge, Cambridge University Press.

Young, K. (1988) 'Patterns of service provision and recruitment: ethnocentrism, professional cultures and affirmative action', in Allen, S. and Macey, M. (eds) *Race and Social Policy*, London, ESRC.

Young, K. and Connelly, N. (1981) *Policy and Practice in the Multi-racial City*, London, Policy Studies Institute.

Young, K. and Connelly, N. (1984) 'After the Act: local authorities' policy reviews under the race relations act, 1976', *Local Government Studies*, **10**(1), pp. 13–25.

Source: Ball, W. and Solomos, J. (eds) (1990) *Race and Local Politics*, London, Macmillan.

5 RACIAL INEQUALITY AND THE LIMITS OF LAW

L. LUSTGARTEN AND J. EDWARDS

Race and the law

In writing the conclusion to *Legal Control of Racial Discrimination*[1], the mood of the study was described as one of qualified pessimism. A decade on, the adjective would have to be deleted. It seems fairly clear that the effect of the Race Relations Act 1976 (RRA) in diminishing racial inequality has been minimal, at best. This article is an attempt to explain why that is so, and what more promising measures might be taken.

Confronted with compelling evidence of widespread racial discrimination and disadvantage, successive British Governments have made use of legal weapons as the primary means of attacking it. They have enacted legislation enabling sanctions to be invoked through the legal process against those found to have committed violations. The legal process can be mobilized either by an individual asserting the right not to be subject to discriminatory treatment, or by a specially created administrative body, either acting on behalf of an aggrieved individual[2] or exercising its own powers separately defined.[3] Except in the latter instance, the legislation has proceeded by altering the rights and obligations of private parties and treated discrimination as essentially a matter of private law. Discrimination has in effect been made into a specific statutory tort, a point recognized in the remedial provision of the Act which explicitly drew the analogy.[4]

Measuring the impact of any piece of legislation, or any particular social intervention, is notoriously difficult. Nonetheless, the ineffectiveness of the RRA seems beyond doubt. Whether one looks at studies of the incidence of discrimination undertaken after it came into force,[5] or at the rate of success of individual complaints,[6] or the extent and influence of the enforcement efforts of the responsible administrative body, the Commission for Racial Equality (CRE),[7] or seeks evidence of *in terrorem* effects of the law on employers' behaviour,[8] the same conclusion is inescapable.

Several plausible reasons for this ineffectiveness can be suggested: incompetence of the CRE and of those who have represented complainants; unfamiliarity with the legislation in the early years of its existence, or hostility, outright or tacit, to its objectives, on the part of tribunals and judges[9]: and substantive defects in the Act itself, which are many and various. Numerous specific suggestions for alteration and reform have been made.[10] Acting upon them might indeed make marginal improvements in enabling individuals to indicate their statutory rights, or enhancing the effectiveness of the CRE. But perpetual patching up will not do: the problem goes very much deeper. Ultimately, it is embedded both in the nature of discrimination and in the nature of law, or at any rate of a legal system underpinned and structured at every level by the traditions and presuppositions of the common law.

It is obvious that legislation to strengthen the rights of workers in this or any other aspect of employment is not on the present Government's agenda. We are thus at an hiatus in terms of reform. We stand at a convenient as well as a very necessary stopping point from which we can reflect upon the effectiveness of attempts in the 1960s and 1970s to protect weak groups in society by means of statute. Lawyers tend instinctively to propose legal changes as a cure for social ills. Yet law is only one form of intervention strategy; and one we believe it is increasingly clear is of limited effectiveness.

Regulation through legal mechanisms is also a process of which our understanding seems to be surprisingly sparse. There is virtually nothing in the voluminous social science literature purporting to address the problem of law and social change[11] which helps one understand how legal intervention in social relations actually works at the sharp end. It is imperative that we begin by recognizing our ignorance. As a tentative step forward, it may be helpful to identify the various contexts within which legal regulation operates. This exercise may assist in the construction of something we need very badly, a theory of legal change. By legal change we mean the imposition of a rule emanating from some organ of the state, including the judiciary, which requires individuals to act in a manner different from how they would have preferred to act, on pain of some sort of sanction; or conversely enables them to act in a certain way without fear of adverse consequences that otherwise would have existed. A variant, which may be called a public law type of legal change, involves the creation of some administrative entity with legal powers to do certain things within prescribed limits.

The various contexts within which legal change operates include the following. First, where the legal system itself is so to speak the primary actor, as with criminal law, procedural rules, or custody and divorce, one would expect the clearest impact of legal change on behaviour, though even here that depends on how deeply the legal system itself penetrates the society. One can think of examples of colonial societies where the law of the occupying power was just a sort of icing on the cake, and there are also instances of countervailing pressures within the legal system such as judicial or jury resistance or non-cooperation by police or some other enforcing agency.

A second context is where the law seeks to regulate behaviour not directly related to the legal system by adjusting individuals' capacities to act. Legal change may impose or remove penalties for acting in a particular way or enable certain legal relations to be created. There seem to be two distinct types of legal change here. The first may be called *facilitative*. A powerful group is freed from some imposed restriction or enabled to act in a certain way not previously permissible. Examples include the enclosure acts, creation of limited liability company, validation and recognition of the trust device, removal of equitable notions of contract law that had prohibited certain types of agreements, and changes in tax law to lessen or eliminate liability for some type of transaction. This type of intervention is likely to be relatively effective because the beneficiaries are enabled to carry on the preferred course of action without hindrance. They have the material power, need no assistance, and will almost certainly be aware of the change and be capable of taking advantage of it. The second type may be called *protective*. It involves the creation of rights, which the weaker party can assert by means of litigation, in the traditional mode of private law. The protected person must invoke the legal process or the penalties must be so credible that the very existence of the law is a goad or a deterrent itself – the *in terrorem* effect.

For reasons we shall spend much of this article trying to explain, protective legislation is much less effective. Put broadly, there are problems of mobilization of the legal process that are severe, indeed debilitating, and do not arise with facilitative law. Three examples of this protective intervention by means of a rights or private law approach are employment protection legislation generally, such as the unfair dismissal and other provisions of the Employment Protection (Consolidation) Act 1978, the Rent Acts, and anti-discrimination law. There is also public law intervention, which may take two forms. The first is where a state institution itself becomes the primary actor by directly providing a service, as with the creation of National Health Service or compulsory schooling until a prescribed age. The law here, although occasionally giving rise to litigation, essentially provides a structure within which bureaucracies operate. Legal considerations are not prominent in the actors' minds. The second is where the institution regulates, investigates or otherwise may direct or influence the operation of private entities.

We hope these analytical distinctions may prove helpful in exploring some of the problems that have emerged as the complex realities of racial equality have had to be translated into legal concepts and otherwise wrenched, pressed, squeezed, pounded and torn to fit within the framework of English law.

The law and discrimination

In principle, cases of direct discrimination, adverse treatment on racial grounds, raise no novel issues for the function of legal adjudication. Facts must be found, or inferred, about specific past events involving a limited number of individuals, and in cases where the information is not directly available, the courts are accustomed to constructing presumptions or other devices so as not unduly to hinder the plaintiff's proving his case.[12] Indeed, they have done this in discrimination cases.[13] The formal burden of proof is not an unsuperable obstacle. The real problem is the unsympathetic response of tribunals[14] – their unwillingness to draw inferences supporting complainants' claims. In the face of the ambiguity inevitable in such cases they have tended to credit the respondents' explanations. This is a matter of political or personal predilection, not of legal incapacity.

Indirect discrimination, however, is a very different matter. It makes unlawful those policies or practices which are not racist in intent, but which have disproportionate adverse effect upon a racial minority. In its present form it is a somewhat narrow and awkwardly-phrased expression of the idea of institutional discrimination.[15] As such, it requires the courts to find 'social facts' about broader societal relationships – the socio-economic condition of ethnic *groups*, the working of labour markets, the employment practices of firms and industries, and the like. Courts in the United States, from which the concept of indirect discrimination was borrowed, have long experience with evaluating data of this type in the form of the so-called 'Brandeis brief' but this is an activity alien to the English courts and one with which, to judge from the reported cases, they feel profoundly uncomfortable.

Racial disadvantage in the fullest sense is outside the law entirely. By 'racial disadvantage' we mean material, psychological or social inequalities, bearing disproportionately upon racial minorities. Examples are under-achievement in schooling, higher rates of unemployment, or residential concentration in decaying neighbourhoods. Discrimination is both a major element and a continuing long-term cause of disadvantage, but the latter has a self-perpetuating dynamic of its own, and both extends much wider and is the product of several additional and even less tangible influences.

The reason the law cannot extend to racial disadvantage is that no one is formally responsible. In law, one needs an identifiable defendant who has done something, or to whom a decision can be imputed. There are therefore tight limits to what legal regulation can reach; at the least some formally articulated or reasonably clear policy is required. This can be seen even in the much narrower area of litigation under the present statute: a significantly disproportionate number of reported cases[16] has involved public sector employers, who far more commonly than those in the private sector use published criteria, clearly enunciated rules and formal procedures in deciding upon hiring and promotion. Their decisions can thus be more readily subject to critical examination than idiosyncratic judgments made without reference to articulated standards or review of extensive personal documentation.

By definition, discrimination is the antithesis of individualized decision. A person is ill-treated, or shares some social circumstances, because of his involuntary membership of a group. There is therefore a collective dimension to every discrimination case which it is difficult to fit within the traditional processes of law. Adjudication in English law has conventionally proceeded by *individuation*: the realm of relevant evidence is marked with narrow boundaries, and the courts, whilst permitting representative actions, have restricted the number of parties by the narrowness of the 'common interest' test of *Markt & Co. Ltd.* v. *Knight Steamship Co. Ltd.*[17]

This individuation may be partly explicable in terms of managerial rationality, the need to keep litigation manageable in a judicial system that has minimal support services for judges and relies exclusively on oral presentation of evidence and legal argument. But there is also an ideology at work: the exaltation of individualism by the common law. This underpins even quite technical rules of procedure, as in the rule that a third party cannot adduce evidence of even a central finding of fact in an action between the other parties with whom he is not privy,[18] or in the refusal to admit as evidence, let alone accord *res judicata* effect to, judgments against a defendant facing a virtually identical claim from a different plaintiff (as in product liability cases); or even to enter judgment automatically in favour of all plaintiffs in a successful representative action.[19]

Discrimination law is hampered in several ways by individuation, but in none so important as the restrictions on the scope of remedies. These may be backward-looking (compensatory) or forward-looking (changes in discriminatory policies and practices). Because all members of a minority group will have been identically affected by the discrimination, it is reasonable that all such persons adequately qualified and shown to be affected be accorded the same remedy as the individual who has won his particular case. In the United States, this is accomplished by means of the class action, but there is nothing magical about this particular procedural device; it is quite conceivable that the representative action could be adapted to achieve the same result. The practical consequence is that an American employer adjudged to have discriminated will face a large bill for compensation to all those within the class. It therefore often becomes cheaper and easier to obey the law; the employer is forced to bear the true cost of his illegality because its effect is fully taken into account rather than measured only in relation to the individual who has had the courage, persistence and patience to bring an action. This cost-maximizing deterrence is not possible under English law and its absence, by making discrimination cheap, virtually ensures the ineffectiveness of the rights approach.

An analogous point applies to forward-looking remedies. Although the statute permits a so-called 'action recommendation', it is merely a recommendation, not an order. Moreover, it cannot extend to a matter that does not affect the complainant personally. This is explicitly provided in the statute,[20] with the consequence that if the evidence reveals that discriminatory policies have excluded black applicants, tribunals are not empowered to order the employment of those who can be shown to have been victimized, let alone impose any sort of hiring targets based upon labour market percentages. This again flows from the fact that legislation in Britain accepts the assumptions and practices of common law, in this instance its long-standing refusal to order specific performance of the contract of employment. The late Professor Kahn-Freund explained this stance as an application of the doctrine of mutuality: since the common law would not recognize servitude, nor order any person to work for a given employer, it followed that no employer could be compelled to engage any individual.[21] Interestingly, though a partial statutory incursion has been made into this principle by the reinstatement and re-engagement provisions for those unfairly dismissed, these remedies – which are supposed to be primary – are hardly ever used.[22]

The deadening influence of the common law is brought into sharp focus by a comparison with American civil rights law – federal legislation creating causes of action heard in federal courts. Apart from constitutional litigation, those courts concern themselves almost exclusively with interpretation of statute. They do not see that task as one of subtle linguistic analysis, nor do they locate statutes in relation to pre-existing *legal* rules. Rather they treat major statutes as blueprints of *social* policy. Hence they attempt to inform themselves fully about the social reality of the 'mischief', interpret substantive provisions broadly in light of that understanding – not in relation to the pre-existing common law – and even create new remedies in a purposive effort to effectuate the legislative aim. The legislation created a muscular skeleton, but the courts at all levels have put on the substantial flesh.

Moreover, the American Congress, unlike Parliament, has long since abandoned its subservience to the assumptions, values and doctrinal constraints of common law. The breakaway can be traced back as early as the creation of the remedy of treble damages in the anti-trust (restrictive practices) legislation of 1890, and has proceeded apace. In the present context, the most relevant example is the labour legislation in the 1930s, in which the Congress began using reinstatement as a protective remedy for those engaged in trade union activities. It consciously drew upon this precedent when fashioning the much broader remedies involving hiring members of the victimized class in the employment discrimination legislation of 1964.[23]

Another problem that has befallen anti-discrimination efforts in this country arises from the peculiar nature of English administrative law – again a reflection of the common law tradition. The CRE has been given virtually unique powers of enforcement, which combine investigation with the imposition of a sanction – the non-discrimination notice.[24] It is not a very potent sanction, but its novelty lies in the fact that it is imposed by the investigative body itself, subject to challenge in the courts. The judiciary have ensnared the Commission in a spider's web of technicality only partly commanded by the language of the Act. They have taken a much more restrictive approach in comparison with, for example, the latitude they have permitted Department of Trade Inspectors under the Companies Act.[25] We think their attitude reflects a hostility to what they see as an unacceptable amalgamation of executive and judicial functions – the body conducting the fact finding also issues the notice. In this instance, they are not evincing hostility to discrimination legislation as such, but giving effect to an ingrained pattern of thinking about administrative powers. One can see a similar process at work in their attitude to the Civil Aviation Authority as constituted in the 1970s. In a persuasive critique of the *Skytrain* decision,[26] G.R. Baldwin pointed out that the Civil Aviation Authority was a constitutional innovation deliberately designed as a body with considerable discretionary powers which would remain subordinate to central government policies.[27] It was meant to combine what were traditionally understood as executive and judicial methods in a delicately balanced legal framework which the court simply failed to understand. An independent regulatory agency possessing the quasi-judicial power to issue injunctive-type orders and make rules at the same time is something readily familiar to lawyers in the United States and Canada but quite alien to the English courts, which are therefore unwilling to allow a body given such power by Parliament to exercise them in the way that was intended. Thus both protective intervention to enhance rights of individuals, modifying private law, and the public law creation of a novel mechanism of control have foundered badly on the conservatism of the common law.

We have examined features of discrimination and disadvantage which make it particularly difficult to use a private law approach to combat them effectively, or indeed to fit comfortably within the traditional pattern of litigation. Additionally, however, there are several distinctive characteristics of legal expression and adjudication, independent of any particular legal culture, which lawyers tend to take for granted but which cumulatively present serious impediments to the effective use of law to implement social policy. We shall use illustrations drawn from discrimination litigation, but equally appropriate examples could be taken from any complex area, such as housing, industrial relations or planning.

Law demands specificity. It is not sufficient to argue that the defendant is within the spirit or broad policy canvass of the legislation. Unforeseen or marginal cases may fall outside of the precise statutory language, as in the decisions holding that rent officers, JPs, and YOPS trainees, are not covered by the discrimination statutes,[28] or that language may be read in a wooden literal way, as in the reading given the prohibition of victimization.[29] Conversely, it may be argued that the plaintiff is not technically within the protected class even though he has undoubtedly suffered discrimination, as in the controversy over whether Sikhs are an 'ethnic group.'[30]

Legal process involves technical rules of procedure specified by statute, rule of court and, equally important, judicial notions of appropriate procedure grafted on to these. Each particular rule may be 'twisted' by the defendant, i.e. used to his advantage. This has been one of the main things plaguing the CRE in its formal investigations. 'Terms of reference' are required for each formal investigation; and the House of Lords has held that these must be based on some specific evidence and that without such evidence the investigation was without statutory authority.[31] The practical import is to narrow the range of discriminatory practices into which, at least initially, the Commission may enquire. More seriously, the Court of Appeal has read the statute to permit the recipient of a non-discrimination notice to contest the findings of fact upon which the notice is based, notwithstanding Lord Denning's recognition that this might make the whole process so cumbersome that formal investigations would grind to a halt.[32]

Use of the law involves skills which large-scale employers may be expected to command far more readily than complainants. Mark Galanter's well-known article, 'Why the Haves Come Out Ahead',[33] which demonstrates the inherent advantages enjoyed by 'repeat players' over 'one-shot players' in litigation, goes a long way towards explaining both the relative ease with which discrimination claims have been defeated, and also the fact that individual complainants are more likely to be successful if they obtain aid from the CRE – itself a repeat player on the other side. The element of skill also means that each potential loophole will be explored in depth – or is it breadth? – delaying tactics adopted, and the like. This, as the saying goes, is standard operating procedure for good lawyers, and partly accounts for the long delays in formal investigations which so exercized the House of Commons Select Committee in its heavily critical report on the CRE.[34] Yet, short of forbidding alleged discriminators to defend themselves in a legal forum, these tactics cannot be curbed.

Legal decision and reasoning proceed by attempting, so far as seems possible, to draw clear lines and to resolve questions with finality by applications of an abstract rule or principle. Institutional discrimination and racial disadvantage require more subtle, long-term policies which must be capable of alteration as experience replaces conjecture and demographic and economic change alter the condition of ethnic minorities. In this area, primary reliance upon legal tools is like trying to etch figures in glass with a pickaxe.

Law merely imposes minimum standards. Compliance is satisfied by strict adherence to the letter; it is perfectly legal to do nothing more. If great areas of concern are outside the effective reach of the law, as we have argued is inevitably true of racial disadvantage, no one is under any legal responsibility to do anything about them. Moreover, emphasis upon defining minimal compliance may discourage developing and implementing more imaginative and innovative measures directed at the ultimate

al incquality, and certainly channels attention to the narrow
ieving the least that is required.

tandem with the previous point, legal regulation ultimately
gative fashion. It imposes constraints backed by penalties for
nce. Yet as a general principle of human psychology, it is
anything but obvious that punishment, or its threat, is the most effective
means of moulding behaviour. Carrots rather than sticks, or perhaps a
judicious combination, are likely to prove more persuasive. In particular,
financial inducements to profit-conscious employers are far more likely to
overcome resistance and even stimulate voluntary innovation than the
rather remote possibility of mild sanctions. And a few strategically placed
OBEs for managing directors of firms which take the lead in implementation of equal opportunities policies, or even Queen's Awards for Race
Relations, would be worth their weight in gold-plated tribunal victories.

There is a final point to be made about the rights approach, particularly in
the context of discrimination: from the Government's point of view, it is
cheap. It simply ignores the realities of racial disadvantage. It does
nothing to assist in the development of human capital; thus for the most
disadvantaged it is simply irrelevant. And the costs of enforcement are
laid upon the victim. It is an expression of classical liberalism, albeit in an
enlightened form, and its inadequacies expose the severe limitations of
that tradition as the basis of social justice.

An approach to discrimination that relies upon the use of negative legal
sanctions for violation of rights created by statute can at best have modest
impact upon the eradication of discrimination, and virtually none upon
the more pervasive and subtle manifestations of racial disadvantage. An
invigorated administrative enforcement body would certainly be welcome.
But to rely on law enforcement as the primary approach[35] seems to us an
advance commitment to fighting the battle with one hand firmly tied
behind one's back. This is not to deny the need for legislation, which
remains essential as a pressure upon those activated by racial animus, or
who will not act without compulsion to remove unnecessary barriers to
the fair evaluation of the competence of black workers. Legislation is also
required to provide facilitative legal support for the implementation of
remedial policies discussed below. But it cannot by itself bring about any
significant reduction of racial inequality.

The law's potential

Given this gloomy prognosis of the power of the law to affect racial
inequality, what alternative strategies present themselves? Two alternatives come immediately to mind. The first is to step outside the law to see
what an administrative or policy-oriented approach might achieve. The

second is to take on board what the law could be made to achieve from the experience of its use in other countries.

In looking to administrative and policy solutions it may be interesting to attempt a thought experiment, one which we fear will remain in the realm of pure thought for some time to come. It is to imagine a government genuinely and forcefully committed to equalizing the conditions of ethnic minorities. What would be its priorities and its methods?

For reasons already suggested, whilst strengthening the Race Relations Act would be one element in its strategy – especially because the damage done by judicial interpretation needs to be repaired – it would constitute only a secondary and supportive measure. The emphasis of such a government would be on an *administrative* approach – on the use of discretionary polices, rather than legal rules. What follows is a schematic outline of what the critical elements of such a strategy would be.

First, every major policy decision would be vetted in advance for its impact on ethnic minorities. Key economic decisions such as incentives for the establishment of new industries in particular areas or the level of construction of public sector housing, to take but two, are of disproportionate importance to ethnic minorities, who are concentrated in declining inner areas, suffer high rates of unemployment and, in the case of West Indians and Bangladeshis, are disproportionately reliant on council accommodation. To take one important example, much recent growth has occurred in places where blacks are notably absent, like Milton Keynes, at the expense of the inner city areas. This exacerbation of racial inequality might have been prevented by consideration of whether the area was likely to attract black people and, if not, what measures could be taken to encourage and assist reasonable numbers to venture there.

The fundamental point is that the ethnic dimension be considered an essential aspect of all such decisions. Creation of a race-specific administrative body is a recipe for marginalization, a deflection of the responsibility that should be shouldered by those taking the critical decisions, which in present conditions are economic. If ethnic matters are the domain of a specialist body, even inside government, it will follow inevitably that the ethnic factor will become part of the decision process only at a later, reactive stage, and not at the critical point of initial policy formulation, when the issues are defined and the parameters drawn. Hence all government departments should impose upon designated high level officials responsibility for this aspect of policy formulation, and for monitoring the ethnic impact of policies at the stage of implementation. More broadly, a cabinet committee chaired by a senior minister should be established for the same purposes.

One consequence of this enhanced role of government is alteration of the role of the Commission for Racial Equality. It need no longer be an all-purpose body purportedly representing the interests of ethnic minorities. It would be freed to direct its energies primarily to law enforcement, and to training others – workers in citizens' advice bureaux and law centres, trade union officials and social workers – in the intricacies of representing individual complainants. It might also assume the role of watchdog over the effectiveness of remedial action policies adopted by central government, which no other organization presently on the horizon is as well positioned to fill.

Turning to our second alternative of the law's potential, it would be wrong to use the experience of Britain's largely regulatory legislation as marking the potential limits of the law as an instrument for social change, let alone the limits of our extra-legal capacities to effect change. Much more can be, and is being done, as experience elsewhere shows. As examples of what can be done we can turn to the experience of the United States where law has proved to be not only an instrument of change in itself but arguably has also changed the climate of race-conscious practice (though not without some unintended and unhappy consequences), and, closer to home, what has been legislated in Northern Ireland in respect of religious groups. In the latter case, it is too early to say what effects the Fair Employment (Northern Ireland) Act 1989 will have, but it does present us with a model of how the law could be used more aggressively to promote racial equality rather than simply as a regulatory mechanism. (There is nothing in the Fair Employment Act and accompanying Code of Practice (Department of Economic Development, 1989a) other than technical issues concerning monitoring and the identification of groups that would not easily translate from religion to race.)

But what the experience of the past twenty years in the US has shown, and what we might hope will eventually be the legacy of the Northern Ireland legislation, is that legal devices and administrative practice are inseparable. Aggressive good practice to promote racial equality will not willingly be adopted on a large scale. It must be required under threat of sanction. But what may grudgingly be done to begin with, we might hope – as the American experience gives us reason to – will become normal practice, a part of corporate and institutional culture.

Before turning to take a closer look at what practice and law can achieve elsewhere, we must be clearer about what it is we want to achieve. The law, it will turn out, is better at some things than others. Racial inequality, racial discrimination, and racial disadvantage are not interchangeable terms; though closely related, they have distinct meanings. Racial inequality is the most general; it can include inequalities of treatment (including discrimination), status, wealth, positions, welfare, rights and so on. Racial disadvantage and racial discrimination have more particular meanings, the former (usually) denoting a disadvantaged socio-economic position for some groups, and the latter, the morally arbitrary use of 'race' in the distribution of goods, positions, statuses, liberties and so on. Racial discrimination (of an adverse kind) will contribute to racial inequality (and, *ipso facto*, to disadvantage) but not all racial inequalities will be the result of negative discrimination. What effective role the law may play therefore (as opposed to more administrative or policy-orientated mechanisms) will depend upon what our primary purposes are. It *may*, for example, prove to be a more effective agent at reducing discrimination than at directly reducing inequalities. Indeed, as we have already noted, racial disadvantage as such, lies quite without the law's reach (as would social disadvantage) though it may be thought to have an indirect impact in so far as discrimination is seen as a cause of disadvantage and the law may affect the latter by its control of the former. But we should not automatically expect the removal of discriminatory barriers to produce racial equality across all its dimensions. Removing discrimination would result in greater equality of racial treatment and more equal effective rights, but it would not remove all disadvantage or create equality of status, wealth, positions and so on between races.

The law and affirmative action in America

There are always dangers in attempting to translate the American experience to the British context, though it has been done at least partially, in the case of Northern Ireland. What distinguishes Great Britain from both the US and Northern Ireland, however, and what provides the spur to action in the latter, but not the former, is a simple fact of demography: approximatley 33 per cent of the population of Northern Ireland is Roman Catholic and 26 per cent of the population of the US (excluding Hawaii) consists of ethnic minorities, as opposed to only 6 per cent of the population in Great Britain. In straightforward statistical terms therefore, it would appear that the task of promoting racial equality and relieving the burden of discrimination ought to be that much more manageable in Great Britain than in the other countries but experience tells us that this is not the case and the reason, as we have suggested, lies in the same figures. The political, moral and prudential pressure to do *something* is much greater when a quarter or a third of the population are suffering discrimination or net inequalities because of their race or religion than when it is only 6 per cent. There are other salient differences between the US and the UK but notwithstanding these, and the demographic factor, the methods adopted in America are of relevance and useful as a guide to what can be done legislatively, legally and administratively (as the translation into the Northern Ireland context has shown).

Major inequalities remain between ethnic groups in America in education, employment, housing, health, wealth·and status, but progress has been made in a number of areas, not least in civil rights (see, for example, Claiborne, 1983) but it is in the field of employment that the influence of law is particularly instructive. The employment participation rates for both blacks and Hispanics increased significantly (though not dramatically) over the period 1966–1988. The participation rate for blacks in the workforce of private establishments with over 100 employees increased from 8.2 to 12.4 per cent in this period; for Hispanics the increase was from 2.5 per cent to 6.2 per cent (though in the case of African-Americans, all the increase was accounted for by female participation) (see Equal Employment Opportunity Commission, 1989). Some of this increase (although how much is impossible to say) has been firmly attributed to Affirmative Action Programs required of federal contractors under Executive Order 11246 (Office of Federal Contract Compliance Programs, 1987) in particular (see, for example, Leonard, 1985; Potomac Institute, 1984; Leonard, 1986; Organisation Resources Councellors, 1984).

Now to the extent that affirmative action practices of one sort or another have contributed to the gains made in minority participation in employment, then we see the influence of the law at work; presidential Executive Orders are legal instruments and have the force of law. But what distinguishes American practice from British is that the former threatens legal sanctions if certain positive things are not done to promote equality (and hence legally required affirmative action) while the latter by and large only requires desistance from negative practices. There is all the difference (in approach and potential outcome) between using the law simply as a regulatory device and using it to promote practices which (in the present context) will have an equalizing effect.

What is significant about the lessons from America is not that the law provides new ways of pursuing equal employment opportunity – it does not – but rather that the threat of legal sanctions appears to work. There is nothing that American companies do by way of affirmative action that could not be (and on occasion has been) done in the United Kingdom. Success (even if only relative success) has come because they have been required to do these things – but with the Equal Employment Opportunities Commission and the Office of Federal Contract Compliance Programs (OFCCP) playing as much supportive as policing roles. More significant than the direct effect of sanctions, however, has been the longer term legacy of legal enforcement – the development of what might be called a 'culture of affirmative action'. Affirmative action practices in the US are now normal practice for probably the majority of medium-to-large employers in both the public and private sectors (see Edwards, 1990a, 1990b). As a matter of everyday good practice, many employers now go well beyond the target and timetable requirements laid down by the OFCCP and much further than 'good faith efforts' would demand. It is a reasonable assumption that this would not have happened had not legal sanctions forced the pace in the first instance and made affirmative action practices widespread and familiar practices (see Fullinwider, 1986). It is also a reasonable assumption that were the legal sanctions now removed, most private sector employers, and the great majority of those in the public sector, would continue with their affirmative action efforts. (It is worth noting that it was only fierce lobbying by the National Association of Manufacturers that dissuaded President Reagan in the mid-1980s from closing down the whole affirmative action apparatus, including the OFCCP.) In this instance, therefore, the reach of the law has gone well beyond the immediate domain of legal sanctions to create a climate in which the law itself has become, if not wholly, then at least largely otiose. Lest we be too sanguine however, it is worth repeating that the demographic situation (i.e. the prospect of labour shortages) injects a good deal of self-interest into affirmative action efforts – a point which the Hudson Institute report *Opportunity 2000* is at pains to convey to employers (see Hudson Institute, 1988, Ch. 6).

What has the law required, encouraged, and eventually persuaded employers to do of their own accord? Nothing, in fact, with which we in the UK are not familiar (by repute if not practice). We are concerned here with just one component of racial inequality – but an important one – that is, inequality in employment. The starting point is the conspicuous fact that some ethnic minorities have higher unemployment rates than others, and that they are over-represented in unskilled and semi-skilled occupations and unpleasant, low status jobs and under-represented in the professions and the higher reaches of management and administration. It is the purpose of affirmative action practices to produce a distribution of minorities over the whole range of occupations and statuses that more closely resembles that of the majority population (on the assumption that in the absence of discrimination and disadvantage, this would represent a more 'normal' state of affairs – see Edwards, 1991).

The main components of employment affirmative action are fairly standard and are found in both US and Northern Ireland practice, and in Great Britain when it is pursued voluntarily. Very briefly, they consist of the following: first, an analysis of the workforce (of a company, city administration, university, etc.) to establish the proportions of minority groups at each level, shift, workshop and so on; secondly, an availability analysis, (which in the US consists of a fairly complex eight-factor analysis of the numbers and proportions of qualified minorities in the relevant labour catchment area for any given position – see OFCCP, 1987). The relevant catchment area for senior management or faculty posts in universities, for example, would be the whole of the US; for clerical assistants it might be a five or ten mile radius from the work location. A comparison of these two analyses then gives a measure of 'utilization' of minorities. If proportions in the workforce are significantly below availability for any given position then this 'under-utilization' can trigger the requirement by the OFCCP for an Affirmative Action Plan to be put in process (see Levin-Epstein, 1987). This plan will consist of a number of components, none of which again are wholly unfamiliar to us in the UK but which, though they have proved effective in America, are not widely used in Great Britain because of the absence of sanctions to enforce their implementation. At a passive level they will include steps to ensure that no part of the hiring, promotion and redundancy processes is indirectly discriminatory (or has 'disparate impact' – otherwise known as the Griggs Doctrine following the Supreme Court finding in *Griggs v. Duke Power* in 1971), including the validation of all tests to ensure neutrality between groups, training in racial awareness for all involved in the personnel process, strict adherence to job and person-specifications and qualification requirements that are no more than the particular job requires. More actively, an Affirmative Action Plan will include steps to increase the pool of qualified minority candidates for a job or position. In this respect, much depends on the ingenuity and motivation of the employer but extant practice includes targeted job advertising, outreach to minority schools, clubs, churches and community centres, vacation placement schemes for minority students, mentoring and a variety of training schemes for minorities (see Levin-Epstein, 1987; OFCCP, 1987; Fullinwider, 1980; Kirp and Weston, 1987). In addition, many universities will offer financial inducements to departments that can find and hire qualified minority faculty – as well as creating new posts for them to fill. And it is not unknown for companies to head-hunt minority personnel from rival establishments in order to reach a self-imposed target.

Some of the less orthodox of these practices are 'unofficial' in the sense that they are not required, or in some cases even condoned by the OFCCP. Indeed, there is little doubt that some, if tested against Title VII of the Civil Rights Act 1964 or the Fourteenth Amendment of the Constitution, would, especially given its present political orientation, be found unlawful or unconstitutional by the Supreme Court. There is a certain irony, therefore, in the fact that the law, in constant application, has spawned a 'culture of affirmative action' (and some preferential treatment) that has developed a momentum of its own, which would no doubt survive the demise of the legislative apparatus that gave it birth, and which includes some practices which would themselves if tested, be found to be unlawful.

The American experience translates to Northern Ireland

We now have in place in one part of the United Kingdom, legislation to promote equal opportunities for religious groups which in the remainder of the Kingdom would (at least for the present) be practically unthinkable if applied to ethnic groups. Northern Ireland has had legislation to deal with religious discrimination since the time of the Race Relations Act (1976) in Great Britain, but whereas the Race Relations Act remains the latest legislative device to deal with discrimination in Great Britain, Ulster in 1989 (effective from 1 January 1990) acquired a much more radical statute, governing practice in the field of employment (the Fair Employment (Northern Ireland) Act). We noted earlier that it is far too soon to begin to see the effects of this Act on equal employment opportunity and we are in no position (as we are in respect of the American experience) to demonstrate the effects of legal devices on the pattern of equality of opportunity, on attitudes and prejudice, or on the position of minorities more generally. However, the exercise of legal sanctions in pursuit of equality of opportunity (or fair employment) in Northern Ireland cannot go without comment.

Whereas the 1976 Fair Employment (Northern Ireland) Act (parts of which remain in force – see Department of Economic Development, 1989b) required much the same in the field of employment for religious groups as the Race Relations Act did on a broader front for ethnic groups – that is, broadly speaking – that providers of services and goods (including employments and emoluments) desist from discrimination on morally arbitrary grounds (see Standing Advisory Commission on Human Rights, 1987, Ch. 5), the 1989 Act goes much further in its demands and is broader in its reach even than the American Executive Orders. To take the latter point first, Executive Order 11246 introduced in the Kennedy administration (as amended by Executive Order 11375) applies only to Federal contractors (as the title of its policing agency – the Office of Federal Contract Compliance Programs – suggests). Only contractors are required to monitor their workforce and if necessary, implement the Affirmative Action Programs we have described above. The Northern Ireland legislation, on the other hand, requires the same action of all private sector employers with more than 25 employees (and all public sector employers) whether or not they hold contractual arrangements with government agencies or are in receipt of government grant or subsidy. (The corollary of this is that the sanctions for non-compliance include straightforward financial penalties for both contractors and non-contractors as well as non-renewal of contract for the former – see Department of Economic Development, 1989a.)

What the Northern Ireland legislation demands and permits bears close similarity, however, with the demands of American Executive Orders – a not surprising fact given that pressure from America was instrumental in the decision to look for a legislative solution (see Osborne and Cormack, 1989) and that it was the American experience of affirmative action upon which the formulators of the 1989 Act draw heavily (McCrudden, 1986; Standing Advisory Commission on Human Rights, 1987; Osborne and Cormack, 1989). Indeed, it is probably true to say that the new Northern Ireland legislation owes more to Washington than to Whitehall. In all respects but one, the Fair Employment Act goes a great deal further than the Race Relations Act. The exception is that the latter Act permits, in Sections 37 and 38, training provision for specific racial groups, something that, in respect of religious groups, is not allowed in the Northern Ireland legislation (nor in the American Executive Orders), though the Fair

Employment Act does make provision for training located in areas predominantly inhabited by one or other religious group.

Should the statutory monitoring reveal the under-utilization of either religious group (as determined by the Fair Employment Commission, playing a role similar to that of the OFCCP in the United States), the Fair Employment Commission will require a company to review its personnel practices (something which all companies and public sector institutions must do anyway) and it may require the setting of goals and timetables and the implementation of affirmative action practices including specifically: training, the encouragement of applications from the under-represented group, and negotiated redundancy schemes to preserve fair representation or gains made by other affirmative action measures (Fair Employment Act, 1989, Section 36, Department of Economic Development, 1989 (Code of Practice) Section 6). Failure to comply with any one of a number of requirements, including registration with the FEC, monitoring, requests for information, and affirmative action requirements, may lead to criminal prosecution and the imposition of fines and economic sanctions. (There are more than twenty criminal offences included in the Act.)

Now all of this will sound more familiar to American than to British ears. In Great Britain the law requires only that we desist from negative discrimination; in Northern Ireland and the United States it requires, in the field of employment, that we take active steps to *promote* fair employment or equality of opportunity. And we have noted that experience in the US strongly suggests that legal sanctions have contributed in no small part to the widespread implementation of affirmative action and more generally to good personnel practice. More than this, however, continuous application of Executive Orders has turned grudging compliance into accepted practice such that affirmative action has become normal action. Might the same apply in Northern Ireland? The kinds of practice that law now requires have for some time been followed voluntarily by the Northern Ireland Civil Service with considerable success (principally on the grounds of getting your own house in order before telling others to do so). Following an investigation by the Fair Employment Agency (the predecessor of the FEC) into the employment patterns of non-industrial civil servants in 1983, the Service established an Equal Opportunities Unit which published its first review in 1986 (see Osborne, 1987, pp. 276–7). The Service had been making quite strong efforts to increase the percentage of Roman Catholics since the beginning of the 1980s, but with the establishment of the new unit these efforts became more formalized and included more affirmative action-type practices (see Northern Ireland Civil Service, Equal Opportunities Unit, 1986, 1987). The result has been a steady increase in the proportion of the non-industrial Civil Service who are Catholic, from 27.7 per cent in 1981 to 35.2 per cent in 1989 (see Osborne, 1990). This figure reflects representation in the labour force as a whole but there is still some way to go in terms of representation of Catholics in the upper reaches of the Service. Nevertheless, change has been marked over the decade and has undoubtedly been brought about largely by the implementation of policies and practices which will in future be required of all employers (public and private) who are under-utilizing. It has to be done with a will of course, but the Civil Service case has shown that it can work.

Further evidence that to enshrine affirmative action and good personnel practice in law will provide results that reliance on voluntary action will not, comes from the first six months experience of the new legislation in Northern Ireland. At the time of writing, the first two statutory requirements of the Act have been completed. All companies with more than 25 employees have registered with the FEC and all but a very small number have filed their monitoring returns (numbers and percentages of Protestants and Roman Catholics at each level in the company hierarchy). Both of these procedures were effected more successfully and with greater ease than most commentators (and the Department of Economic Development) had ever hoped. The extensive use of advertising in all the media and free (to companies) access to consultancy firms to help establish monitoring and good personnel practice, contributed a great deal to this success but there can be no doubt that the lever of a statutory requirement was instrumental in companies being able to persuade their employees to participate in the monitoring exercise and in producing an almost 100 per cent response rate from companies. These are only the initial (but necessary) steps in the whole process and only time will tell whether good practice and some affirmative action will have the required effect, but on the evidence so far there is reason to be optimistic. The stakes have been raised, and high expectations implanted; the stumbling block may be the factor that neither the US nor Great Britain has to contend with – the threat of retaliation from sectarian paramilitary groups.

We can only speculate on whether what has been translated from America to Northern Ireland can now be transferred to the mainland. There are a number of factors that suggest it will be difficult and unlikely at least in the near future. First, as O'Callaghan points out, there is no equivalent strong pressure group in the area of race comparable in its power and economic leverage to the American–Irish caucus that was so instrumental in bringing about change in Northern Ireland (O'Callaghan, 1988). Secondly, as we noted earlier, the differences in the proportions of the total population that are composed of minorities in the three countries makes less imperative in Great Britain, what has been done in the US and Northern Ireland. Quite simply, there is less pressure to do something about 6 per cent of the population than about 25 per cent or 33 per cent. And thirdly, intermittent civil disturbances in areas of ethnic minority concentration notwithstanding, racial differences and disadvantage do not present the Government with the festering security problems of religious sectarianism that beset Northern Ireland, the solution of which (including in part legally backed sanctions to promote fair employment) is now seen as a necessary pre-condition of further economic investment in the province.

The reasons we have rehearsed above, however, are all extraneous to the question of whether Northern Ireland-type legislation, if it were introduced into mainland Britain and applied to racial groups, would achieve the desired result. We can only speculate on the answer with a series of sub-questions. Would there be a majority backlash? Would resentment at the threat of criminal sanctions be such as to lead to large-scale non-compliance? Would there be the requisite amount of goodwill and consensus that the purpose of the legislation was laudable and worth-while, and that it justified the use of the law to achieve it? The law, after all, does not guarantee success. The costs of policing affirmative action are high and the mechanisms cumbrous. Unless there is general acknow-ledgement that the purposes are valuable and valued, the motivation to circumvent the law will be high, and as all previous legislation in the field of race has demonstrated, circumvention is not difficult. None of this is to say that affirmative action legislation in Great Britain would not work; it is simply to enter some notes of caution. It has worked in the US; it has got off to a good start in Northern Ireland, but past experience in Great Britain should persuade us not to be too sanguine.

The role of law in promoting equality

One factor, more than any other should be borne in mind when considering the role of the law in promoting equality between ethnic groups. It is simply that in this area, the law is not creative; it will add nothing to our armoury of policies and practices by itself. What it will do is (we hope) to persuade people that the costs of not doing something (or doing something) are too great and that wisdom lies on the side of compliance. The law, in other words, is a stick, the use of which (or the threat of such) may, given the American experience, in the long run change long standing habits for the better. But unless what the law requires us to do is itself carefully crafted to achieve the desired results, then it will serve no purpose; it will be impotent, futile. Now, ironically, it may be that a law that requires people to do certain specific, encoded things (such as step-by-step affirmative action) will prove more successful in this respect than any that merely requires that they desist from doing other things when this requires nothing specific and tangible. And lest this appears arcane, we have only to compare the policing of the two types of law. In the latter case (not discriminating) this must rely on individual complaints which, evidence of the Race Relations Act suggests throw up only a minuscule proportion of discriminatory acts or, a comic prospect, some regulatory body going around asking employers or whoever, whether they have discriminated in the past six months or year. When sanctions are tied to specific activities, however, the policing can take the much more effective form of 'why have you not sent in your monitoring return?'; 'why have you not completed steps x, y, z, of the affirmative action plan that you agreed to implement by last November?' and so on. Clearly, there is far more bite to this sort of requirement.

In the latter part of this article we have focused on the experience of using the law to promote affirmative action in pursuit of greater equality (and equality of opportunity) in the field of employment. But might what holds for employment apply to other areas involving the allocation of goods, services, and statuses to individuals and groups? Employment almost selects itself as an exemplar because it is here that we find the clearest evidence of the use of law to *promote* certain actions as opposed simply to requiring desistance from others. Of course, employment is a crucial determinant of equality because income and status follow on its coat-tails. But it is only one (an important one) of life's domains that determine the extent of equality between individuals and groups. Whether the law could gain a similar sort of purchase in education, housing, health provision and other areas of social and welfare provision must for the moment remain a matter of conjecture. We know that the Race Relations Act 1976 has had only a limited effect in these areas; what must now be at issue is whether the law as a *promotional* agent can do for these what it appears to have done (and is doing) in the field of employment. Indeed, what may be of greater significance in the longer term for the promotion of racial equality is not so much *whether* the law is pressed into service as a promotional agent, as in *which* domains of life it is applied. It is worth noting in this respect, the view, increasingly aired in the United States, that affirmative action in employment will from now on produce diminishing returns until such time as the available pool of qualified minorities increases substantially. And this means that the pressure point for race conscious policies must shift to the field of education. This will prove to be a much more intractable area and may well define the limits of the effectiveness of law as a promotional agent.

As to the current state of affairs in Britain however, for twenty years, governments have contented themselves with enacting legislation creating individual rights and imposing limited negative requirements on private employers. They have done very little to put their own house in order and have done even less to assist and encourage the private sector, or to offer a credible model of successful practice. It is impossible to say whether the preference for a legal approach was based upon an exaggerated faith in the efficacy of law; or the need, for political reasons, to be seen to do something highly visible, such as enacting a statute; or was a conscious alternative to taking on a wider long-term expensive and controversial commitment. It does seem tolerably clear, however, that continued reliance on the legal approach in the future will signal a decision that racial equality has been accorded low priority, and perhaps also that greater importance has been accorded to being seen to be doing something rather than actually doing it.

Notes

1 Lustgarten, L. (1980) *Legal Control of Racial Discrimination*, London, Macmillan, p. 253.

2 The Commission for Racial Equality is given powers under the Act to advise, assist and/ or represent individual complainants. Under the 1968 Act its predecessor, the Race Relations Board, had the exclusive power to bring legal action. Most successful litigation under the present law has involved CRE support.

3 Under present law this is done by means of the so-called formal investigation, RRA 1976, ss. 48–52, 58–60.

4 RRA 1976, s. 57(1).

5 Especially that conducted by the Nottingham CRC and published by them under the title *Half a Chance?* in 1980.

6 In 1982, 200 cases heard in industrial tribunals produced only 30 successes, a proportion markedly lower than 25 per cent, achieved in the staple of those tribunals, unfair dismissals. From 1977 to 1982, discrimination complaints won only 106 cases. These data come from the CRE Consultative Document *The Race Relations Act – Time for a Change?* (1983), p. 9.

7 Many of the scathing criticisms of the CRE in the Report of the House of Commons Select Committee on Home Affairs were justified (first Report, 1981–82 Session, HC 46). See further, Lustgarten, 'The CRE under attack' [1982] PL 229. However, the courts have severely restricted the Commission's ability to conduct formal investigations by their interpretation of the relevant statutory provisions in cases such as *CRE* v. *Amari Plastics* [1982] QB 265; *Hillingdon Borough of London* v. *CRE* [1982] AC 779; and *CRE* v. *Prestige Group Ltd.* [1984] 1 WLR 335. These legal obstacles were wholly ignored in the Select Committee Report.

8 The Policy Studies Institute Report, Daniel, W. and Stillgoe, E. *The Impact of Employment Protection Laws* (PSI, 1978) reported that most personnel managers and others who would be responsible for implementation of the Act had only the vaguest idea of its substance, and had done nothing to change their practices in light of it. It is possible that a similar survey conducted in 1985, particularly with the Code of Practice in force since April 1984, would reveal considerably greater awareness. See also, Young, K. and Connelly, N. *Policy and Practice in the Multi-Racial City* (PSI 1981) documenting widespread ignorance and inaction in many local authorities, who under s. 71 have an explicit statutory responsibility to eliminate discrimination and promote equal opportunity.

9 Expressed most openly in the Court of Appeal judgements in *Ojutiku* v. *MSC* [1982] ICR 661, and *Mandla* v. *Dowell Lee* [1983] QB 1. The *Hillingdon* case (see note 7) manifests the same attitude more subtly. This began to change in the late 1980s.

10 Notably in the CRE Consultation Document (see note 6) and in the strengthened *Review of the Race Relations Act: proposal for change*, adopted by the Commission after the consultative process and published in July 1985.

11 For example, in the articles extracted or cited in Friedman, L. and Macaulay, S. (eds),

Law and the Behavioural Sciences (2nd edn, 1979); Schwartz R. and Skolnick, J. (eds), *Society and the Legal Order* (1970), and Campbell, C. and Wiles, R. (eds), *Law and Society* (1979). A good review of the findings and analytical shortcomings of various 'law and social change' theorists may be found in Cotterrell, R., *The Sociology of Law: an introduction* (1984), Chap. 2. The essay by William Evan, 'Law as an Instrument of Social Change' in Gouldner, A. and Miller, S. (eds), *Applied Sociology* (1965) is interesting and suggestive, but is either speculative or based on extrapolations of one specific instance. A more common flaw is the creation of 'models' which either state the very, very obvious or are vague to the point of vacuity, e.g. the twelve-factor model of Maxmanian, D. and Sabatier, P., *Effective Policy Implementation*, p. 89.

12 For example, the doctrine of *res ipsa loquitur* or the sort of presumption used in *McGhee v. National Coal Board* [1972] 3 All ER 1008, a case of breach of statutory duty.

13 As in *Khanna* v. *Ministry of Defence* [1981] ICR 653; *Wallace* v. *South Eastern Education and Library Board* [1980] IRLR 193 (NI) and *Oxford* v. *DHSS* [1977] IRLR 225.

14 Although county courts hear housing discrimination cases, there have been only about a score of these in seven years. Discrimination law is essentially employment law, within the domain of industrial tribunals with appeal on questions of law to the Employment Appeal Tribunal.

15 See further, Lustgarten, L. *supra* note 1, pp. 8–14, and McCrudden (1982), 'Institutional Discrimination', *Ox. J. Leg. Studs.* **2**, p. 303.

16 We base this statement on the admittedly arbitrarily-selected sample provided by the editors of the *Industrial Relations Law Reports*.

17 [1910] 2 KB 1021.

18 *Hollington* v. *Hewthorn and Co. Ltd.* [1943] KB 587.

19 A valuable discussion of these procedural limitations may be found in Miller, 'Some Problems of Individual and Collective Consumer Redress in English Law' in Anderman, S. (ed.) (1983), *Law and the Weaker Party*, **2**, pp. 127–9.

20 RRA 1976, s. 56(1)(c). See *Bayoomi* v. *British Rail* [1981] IRLR 413.

21 Kahn-Freund, 'On uses and misuses of comparative law' (1974) 37 MLR 1, 24.

22 Dickens *et al.*, (1981) 'Re-employment of unfairly dismissed workers: the lost remedy' **10**, ILJ, 160.

23 See *Albemare Paper Co.* v. *Moody*, 422 US 405, 419 n.11 (1975).

24 RRA 1976, ss. 58–59.

25 For example, *Re Pergamon Press* [1971] Ch. 388; *Norwest Holst Ltd.* v. *Department of Trade* [1978] 3 All ER 1280, both Court of Appeal decisions.

26 *Laker Airways Ltd.* v. *Department of Trade* [1977] QB 643.

27 Baldwin 'A British independent regulatory agency and the "Skytrain" decision' [1978] PL 57.

28 *Department of the Environment* v. *Fox* [1980] 1 All ER 58; *Knight* v. *Attorney-General* [1979] ICR 194; *Daley* v. *Allied Suppliers Ltd.* [1983] I.C.R. 90.

29 *Kirby* v. *Manpower Services Commission* [1980] 1 WLR 725. This, and the three cases cited in the preceding note, were all EAT decisions.

30 Finally decided in the affirmative by the House of Lords in *Mandla (Sewa Singh)* v. *Dowell Lee* [1983] 2 AC 548.

31 In the *Hillingdon* case (see note 7).

32 In the *Amari Plastics* case (see note 7).

33 (1974) 9 *L. & Soc. Rev.* 115. A useful extract appears in the Campbell and Wiles collection (see note 11).

34 See note 7.

35 We would not quarrel in principle with McCrudden's view ('Anti-discrimination goals and the legal process' in Glazer, N. and Young, K. (eds), *Ethnic Pluralism and Public Policy* (1983), p. 58) that legal action may be a useful adjunct to political and administrative effort, though I am far less optimistic than he that a group which is politically weak can exercise a louder 'voice' in the courts, which seem to us even less responsive to the needs/claims of the poor and lowly. There is also the boomerang problem: when an authoritative legal ruling interprets the statute so as to narrow its scope or application, it may lead to greater future resistance or even abandonment of changes undertaken in the mistaken view that the law, then unsettled, required them. For a general overview of this issue, see Prosser, T., *Test Cases for the Poor* (CPAG, 1983).

References

Claiborne, L. (1983) *Race and Law in Britain and the United States*, London, Minority Rights Group.

Department of Economic Development (Northern Ireland) (1989a) *Fair Employment in Northern Ireland: The Fair Employment (Northern Ireland) Act 1989: code of practice*, Belfast, HMSO.

Department of Economic Development (Northern Ireland) (1989b) *Fair Employment in Northern Ireland: The Fair Employment (Northern Ireland) Act 1989: key details of the Act*, Belfast, HMSO.

Edwards, J. (1990a) *Affirmative Action and Preferential Treatment: an evaluation of costs and benefits*, Delaware, College of Urban Affairs and Public Policy, University of Delaware, USA.

Edwards, J. (1990b) 'What purpose does equality of opportunity serve?', *New Community* **16**(2).

Edwards, J. (1991) 'US affirmative action alive and well despite Supreme Court', *Equal Opportunities International* **10**(1), pp. 11–13.

Equal Employment Opportunities Commission (1989) *Indicators of Equal Employment Opportunity Status and Trends*, Washington DC, EEOC.

Fullinwider, R. K. (1980) *The Reverse Discrimination Controversy*, Totowa, New Jersey, Rowman and Littlefield.

Fullinwider, R. K. (1986) 'Reverse Discrimination and Equal Opportunity' in DeMarco, J. P. and Fox, R. M. (eds) *New Directions in Ethics: the challenge of applied ethics*, New York, Routledge and Kegan Paul.

Griggs v. *Duke Power Co.* (US Supreme Court Case) (1971) 401 US 424.

Hudson Institute (1988) *Opportunity 2000*, Indianapolis, Hudson Institute.

Kirp, D. and Weston, M. (1987) 'The political jurisprudence of affirmative action', *Social Philosophy and Policy* **5**(1), pp. 223–48.

Leonard, J. S. (1985) 'What promises are worth: the impact of affirmative action goals', *Journal of Human Resources* **20**(1), pp. 3–20.

Leonard, J. S. (1986) 'Contract compliance in the USA: an evaluation of impact and cost', *Euqal Opportunities Through Contact Compliance: the British and American experience: National Symposium*, London, Inner London Education Authority.

Levin-Epstein, M. D. (1987) *Primer of Equal Employment Opportunity* (4th edn), Washington DC, Bureau of National Affairs.

McCrudden, C. (1986) 'Rethinking positive action', *Industrial Relations Law Journal* **XV** (4), pp. 219–43.

Northern Ireland Civil Service, Equal Opportunities Unit (1986) *Equal Opportunities in the Northern Ireland Civil Service : first report*, Belfast, NICS/EOU.

Northern Ireland Civil Service, Equal Opportunities Unit (1987) *Equal Opportunities in the Northern Ireland Civil Service: second report*, Belfast, NICS/EOU.

O'Callaghan, D. (1988) 'From Belfast to Brixton', *Personnel Management*, August, pp. 44–7.

Office of Federal Contract Compliance Programs (1987) *Equal Opportunities and Affirmative Action: guidance manual*, Washington DC, OFCCP.

Organisation Resources Counsellors Inc. (1984) *Managing Diversity: the challenge of equal employment opportunity to 1990*, New York, ORC.

Osborne, R. (1987) 'Religion and employment' in Buchanan, R.H. and Walker, B.M. (eds) *Province, City and People: Belfast and its region*, Antrim, Greystone.

Osborne, R. (1990) 'Equal opportunities and the Northern Ireland civil service', *Public Money and Management* **10**(2), pp. 41–5.

Osborne, R. and Cormack, R. (1989) 'Fair employment: towards reform in Northern Ireland', *Policy and Politics* **17**(4), pp. 287–94.

Potomac Institute Inc. (1984) *A Decade of New Opportunity: affirmative action in the 1970s*, Washington DC, Potomac Institute Inc.

Standing Advisory Commission on Human Rights (1987) *Religious and Political Discrimination and Equality of Opportunity in Northern Ireland* Cm. 237, Belfast, HMSO.

Source: The first half of this paper appeared in Jenkins, R. and Solomos, J. (eds) (1987), *Racism and Equal Opportunities in the 1980s*, Cambridge, Cambridge University Press.

LIST OF CONTRIBUTORS

Gideon Ben-Tovim is senior lecturer in the Race and Social Policy Unit, University of Liverpool. He is chair of the Education Committee Equal Opportunities Sub-Committee, Liverpool City Council. He is co-author of *The Local Politics of Race* (Macmillan, 1986) and *The Racial Politics of Militant in Liverpool* (Runnymede Trust, 1986).

Avtar Brah teaches in Birkbeck College, University of London. She was previously lecturer in education at the Open University and has held research posts at the Universities of Leicester and Bristol. She has published widely on gender, 'race', and ethnicity and on education and employment issues. Her latest publication is *Working Choices: South Asian young Muslim women and the labour market* (Department of Employment, 1992).

Colin Brown is manager of the Public Interest Research Group at the Consumers Association. As senior fellow at the Policy Studies Institute (PSI), he was author of *Black and White Britain: the third PSI survey* (Heinemann/Gower, 1984) and co-author of *Racial Discrimination: 17 years after the Act* (PSI, 1985). He has recently co-authored *Racial Justice at Work: enforcement of the Race Relations Act 1976 in employment* (PSI, 1991) and *Training for Equality: a study of race relations and equal opportunities training* (PSI, 1991).

Lena Dominelli is professor of social administration at the University of Sheffield. She has been a social worker, probation officer and lecturer in social work and social policy at the University of Warwick. Her most recent books include *Anti-racist Social Work* (Macmillan, 1988), *Feminist Social Work* (Macmillan, 1989) with Eileen Mcleod, and *Women across Continents: feminist comparative social policy* (Harvester Wheatsheaf, 1990). She also sits on the Board of the International Association of Schools of Social Work and on the editorial board of several journals. Her current research covers racism and social work in Europe, child sexual abuse and interactive language technology relevant to social work.

John Edwards is head of the Positive Action and Equal Opportunities Evaluation Programme at Royal Holloway and Bedford New College, University of London. He previously worked at the Centre for Research in Ethnic Relations at the University of Warwick. He is author of *Positive Discrimination, Social Justice and Social Policy* (Tavistock, 1987).

John Gabriel is lecturer in cultural studies at the University of Birmingham. He is co-author of *The Local Politics of Race* (Macmillan,

1986). He has been vice-chairperson and vice-president of the Wolverhampton Council for Community Relations (now Wolverhampton Race Equality Council) and is active in local politics.

Peter Gibbon is research fellow at the Scandinavian Institute of African Studies in Uppsala, Sweden. He formerly worked as lecturer at Sheffield Polytechnic and with Sheffield City Council on employment and 'race' issues.

Norman Ginsburg is principal lecturer, Social Sciences Department, South Bank Polytechnic. He is a founder member of the editorial collective of the journal *Critical Social Policy* and is a regular contributor to the journal. He is author of *Class, Capital and Social Policy* (Macmillan, 1979) and *States of Welfare Division* (Sage, 1992).

Paul Gordon has been research officer at the Runnymede Trust since 1980. He was previously research officer with the Scottish Council for Civil Liberties. He is the author of numerous publications on policing, civil liberties and 'race' issues, including *White Law: racism in the police, courts and prisons* (Pluto Press, 1983), *Policing Immigration* (Pluto Press, 1985), *Racial Violence and Harassment* (Runnymede Trust, 1986) and *Fortress Europe? The meaning of 1992* (Runnymede Trust, 1989).

Richard Jenkins is senior lecturer in sociology, University College, Swansea. He was previously research associate at the SSRC Research Unit on Ethnic Relations. He is currently engaged in a study of the transition to adulthood of young people with learning difficulties. His latest publication is *Pierre Bourdieu* (Routledge, 1991).

Nick Jewson is lecturer in sociology and co-director of the Ethnic Minority Employment Research Centre at the University of Leicester. He is co-author (with David Mason) of *Ethnic Minorities and Employment Practice: a study of six organisations* (Department of Employment, 1990).

Ian Law is lecturer in sociology at the University of Leeds. He was previously co-ordinator of racial equality units in the housing and education departments of Leeds City Council and worked on various race relations research projects. He is author of *Race and Housing in Liverpool* (CRE, 1984) and co-author of *The Local Politics of Race* (Macmillan, 1986) and *Local Government and Thatcherism* (Routledge, 1990).

Laurence Lustgarten is reader in law at the University of Warwick. He has also occupied visiting posts at universities in Canada, Tanzania and Australia. His publications include *The Legal Control of Racial Discrimination* (Macmillan, 1980), *The Governance of Police* (Sweet & Maxwell, 1986) and (with Ian Leigh) *In from the Cold: national security, secrecy and democracy* (OUP, 1993).

Amina Mama is lecturer in women and development at the Institute of Social Studies, The Hague. She was previously responsible for the Domestic Violence Project at the London Race and Housing Research

Unit. She is currently preparing for publication her doctoral thesis *Race and Subjectivity: a study of black women* (Routledge, forthcoming).

David Mason is lecturer in sociology and co-director of the Ethnic Minority Employment Research Centre at the University of Leicester. He has been involved in several major research projects on ethnic minority employment and equal opportunities issues and has published numerous papers dealing with these as well as theoretical and conceptual issues in the field of 'race' and ethnic relations. He is co-editor (with John Rex) of *Theories of Race and Ethnic Relations* (CUP, 1986) and co-author (with Nick Jewson) of *Ethnic Minorities and Employment Practice: a study of six organisations* (Department of Employment, 1990).

Robert Miles is reader in sociology and director of the Research Unit on Migration and Racism at the University of Glasgow. He was previously research associate at the SSRC Research Unit on Ethnic Relations. He has published extensively in the field of racism, politics and migrant labour. His most recent publications in English are *Racism* (Routledge, 1989) and (with D. Kay) *Refugees or Migrant Workers: the recruitment of displaced persons for British industry 1946–51* (Routledge, 1992).

Annie Phizacklea is lecturer in sociology at Warwick University. Her main research interests have been in migration, racism and employment, with particular reference to minority women. Her most recent book is *Unpacking the Fashion Industry: gender, racism and class in production* (Routledge, 1990).

John Solomos is senior lecturer, Department of Politics and Sociology, Birkbeck College. He was previously research fellow at the Centre for Research in Ethnic Relations. He has written widely on the topic of 'race' and racism.

Kathleen Stredder is staff tutor in education for the West Midlands region of the Open University. She is co-author of *The Local Politics of 'Race'* (Macmillan, 1986). She is a member of Wolverhampton Race Equality Council.

John Wrench is senior research fellow at the Centre for Research in Ethnic Relations, University of Warwick and lecturer in the Management Centre at the University of Aston in Birmingham. He is editor of the *Research in Ethnic Relations* series (Gower).

Ken Young is professor of politics at Queen Mary and Westfield College, University of London. He is co-author (with N. Connelly) of *Policy and Practice in the Multi-Racial City* (Policy Studies Institute, 1981).

INDEX

abuse *see* domestic violence; male violence

acceptability criteria in recruitment, 149–52, 155, 159

administrative law, 275–6

affirmative action, 281–5, 288

affray charges, 180, 182

Africa Liberation Committee, 79

African women, and domestic violence, 89

African-Americans, and unemployment (USA), 282

Afro-Asian unity, 79

Afro-Caribbeans: employment, 43, 48–9, 59–60, 81–6, 136, 156–7; homelessness, 122; immigration, 10, 33–5, 51–2; and legal system, 93–7, 183, 186–9; as parents, 91; psychiatric treatment, 92–4; women, 77, 79, 81–6, 89, 93, 97

after-care of prisoners, 179

age criteria in recruitment, 151

Aliens Act (1904), 32

Aliens Order (1920), 8

alliances, antiracist, 212–13

Amalgamated Union of Engineering Workers (AUEW), 38–9

American-Irish caucus, 287

anti-depressant drugs, 93

antiracism: alliances, 212–13; careers service, 138–9, 142–3, 145; in education, 257, 289; as extremism, 204–5; in local government, 130, 171, 201–16; marginalization of, 202–16, 279; by tenants, 126–7

apprenticeships, 107, 134

arranged marriage, 70, 72, 92

Asians: as 'black', 79–80; employment, 36–7, 43, 136; and legal system, 183, 184, 186–9; *see also* South Asians; East African Asians

assault *see* violence

AUEW (Amalgamated Union of Engineering Workers), 38–9

avoidance strategies in social work, 167, 170

bail, and black people, 179, 183–5

Bangladeshis, 23, 59–60, 83, 122–3; *see also* South Asians

banks, policies towards black people, 118–20

Barbados, returned immigrants, 94

Bedford, housing, 112, 118–19

benefits, child, 91

Bengalis, housing, 112–13; *see also* South Asians

Birmingham, 115–17, 127–8

birthrates, 88

black, meaning of, 79–80

Black Female Prisoners Scheme, 97

Black Power movement, USA, 110

black resistance movements, pathologization of, 92

black specialist model in social work, 172–3

Black Trade Union Solidarity Movement, 43

black unity, 79–81

black women's movement, 77, 79, 96–7

Black Workers Association, 43

Black Workers' Charter, 41

black workers' groups, 43

Böhning, W.R., 4–5

borstals, 186–7, 188

'Bradford 12', 181, 184

Brent, housing, 122, 124–5

Breugel, Irene, 85

Bristol, riots, 180, 185

British Leyland (BL), 38, 152

British Medical Association, 86

British Nationality Act, 9–11

British subjects, and immigration, 9, 10, 21, 25

'Britishness', 12

Brixton, 95, 121, 183, 256

Brixton Black Women's Group, 79, 96

Brixton Defence Campaign, 79

building societies, policies towards black people, 118–20

bureaucratization, equal opportunities, 224–6, 242, 243, 248–9, 258–9, 263–4

Camden Black Sisters, 79

Campbell, Richard 'Cartoon', 95

cannabis psychosis, 92

capitalist interests, and immigration, 14, 30–2, 47, 191

careers service, 133–46

Caribbean *see* Afro-Caribbean

caring services, and racism, 166
Carmichael, Stokely, 110
Census, Sample (1966), 48–9
central government, 61, 120–3, 206–7, 257, 279
children, 71, 81, 89–91, 174–5
Chinese, immigration, 62, 110
Chix Sweets, 68
Civil Aviation Authority, 276
civil disturbance: and criminal justice system, 179, 180–6, 191, 192; inner city (1958), 11, 12–13, 34; inner city (1981–85), 24–5, 191, 235, 256; and local politics, 210
civil rights law, USA, 275
Clark, Alan, 185
class actions, USA, 274
coded language see language
colonial policy, women, 69
colonies, immigration from, 9–12
'colour blindness', 167, 169, 206–7, 211–12
Commission for Industrial Relations, 37
Commission for Racial Equality (CRE), 38–9, 41, 55, 107; and employment, 136, 152, 157; and equal opportunities, 214, 235, 237, 239–40, 249; and housing, 112–13, 119–20, 122, 124–8; and local authorities, 257; powers and functions, 270–1, 275–7, 279–80
committees, marginalizing antiracism, 203–4
common law, 275
common sense racism, 110, 165
Commonwealth immigration, 9–12, 14–17, 19–25, 32–6
Commonwealth Immigrants Acts, 11–12, 13–16, 17–18, 35
communities, establishment and consolidation, 50, 52, 58
community care by women, 81
community consultation, marginalizing antiracism, 203–4
community networks, as racism, 166
Community Relations Commission, 55, 253
community resources, and antiracism, 210–11
community service orders, 188, 189
Confederation of British Industry (CBI), 37
consciousness-raising, 228–9
Conservative Party, 10–27, 34–5, 48, 120, 235
conspiracy charges, 180–2
consultation marginalizing antiracism, 203–4
contraceptives, 75, 89
council houses sales, 110, 120–1
councillors see local government

counselling, of black psychiatric patients, 93
courts see law courts
Cricklewood affray, 180
criminal justice system, 93–6, 175, 179–92
criminalization of black people, 179–92
Crown Court sentencing, 187–8
cultural initiatives, marginalizing antiracism, 205
cultural racism, 110, 165, 169
culture, meaning of, 80
curfews, 184
cuts see public expenditure

death in police custody, 95
decentralization and equal opportunities policies, 264–6
decontextualization strategies in social work, 167, 169
Deedes, William, 14
demographic downturn, effect on unemployment, 59, 144
denial strategies in social work, 167, 169
Denning, Lord, 185–6, 277
dentists, 82–3
Department of Social Security officials, and racism, 91
Depo-Provera, 75, 89
deportation, 18, 85, 90, 94, 191
depression in women, 93
deskilling, 223, 238
detention, under Mental Health Act, 92
detention centres, ethnic monitoring, 186–7, 188
disorder, public see civil disturbance
dispersal policies in housing, 115–17, 124–5
displaced people, 8
doctors, 82–4, 89
doctrine of mutuality, 275
domestic violence, 89–90, 95, 166
domesticity ideology and labour market, 67, 81
drapetomania, 92
drug offences, 187
drug treatment, of black psychiatric patients, 93
dumping strategies in social work, 167, 170

earnings see wages
East African Asians, 17–18, 21, 49–50
East London Black Women's Organization, 79
Economic League, 235
economic nationalism, trade unions, 30, 34, 44

education: admission requirements, 175; antiracism, 289; educationally subnormal, racism in, 166; equal opportunities, 265; free market approach, 133; national curriculum, 133; sexual discrimination, 74–5; of social workers, racism in, 173–6; South Asian girls, 74–5
educational qualifications, and labour market, 85, 222–3, 237–8
Educational Reform Act (ERA) (1988), 133
elections, 16–17, 19, 20, 38
electro-convulsive therapy (ECT), and black patients, 93
emigration, 25, 47
Employment for the 1990s, 135, 144
employment: Afro-Caribbeans, 48–9, 59–60, 81–6, 136; apprenticeships, 107, 134; Asians, 36–7, 43, 48–9, 59–60, 66–8, 81–6; domesticity ideology, 67, 81; entry qualifications, 85, 222–3, 237–8; equal opportunities, 218–30, 235–50, 259, 281–8; ethnic minorities involvement, 83; ethnic monitoring, 283; European labour mobility, 62; gender analysis, 82–8; Greeks, 53; home-workers, 67, 81; job-search patterns, 156–7; legal control of inequality, 47, 281–90; Northern Ireland, 280, 281, 284–8; part-time women workers, 67, 81; positive discrimination, 61; effect of public expenditure cuts, 81; racial discrimination, 30–44, 46–63, 133–46, 148–62; regional patterns, 53, 58, 66; selection and recruitment, 53, 55, 60–1, 134–46, 148–62, 224, 235–50, 260–2, 264; Sheffield, 240–2; women, 66–8, 81–6; young people, 133–46; see also job levels; workers
employment agencies, 153
Employment Protection Acts, 272
Employment Services, 153, 156–7, 158–9, 160
employment vouchers, 16, 51
Engels, Friedrich, 32
English see language skills
entry certificates, 19–20
Equal Employment Opportunities Commission, 282
equal opportunities, 218–30; definition, 197; in employment, 218–30, 235–50, 259, 281–8; in local government, 201–16, 239, 252–68; perceptions, 220, 228–9, 259–61; policies, 235–50, 252–68; religious groups, 284–8; training in, 224, 228–9, 245

Equal Opportunities Commission (EOC), 235, 237, 240, 249
equal opportunity employers, 236
estate agents, and racism, 118–20
ethnic minority officers, trade unions, 42
ethnic monitoring: careers service, 141, 143; council housing, 125; employment, 283; equal opportunities, 227, 236; prisons, 186–7, 188; trade unions, 42–3
ethnicity, meaning of, 80
European Commission of Human Rights, 70
European labour mobility, 62
European Volunteer Workers, 9, 33
exclusive channel, social work interaction, 166, 169
exclusive racism, 166
Executive Orders (US), 282, 285–6
expenditure see funding; public expenditure
extended household, 71–2, 168, 170
extremist labelling of antiracism, 204–5
extremists, right-wing, 13, 35, 36, 37, 38
eye contact, cultural differences in, 151

Fair Employment Commission/Agency (FEC), 286
Fair Employment (Northern Ireland) Act (1989), 280, 284–8
families, 68–73, 85, 115
family size, effect on council house allocation, 112, 115
feminism see women
finance for housing: racism in allocation, 118–20
financial sector, equal opportunities, 243
fostering, 91, 174–5
Fowler, Norman, 135
free market approach to education, 133
funding, for race relations initiatives, 80, 205–8, 253–5

Gaitskell, Hugh, 15
gender analysis: criminal justice system, 93–6; employment, 82–8; mental health services, 93
gender distribution of immigration, 49–50, 66
gender monitoring, 236
Ghanaians, immigration, 23
Gill, Ken, 40
girls, South Asian, 74–5
Gordon Walker, Patrick, 16
government see central government; local government
Grassroots, 79

Greater London Council, 41–2, 85, 113–14, 129–30, 130
Greek workers, 53
Griffiths, Peter, 17
Griggs Doctrine, 284
Groce, Cherry, 95
Grunwick Film Processing, 43, 68

Hackney, 113, 127, 128, 171
Hall, Stuart, 69
Hamilton, Charles V., 110
harassment: by immigration service, 70, 85, 88, 94; by police, 180, 188; on housing estates, 65, 109, 118, 123–7
Harris, C., 12
Harwood Cash Lawn Mills, 37
Hawley Report (1976), 23
health service workers, and ethnic minorities, 48–50
health services to black women, 86–94
Hen, Lisa, 90
Hindu women, 66
Hispanics, unemployment (US), 282
home help service, 166
home-workers, 67, 81
homelessness, 122–3, 190
Hong Kong Chinese, 62, 110
housework, South Asian women, 71
housing: racism, 47, 50, 90, 109–30, 166; regional patterns, 58; social reports misused, 90, 94, 95; tenure patterns, 50
Housing Acts, 121, 122, 128
housing associations as equal opportunities employers, 247–8
Housing Corporation, 128, 129
Housing for Wales, 128
Hudson Institute, 283

immigrants: crime by, 11, 24; deportation, 18, 24, 85, 90, 94, 191; illegal, 24, 31, 70, 89
immigration, 7–27; Afro-Caribbean, 10, 33–5, 51–2; Asians, 10, 17–18, 23, 33–5, 48–50, 64–5; capitalist interests, 14, 30–2, 47, 191; Chinese, 62, 110; Commonwealth, 9–12, 14–17, 19–25, 32–6; Conservative Party attitudes, 10–27, 34–5; control, 7–27, 30–6, 70–1, 166, 191; East African Asians, 17–18, 49–50; employment vouchers, 16, 51; gender distribution, 49–50, 66, 82–3; Ghanaians, 23; Irish people, 8, 10, 16, 31–2; Labour Party attitudes, 10, 11, 13, 15–18, 19–20, 25–6, 30, 33, 35; Liberal Party attitudes, 13; and local government, 253; right-wing attitudes, 13, 35; sexism of controls, 21, 70; trade

unions attitudes, 30–6; *see also* migrant workers
Immigration Act (1971), 20, 21, 23, 35, 70
Immigration Appeals Act (1969), 19
Immigration Rules, 21, 23, 70
immigration service, harassment by, 70, 85, 88, 94
Immigration Widows' Campaign Group, 71
Imperial Typewriters, 37, 43, 68
inclusive racism, 166
Indian Workers Association, 43
Indians: employment, 36–7, 48–9, 59–60, 83; immigration, 10, 23, 51–2; unemployment, 59; women, 83; *see also* South Asians
individual racism *see* subjective racism
individuation in law, 274
industrial disputes, Indian workers, 36–7; *see also* strikes
informal worker recruitment, 154–60, 224, 246–7
inner city: social problems, 23; Urban Programme, 205, 207, 254–5; *see also* civil disturbance
institutional racism, 105–11, 165; housing, 109–120, 111–18, 127–130; social work, 165, 169
internal labour market (ILM), 153–4, 156–7, 158–61, 224, 248
interviews, 149, 153, 154, 175
Ireland, nurse recruitment, 83–4
Irish people: as 'black', 80; immigration, 8, 10, 16, 31–2; workers, 31–2
'Islington 18', 181, 183

Jamaica, returned immigrants, 94
Jarret, Cynthia, 95
Jenkins, R., 237–8
Jewish political refugees, 32
Jewson, N., 239–40
Job Centres *see* Employment Services
job levels, 48–63, 155–6, 159–60, 243–5; National Health Service, 84; social work, 166, 167, 172
job-search patterns, 156–7
Jones, Jack, 37
judges, and racism, 179
juries, 181, 185–6

Kauffman, Gerald, 25
Kentish Town, 126
Kenya, 92
Kenyan Asians *see* East African Asians
kinship, West African families, 91
kinship networks, as exclusive racism, 166, 168

labelling *see* language of discrimination
labour *see* employment; workers
labour movement and racism, 30–44; *see also* trade unions
Labour Party: antiracism, 37, 201–16; and disadvantage, 235; housing policy, 120; immigration control, 10, 11, 13, 15–20, 25–6, 30, 33, 35, 48, 55–6; racism, 55–6
Labour Research Department, 41–2
Lambeth Black Families Unit, 174–5
Lancashire Association of Trades Councils, 41
Land and Freedom Army, 92
language: of discrimination, 14, 23; of equal opportunities policies, 267–8
language skills, 150, 151, 152
large families *see* family size
law: limits of, 270–90; promoting equality, 288–90
law courts, and racism, 93–4, 175, 179–92
Leeds affray, 180, 183
Lees, Sue, 72
legal measures combating racial inequality, 270–90
legal system: racism, 93–4, 175, 179–92; United States, 274–5
legislation: marginalizing antiracism, 206–7; on racial inequality, 270–90
Leicester, 37, 125
Leicester Racial Attacks Monitoring Project, 125
leisure services, equal opportunities, 246
'Lewisham 19', 181
Liberal Party, immigration control, 13
liberalism, equal opportunities, 218–30
Liff, S., 239
literacy *see* language skills
'Little England' policy, 16
Liverpool, 112, 127, 201–16
Liverpool Trades Council, 213
loans for housing, and racism, 118–20
Local Authorities Race Relations Information Exchange, 257
local government: equal opportunity policies, 201–16, 239, 252–68; ethnic minority involvement, 61; funding, 80, 205–8, 253–5; and immigration, 253; and riots, 210
Local Government Act (1966), 207–8, 253–4
local government bureaucracy, and racism, 208, 258
Local Government and Housing Act (1989), 122, 142
London Race and Housing Research Unit, 89
London Transport, 33

London Underground, 107
Loughborough, 36–7

magistrates, 93–4, 179, 182–3, 187–8
Malaysia, nurse recruitment, 83–4
male violence, 76, 87–9, 95
Malmic Lace, 37
managerial *see* professional
Mangrove trial, 185
Manpower Services Commission (MSC), 134, 140
Mansfield Hosiery Mills, 36
manual workers, ethnic minorities, 48–50, 52–4, 56–7, 59–60, 61–2
manufacturing industries, recruitment, 150, 153–4, 243
marginalization of antiracism, 202–16, 279
marital psychosis, South Asian women, 92
marital status, and recruitment, 151
market forces in education, 133
marriage, 70, 72, 92
Mason, D., 239–40
Mau Mau, 92
meals on wheels, 166
members of parliament, black, 61
mental health, 91–4
Mental Health Act (1983), 92
Michael X, 185
migrant workers, 8–9, 10, 14, 20, 30–5, 46–9, 51–2, 82–3, 191
migration *see* emigration; immigration
mobility agreements in internal labour market, 158–9
monitoring *see* ethnic monitoring; gender monitoring
Morrison, Peter, 140
mortgage finance allocation, racism in, 118–20
mortgage tax relief, 120–1
multiculturalism, 257
Muslims, 62, 66–7
mutuality, doctrine of, 275

NALGO, 43
National Abortion Campaign, 75–6
National Association of Probation Officers, 42
National Committee for Commonwealth Immigrants, 253
national curriculum, 133
National Front, 36, 37, 38
National Health Service, 81–9
National Joint Advisory Council, 34
National Prisoners Movement (PROP), 187, 191
National Union of Hosiery and Knitwear Workers, 37

National Union of Public Employees (NUPE), 41, 42
Nationality Act (1981), 89
new vocationalism, 133
'Newham 8', 182
Newham Monitoring Project, 125
Nigerians, immigration, 23
non-patrials: immigration, 20
Norplant, 89
Northern Ireland, 280, 281, 284–8
Northern Ireland Civil Service, 286–7
Notting Hill, 11, 12–13, 34, 180, 181, 183, 185
Nottingham, 11, 12–13, 34, 112, 183
NUPE (National Union of Public Employees), 41, 42
nurses: recruitment overseas, 82–4

Office of Federal Contract Compliance Programs (OFCCP), 282–4, 285
Oldham, 119
omission strategies in social work, 167, 169
opening the door model in social work, 172–3
Organization for Economic Cooperation and Development (OECD), 22
Organization for Women of African and Asian Descent (OWAAD), 79, 96
Osborne, Cyril, 13
owner-occupation and institutional racism, 118–20

Pakistanis: employment, 48–9, 59–60, 83; immigration, 10, 23; women, 83; *see also* South Asians
paranoia, 92
parents, 74, 91, 122
part-time women workers, 67, 81
pathologization of black cultures and movements, 92, 166, 174, 189
patrials, immigration, 20
patronization strategies in social work, 167, 170
pay differentials, white and black women, 85
PEP *see* Political and Economic Planning
perception of equal opportunities, 220, 228–9, 259–61
personnel specialists, 154–5, 235, 239, 260, 264–6
Philippines, nurse recruitment, 83–4
police: and black people, 94–6, 175, 179, 192; evidence, 183; harassment, 180, 188; violence by, 95
policy making and antiracism, 211–15
Policy Studies Institute (PSI), 42, 56, 60

Political and Economic Planning (PEP), 47–8, 56
political ideologies marginalizing antiracism, 206–7
political refugees, 32
politicization of equal opportunities, 224–6, 266
politics: of immigration, 7–27; of racial inequality, 201–16; racialization of, 22–4
positive action, 226–7, 236, 242, 246, 247, 257
positive discrimination, 61, 226–7, 247
postgraduate social work courses, 175–6
Powell, Enoch, 16–17, 18–19, 24
prejudice *see* subjective racism
prisoners: after-care, 179; black people, 184, 186–9; women, 93–7
prisons: ethnic monitoring, 186–7, 188; racism, 166
private sector, and equal opportunities, 242
privatization, National Health Service, 84
probation, 188, 189–90
probation officers, 171–3, 179, 189–90
professional and managerial workers from ethnic minorities, 48–50, 52, 56–7, 61, 83, 243–5
PROP, 187, 191
propaganda, right-wing extremists, 13
PSI *see* Policy Studies Institute
psychiatric services *see* mental health
psychotic disorders, 92
public disorder *see* civil disturbance
public expenditure cuts: employment, 81; equal opportunities, 208; housing, 110, 121, 129; National Health Service, 84
public meetings, marginalizing antiracism, 203–4
public opinion on immigration, 14
public order charges, 180
public sector, recruitment, 81–6, 150, 153–4

qualifications *see* educational qualifications

Race Relations Acts (RRA), 22, 39, 55–6, 61, 128, 207, 214, 255, 270–1, 285–9
Race Relations Board, 55–6
race relations units, 260, 265, 266
race riots *see* civil disturbance
racial attacks, 65, 75, 123–9
Racial Attacks Group, 129
racial harassment *see* harassment
racialization of politics, 22–4, 257–8
racism, definition of, 165
racism-awareness, 229
radicalism in equal opportunities, 218–30

rape *see* male violence
Rastafarianism, pathologization of, 189
recession, effect on unemployment, 148
recruitment, 134–46, 148–62, 224;
    discrimination, 53, 55, 60–1; equal
    opportunities policies, 235–50, 260–2,
    264; informal, 154–60, 224, 246–7;
    overseas, 8–9, 10, 14, 20, 30–5, 32–5,
    46–9, 51–2, 82–4, 191
redundancy agreements, 84, 158–9, 161
refugees, 8, 32
regional patterns: employment, 53, 58;
    housing, 58
religious groups, and equal opportunities,
    284–8
religious mania, 92
remand, black people on, 183–5
Rent Acts, 272
rents, 121, 122
repatriation *see* deportation
repossession of mortgaged property, 120
reproduction: slaves, 87–8
reproductive rights, 75, 88
retailing, 150, 153–4, 241
right-wing extremists, 13, 35, 36, 37, 38
riotous assembly charges, 182
riots *see* civil disturbance
'rivers of blood' (Powell), 18
Roach, Colin, 95
Rochdale, mortgages, 119, 120
Rose, Winston, 95
Rushdie, Salman, 62

Salisbury, Marquis of, 12–13
Sample Census (1966), 48–9
Satanic Verses, 62
Scarman, Lord, 22, 121
schizophrenia, 92
schooling *see* education
seaports, black settlement, 7
segregation in housing, 115–17, 124–5
Select Committee on Race Relations, 23,
    277
self-employed ethnic minorities, 48–9, 60,
    62
self-help groups, as exclusive racism, 166
sentencing: of black people, 93–4, 179, 181,
    183, 186–9; of unemployed people, 183,
    190
sexism, 174, 175, 229
sexual discrimination, 21, 40, 74–5
sexual division of domestic labour, 71–2
sexual harassment, 68
sexuality stereotypes of black women,
    72–3, 87, 89
Sheffield, 240–8
sheltered accommodation, 166

Sierra Leone High Commission, 181
Sikh women, 65, 66
Single Homelessness In London, 122
single parents, homelessness, 122
slaves, 87–8, 92
Smethwick byelection (1964), 16–17
social control, social work as, 166
social inquiry reports, 188, 190; misuse by
    housing departments, 90, 94, 95
Social Security Acts, 89
social security benefits, 71
social services, black women as clients,
    89–91
social work, and racism, 164–76
social workers, racism in employment of,
    171–3
soldiers as immigrants, 8
South Asians: as 'black', 79–80; education,
    74–5; parents, 74; women, 64–77, 79, 85,
    89, 92, 97
Southall Black Sisters, 79
Southall Monitoring Project, 125
Spitalfields, housing, 113–14
Standard Telephone and Cables, 37
state racism, 10–27, 68–71, 79–99, 120–3
stereotypes: ethnic groups, 13, 61, 120,
    143, 152, 166; South Asian women, 67,
    69, 74, 75; women's sexuality, 72–3
Stone, I., 238–9
strikes: by black workers, 36–7, 43, 68, 75;
    strike-breaking, 43; *see also* industrial
    disputes
structural inequality, 221
structural racism: housing, 109–10, 120–3,
    130
subjective racism: housing, 109–10,
    112–15, 123–30; social work, 165, 169
supervisors *see* professional and
    managerial
Supreme Court (US), 197
sweatshops; South Asian women, 67

Tanzanian Asians *see* East African Asians
tariff system, 166
tax relief on mortgages, 120–1
Tebbit, Norman, 110
tenants, antiracism, 126–7
tenants' associations, 126
Tenants Tackle Racism, 126
Tewson, Sir Vincent, 34
Thatcherism in immigration control, 21–6
therapy, black psychiatric patients, 93
Tottenham, police racism, 95
Tower Hamlets, 113–14, 122–3, 126,
    129–30
Trades Union Congress (TUC), 32–7, 40–3
trade unions: black workers' groups, 43;

and civil disturbance, 34; collaboration with capitalism, 30–2; economic nationalism, 30, 34, 44; equal opportunities, 42–3, 213, 237, 266; ethnic minority officers, 42; ethnic records, 42–3; immigration control, 30–6; and racism, 30–44; racist behaviour, 36–44, 161; redundancy agreements, 158–9, see also labour movement
training: in equal opportunities, 224, 228–9, 244; of social workers, racism in, 173–6
transfer policy, council housing, 124–5
Transport and General Workers Union (TGWU), 37, 42
transport services, 81
trespass charges, 181
trials see law courts
Trivedi, Parita, 72

Ugandan Asians see East African Asians
unemployed people, sentencing, 183, 190
unemployment: demographic down-turn, 59, 144; ethnic minorities, 33, 54–5, 58–9, 67, 241, 282; public expenditure cuts, 81; recession, 148
United States: affirmative action, 281–4; legal system, 274–5, 280
United States Supreme Court, 197
universities, and equal opportunity policies, 239
urban see inner city
Urban Programme, 205, 207, 254–5
urban unrest see civil disturbance

violence see civil disturbance; death in police custody; domestic violence; harassment; male violence; racial attacks
virginity tests by immigration service, 70, 88
visas, immigration control, 23–4
vocationalism, 133

voluntary sector, equal opportunities, 242
vouchers, immigration control, 16, 51

wage differentials, white and black women, 85
Webb, T., 239
welfare state, and black women, 81–99
West Africans, 91
'West Indian psychosis', 92
West Indians see Afro-Caribbeans
West Midlands, labour market, 148–62
West Midlands Regional TUC, 41
white people, migration, 8–9, 14, 25, 47
white-collar see professional
Wilson, Harold, 16, 254
Wilson, Sir Roy, 19
Wolverhampton, 201–16
women, 79–99; Asian, 64–77, 83; black women's movement, 77, 79, 96, 96–7; domestic violence, 89, 95, 166; education, 74–5; employment, 66–8, 81–6; health, 86–94; and police, 94–6; refuges, 97, 166; sexuality stereotypes, 72–3, 87, 89; state racism, 79–99
Woolfe's rubber factory, 68
word of mouth worker recruitment, 154–60, 224
work permits, immigration control, 20
workers see employment; labour movement; migrant workers; trade unions
Working Together for a Better Future, 134–5
World War 2, and immigration, 8

X, Michael, 185
X-ray examinations by immigration service, 70

Young, K., 239–40
young people: employment, 133–46
Youth Training Scheme (YTS), 134–45